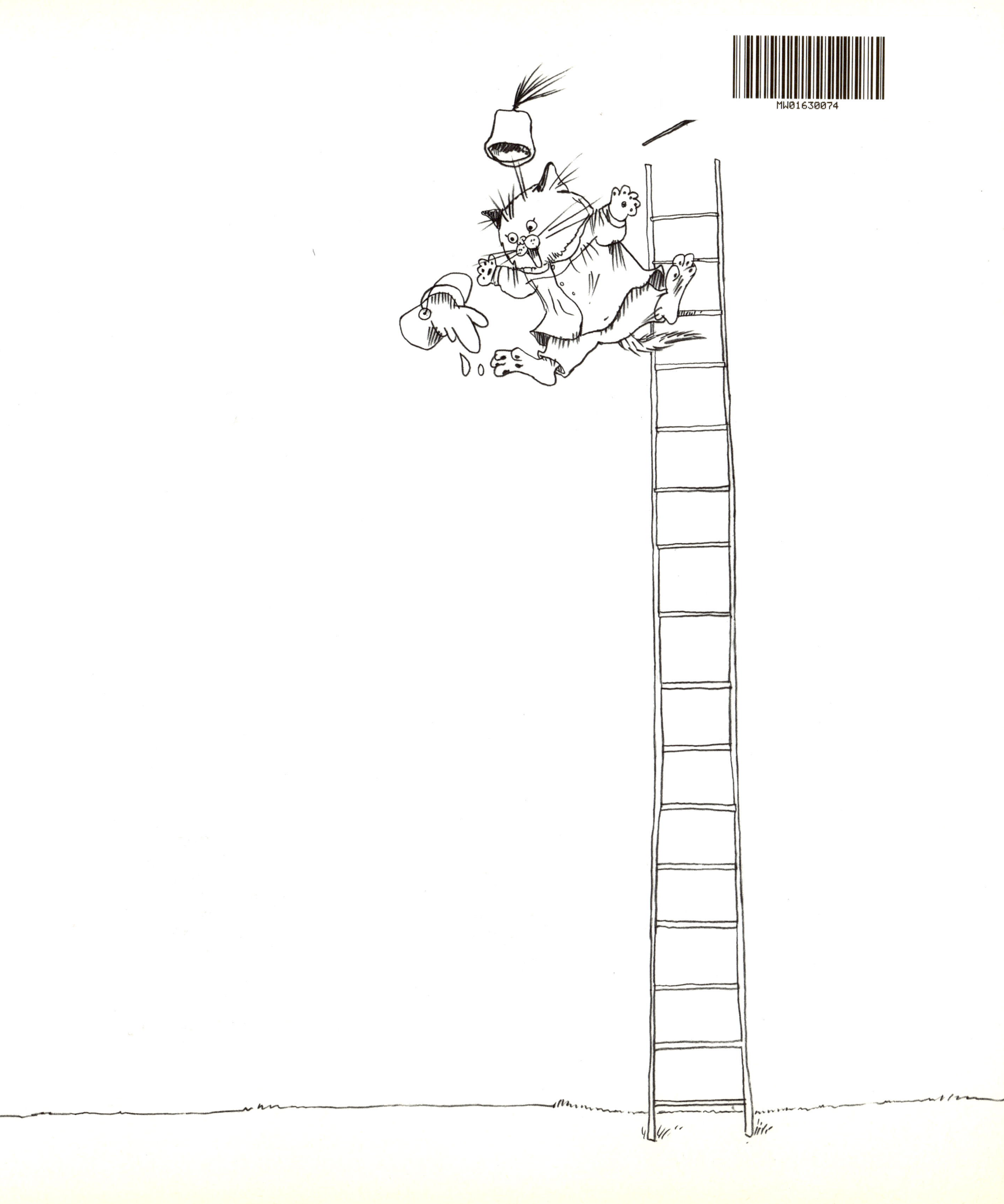
Do

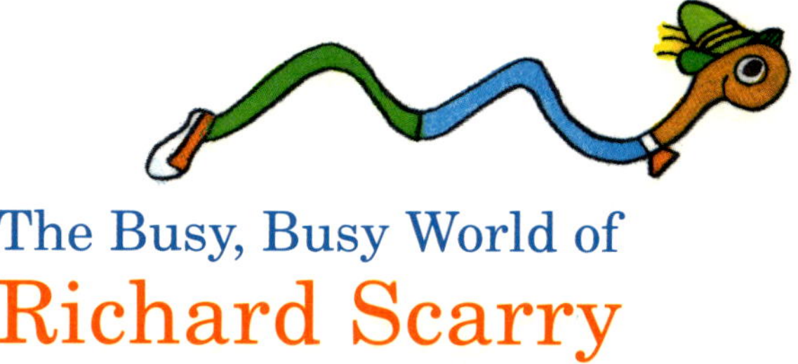

The Busy, Busy World of Richard Scarry

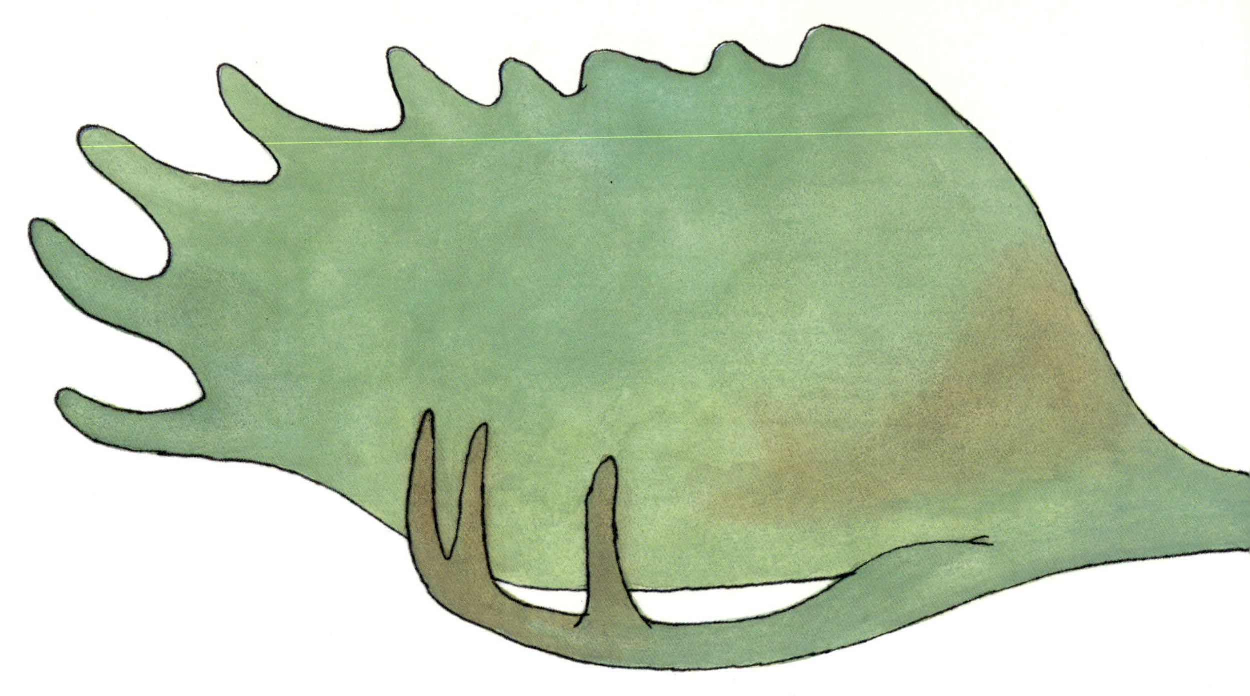

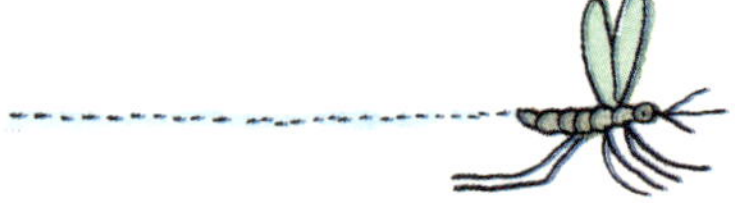

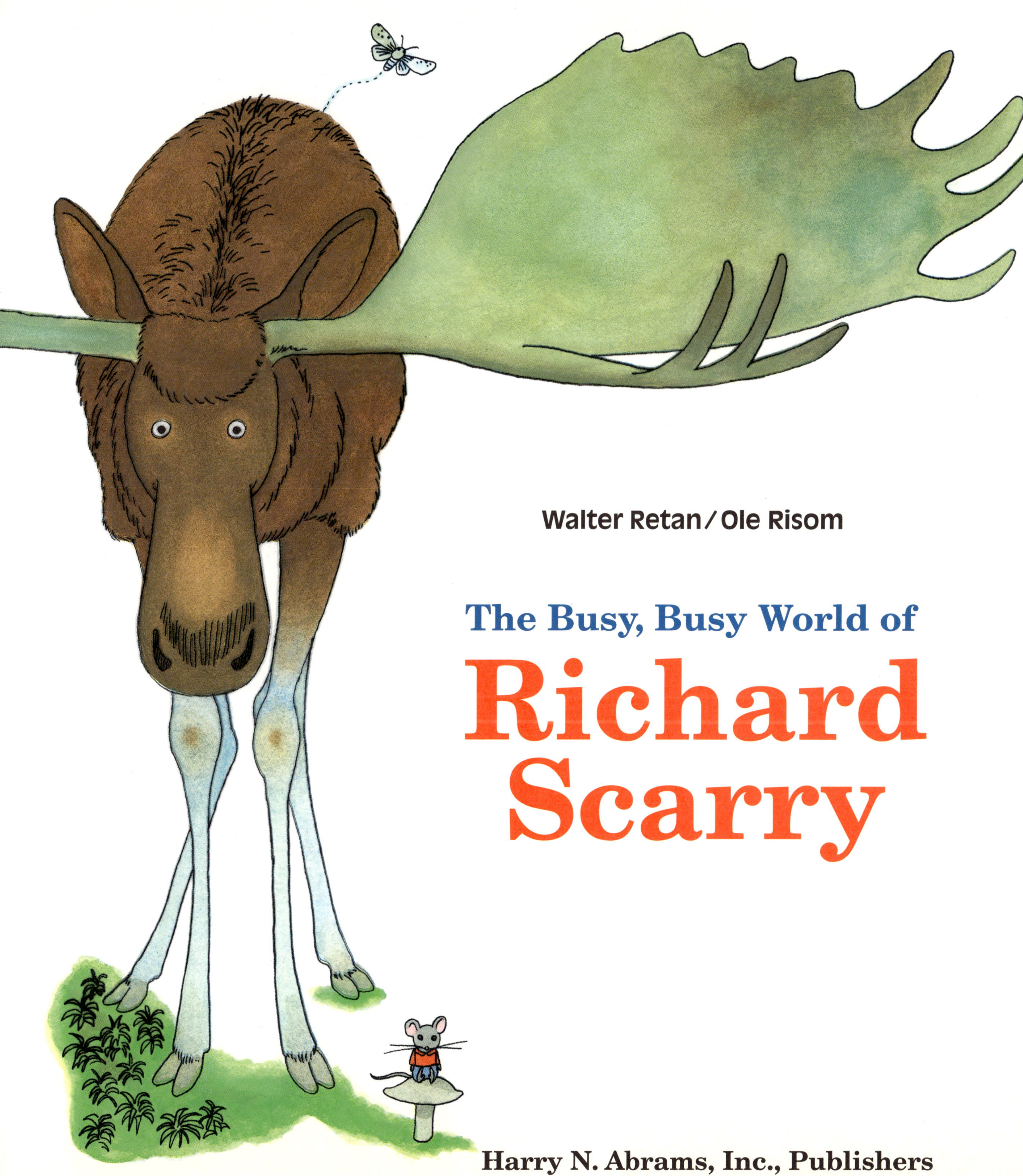

Walter Retan / Ole Risom

The Busy, Busy World of Richard Scarry

Harry N. Abrams, Inc., Publishers

Editor: Robert Morton
Art Director: Ellen Nygaard Ford

Library of Congress Cataloging-in-Publication Data

Retan, Walter.
The busy, busy world of Richard Scarry / by Walter Retan and Ole Risom.
p. cm.
Includes bibliographical references (p.) and index.
ISBN 0-8109-4000-0
1. Scarry, Richard. 2. Authors, American—20th century—Biography. 3. Illustrators—United States—Biography. 4. Children's stories—Illustrations. 5. Children's stories—Authorship. I. Risom, Ole. II. Title.
PS3569.C3247Z86 1997
813'.54—dc21
[B] 97-1756

Published in 1997 by Harry N. Abrams, Incorporated, New York

Printed and bound in Japan

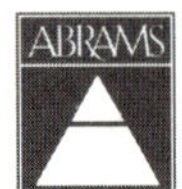

Harry N. Abrams, Inc.
100 Fifth Avenue
New York, N.Y. 10011
www.abramsbooks.com

Endsheets: From *Richard Scarry's Storybook Dictionary*
Page 1: From *Richard Scarry's Best First Book Ever*
Pages 2–3: From *Richard Scarry's Best Word Book Ever*
Pages 4–5: From *Richard Scarry's Storybook Dictionary*
Pages 8 and 120: From *Richard Scarry's Great Big Schoolhouse*

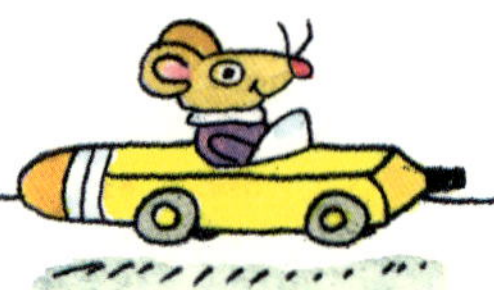

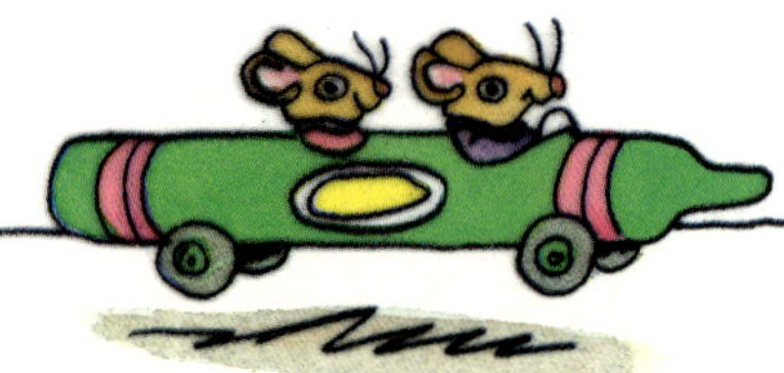

CONTENTS

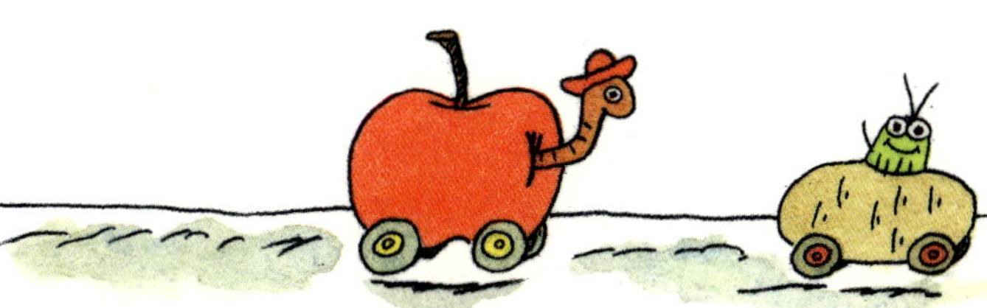

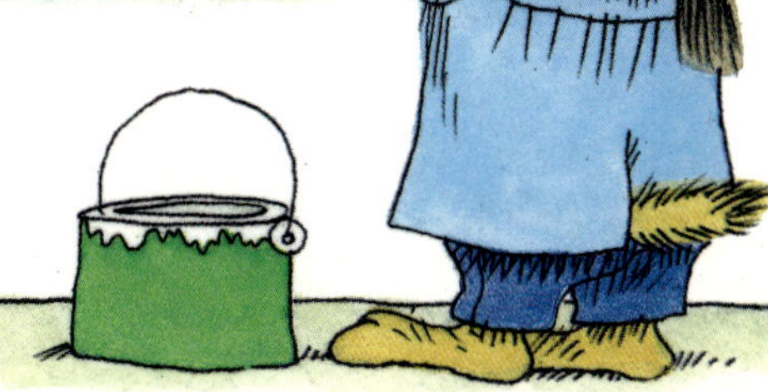

To the Best Mountain-Climber Ever —
from the Second Best
Mountain Climber Ever.
Oncle Dick Scarry
Mürren, Switzerland
1970

PREFACE

In the mid-seventies, Richard Scarry, his son, Huck, and I traveled by train to Lapland for some cross-country skiing. It was springtime, and the days were long enough for us to ski for many hours on the powdery white snow. In the evening we would return to our hotel, located on a large, snow-covered lake that was excellent for skiing.

One night we were settled at the bar for a drink when we suddenly heard loud bursts of childish laughter coming from the hotel lobby. Dick immediately went off to investigate; he loved anything that sounded like fun. A father sat in the lobby reading to his son, who was laughing uproariously. What was he reading? The Finnish edition of Richard Scarry's *Funniest Storybook Ever.* I went over to the father and explained in Danish that the man with me was the author/artist of the book. Both he and his son were delighted to meet the man who had written and illustrated the book that they were enjoying so much.

This was not as unique a coincidence as you might think. Over the years Dick created more than eighty major books; many were translated into as many as twenty-eight languages, ranging all the way from Japanese to Finnish, Icelandic to Italian, Swedish to Spanish, and so on. These books were beloved by children (and parents) everywhere. Nobody knows exactly how many copies of Scarry books have been sold—but certainly more that 150 million copies. He is one of the most popular children's book authors of all time.

In a sense, Dick really wrote and illustrated his books to satisfy the child in himself. He derived a childlike pleasure out of human absurdities, and he enjoyed nothing more than getting up early in the morning to start work on a new book about the busy, busy world around him. He enjoyed life to the fullest, and he wanted his young readers to enjoy it, too. He also wanted them to learn, and he had an amazing ability for teaching children in a funny, effortless manner.

This book will introduce readers to some of the major incidents in Richard Scarry's life, some of his basic beliefs about creating children's books, and some interesting facts about his illustrating and writing techniques. Nothing happened by accident in Richard Scarry's books. He always knew exactly what he was doing and why. Children all over the world have responded enthusiastically, reading and rereading the books until they are tattered and held together by Scotch tape: the greatest compliment a children's book author can receive.

Richard Scarry was one of that very rare breed in our world—a genius.

—Ole Risom

Richard Scarry *(left)* and Ole Risom take a break during a hike in the Swiss Alps.

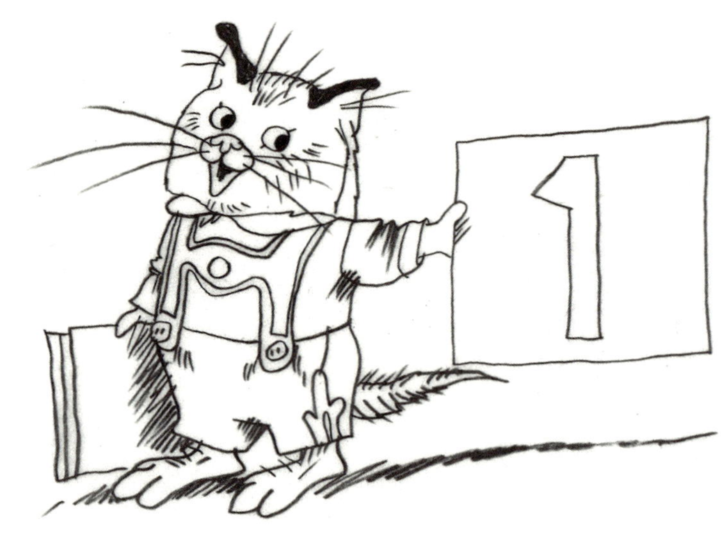

AN ARTIST'S LIFE

GROWING UP IN BOSTON

As a boy Richard Scarry already showed the strong visual sense and interests of an artist. When his mother sent him to the store, he never bothered to write out a shopping list. Instead, he drew little pictures of everything she wanted—a bottle of ketchup, a loaf of bread, a package of raisins. At the store, he even drew a picture of the grocer, but he was careful not to let the grocer see what he was doing. Almost everywhere he went, he carried a pad and pencil so that he could draw pictures of anything that especially interested him.

On Saturday mornings, when he was still very young, Richard's mother took him to the art school at the Museum of Fine Arts, Boston, where he sat in class, sketching porcelain horses, ancient goddesses, and other antiquities. Sometimes

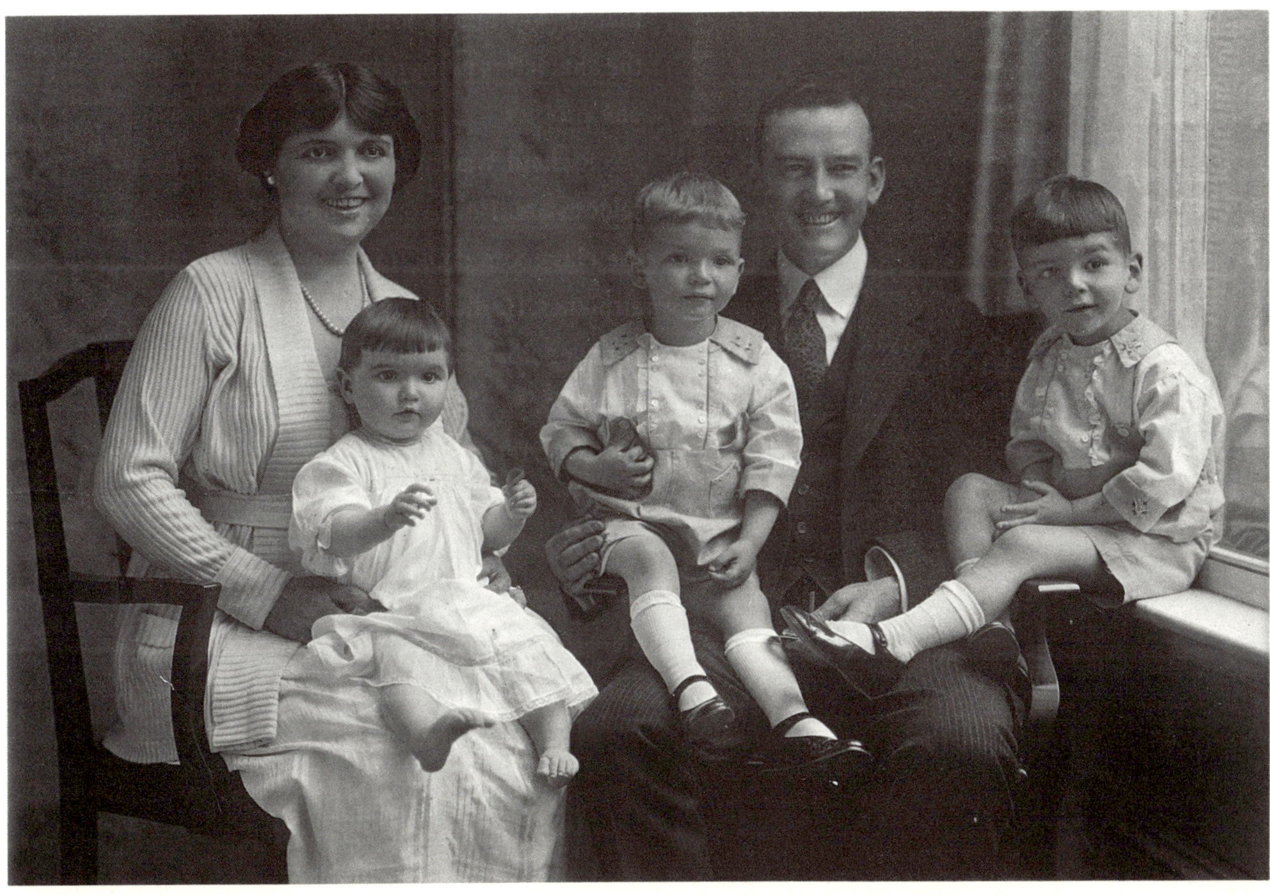

Dick Scarry *(at far right)*, age four, poses with his parents and two siblings.

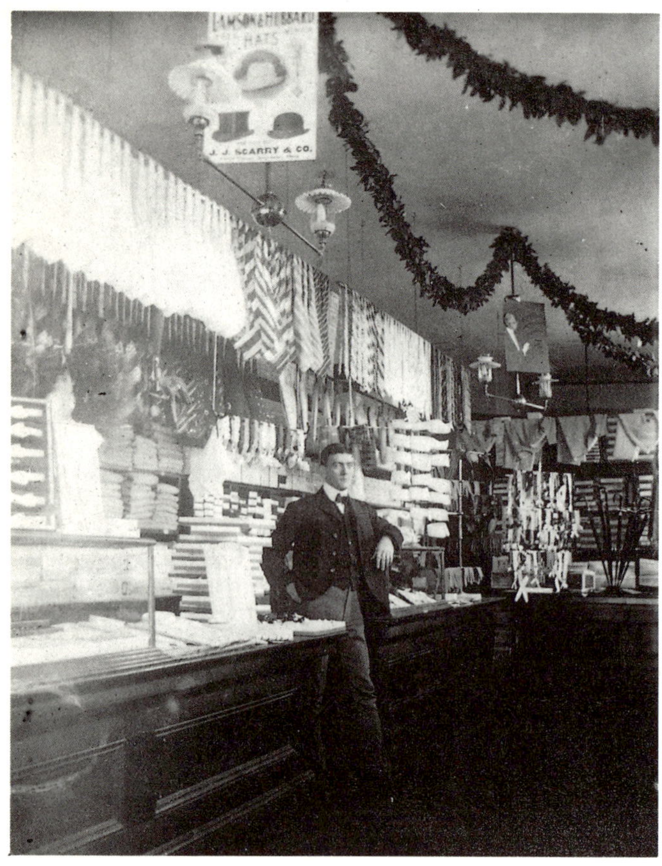

John James Scarry at a counter in his department store at Field's Corner, Dorchester, Massachusetts.

the class roamed the vast museum halls, drawing whatever struck their fancy. "The classes lasted only for an hour," he later wrote, "but one became lost in the atmosphere. And I believe that is where it all began." As a kind of reward, his mother would take him for a ride afterward in one of the pedal boats on the pond in the Boston Common, right in the heart of the city. "Just my mother and I. . . . She was full of fun."

Born in Boston on June 5, 1919, Richard McClure Scarry was the second of five children—four boys and a girl. The Scarry family, including Richard's Aunt May, lived in the neighborhood of Dorchester, the southeast section of Boston. Richard's father, John James Scarry, owned a store in the area called Scarry's Department Store. There he sold men's, women's, and children's clothing. Because of this store, the family lived in comfortable circumstances, even during the Great Depression of the 1930s. "We were a close family," Richard wrote. "My mother was pretty and carefree. My Auntie May did the cooking, spoiling, and general upbringing of the family. We laughed a lot, and had to go to church on Sundays." All in all, the artist felt that he was raised with healthy doses of discipline, love, and respect. As a result, the characters in his future books would show the same kind of care and respect for one another.

Richard was not fond of school. Children who are more visual than verbal seldom are. He preferred football, sketching, and Saturday afternoon movies. In the classroom sometimes, instead of studying his lessons, he drew World War I airplanes. He did enjoy reading, however, perhaps because he had been read to as a younger child. His father often read aloud to him after he had gone to bed, especially the books of Thornton Burgess. Two favorites were *The Adventures of Buster Bear* and *The Adventures of Jerry Muskrat.* Young Richard loved the stories about the animals' adventures and the illustrations that accompanied them.

Frequently he went to the Boston Public Library. "I spent a good deal of time there, sometimes reading, sometimes fooling around with my classmates under the glare of our librarian." He recalled that one day, on his way to the library, he passed a small pond where he discovered a pretty little garter snake. Picking it up, he took it along to the library. Several of his mischievous pals were already there.

"To impress them," Richard wrote, "I let the garter snake loose on the table. It wriggled over the smooth surface, and all the girls screamed. So did the librarian. And the head librarian banished me from the library forever." But many years later,

Opposite: A drawing that Dick Scarry gave to Ole Risom of Father Cat reading to his son. John Scarry had read bedtime stories to his children.

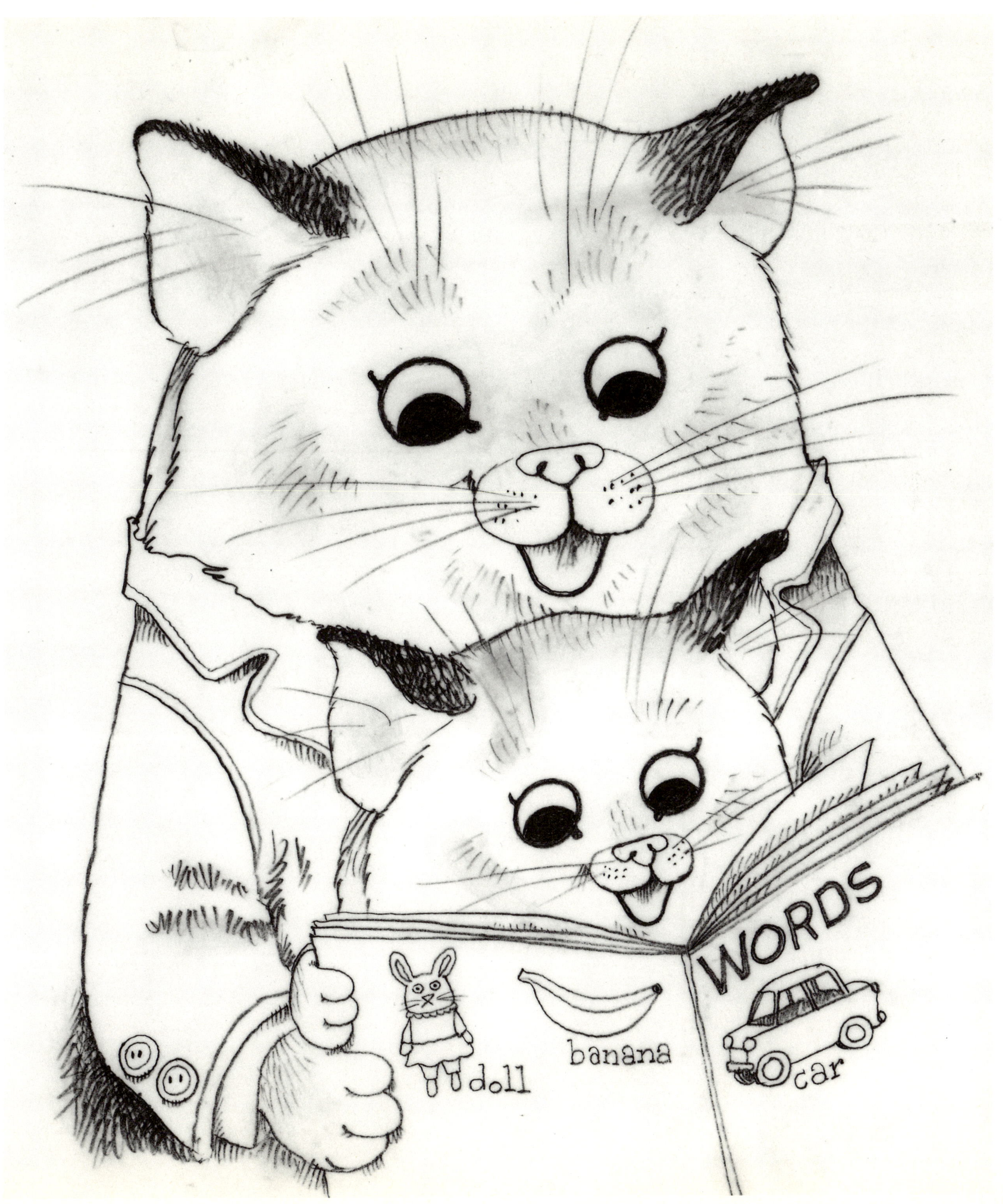
WORDS
doll
banana
car

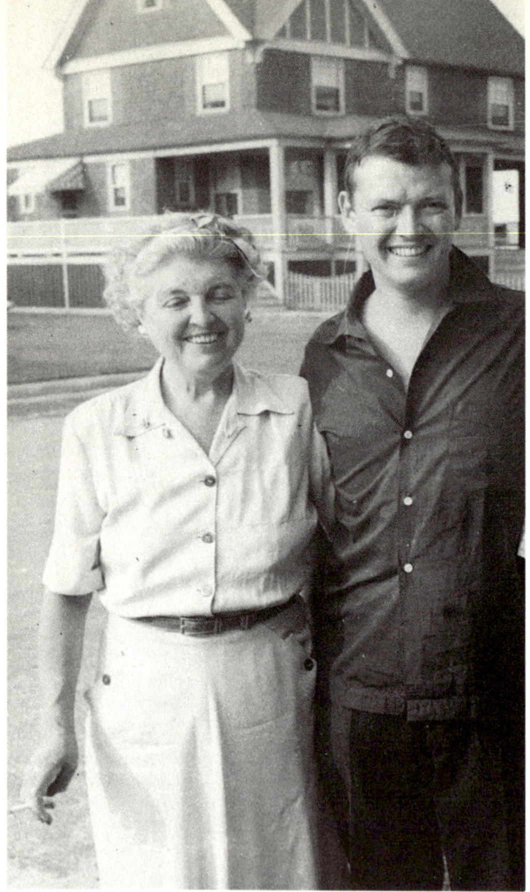

Above: Richard Scarry with his mother, whom he described as "full of fun."

Below: Scarry's dapper Uncle Arthur, this time not wearing his white linen suit.

Richard could certainly feel that he had gotten his revenge. The library stacks were full of Scarry books, and they were all extremely popular with young readers.

Richard's high school career was also undistinguished. He took five years to earn the usual four-year diploma. Algebra was his downfall. He had to repeat the course twice before he passed. What with sailing small boats around Boston Harbor, fishing, and pursuing and dancing with attractive girls, he had little time for his schoolwork. But after he learned to copy his mother's handwriting, it was easy to skip classes. "Dear Miss O'Conner," he would write, "Richard couldn't attend school yesterday. He had a bad cough. Mrs. Scarry."

Sometimes he skipped school in order to go to the burlesque shows at the Old Howard in downtown Boston's Scollay Square. He had discovered the mysteries of sex. To him the girls who took off their clothes while they strutted around the stage were beautiful. He later admitted, "There was one girl there I thought about night and day. She crowded my mind. I had no time for algebra when I could think about her. I tried drawing her swinging her tassels. Countless pictures. And of course my parents found them."

"What is going to become of you?" his father asked.

"If I'm going to be an artist, sir," Richard replied, "I have to learn to draw the human form."

"If you try to be an artist you will live in a garret and eat nothing but spaghetti," his father answered. He was a serious and conservative man, whose own experience had given him confidence only in a businessman's career.

According to Richard, the only useful advice he ever received from his family came from his popular Uncle Arthur, a white-haired, sun-tanned ladies' man who lived in New York. In Uncle Arthur's stories, all the women swooned for him, and Richard planned to be just like him. Uncle Arthur's advice was:

"Buy a natural linen suit at Brooks Brothers, with a pale blue shirt to wear under it. This is the only thing you need to learn in life."

"I did exactly what he said," Richard later wrote, "and I paid for the suit by selling neckties at my father's department store. Long, long hours. In between I tied parcels in the basement of Filene's department store."

But the white suit and the blue shirt failed to impress the admissions officer at Harvard University, where Dick's father had hoped he could enroll. His grades were not good enough. Instead, at his father's insistence, he attended a local business

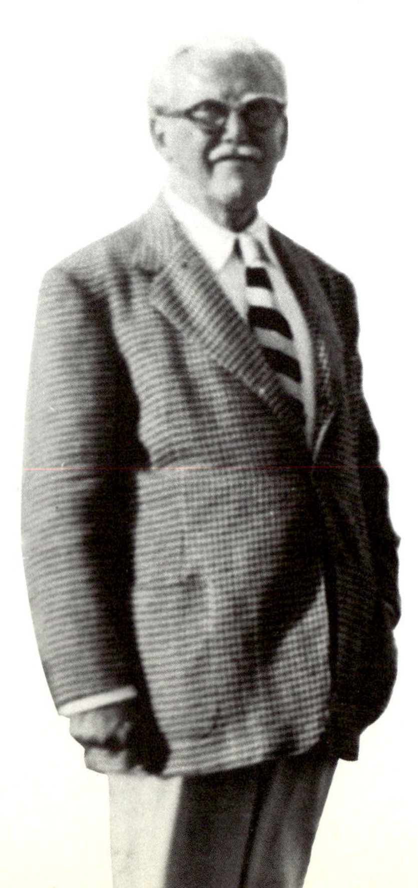

college. Richard hated business school so much that he quit before the end of the first year. Finally his father gave up. If his son was determined to be an artist, he might as well go back to Boston's Museum of Fine Arts art school. But he warned his son once again of a life doomed to attics and spaghetti.

To Richard, the return to art school was like going back to an old friend. He flourished in the midst of the welcoming atmosphere of drawing pencils, charcoal, and paint. Unfortunately, the outbreak of World War II ended his art studies prematurely. After completing just three years of the course (1939–42), he was drafted into the army, so he never received his diploma.

AT WORK IN THE WAR

Richard had already tried to volunteer for military service, but the armed forces had rejected him on account of poor eyesight. This time they pronounced him fit for service and ordered him to report in ten days. When he was told to list his occupations and talents on a questionnaire, he wrote just one word—ARTIST. The army, true to its reputation, immediately shipped him off to Radio Repair School in Fort Monmouth, New Jersey.

"I could never repair anything, even my mother's toaster," Dick later wrote. And he proved it by earning the memorable grade of minus thirteen on his exam. He hated everything about radio repair school: the huge, dismal barracks; the lessons in proper bedmaking; and—most of all—the constant drilling, *left, right, left, right,* and the loathsome drill sergeant.

Then a miracle happened. One day he was suddenly ordered to report to the major's office. Wondering what he had done wrong, Richard tried to give a smart salute, but he was so nervous his hand trembled. The officer busied himself shuffling papers about on his desk. "I see you're an artist, Scarry," he said at last. "Can you paint letters . . . A, B, C . . . that sort of thing?"

"Yes, indeed, sir," Private Scarry answered.

"Then you've got a job," the major declared. "There's a sign outside that needs to be changed. I want the background to be in black and the letters painted in silver, so they will really stand out."

Richard couldn't believe the size of the sign. It must have been thirty feet long:

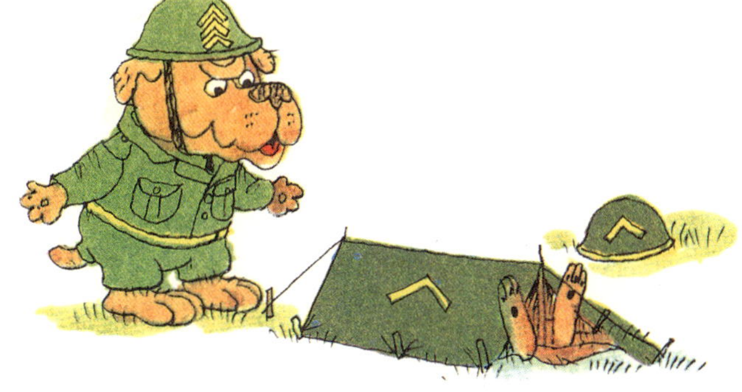

Here and on the following four pages: From *Richard Scarry's Cars and Trucks and Things That Go.* Scarry's army experience reveals itself in these illustrations.

WELCOME TO THE SEVENTH ENGINEERS

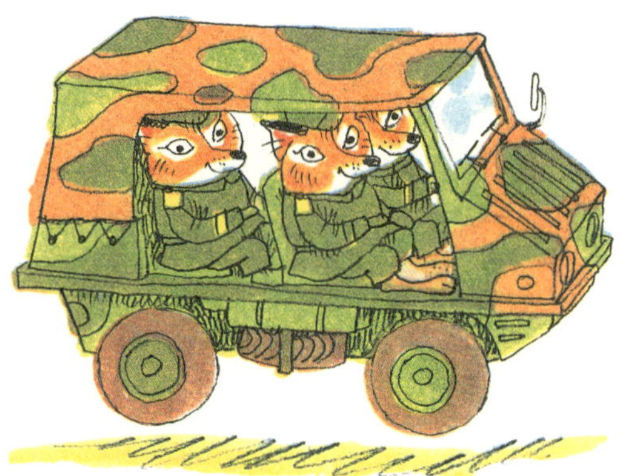

WELCOME TO THE SEVENTH ENGINEERS OF FORT MONMOUTH, NEW JERSEY, U.S.A. He figured that painting a sign like that ought to keep him busy for at least one whole war. Equipped with a bucket of black paint and a bucket of silver, he went to work. The black paint was as thick as tar; it wouldn't spread. He had to fling it out of the bucket and drag it over the sign with a broom. It took weeks to dry.

Nevertheless, Richard was delighted with his job. Finally the army had seen fit to recognize his talents as an artist. Every morning he painted while the drill sergeant shouted at his less fortunate buddies: *"Left, right, left, right."* And every Saturday he got a pass to take the bus to New York City, where he could dance with the young women at the U.S.O. Tall, broad-shouldered, with a wide forehead and a mischievous twinkle in his eyes, Dick had no difficulty attracting partners.

A few months later he applied to, and was accepted by, the Army Administration Officer Candidate School. That was the place where everyone dreamed of going. According to Dick, it was a "three-month snap course" (whose graduates were dubbed "90-day wonders") from which he emerged as a second lieutenant. Assigned to Special Services, he had the good fortune to be sent to Washington and Lee University in Lexington, Virginia. There soldiers were trained to entertain the troops and bolster their morale—the function of the Special Services units. The university campus was covered with green grass, trees, and flowers. Better yet, there were many young women from the Red Cross and the Nurses Corps who were also receiving Special Services training.

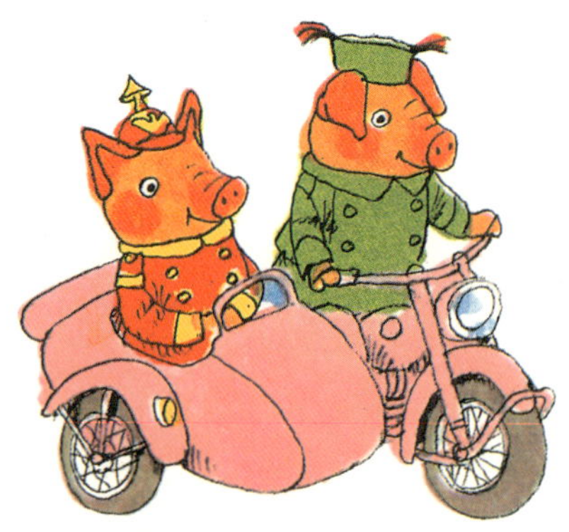

During his month of training, Richard learned to hand out baseball bats and balls, volley balls, and Ping-Pong balls. He was also instructed in the techniques of sending news and information to the men overseas, and he was trained to select movies for the entertainment of the fighting troops. Just as his training stint was about to end, word came from army headquarters in North Africa that they needed an art director to help prepare informational materials. There was just one problem for Richard: the art director must be a captain. The officer in charge of the assignment solved that problem very quickly. "You will be a captain in no time," he said. "Pack your gear and get ready to go to the staging area at Norfolk."

OF FORT MONMOUTH, NEW JERSEY, U.S.A.

At the staging area, Scarry went to the medical section to get new eyeglasses. While he was there, the doctors discovered an abscess on his hip, so they sent him to the army hospital for treatment. His travel orders had assigned him to a special staging unit that included one colonel (chief medical officer), as well as a lieutenant colonel, a major, two captains, and one lowly second lieutenant (Scarry himself). The colonel telephoned Richard in the hospital and advised him to get out of the place as quickly as possible, or he would miss the ship to North Africa. Richard wasted no time in getting a medical discharge. The doctor also gave him a note excusing him from any strenuous physical activity until the abscess had healed.

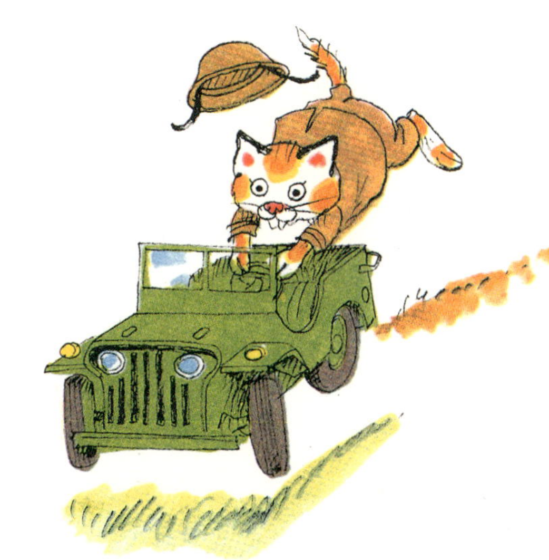

Back at the staging area, Scarry packed his duffel bag and prepared to board the ship with the rest of his special unit. The *Maraposa*, the sleek, streamlined ship that carried him to the port of Casablanca in North Africa, was so fast that she didn't require the protection of a naval convoy. The ship's captain plotted a zigzag course to confuse any enemy submarines that might be lurking in the area.

Scarry was assigned to bunk 11, Cabin A, which was right behind the ship's captain's suite. Ten other officers—all of higher rank than Richard—shared the cabin. Before the war, Cabin A had been the honeymoon suite. Because it was so close to the captain's quarters, the men had hot water for shaving and washing their underwear; in fact they even had their own sun deck. The soldiers, nurses, and Red Cross girls aboard the ship spent most of their days on deck sun-tanning and playing gin rummy. Except for the lack of privacy and the cramped quarters, the five-day crossing was almost as pleasant as a peacetime cruise.

The luxury tour ended abruptly, however, when they arrived at Casablanca, the chief seaport of Morocco. All Special Services personnel were assigned to tents, where they sweltered in the intense heat while waiting for orders to proceed to Algiers. About a week later all of the group except Scarry received their orders and boarded boxcars (without seats) headed for Algiers and Oran. Richard was the only one not included in the orders. He had to remain all alone in the hot, steamy port; as far as he was concerned, the fun had ended.

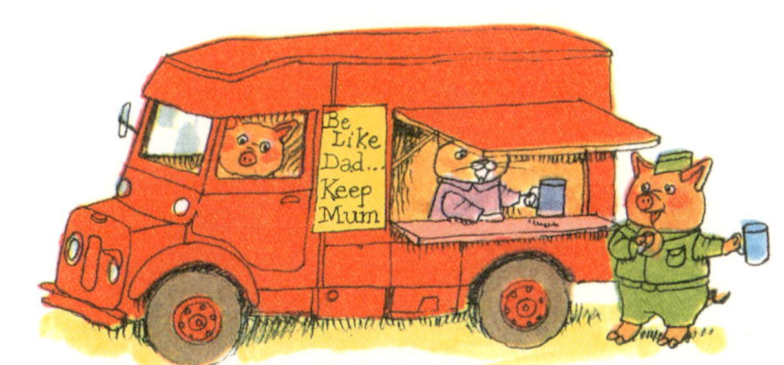

The next morning the army produced a second miracle. Scarry received orders

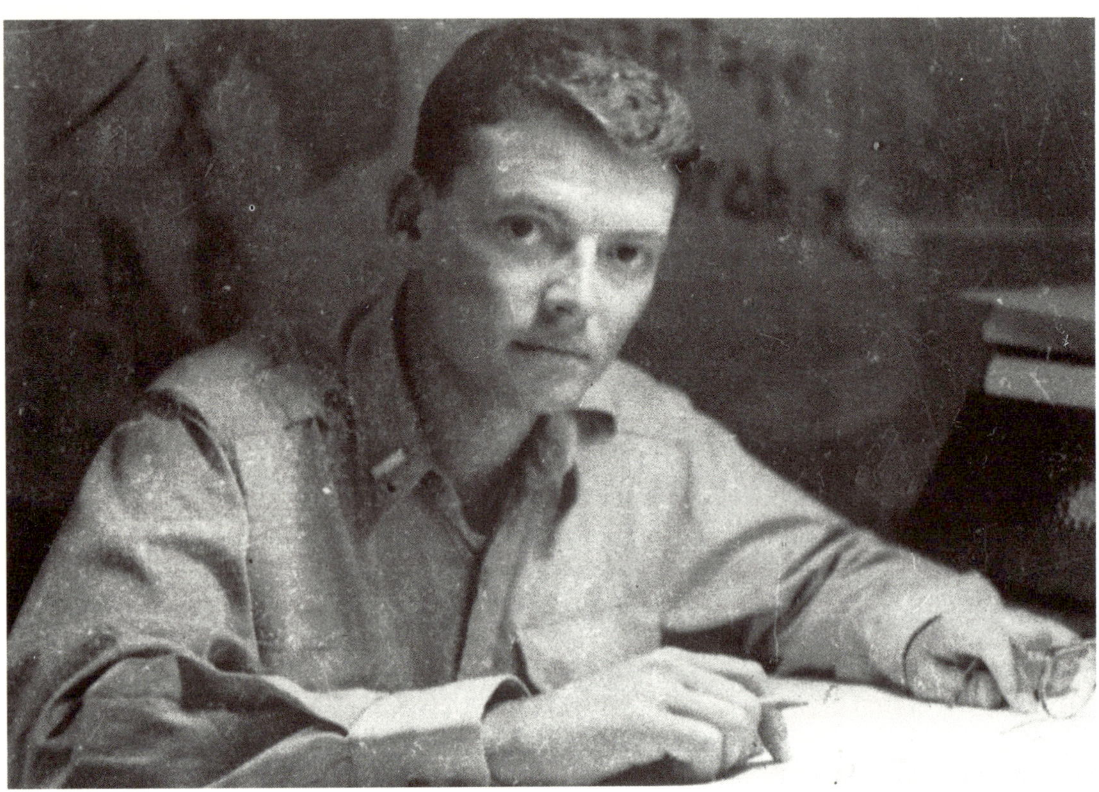

A serious-looking Lieutenant Scarry works at his drawing board in Caserta, Italy, in 1945.

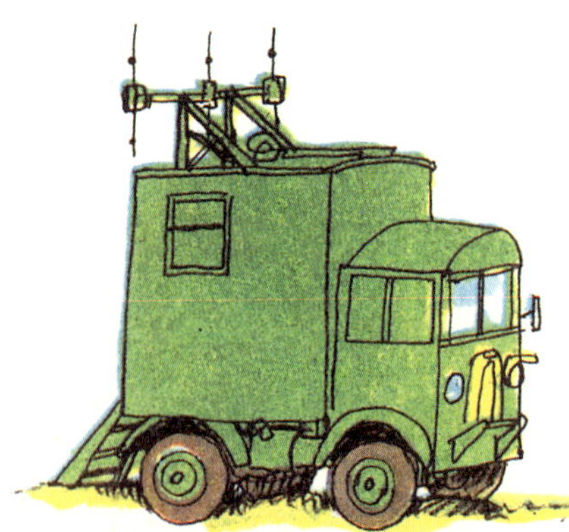

to board a flight headed for Algiers—the first time he had flown in a plane. From the windows of the aircraft he could see the boxcars filled with his friends weaving along the railroad tracks below. He would be in Algiers before they got there. He couldn't wait to tell them how he had traveled in real style.

At army headquarters in Algiers he was quickly assigned to a room in a comfortable apartment belonging to a French widow. Three other young officers were billeted in other bedrooms in the same apartment. On the front door of the building, a brass sign said—VERDUN. The landlady's husband had been killed there during World War I.

One night, soon after Scarry arrived in Algiers, enemy planes started bombing the city. His landlady asked Richard and the other three officers to come to her living room to sip a little wine. Through the French doors they had a spectacular view of the fireworks. "It was like the Fourth of July," he said. "Suddenly a bomb landed not far from the house. The earth shook, the house shuddered and swayed." The little group ran for the safety of their own rooms, where they hid under the beds. This little adventure created a strong bond of camaraderie among them. More important, the young man from Boston experienced his first taste of real warfare.

When Scarry reported for duty, he had no idea what sort of work would be expected from an art director in Algiers. He was quickly assigned to an office, where he discovered that an inexperienced young soldier had already been sent to assist with the job. Since the other man knew as little about the work as Richard, they decided they might as well enjoy themselves. For the first few days they clowned around, wasting time and in the process becoming great chums. Finally, a colonel from headquarters stopped by to give them their orders. "You are supposed to tell the troops why they are fighting," he explained, "and send them news from home."

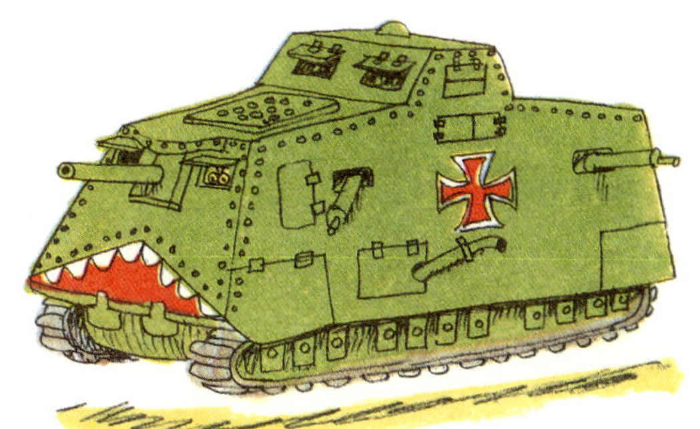

Up to that time Scarry hadn't even received a letter with news of his own family, so he very respectfully asked the colonel, "How are we supposed to do that, sir?"

"By post!" the colonel shouted, as he slammed the door behind him.

Scarry and his colleague were stunned. How could two completely inexperienced young soldiers hope to bolster the morale of the entire American fighting force in Africa? It looked like a totally impossible assignment. Then Art Director Scarry had a brilliant idea. He arranged to have a copy of *Time* magazine flown to their office every week. The magazine was full of the latest news, which the two men paraphrased, illustrated, and turned into a flier that they duplicated on a mimeograph machine. The fliers were sent to American troops all over North Africa. The fledgling art directors also made posters—sometimes with their own pens and paint brushes, sometimes with the help of American news magazines.

As they threw themselves into their work, they began to love it. So did the colonel. He commended the young lieutenant for the fine job he was doing. Scarry decided that, if he had to be in the armed forces, this was certainly the best assignment he could have gotten. As art director, editor, and writer of information publications for U.S. Troops, Information and Morale Services Section, Allied Force Headquarters of the North-African and Mediterranean Theaters of Operation, he helped design, write, and illustrate information manuals and guidebooks for GIs stationed or fighting in Northwest Africa. He also drew maps that showed the troops how Allied fighting was progressing all over the world.

While he was in Algiers, Dick achieved one rather offbeat distinction. As part of its effort to improve the morale of troops in the area, the Morale Services Center,

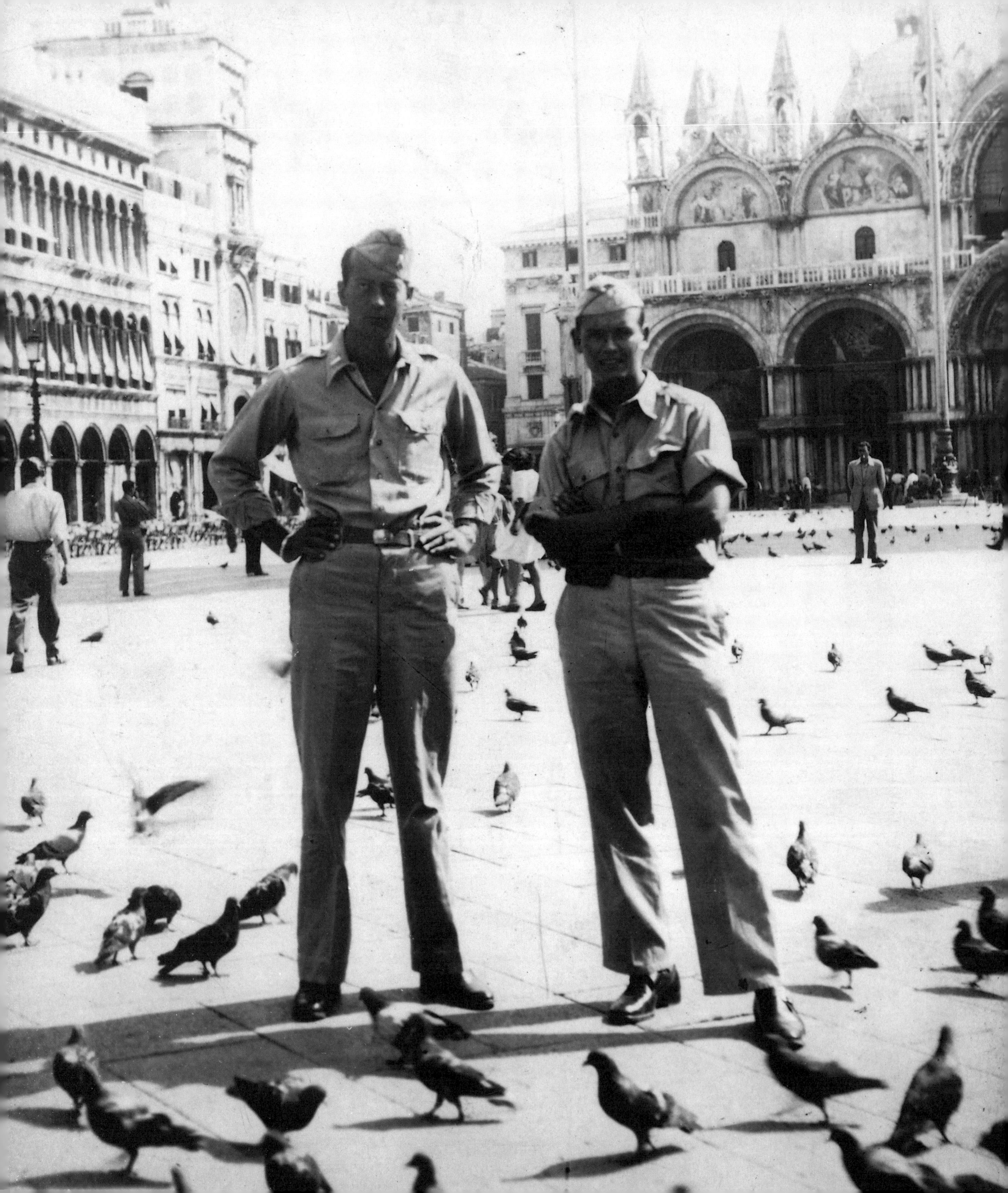

Headquarters, decided to stage a boxing match. In connection with this event, they also sponsored a contest to see who could create the best design for a victory belt. Dick decided to enter the design contest. He came up with the idea of a very wide red belt with a huge brass clasp in front. To his amazement he won the contest. The champion who earned this so-called "Algerian Belt" was none other than the Algerian boxer Marcel Cerdan, then still an amateur. (After the war, Cerdan went on to win the National Boxing Association—now the World Boxing Association—middleweight title for 1948–49.)

After about six months, the section of headquarters to which Scarry was assigned moved to Oran, another Algerian seaport city on the Mediterranean, approximately two hundred miles west of Algiers. In addition to their regular duties, his group was now responsible for the army radio station in Oran.

By this time Richard and his fellow officers had become wise to the ways of the army. Instead of accepting lodgings provided by headquarters, they decided to look for something more desirable on their own. About twenty miles outside the city, there was a group of villas or summer cottages which the army had requisitioned for its use. Richard and his friends found an attractive villa that seemed to be empty and obtained permission to be billeted there. Just one problem remained: how could they get to their office in the city? Twenty miles is a long way to walk twice a day. They solved this by obtaining the colonel's permission to use his Buick. The Buick not only solved their transportation problem; it was also very useful for their dates with the nurses billeted in the villa next door.

Algiers and Oran fascinated Richard, especially the older parts of the cities. When he had time off, he wandered through the narrow, winding streets, tried the exotic foods in restaurants, and observed a culture that was completely different

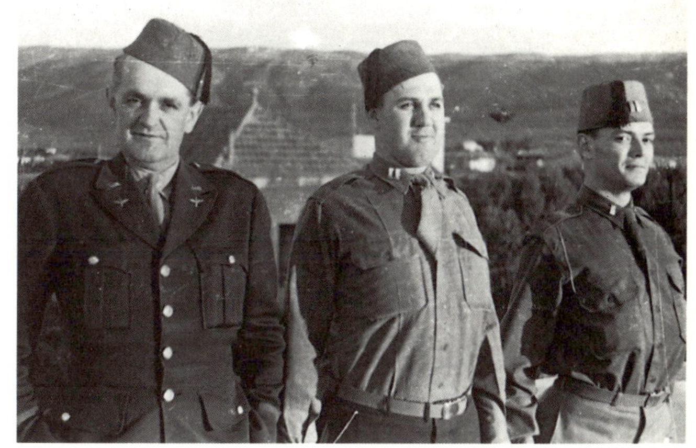

Above: First Lieutenant Scarry *(far right)* poses in a French army cap alongside his captain and major. On the back of the photo Dick wrote, "three of the U.S. Army's finest."

Opposite: On leave in Venice, Scarry stands with an unidentified army buddy in the Piazza San Marco. He developed a lifelong love for this beautiful Italian city.

Below: From *Richard Scarry's Busy, Busy World*

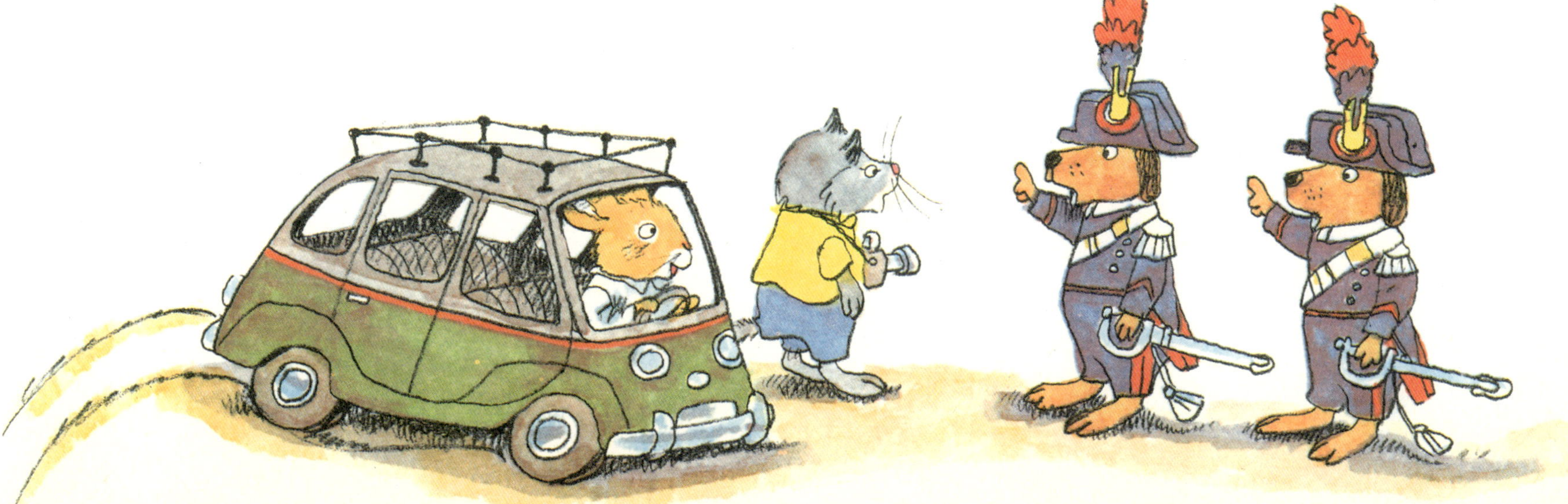

from the one in which he had grown up. On his sightseeing excursions he made frequent use of his sketching pad and pencil. It was no accident that one of the first stories in his big picture book *Busy, Busy World* was set in Algiers, for Northern Africa had made a lasting impression on him.

Several months after the transfer to Oran, Scarry's unit moved again, this time to Caserta, Italy: the Allied Forces had secured a strong foothold on the peninsula. Naturally, the first time he got a chance, Dick paid a visit to Rome. Rome proved

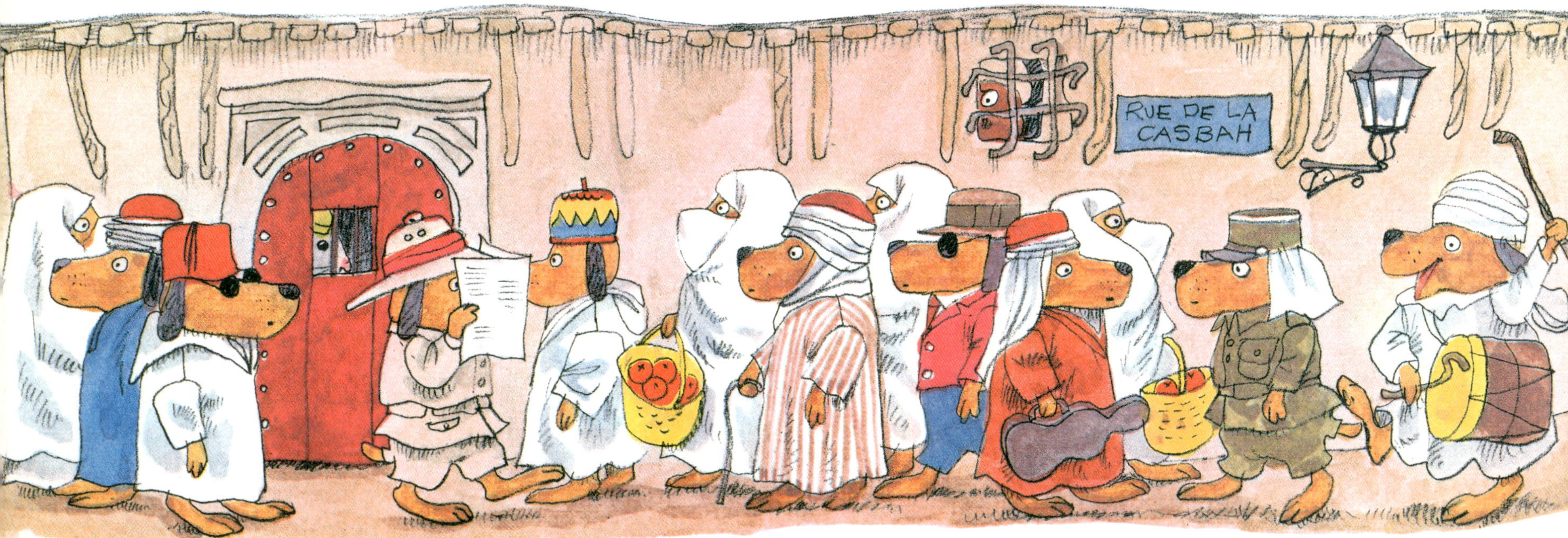

From "Couscous, the Algerian Detective"
in *Richard Scarry's Busy, Busy World*

to be even more fascinating than Algiers and Oran. He went for long walks, studying the ancient Roman ruins and visiting art museums and churches. While stationed in Italy, he was even able to make side trips to a few other historic cities such as Siena and Venice. For an aspiring artist, Italy offered unique sights and opportunities.

Several months after the end of the fighting in Europe on May 8, 1945, Scarry was sent to Paris. When he arrived in the French capital, he discovered that the army had goofed again. He wasn't supposed to be in Paris at all. But the colonel to whom he reported shrugged his shoulders and said, "You may as well stay here. You'll be going back to the States in a month's time. You've got enough points to be discharged from the service."

For Scarry that month was a wonderful opportunity to visit some of the Parisian museums and admire the many historic buildings. He wandered for hours through picturesque streets or sat in street cafés, watching the passing crowds.

"For me," he once admitted in an interview, "that was the best war ever." His army experience instilled in him a great love of travel and foreign sights. It was a love that stayed with him all his life—and was later reflected in his many books. His friends, editors, and art directors were constantly receiving postcards from exotic locales with funny Scarry drawings and messages on the reverse side.

GETTING STARTED IN NEW YORK

On August 14, 1945, Japan surrendered. World War II had finally ended. And on the twenty-fourth of March, 1946, Captain Richard M. Scarry became a civilian again. Now the twenty-seven-year-old artist, art director, and editor, who had been providing information materials for an audience of more than a million readers every week, had to decide what to do with the rest of his life.

Like many returning veterans, he was eager to get started on a real career. He didn't want to go back to art school. Because he had enjoyed being an art director in the army, he applied for and got a job in the art department of *Vogue* magazine at Condé Nast Publications, Inc. But after just three weeks on the job he was fired. When they told him he wasn't right for the position, he asked why they had hired him in the first place. The personnel officer explained that they had been impressed by his white suit and blue shirt. (Richard could thank his Uncle Arthur for that.)

Next he got a job in an advertising agency, pasting up photographs for layouts, but the work proved to be boring and uncreative. He stuck it out for just three months before quitting. Finally he decided to devote himself to free-lance illustration and acquired an agent, Hans Fybel. With the agent's help, he received a few assignments to provide art for advertising promotions and magazines. So far he had been earning very little money, but he had found a small apartment on Manhattan's

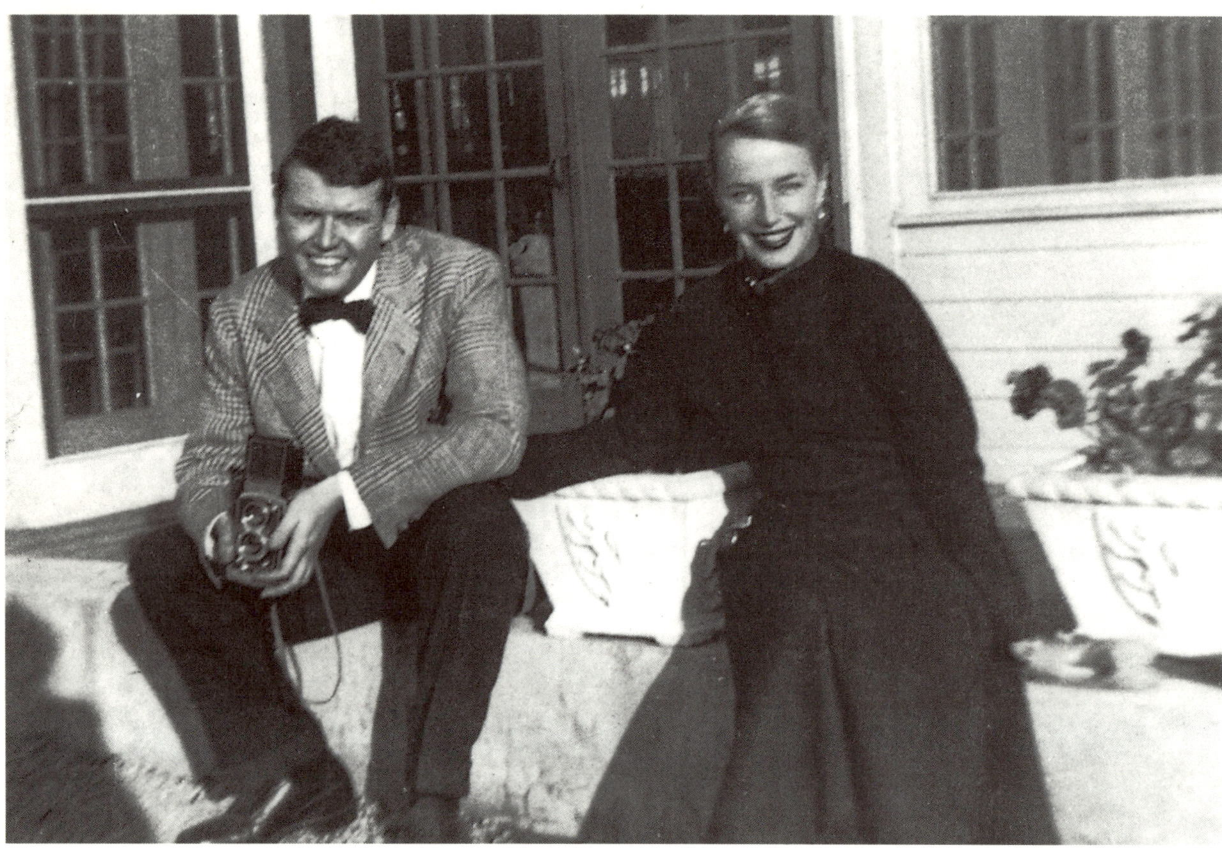

Newlyweds Dick and Patsy pose for a friend's snapshot.

East Side, for which he paid only fourteen dollars a month. "In those days you could live on $1,000 a year," he said, "and I lived well."

Then his luck seemed to change; the agent secured an assignment at *Holiday* magazine which paid him the unbelievable fee of $2,000. That gave him enough money to move to a better apartment overlooking Washington Square. It also covered his living expenses for a considerable amount of time.

Dick's life wasn't all work. Having gradually collected a large group of friends in New York, he maintained an active social life. Once his working day had finished, he enjoyed going to parties, good restaurants, and taking in all the sights of the city. Attractive young women had never lost their appeal for him, and he dated frequently, but so far he hadn't settled on any one woman. However, that situation was about to change.

In the late summer of 1948 he was invited to a large, rather elaborate cocktail party. His best friend arrived, escorting a petite ash blonde with sparkling blue eyes and a very appealing smile. Her name was Patricia Murphy (Patsy to her friends). Originally from Canada, where she had been an actress on radio, she had lived in New York long enough to have a very good job as a writer at the advertising agency of Young & Rubicam.

Patsy later wrote, "Upon being introduced to Dick, I knew instantly that THIS was the man for me. He asked me out for dinner the next night. And the next night, and he seemed immensely sure of himself. Sure of ME, too."

She decided to put his affection to the test. A few weeks earlier she had accepted an invitation from a "nice young Yale man" to spend the Labor Day weekend at the home of Eugene Du Pont in Delaware. It would be a four-day house party. To Dick's great surprise, she decided to go. (She hoped he would miss her.) "It was the dullest weekend I could ever imagine," she wrote. "I kept looking at the telephone, and it just would NOT ring."

On the very last day, the guests all went to see another magnificent Du Pont house called Mount Cubs. While they were eating lunch, Eugene Du Pont himself appeared and extended his best wishes to the partygoers, and at practically the same moment, a butler came into the dining room and placed a telegram on Patsy's plate. It said: "MUST MOVE GRAND PIANO. HEAVY. NEED HELP. COME IMMEDIATELY. . . . DICK."

"I got up from the table and announced to all," Patsy said, "I am about to be married!" (She knew a marriage proposal when she saw it.) She caught the next train for New York.

It was a classic case of "opposites attract." Dick tended to be quiet and withdrawn, not given to expressing his feelings through talk. Patsy was outgoing and gregarious. She could get along with anyone and cope with any social situation. Often she acted as a kind of buffer between Dick and his publishers as well as his fans: his life would always be centered around his work.

Patsy and Dick were married September 11, 1948, at the end of the same week that he had proposed, at the First Presbyterian Church on Fifth Avenue. The reception was held at Dick's apartment on Washington Square. The bridal couple traveled by taxi from the church to the reception, picking up friends and acquaintances —and anyone else they saw and liked—along the way. The taxi driver became a guest of honor at the party.

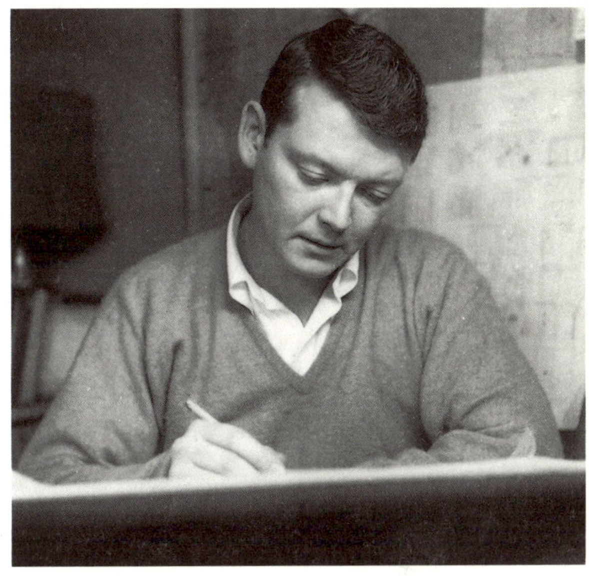

As a civilian, Dick returned to his drawing board, at first to work in the world of advertising.

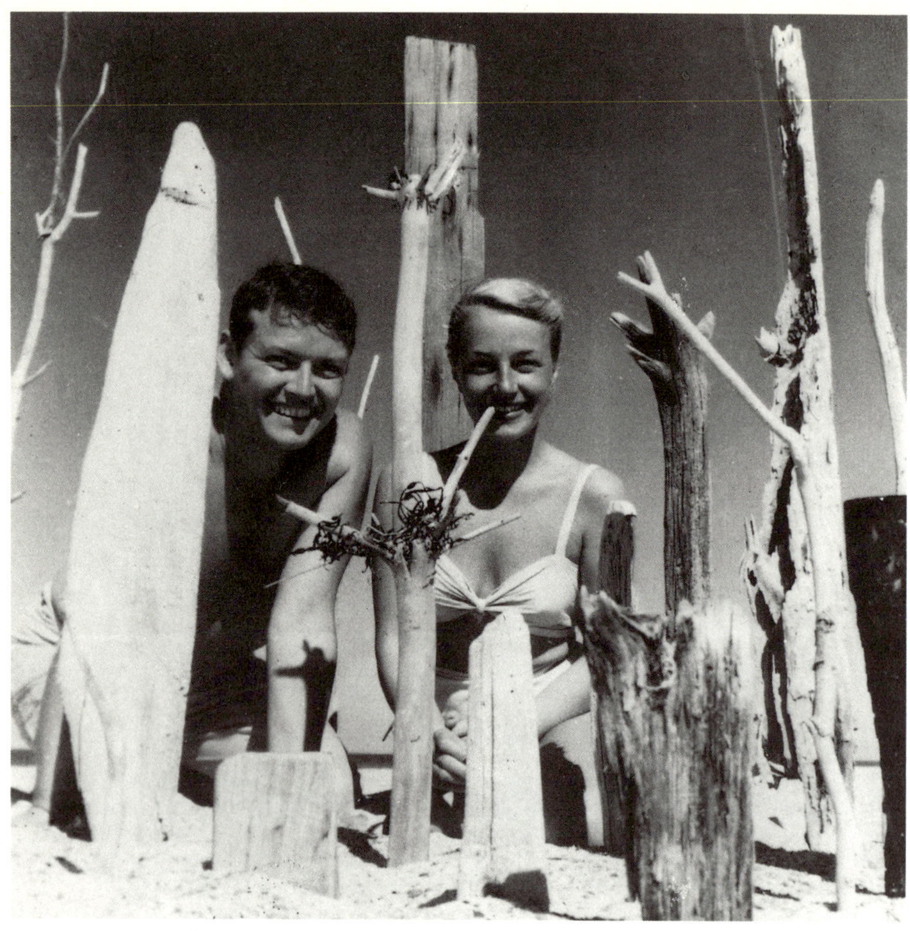

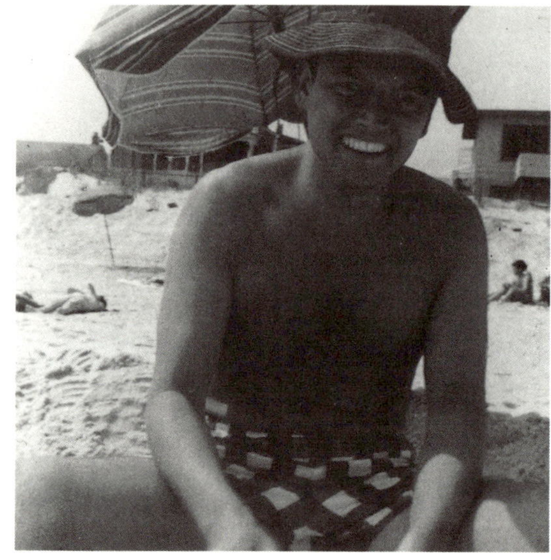

A group of snapshopts from Dick and Patsy's honeymoon on Martha's Vineyard island, off the coast of Massachusetts

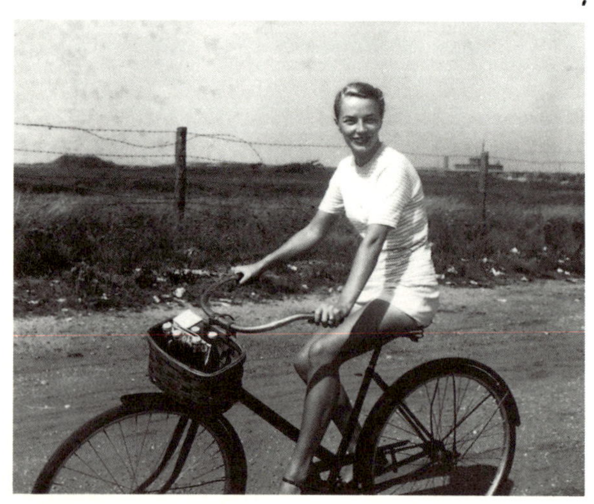

After the wedding festivities, the young couple went off for a brief honeymoon on the island of Martha's Vineyard, but as soon as they got back to New York they had to start thinking about their future. Everything had happened so quickly that they'd had no opportunity for much planning. Dick decided that they should live in Patsy's apartment on Ninth Street. The rent there was cheaper. He also wanted Patsy to continue working at the agency. As a child of the depression years, he tended all through his life to be cautious about spending more money than necessary.

There was another, more immediate reason for his caution. After his job for *Holiday* magazine, Dick's agent hadn't produced many additional assignments. Work was thinning out again. One day the agent suggested that he create some sample illustrations for children's books. The idea appealed to Richard, and he immediately set to work preparing a portfolio. While he toiled at the drawing board mastering the new subject matter, Patsy worked at the agency.

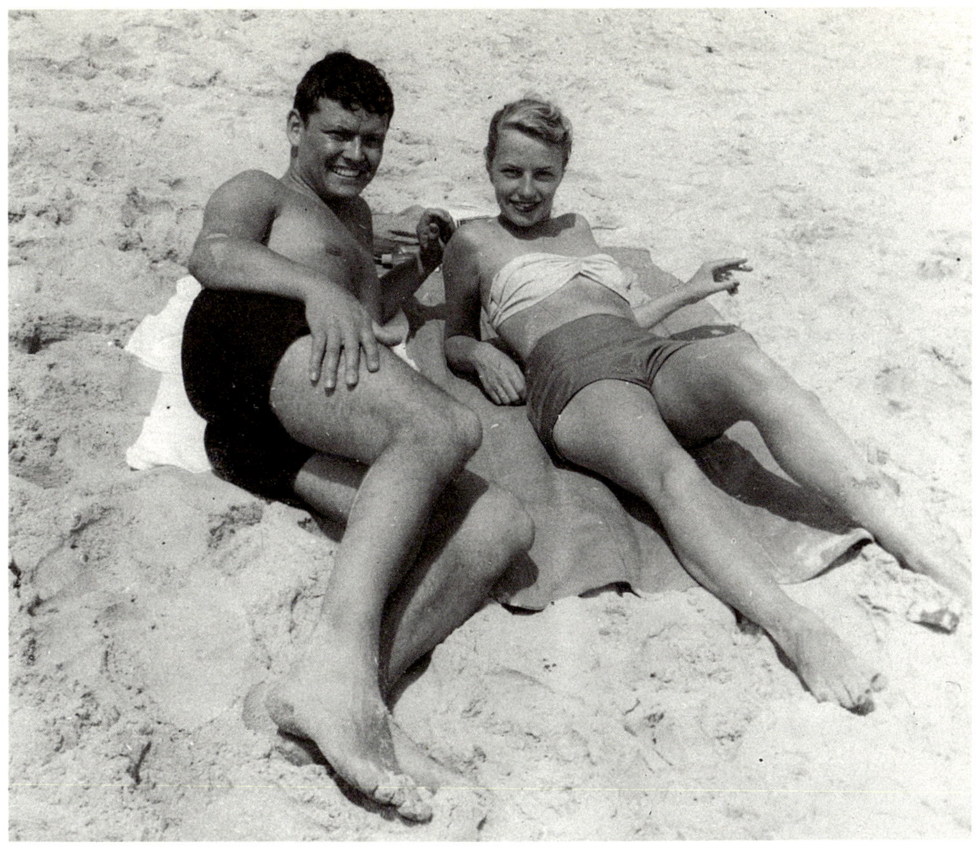

Finally, in the late summer of 1948, Scarry got his first big break, and it came through the new art samples he had been preparing for children's books. His agent made an appointment for him to show his artwork to Lucille Ogle at Artists and Writers Guild. Artists and Writers was a small editorial subsidiary company set up in New York City and financed by Western Printing Company, which had huge printing presses in both Racine, Wisconsin, and Poughkeepsie, New York. Western also owned a publishing division called Whitman in Racine. It produced mass-market activity books and games, but the company needed more material to keep its presses running full time. The books created by Artists and Writers, under the direction of Georges Duplaix and Lucille Ogle, would be unique. Because of Western's printing resources, they could afford to include many full-color illustrations.

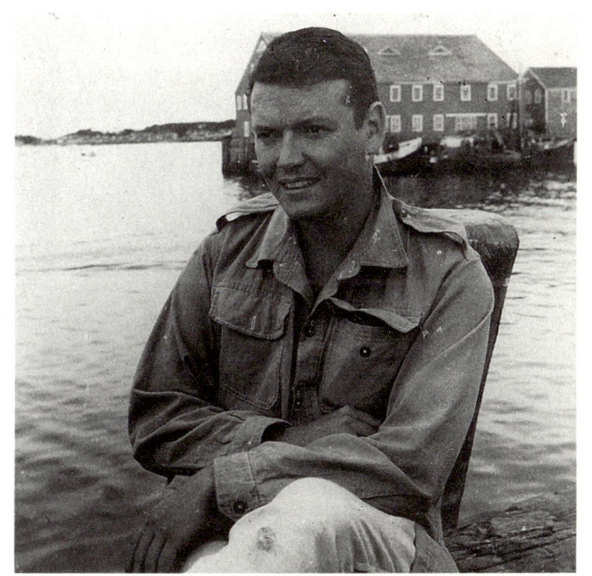

At first Artists and Writers placed their books with a number of different publishers, including Random House, Simon and Schuster, Harper and Brothers, and Grosset & Dunlap. One of the early products they created was Little Golden Books. These were small hardcover books that sold for just twenty-five cents. Albert Leventhal, vice president and sales manager at Simon and Schuster, was immediately excited by the concept. Such a line of children's books would provide a perfect complement to the twenty-five-cent adult Pocket Books that Simon and Schuster was already distributing.

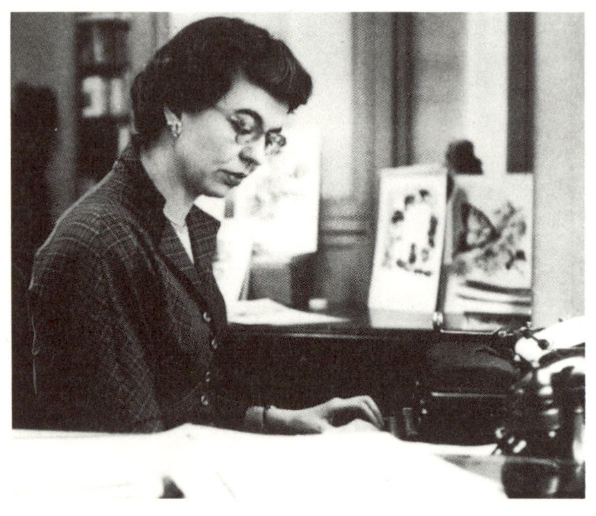

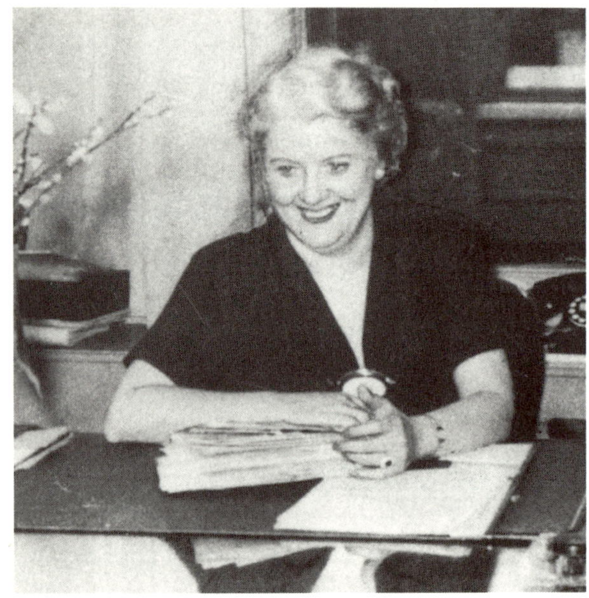

At top: Jane Werner Watson, in charge of the editorial staff at Artists and Writers Guild during the 1940s

Above: Lucille Ogle, the talented cofounder of Artists and Writers, gave Scarry his first assignment as a children's book illustrator.

The first list of Little Golden Books was launched in 1942, and the sales immediately surpassed everyone's expectations. The initial list consisted of just twelve titles, but within five months of publication, one and a half million books had been sold. The huge demand meant that more and more books had to be created. This, in turn, created work for more and more authors and illustrators. By 1947 total sales had reached thirty-nine million copies. Richard could not have arrived in Lucille Ogle's office at a better time. Jane Werner Watson, who was then in charge of the editorial department, later wrote a first-hand account of the meeting:

> *In the mid-1940s, wartime staff dislocations and other circumstances put Lucille Ogle in command of the Artists and Writers Guild office, and I (for the duration) was in charge of the editorial side. Lucille loved her lunch-hour shopping excursions, and I was quite accustomed to being summoned to her sanctum for a viewing of the latest, often a new hat. (Hats were very big in those days!) So I was not surprised one quiet afternoon to receive another such summons.*
>
> *Of course Lucille also kept her door open to artists and their agents. Young hopefuls bearing bulky portfolios were always made welcome—and sometimes invited to share Lucille's excitement over her latest purchase.*
>
> *This particular day it was indeed a young hopeful I had been asked in to meet, and give an opinion on his art samples. He was a tall, meticulously groomed, solemn young man, round-faced and wide-eyed, fresh from a Boston art school and the army, and very much the Proper Bostonian of half a hundred years ago.*
>
> *His portfolio, samples from which were spread out on Lucille's broad desk top, clearly showed particular promise, so he was promptly given an assignment. This was Richard Scarry, whose long-lived success has been a delight to us all.*

To Richard's great delight, Artists and Writers signed him to a one-year exclusive services contract, dated December 8, 1948. It guaranteed him an annual income of $4,800, payable in monthly installments of $400. (The agreement was renewable for up to five years.) By the terms of the contract he was to provide the artwork for two Golden storybooks and two Little Golden Books. Finally the young army veteran was doing what he loved to do and getting well paid for it.

For the next several months, Dick spent long hours bent over his drawing board. Simon and Schuster published a total of six books illustrated by Richard

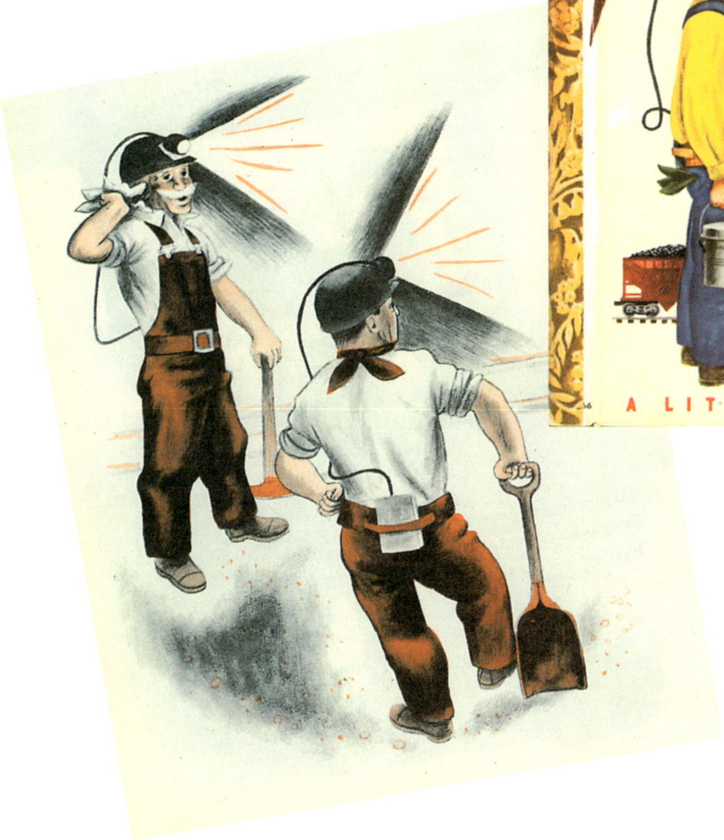

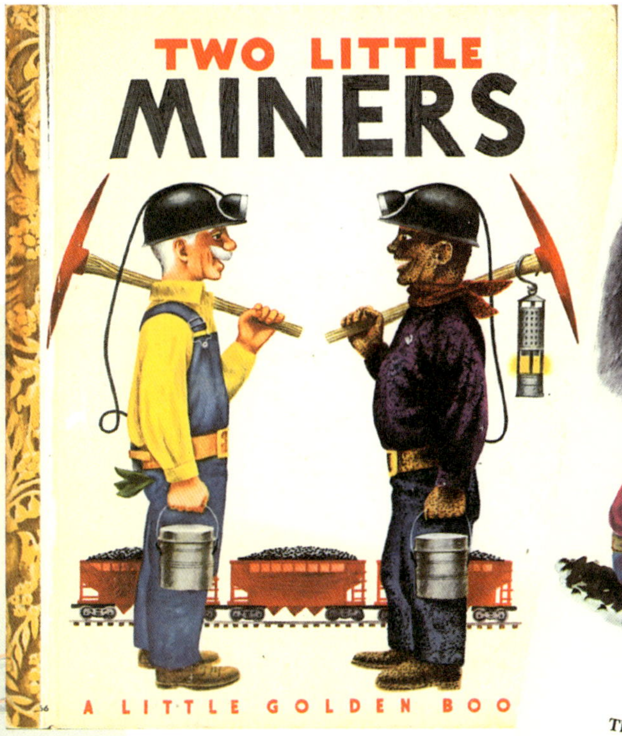

TWO LITTLE MINERS

A LITTLE GOLDEN BOO

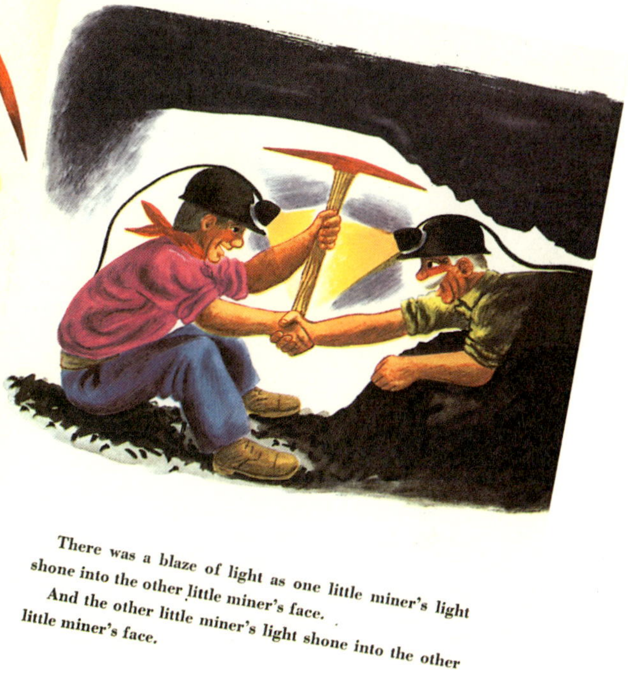

There was a blaze of light as one little miner's light shone into the other little miner's face.

And the other little miner's light shone into the other little miner's face.

Above: The cover and two inside illustrations from *Two Little Miners,* the first Little Golden Book illustrated by Richard Scarry

Below: Scarry at work.

Scarry during 1949. As soon as he finished the artwork for one manuscript, the editors at Artists and Writers would send him another. Obviously, they liked his work. His first Little Golden Book, published on June 7, 1949, was called *Two Little Miners.* The text was by Margaret Wise Brown, who had already made quite a name for herself as a children's book author, and Edith Thacher Hurd. In several interviews Dick himself said that the first story he illustrated was a storybook called *The Boss of the Barnyard.* However, the official publication date for *The Boss of the Barnyard* was September 15, 1949. This discrepancy is quite possible. Simon and Schuster shipped Little Golden Books in assortments—a mixture of old and new titles—and they selected books on the basis of how they would fit into the overall assortment.

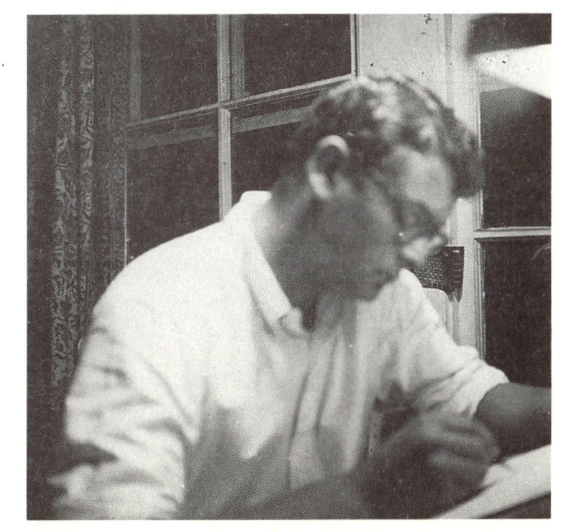

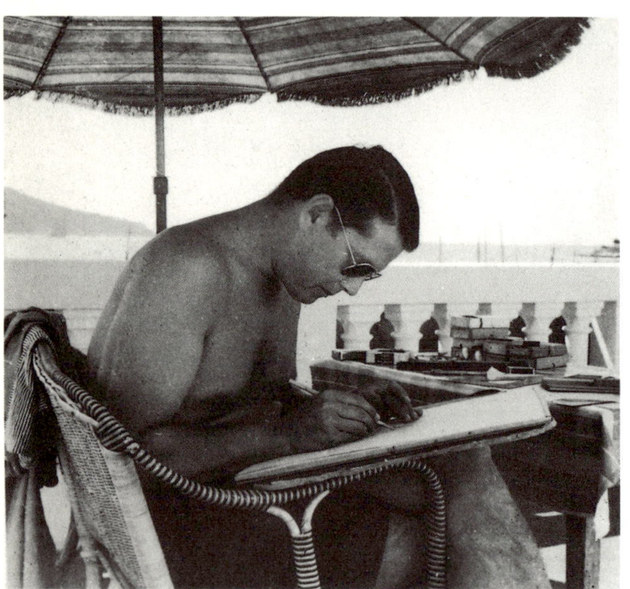

Even at the beach, Dick could often be found working with his sketchbook and paints.

Frequently they delayed the shipment of a new title until it fit the special needs of a particular assortment.

In spite of the hard work, the newly married couple enjoyed living in New York. Dick was gradually acquiring a circle of friends among the young authors and artists working on books for Simon and Schuster. Alice and Martin Provensen, John Parr Miller, Mike Smollin, Mary Blair, and Aurelius Battaglia all lived in the New York area; Feodor Rojankovsky made frequent trips to the city from his home in Florida, and Gustaf Tenggren came regularly from Maine. In addition, Patsy had many good friends from the advertising world. They led an active social life, centered in Greenwich Village, and frequently went out to dinner at first-class restaurants, using Patsy's salary for special entertainment expenses.

After he finished the first six books for Artists and Writers, there was a fairly long break before Richard could expect another manuscript. Although he and Patsy had already had an "official" honeymoon, Dick was very eager for them to take a real honeymoon trip to Europe, so they decided to book passage on an ocean liner to England. They financed the trip with the money Patsy had saved from her salary.

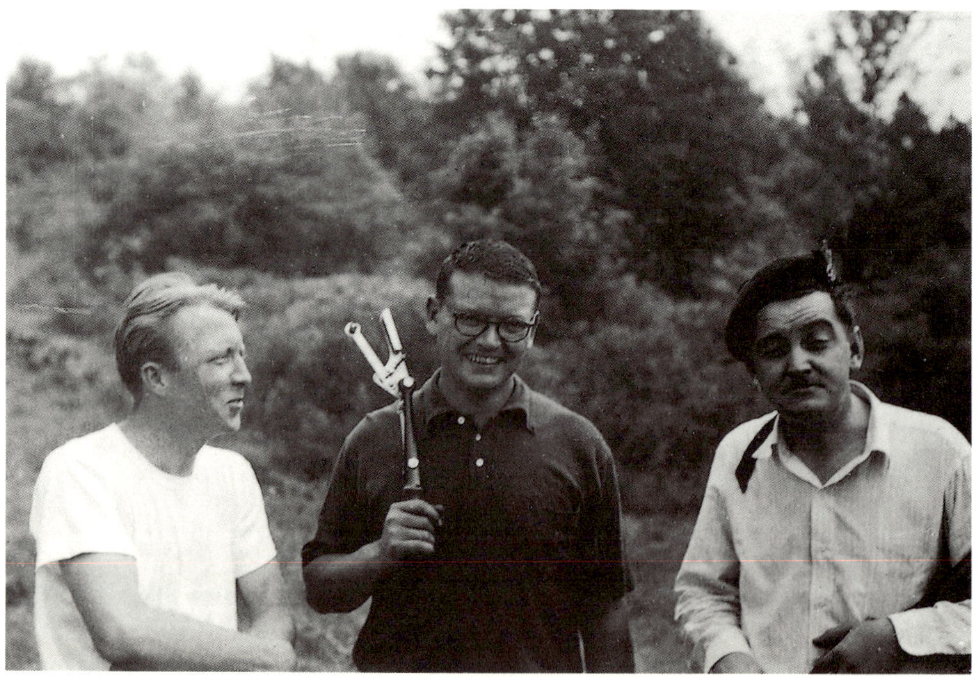

Scarry poses in the country with two artist friends, Martin Provensen *(left)* and John MacLeish

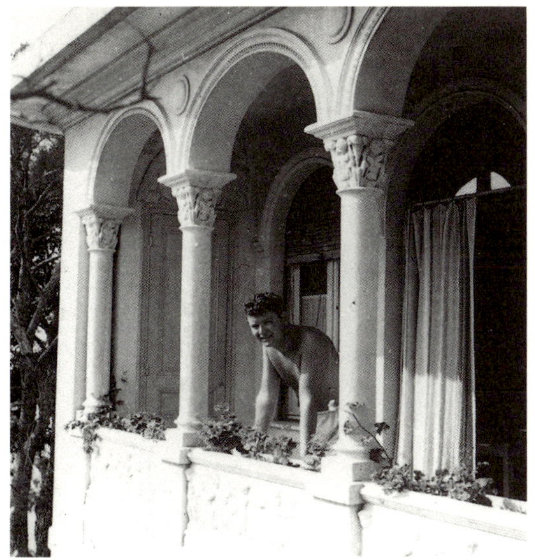

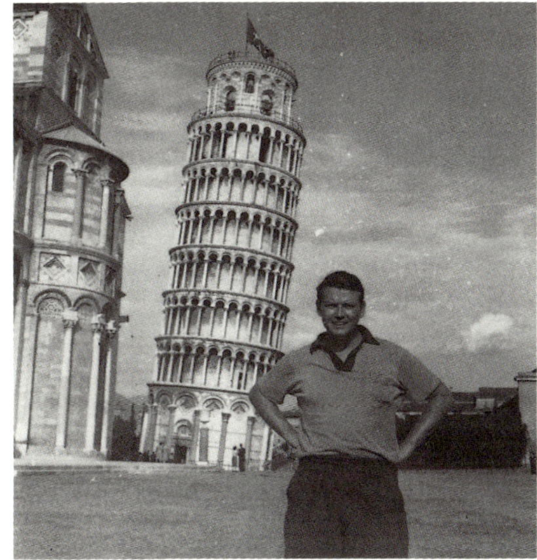

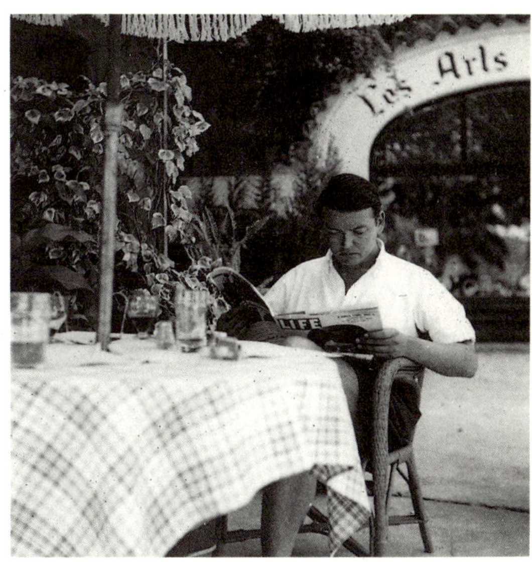

Three photographs of Scarry taken during the couple's first trip to Europe: *(left)* leaning over a balcony at St Jean Cap Ferrat, *(center)* standing in front of the famous leaning tower of Pisa in Italy, and *(right)* sitting in a café at Villefrance on the Riviera

It was an exciting voyage; the night before they landed at Southampton they danced until dawn, and they were still wearing evening clothes when the ship docked. A friend of Dick's had come to the pier to meet them, and Patsy tried to attract his attention by jumping up and down in her evening pumps, waving her arms and screaming as loudly as possible. At last, the pilot of the tug boat shouted through his megaphone, "If the lady in the long pink dress would just be silent for a moment, we could dock this ship!"

The trip proved to be a perfect honeymoon. They went everywhere, and Dick had a wonderful time sharing with Patsy all of the favorite haunts he had discovered during his wartime experiences. They made one new joint discovery, however, which would prove to have great significance in future years: St. Jean Cap Ferrat, a tiny, unspoiled village on the French Riviera. They rented a sunny apartment with a view of the sea and a small beach. The area attracted an interesting mix of artists, writers, actors, and deposed members of royalty from different European countries, and everybody got acquainted either on the beach or at the Hotel Brise Marine. They decided that St. Jean Cap Ferrat was definitely a place they would return to.

The last stop on the "grand tour" was Paris. From there they would go directly to the port to board their ship back to the States. Unfortunately, they had spent nearly all their money, so there was very little they could do during their last ten days in France. No glittering night clubs, no fancy four-star restaurants. In fact, they could

Dick and Patsy sightseeing in Paris near Notre Dame Cathedral

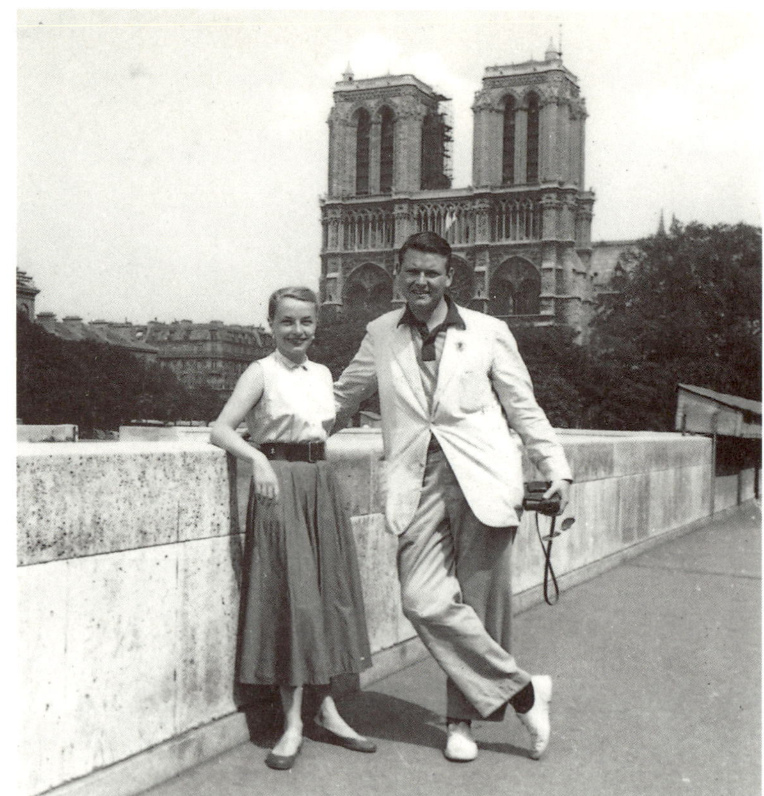

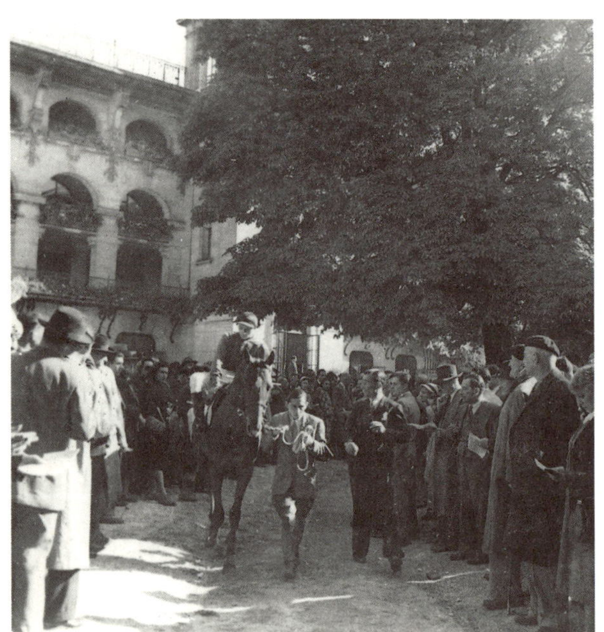

The miraculous racehorse winner, Buffalo Bill, replenished the empty Scarry pocketbook.

barely afford a cup of coffee and a thin slice of ham on French bread. They weren't even sure they could pay their hotel bill.

Despite their lack of funds, Dick decided they should go to the racetrack. Buoyed by the bustle and excitement, he recklessly bet their last five-franc piece on a horse named *Buffalo Bill.* With a name like that, Dick insisted, how could the horse fail to win? Not many bettors agreed with him. *Buffalo Bill* was definitely a very long shot, but—wonder of wonders—he won. Suddenly the Scarrys were rich! They could pay their hotel bill, they could go to the Folies Bergère, and they could eat in some really good restaurants. But all too soon they had to board the ocean liner and return home. The trip had been perfect, so perfect that Dick announced he wanted to live in Europe someday.

When they disembarked in New York City, the racket, the traffic, the dirt in the streets hit them with a bang. Worse yet, their taxi driver tried to cheat them. Deciding that they were tourists who wouldn't know any better, he headed for Wall Street after Dick had instructed him to go to Ninth Street. It was on that taxi ride, Dick later said, that he first began to think about moving to a house in the suburbs, maybe Connecticut. They wanted to start a family, and they didn't think that the city would be a great place for a child.

MOVING TO EXURBIA

About a year and a half after their marriage, the Scarrys rented a small one-story house on the Conklin Farm in Ridgefield, Connecticut. Alongside the house stood a long, narrow building that housed a garage, workroom, and separate storage room. They called it "the barn." Both the barn and the house were painted white when they moved in. Later the Scarrys had the buildings painted red.

The Conklin Farm was an old-fashioned kind of farm (the type that Dick would later draw in his books) complete with chickens and a chicken coop, cows that grazed in the meadow behind the Scarry house, and a horse called Pepper. There were many beautiful tall elm trees scattered around the property, and a true old-fashioned barn close to the Conklins' house.

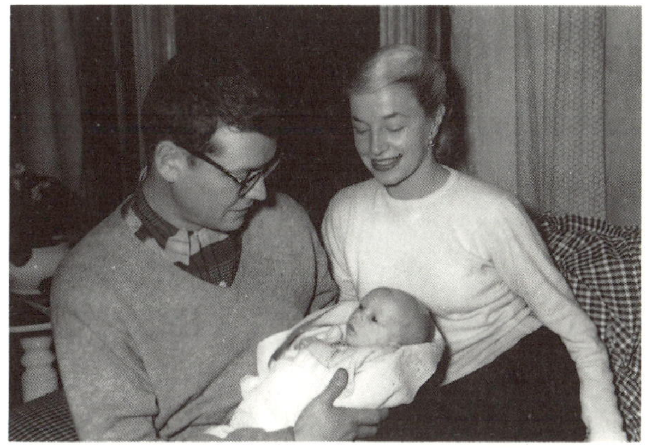

Dick and Patsy gaze fondly at their new son, Huck.

Dick had recently bought a sporty, black MG-TC. They loaded the little MG with the few fragile possessions they could squeeze in and started off early one morning for their new home. Ridgefield in those days was a small farming community, near enough to Long Island Sound for Dick to go sailing. Except for a few airline pilots and their wives, not many congenial young couples were living in the area. One illustrious businessman, Henry Luce, lived down the road in a much fancier house, along with his famous playwright wife, Claire Booth Luce. Luce, of course, was the owner and publisher of *Life, Time,* and *Fortune* magazines. Patsy had met Mrs. Luce while working on commercials for *The March of Time,* a special news feature prepared by *Time* magazine for showing in movie theaters, but she didn't really know her. So the Luces couldn't be numbered among their neighborhood friends. For social life they had to rely on visitors from New York.

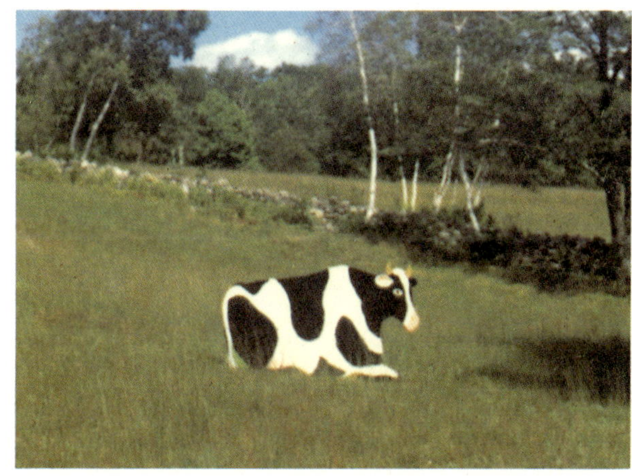

John Miller's painted, wooden cutout of a cow looked absurdly real lying in the Scarry yard at Ridgefield, Connecticut.

John Parr Miller was one of their artist friends who often came to visit. Dick admired John's artwork, which had appeared in many Golden Books, and later said that his illustrations had considerable influence on his own style. John was a short, wiry man with a quirky sense of humor, and during one visit he decided to paint a prancing black horse on the side of the barn. It naturally attracted an enormous amount of attention, both from curious local residents and friends from the publishing world who drove up from the city. In addition, he painted a wooden cutout of a black-and-white cow lying on its side, which the Scarrys placed on their lawn. It looked absurdly real.

The new Scarry quarters at Ridgefield, complete with a prancing black horse painted by John Miller.

Below: Dick shows John how his new gun works.

Bottom: Richard Scarry, the gentleman skeet shooter.

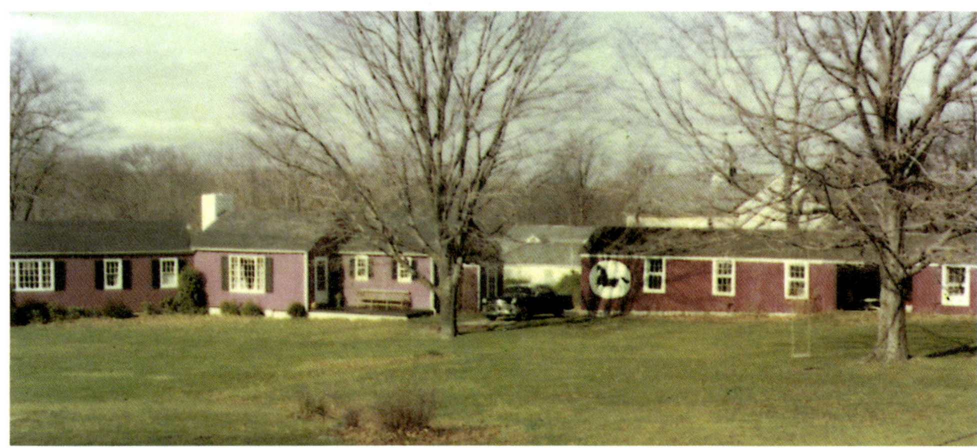

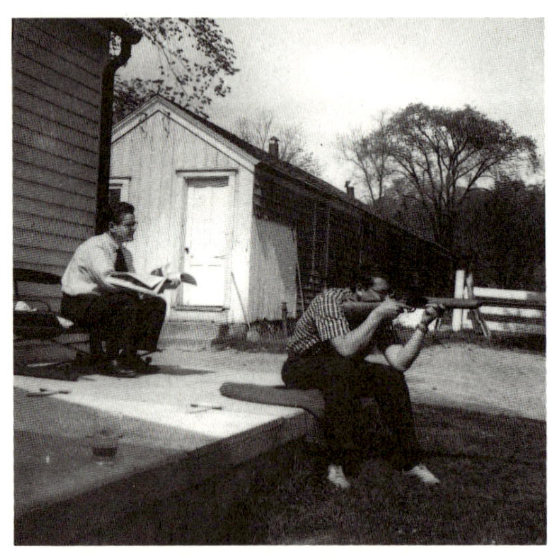

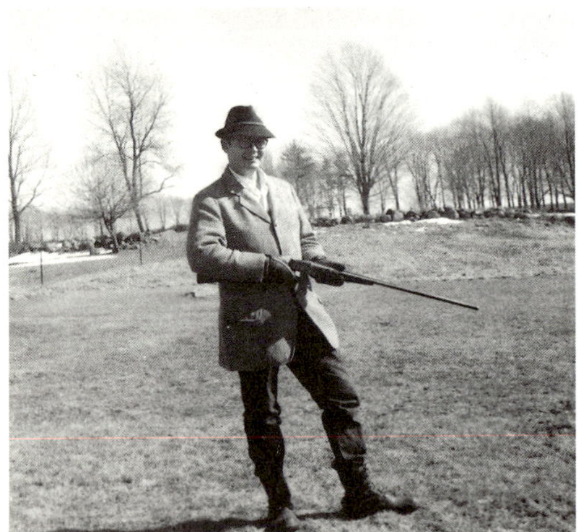

There was always something unusual going on at the Scarrys' in those days. Dick was the kind of fellow who enjoyed acquiring, and even making, new gadgets. He also liked to collect guns, though he had definitely never excelled at target shooting while in the army. His poor vision proved to be a severe drawback on the shooting range. Nevertheless, he suddenly developed an interest in skeet shooting and bought a couple of shotguns at Abercrombie and Fitch.

Skeet shooting is a sport developed to give hunters of game birds practice at hitting moving targets in midair. The targets are called skeets, or clay pigeons, and they are usually flipped into the air by a spring-driven mechanism known as a trap. The trap gives a spinning motion to the clay pigeon.

Dick, with his usual New England thriftiness, didn't want to spend money on a trap. Instead he made Patsy throw the skeet into the air while he tried to shoot it with his gun. This, as Patsy later told the story, was a terrifying job because Dick was such a poor shot. One day, while they were having a practice shoot, Claire Booth Luce came down the road in a long white sedan driven by the Luce chauffeur. Patsy tossed the clay pigeon into the air. Dick shot at it, missing the Luce car by just a fraction of an inch. "Drop everything!" he shouted, and they rushed into the barn to hide like a couple of guilty children. That ended the skeet shooting; Dick realized that he was too much of a menace to the neighborhood. The episode was typical of his childlike sense of fun.

He continued to work hard on his illustration assignments for Artists and Writers, and in 1951 the monthly payments were raised from $400 to $650. That same year Simon and Schuster published his *Great Big Car and Truck Book.* It was the first

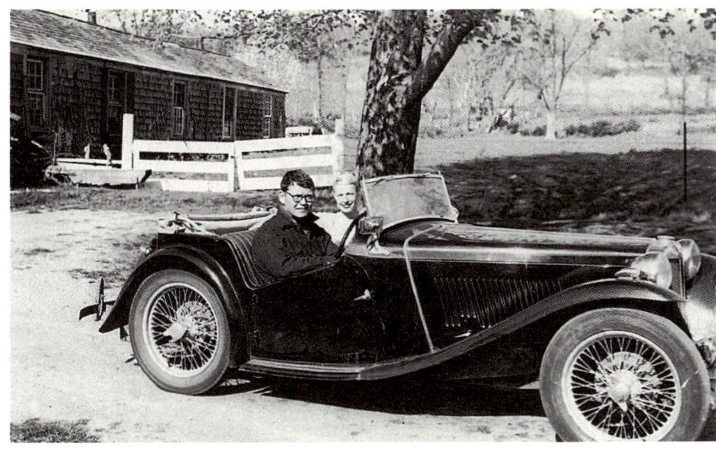

Left: The Scarrys in their sporty new English MG-TC.

Below: The title page, showing Dick and Patsy whizzing along in their little car, from *The Great Big Car and Truck Book,* the first book written and illustrated by Scarry.

Scarry book for which somebody else hadn't provided the words. The text was minimal, consisting of a short descriptive line for each drawing, but Dick had worked out the editorial content himself. The characters were all humans, and it's fun to note that the couple in the small black sports car at the beginning of the book are obviously Dick and Patsy.

The next year, 1952, Artists and Writers drew up a new "exclusive services" agreement to run from 1952 to 1956. It contained a provision that the agreement could be canceled before 1956 on proper notice. Wherever possible, Western liked to keep its popular illustrators from working for competitors. At the same time, it preferred to pay them a flat fee instead of a royalty.

Now that Patsy was no longer working at the advertising agency, she decided to try her hand at writing stories for Little Golden Books. She welcomed a chance to keep writing and, at the same time, earn some extra money. Artists and Writers paid a flat fee for the stories—at first it was only $250—but the payment seemed an unexpected fortune at the time. In 1953, Simon and Schuster published a new Little Golden Book called *Danny Beaver's Secret.* The text was written by Patsy, and Dick provided the illustrations.

Patsy had a special incentive for wanting to write stories for children—she was pregnant. On January 21, 1953, a son was born at Norwalk Hospital. (Dick included a diaper service truck in his *Great Big Car and Truck Book.*) They named their new son Richard, but from the very beginning he was always called Huck. Dick took the nickname from his favorite book and character, Mark Twain's Huckleberry Finn.

The year 1953 was very important for Dick in other ways. Simon and Schuster

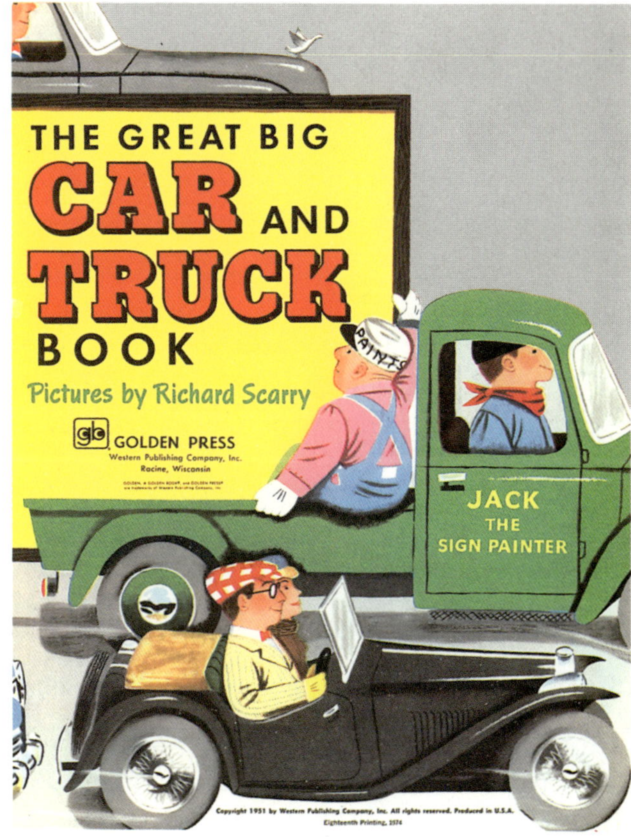

Overleaf: Covers and illustrations from four Little Golden Books written by Patsy and illustrated by Dick.

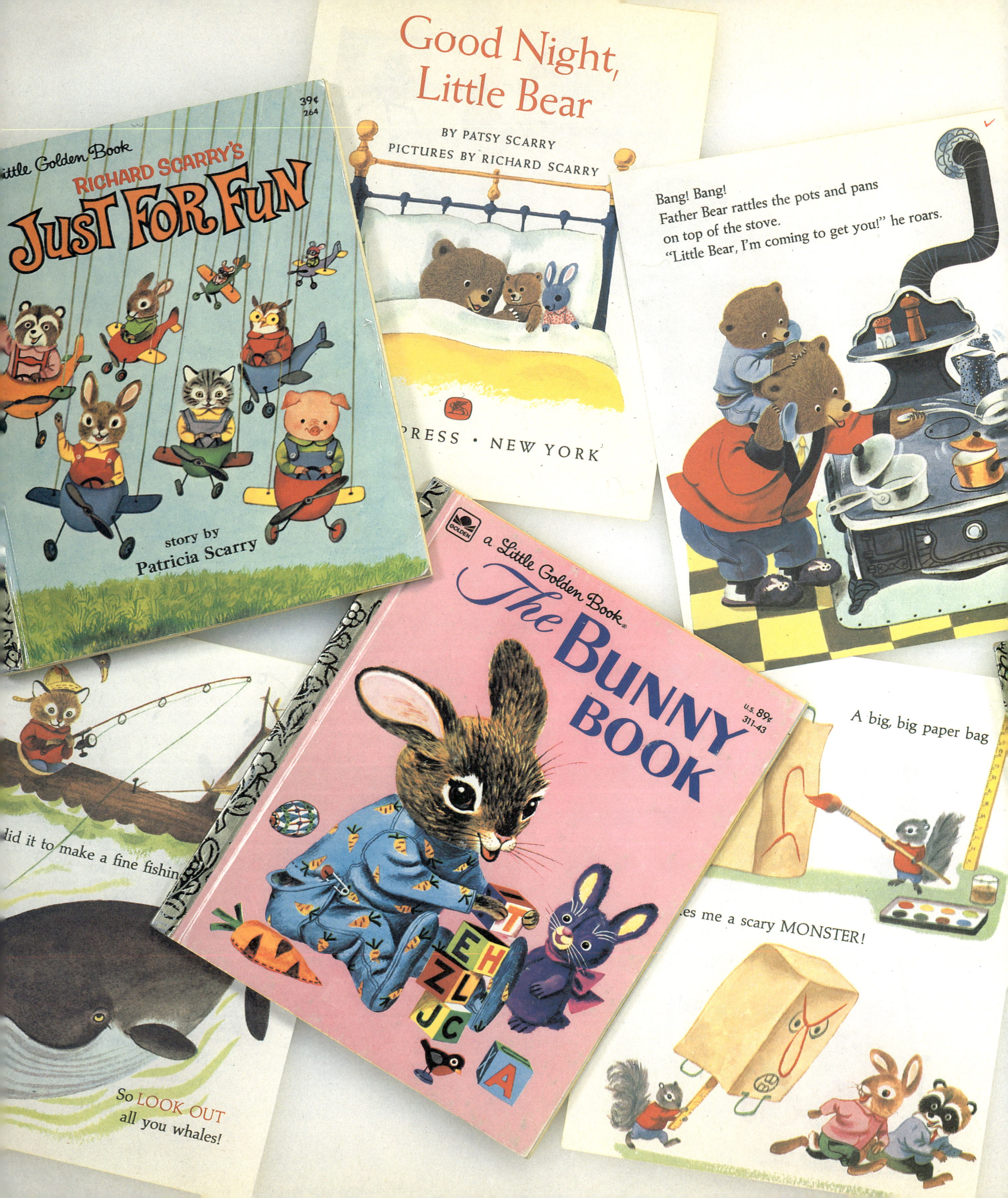
39¢
264
ittle Golden Book
RICHARD SCARRY'S
JUST FOR FUN
story by
Patricia Scarry
Good Night,
Little Bear
BY PATSY SCARRY
PICTURES BY RICHARD SCARRY
PRESS • NEW YORK
Bang! Bang!
Father Bear rattles the pots and pans
on top of the stove.
"Little Bear, I'm coming to get you!" he roars.
GOLDEN
a Little Golden Book
The BUNNY BOOK
U.S. 89¢
311-43
lid it to make a fine fishin
So LOOK OUT
all you whales!
A big, big paper bag
es me a scary MONSTER!

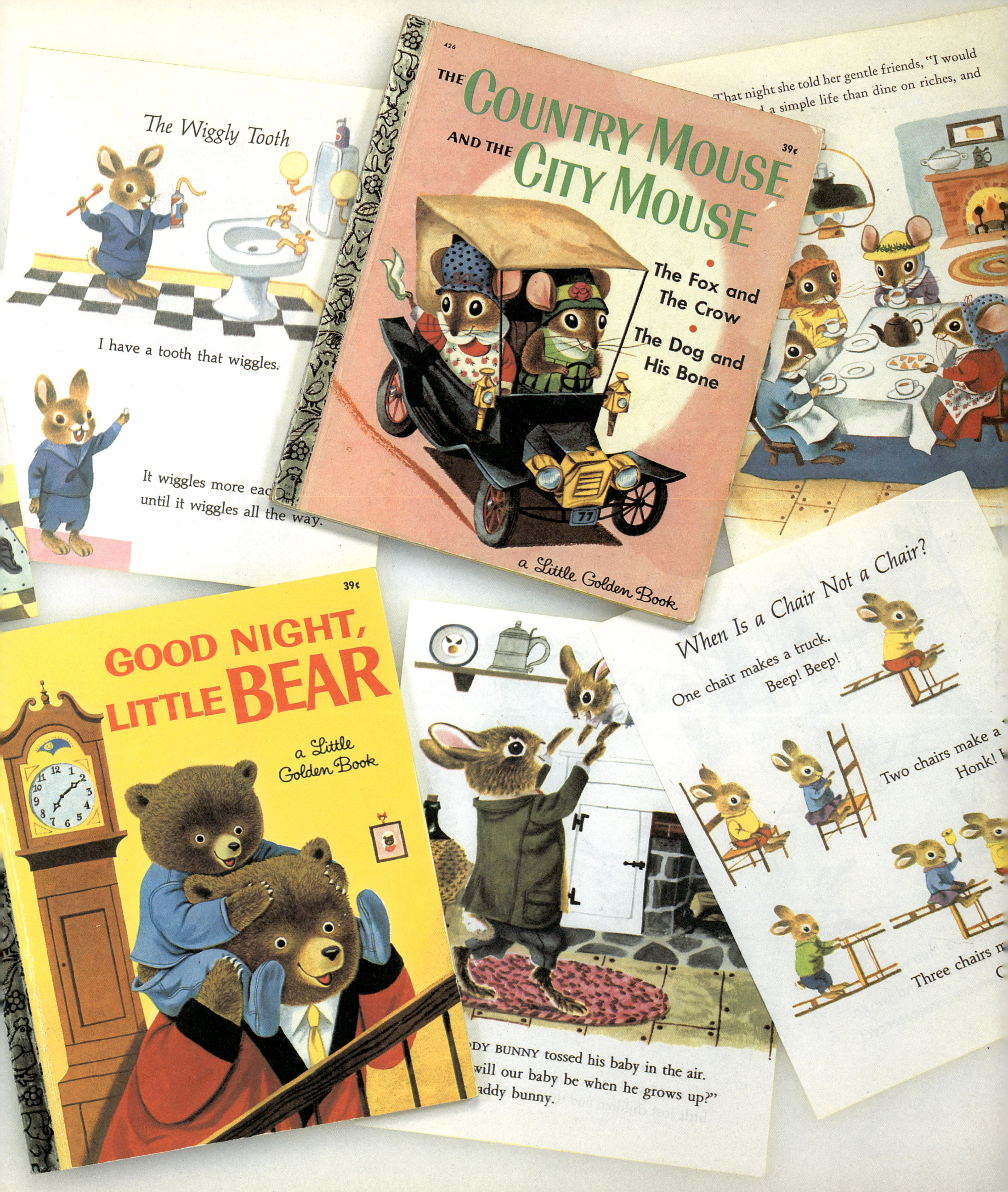
The Wiggly Tooth
I have a tooth that wiggles.
It wiggles more eac
until it wiggles all the way.
426
THE COUNTRY MOUSE AND THE CITY MOUSE
39¢
The Fox and The Crow
The Dog and His Bone
77
a Little Golden Book
That night she told her gentle friends, "I would
a simple life than dine on riches, and
39¢
GOOD NIGHT, LITTLE BEAR
a Little Golden Book
DY BUNNY tossed his baby in the air.
will our baby be when he grows up?"
addy bunny.
When Is a Chair Not a Chair?
One chair makes a truck.
Beep! Beep!
Two chairs make a
Honk!
Three chairs

published six new books with Richard Scarry illustrations. For one of them, a Little Golden Book entitled *Rabbit and His Friends*, Richard also wrote the text. It was a conventional kind of storybook about a rabbit that finds an egg in a "deep, dark, muddy hole." The small furry animal that emerges from the egg mystifies all of rabbit's friends, but eventually they learn that it's a platypus. Although the animal characters all wear a few pieces of clothing, they remain anthropomorphic animal characters. Scarry's illustration style in the book is rather derivative, resembling the stylized, graphic painting of other popular Golden Book artists working at that time. The little storybook is entertaining but scarcely indicative of the really creative work to follow.

The following year there were just three new books with art by Richard Scarry. All of them were Little Golden Books: *Little Indian* had a text by Margaret Wise Brown; *Pierre Bear* was written by Patsy; and Kathryn and Byron Jackson wrote *Party Pig.*

Below and opposite: From *Pierre Bear*, a Little Golden Book written and illustrated by Patsy and Dick and published in 1954. Like the Scarrys, Pierre Bear and his wife have a new baby.

Now that the Scarrys had a baby, the little MG was no longer adequate, so Dick traded it in for a roomier station wagon, nicknamed the "downtown car." Luckily, he didn't park it in the barn. On a weekend when John Miller was visiting, Dick decided to give a demonstration of a new pistol that he had recently bought. The two men went outside. Dick took aim at the barn and fired several shots. The bullets went right through the wall and punctured some paint cans stored inside. Red, yellow, green, and white paint squirted out in all directions, creating a rainbowlike interior.

Toward the end of 1955, Scarry went into New York for a meeting with his agent, Hans Fybel, and Lucille Ogle at the offices of Artists and Writers. Dick was officially terminating his agreement with Fybel, and he had to give due notice of this fact to Artists and Writers. Lucille was a shrewd businesswoman who had had a great deal to do with the success of the company. She had a keen eye for talent and was a never-ending source of creative ideas. She was a short, rather stout woman with a head covered by a mass of white curls (often touched up by a blue rinse). But her most remarkable feature was her wide lavender-blue eyes. The curls and the eyes gave her a cherubic look, but her staff knew better. She had an explosive temper and

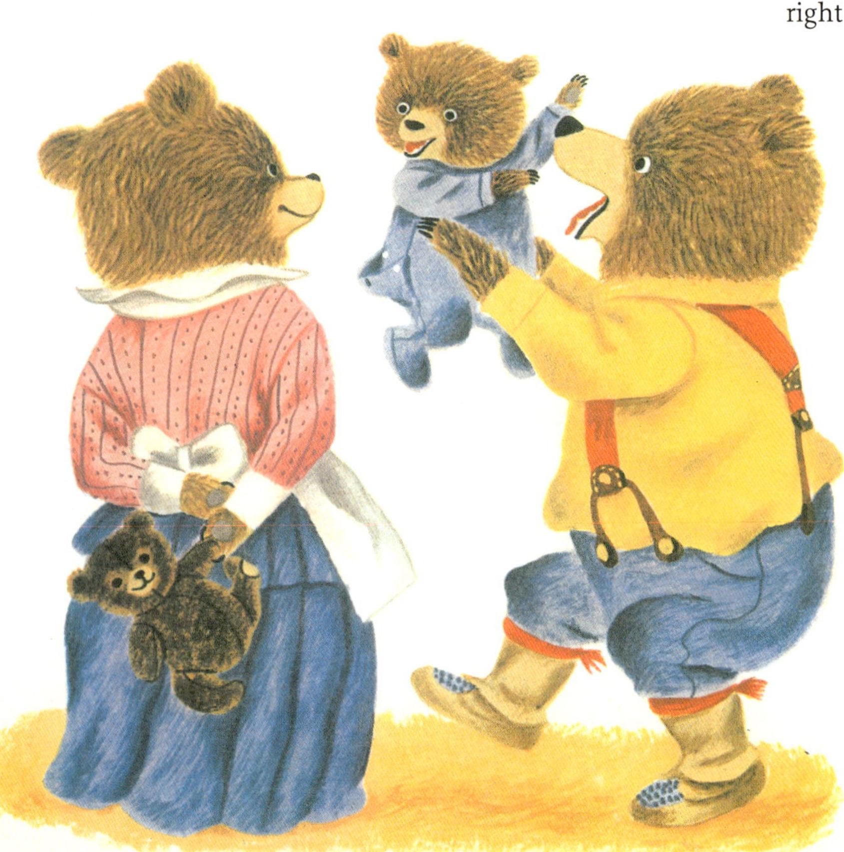

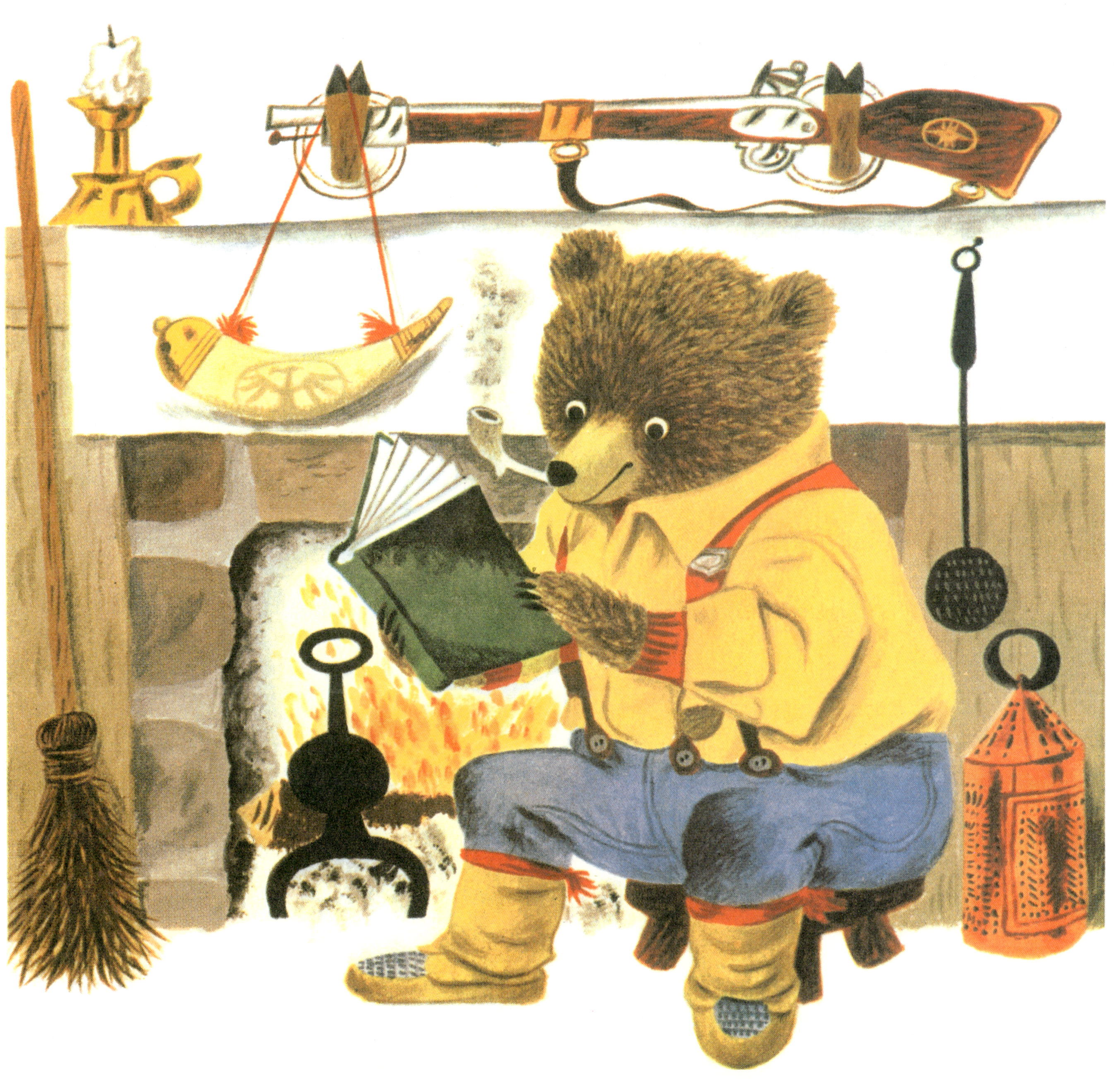

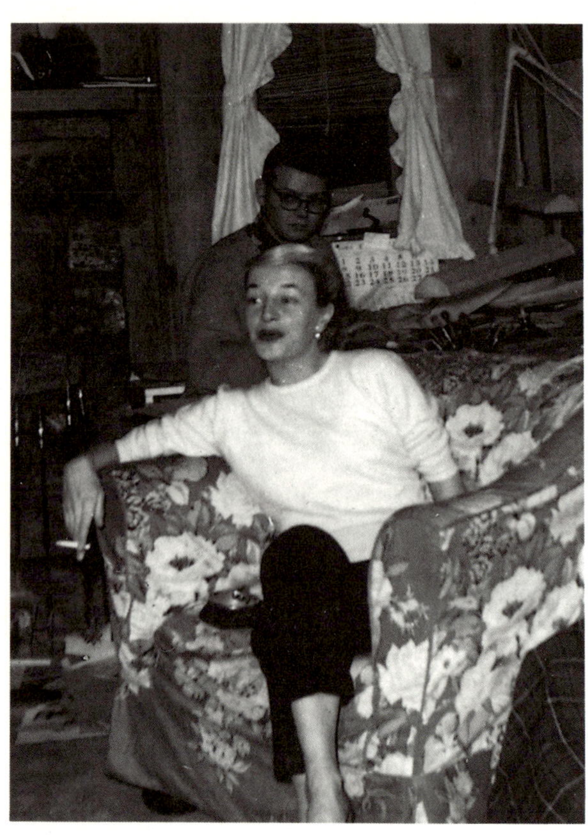

Patsy relaxes in their Ridgefield home while Dick, as always, works at his drawing board.

didn't put up with any nonsense. She was even rumored to have thrown a heavy Scotch tape dispenser at a production man who was irritating her. (She missed him.) But to counter her temper, she also had a delightful sense of humor and could be a great friend and professional advisor.

After Hans Fybel had left, Dick mentioned that he thought he ought to be getting royalties.

"I think you should, too," Lucille responded.

"Then why haven't I been getting them?" Dick asked.

"Because you never asked," Lucille answered.

When Dick told her that now he was asking, she agreed to take care of the problem. On December 31, 1955, the exclusive services agreement of 1952 was terminated; all future books were to be covered by individual contracts with an advance against royalties as a part of each agreement. From one standpoint, 1955 had been a good year for Scarry. He had a new business arrangement with Artists and Writers, and five new books with Scarry illustrations had been published, including *The Golden Bedtime Book* and *Smokey the Bear.* On the other hand, Artists and Writers hadn't sent Dick many new manuscripts to illustrate; for the moment they were cutting down on new assignments. As a result, money was running low in the Scarry household.

Help came just in time from a totally unexpected source. An advertising agency hired Dick and Patsy to fly to Florida, pick up a brand-new Buick and drive from one expensive resort hotel to another, staying a night or two at each. Meanwhile photographers from the agency followed them about taking pictures to be used for a special promotion both for the hotels and the newest model Buick. The job provided Dick and Patsy with a considerable amount of money when they badly needed it, as well as a very nice vacation. Huck stayed at home in the care of a baby nurse.

During the lean period, Dick spent some time developing book ideas of his own. He made pencil sketches for several different projects (including a story about a hippopotamus and a rabbit) and tried to sell them to Golden Books as well as to a few other publishers. But before anything much could come of those projects, Artists and Writers started sending him manuscripts again. For the next few years they kept him busy creating illustrations for both Little Golden Books and big Golden storybooks.

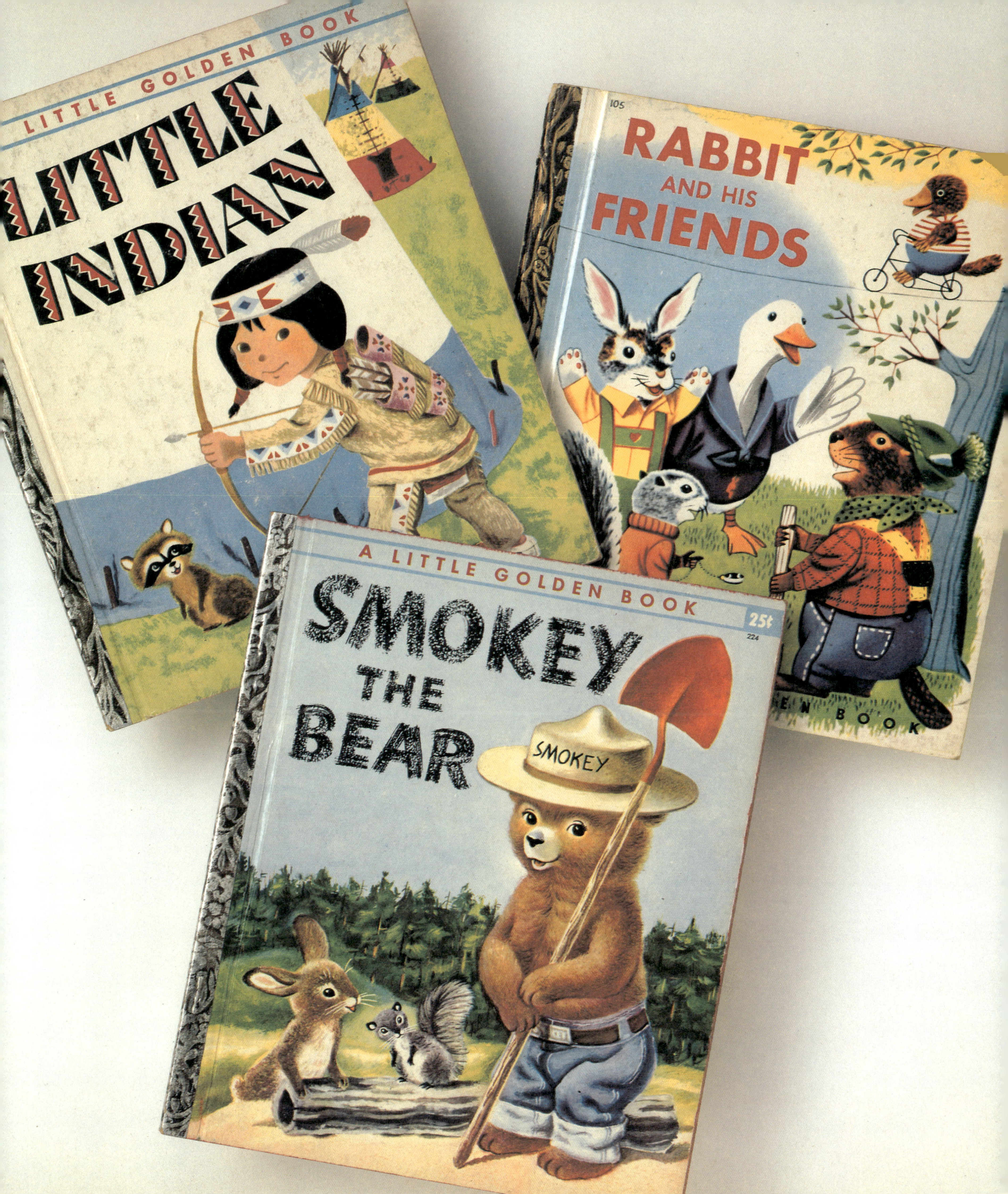

LITTLE GOLDEN BOOK
LITTLE INDIAN
105
RABBIT AND HIS FRIENDS
EN BOOK
A LITTLE GOLDEN BOOK
25¢
224
SMOKEY THE BEAR
SMOKEY

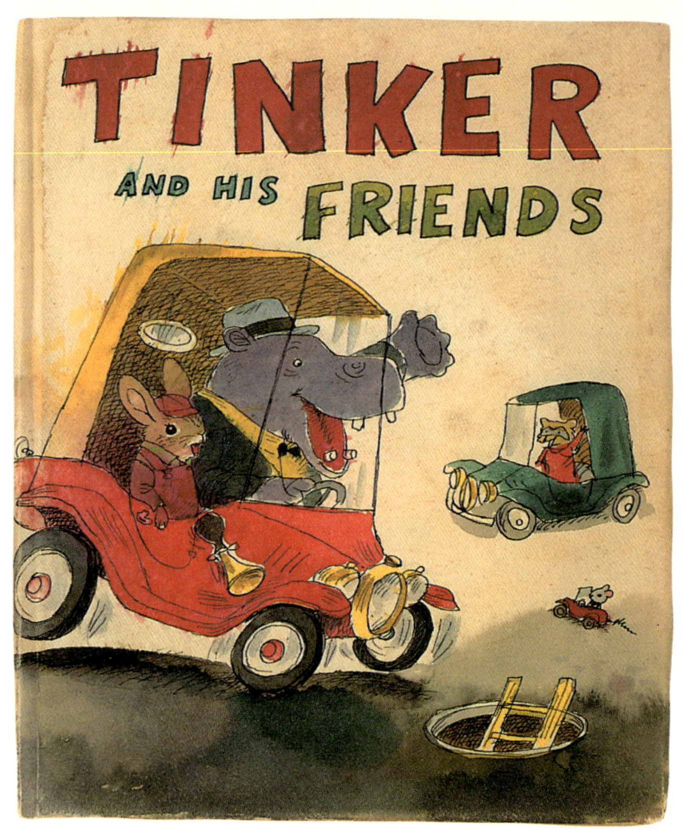

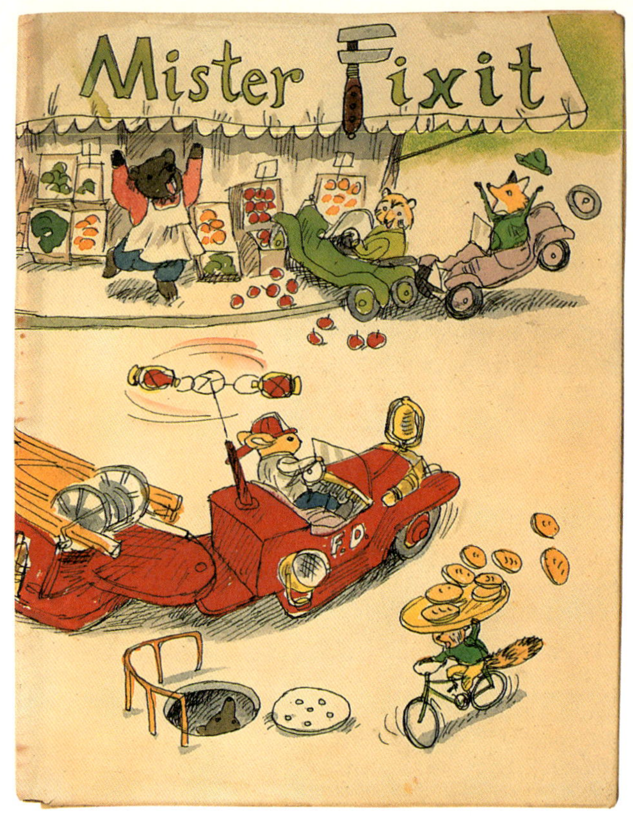

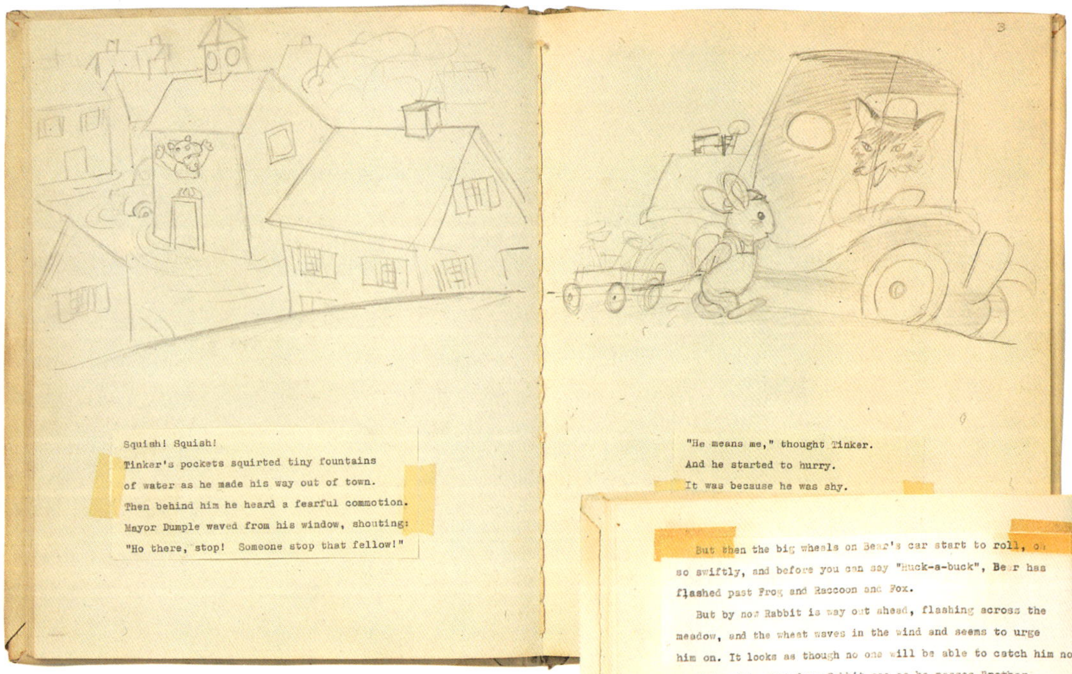

Squish! Squish!
Tinker's pockets squirted tiny fountains
of water as he made his way out of town.
Then behind him he heard a fearful commotion.
Mayor Dumple waved from his window, shouting:
"Ho there, stop! Someone stop that fellow!"

"He means me," thought Tinker.
And he started to hurry.
It was because he was shy.

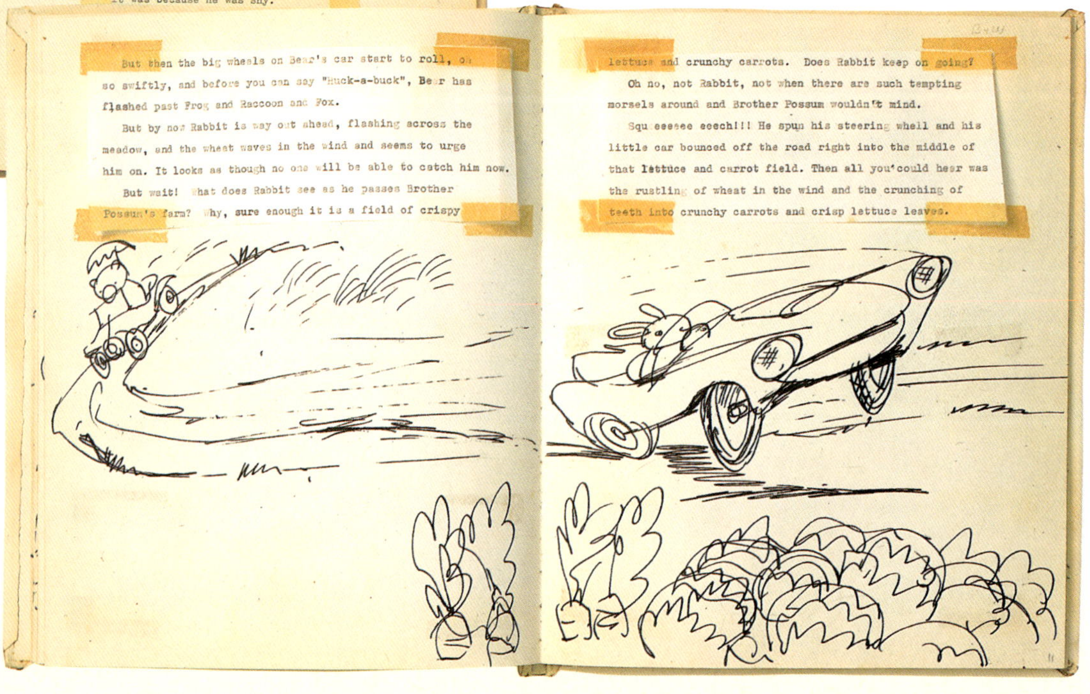

But then the big wheels on Bear's car start to roll, on so swiftly, and before you can say "Huck-a-buck", Bear has flashed past Frog and Raccoon and Fox.

But by now Rabbit is way out ahead, flashing across the meadow, and the wheat waves in the wind and seems to urge him on. It looks as though no one will be able to catch him now.

But wait! What does Rabbit see as he passes Brother Possum's farm? Why, sure enough it is a field of crispy lettuce and crunchy carrots. Does Rabbit keep on going?

Oh no, not Rabbit, not when there are such tempting morsels around and Brother Possum wouldn't mind.

Squeeeeee eeech!!! He spun his steering wheil and his little car bounced off the road right into the middle of that lettuce and carrot field. Then all you'could hear was the rustling of wheat in the wind and the crunching of teeth into crunchy carrots and crisp lettuce leaves.

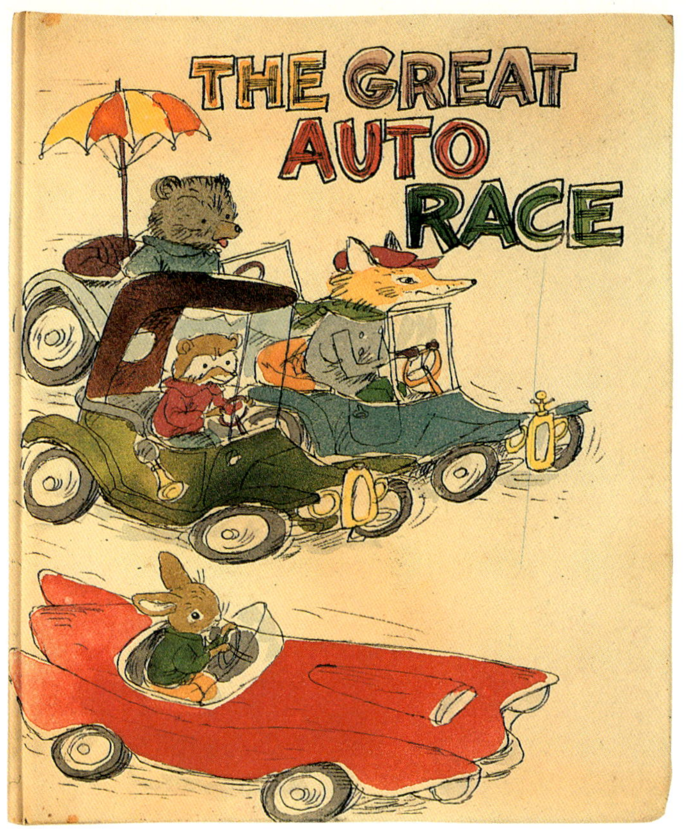

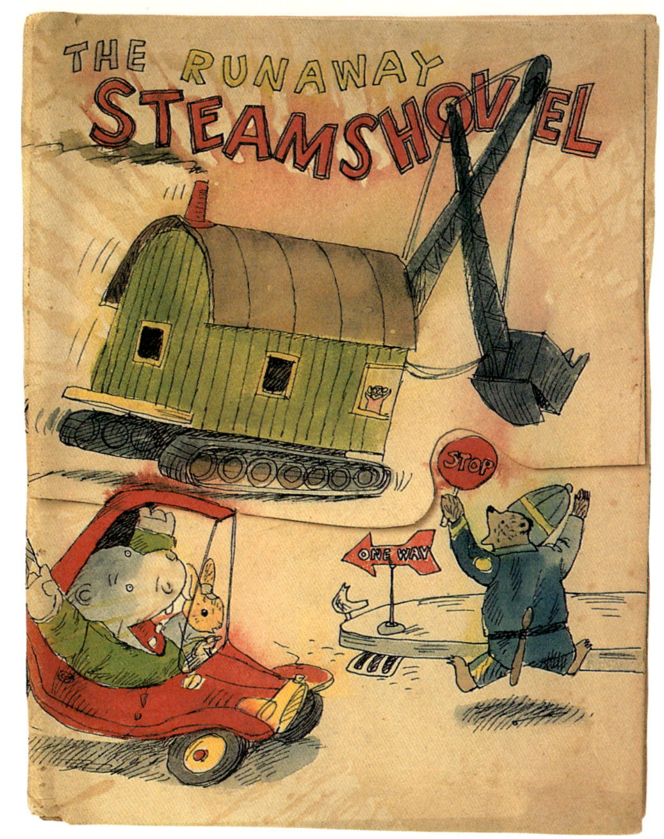

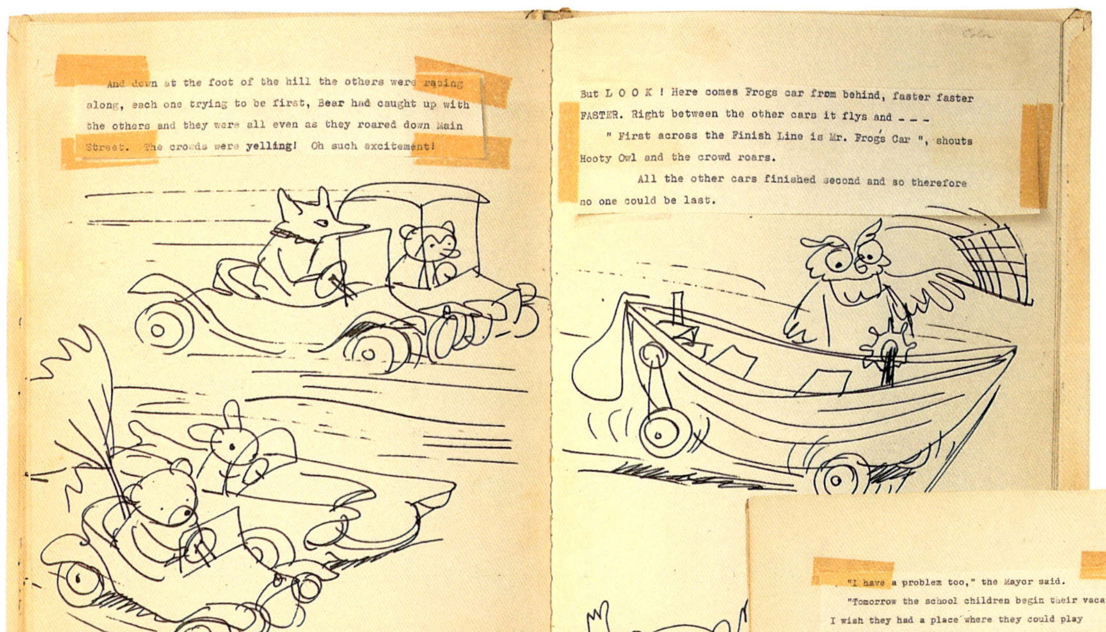

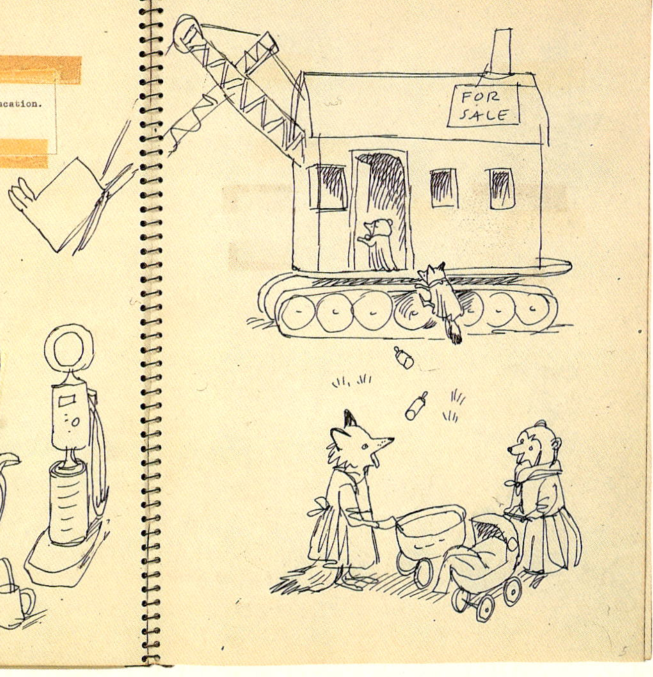

Rough sketches for some book projects that Dick Scarry wrote and illustrated and tried unsuccessfully to sell to publishers when book assignments were scarce. Two of the characters, Mr. Fixit and Tinker, eventually turned up in later books, although Mr. Fixit became a fox, a rather inept one.

Above and opposite: Naughty Bunny was the third book written as well as illustrated by Scarry. In it, for the first time, his animal characters emerged as real people, and Dick showed that lessons in good behavior could be fun.

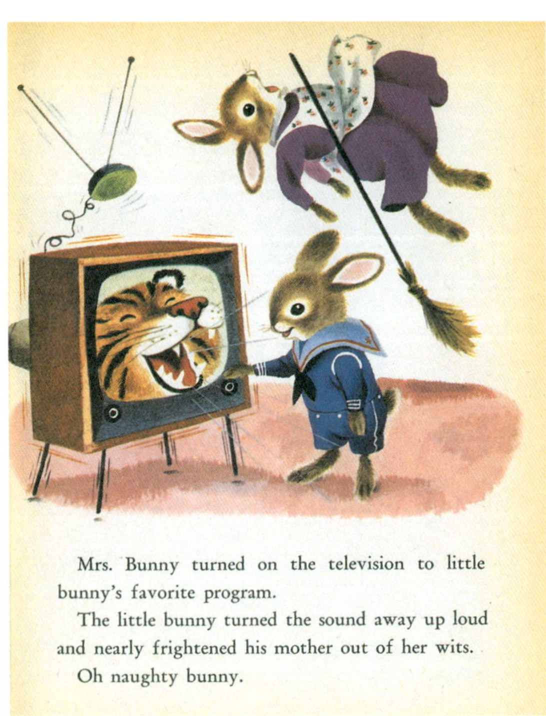

A SUCCESSFUL ARTIST IN WESTPORT

Toward the end of the fifties Dick and Patsy faced a new problem. Their farmhouse had become too small, and they were tired of living so far from the city, away from their friends and professional contacts. There was also Huck to think about. He would soon be old enough to go to school, so they wanted to move to a town with better educational opportunities. They began to search for a new home.

On March 7, 1959, they signed the deed to a house on Bradley Street in Westport, Connecticut. It was an old-fashioned, rambling white house with fourteen rooms and a crow's nest on the third floor from which they had a wonderful view of Compo Beach and Long Island Sound. Dick turned the crow's nest into a studio. From the railing that encircled the little balcony outside the crow's nest, he often flew colorful European flags. The studio was supposed to be off limits to everyone except Dick, but guests had a way of wandering up there, drinks in hand, when the Scarrys entertained.

Patsy had a real flair for finding all kinds of interesting pieces of furniture and bric-a-brac at thrift shops and at the Salvation Army store. With very little money she created a charming, comfortable home. She was also a wonderful hostess, always full of energy, never failing to look after her guests and making sure they had enough to eat and drink.

It was not long before the Scarry house became a mecca for all the authors and artists living in the Westport area, as well as publishing people from New York City. Mike Smollin, whose colorful illustrations brought the Muppet characters to life in many Sesame Street books, lived right across the road from the Scarrys. Niels Bodecker, a well-known Danish illustrator and author, lived a short way down the street with his wife and two young sons. Erik and Lenore Blegvad, Leonard Shortall, and many other artists were also nearby. Weekend guests were frequent: Kathleen Daly, an editor at Golden Press, arrived nearly every Friday afternoon during the summer; so did John Miller, along with other friends from the city. And every Monday morning the guests would return to the city, saying cheerfully, "See you next weekend."

In spite of the partying and the constant interruptions, Dick managed to work very hard. He was an extremely disciplined worker, beginning at eight in the morning and working until at least four in the afternoon, with an hour out to eat the

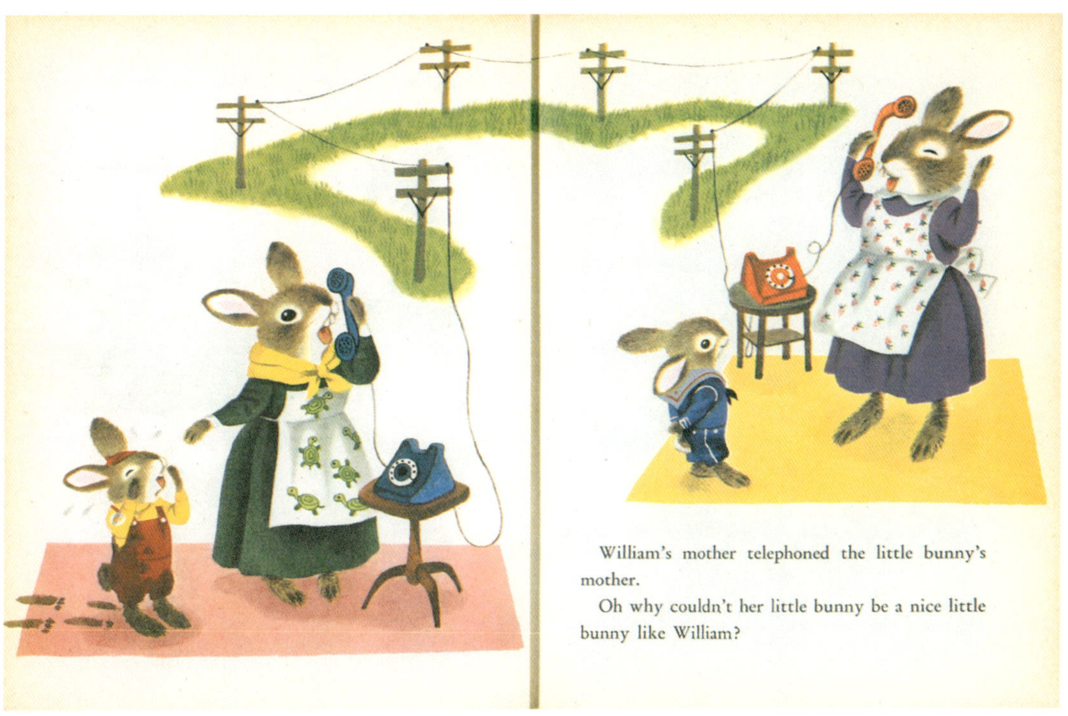

sandwiches and coffee that Patsy brought to him in his studio. Even Patsy wasn't allowed to stop and chat. She simply set his lunch on his desk and went quietly back downstairs. He worked five days a week, taking the weekend off, if possible, like people with regular office jobs. With Huck in the Westport elementary school, Patsy found some free time for writing more Little Golden Book stories.

The books Dick was now illustrating for Artists and Writers had a different publisher. In 1958 Western and Pocket Books had jointly purchased all the Golden Book properties from Simon and Schuster, which had decided it wanted to concentrate on adult books, and set up a new company called Golden Press, Inc. Western continued to create and produce Golden Books, and Pocket Books sold and distributed them. Albert Leventhal, who had already left Simon and Schuster to work at Artists and Writers, was appointed president of the new company.

That same year Dick sold another original story to Golden called *Naughty Bunny.* It was published in 1959 as a Little Golden Book. For the first time, his animal characters emerged as real people, fully clothed and leading a completely human existence. They have much more personality, and the drawings are much looser in style.

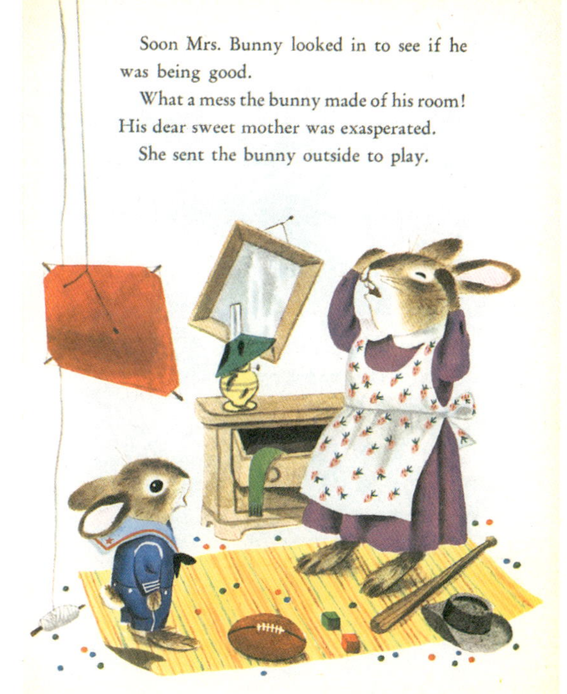

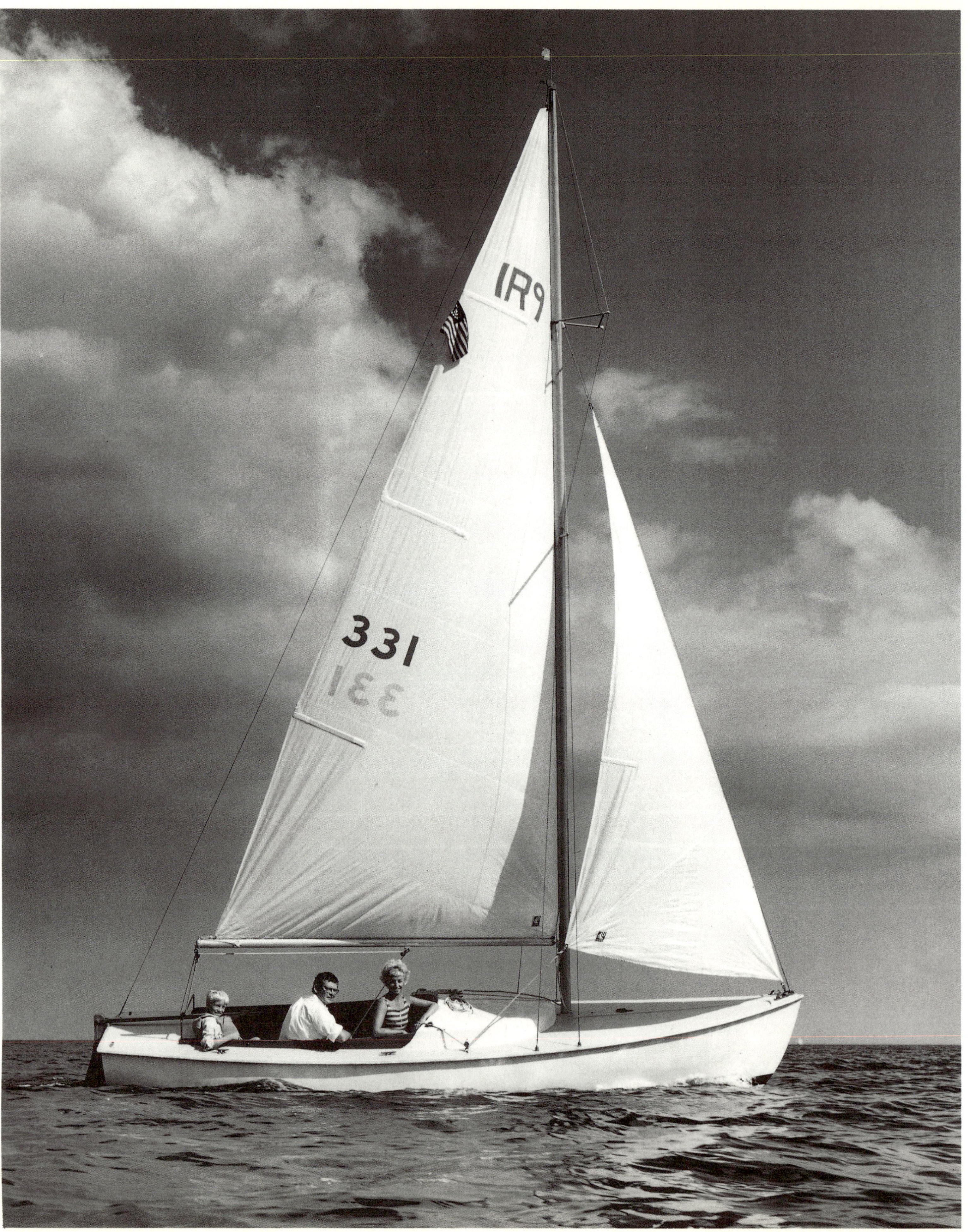
331

In good weather, Dick liked to spend his free time sailing in the Sound. The Cedar Point Yacht Club was within easy walking distance, and Dick kept his sailboat, the *Irish Pennant*, there. Often Huck went sailing with him, and sometimes Patsy joined them. The whole family loved to sail. Many years later Huck recalled that there were often one or two sailboats on the lawn of their Westport home. Dick would be painting them or covering them with fiberglass. Huck often helped. Here is how Mike Smollin remembers Dick the sailor:

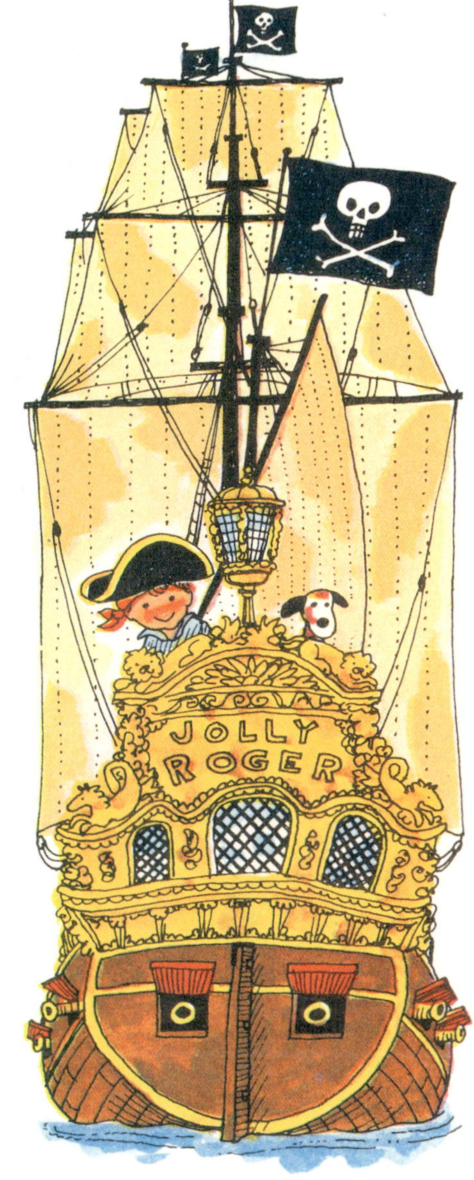

> *Dick's studio was up on the third floor of his house and opened onto a small deck surrounded by a white-painted railing. I would often see Dick poised up there staring out at Long Island Sound and the boat marina. He looked like a captain at the helm of his ship. Each morning he hoisted a flag out on a pole and at sunset he took it in. The flag would indicate wind direction and strength and help Dick decide whether he'd go sailing.*
>
> *My favorite image of Dick is of him striding out of his house and onto Bradley Street, headed for the marina. He'd be wearing a jaunty French blue and white striped shirt, dark blue shorts, waterproof boots or sneakers, and his stand-by bright yellow slicker jacket.* Very *nautical. Sometimes he'd tote a canvas bag of gear to take aboard his boat. Dick always looked as if he were filled with joyous anticipation of his sailing. Very content in his role of sailor. I think he was always at peace at these moments.*
>
> *Dick kept his Rhodes 19 at Cedar Point Yacht Club—directly across the street from our house. He also kept a Sailfish. I recall a time when he was determined to get me out on a Sailfish. It meant I'd have to struggle with getting the Sailfish to sail out of the marina basin, through the entry channel and into the Sound, despite heavy traffic from large sailboats and motor yachts.*
>
> *Finally one day I agreed to make the try. Dick helped me get my Sailfish into the water and his as well. It was his intention to follow me out of the basin, shouting advice as we went. Unsteadily, I tried to navigate my way between the moored and moving craft. Somehow I made it to the entrance channel only to encounter a swift current, a stiff wind, and a large motor craft making her way out to sea. I became nervous. Dick was shouting something I couldn't hear. I turned around in an attempt to hear him better. "For God's sake," he yelled, "don't turn around!"*
>
> *Over I went, into the drink, in the path of the yacht. Somehow I shoved the Sailfish out of the way and swam aside to avoid the fast approaching boat. Talk about embarrassment!*

Above and below: From *Boats*

Opposite: The Scarry family sail in *Irish Pennant*, a Rhodes 19. Scarry also named the ocean liner in *What Do People Do All Day?* (pages 134–35) *Irish Pennant*.

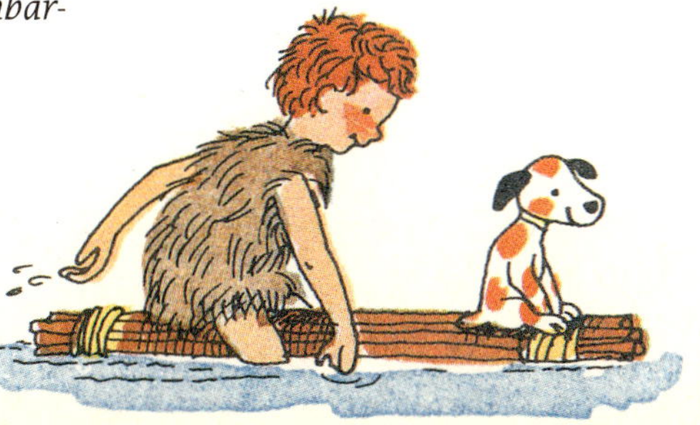

Sometimes Dick and I would go out on his "poop deck," drinks in hand and discuss our careers. At one of those moments, Dick confided that he felt his career had taken a turn for the better after a period of struggle. And he gave full credit to the guidance of Ole Risom [art director and vice president at Western] for the happy change.

In addition to sailing, Dick and another neighbor, Leonard Shortall, decided to take up the game of golf. Neither of them was very good at it. They had trouble keeping the ball where it belonged. It always had a way of landing in the swamp. Since the two men had little money to spare in those days, they certainly couldn't afford to replace their golf balls with new ones. Instead, they would go up to the swamp after dark to hunt for lost balls. Often Huck went with them. They usually returned with two or three buckets full of balls, which Dick immediately marked as his own.

There were other activities that Dick shared with his son. One day he came home with a bow and arrow he had bought, thinking it would be fun to teach Huck the fundamentals of archery. A grass field lay between the house and the beach, and Dick set up a target at one end of it. In the course of showing Huck how to use the bow and arrow, he got the idea of pointing the arrow straight up into the air to see where it would land. He pulled the string back as far as possible and let go. The arrow went straight up but neither of them saw it come down again. They searched all around the field, but without success. Dick was concerned; he worried that the arrow might be found by a child . . . or, worse, that someone might have been hit.

A few days later, Huck finally spied the missing arrow from his bedroom window. It was sticking out of the roof of their neighbor's house. Since nobody was at home, Dick got a tall ladder and climbed up to the roof of the front porch. From there he scrambled onto the main roof. Pulling the arrow loose, he threw it down to the ground. He was just climbing back down the ladder, when a car turned into the driveway. The neighbors had come home. Dick had the embarrassing task of explaining why he had been up on their roof.

There were few dull moments at the Scarry home in Westport. Erik Blegvad, a good friend and neighbor, as well as a uniquely talented artist and author, remembers:

In the early fifties, when Harry S. Truman was still president of the U.S.A., my wife, Lenore, and I began our long friendship with Patsy and Dick Scarry and their little son,

Huck. Westport in those days was a lovely town, and the Scarrys lived by the water in a splendid white house. Upstairs, Dick had a large, airy studio. Both he and Patsy wrote children's books, something Lenore and I had yet to try. But Dick was first and foremost a superlative illustrator with an inexhaustible fund of ideas for books of all sizes and subjects. It was rumored that he started drawing at dawn every day. Some said he drew with a pencil on transparent paper at a terrific rate.

Patsy and he also found some hours every day to write their wonderful stories, and after school Huck would spend hours developing his extraordinarily precocious drawing talent. The whole house seethed with creativity, and at night they threw parties. Such parties! Westport was in those days inhabited by a cross section of America's most talented commercial artists. Practically all were friends and frequent guests in the Scarrys' hospitable home. The talk was animated but only rarely shop. We never saw Dick work. He was, I think, a bit shy about his own drawings, just as he always seemed eager to praise other artists' work.

Although the Scarrys loved their new house, and the life they were leading, they still had worries. Golden Press just wasn't providing enough illustration assignments to bring in the sort of income they needed. It became obvious to Dick that he would have to begin making the rounds again in an effort to drum up more work. He dug out some of the ideas he had been working on at Ridgefield. Among them were the sketches for a series of books about a rabbit (Tinker) and a hippopotamus (Tanker). Another was a collection of Jean de la Fontaine fables that he planned to retell and illustrate with full color paintings. Since his agent hadn't made much effort to place these projects, Scarry decided to try approaching some publishers himself.

Dick's son, Huck, recalls, "... as a child I was often drawn downstairs by curiosity, in my pajamas, to uproarious parties.... But I also recall that times were not always easy. My father would often take the train into New York, wearing a Tyrolean hat and carrying a knapsack, in quest of commissions."

Eventually Scarry found a home at Doubleday for *Tinker and Tanker* and Jean de la Fontaine's *Fables.* A young editor there, William Hall, had been given the job of starting a list of children's books with special appeal for bookstores, and he saw great promise in Scarry's work. Dick was delighted. For nearly eleven years, he had spent most of his time illustrating other people's texts. Although he was happy to

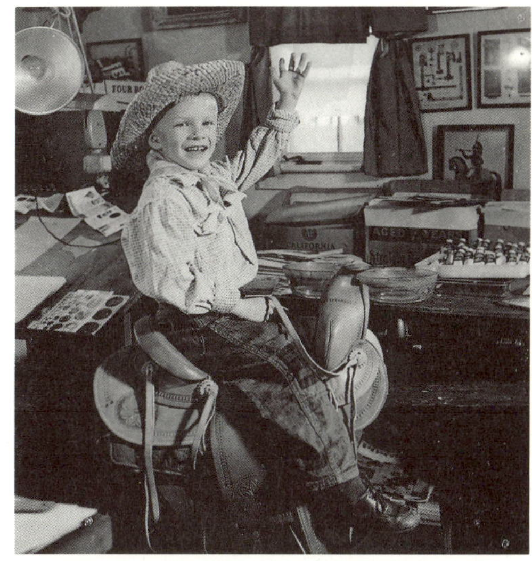

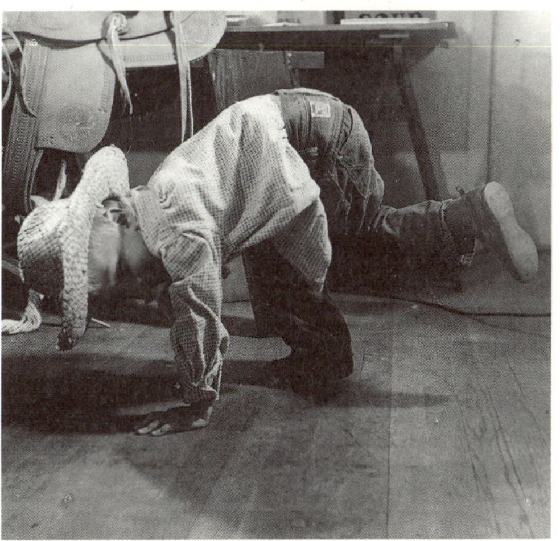

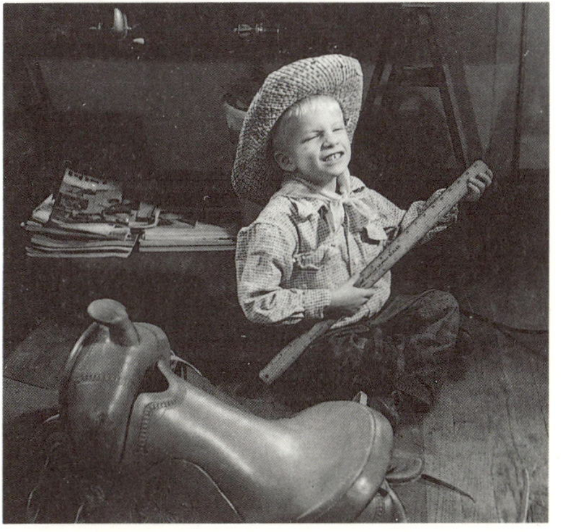

Wearing a cowboy outfit, Huck models for his father.

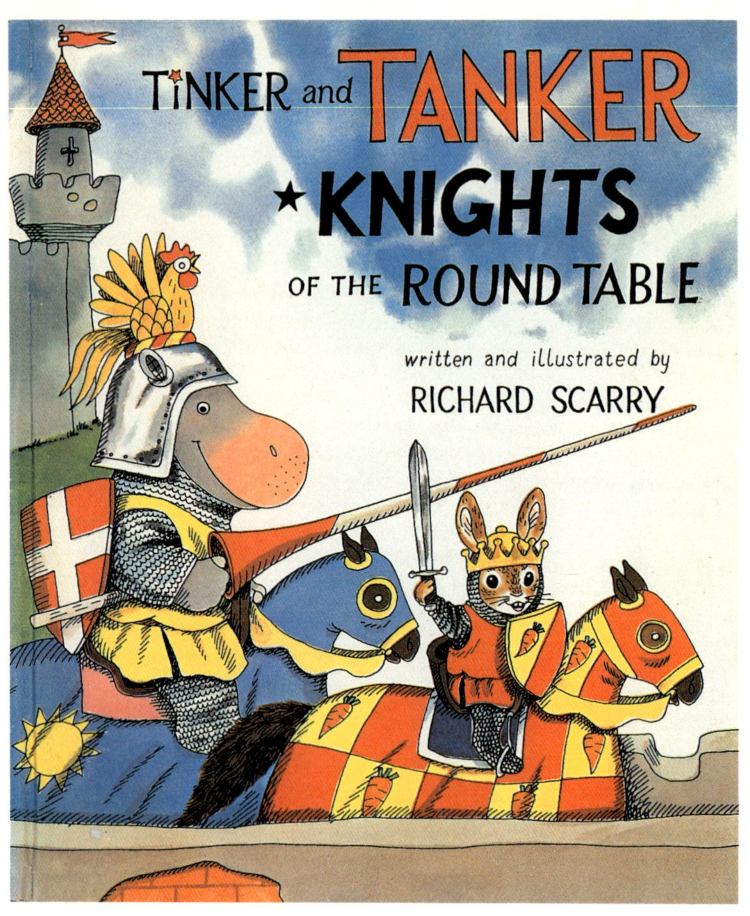

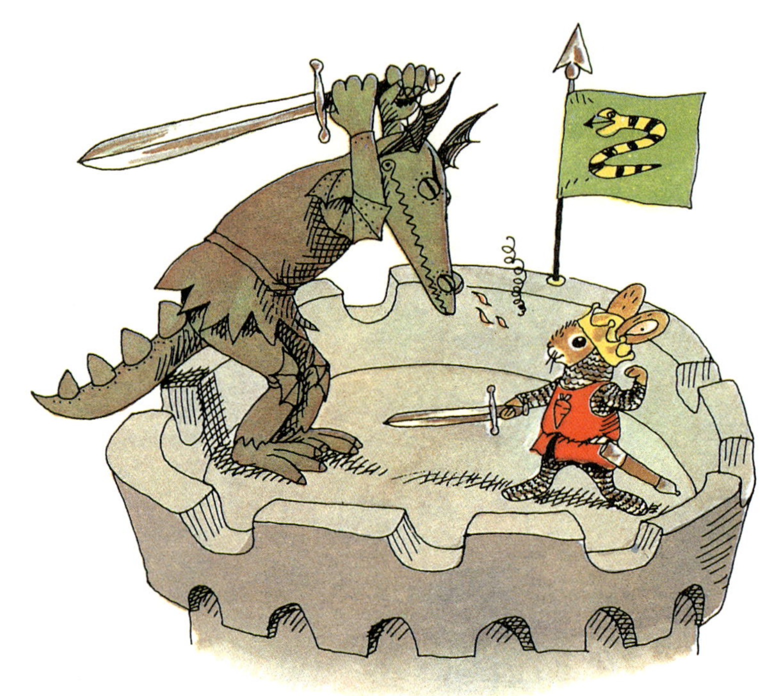

Above: Cover and interior illustration from *Tinker and Tanker, Knights of the Round Table.*

Below: From *Tinker and Tanker*

have work that he liked so much, as well as the income it provided, he was often exasperated by authors' picky criticisms. ("That dog should be black, not white" or "Why is that chicken so big?" and so on.) And, like most illustrators, he frequently felt that he could write stories that were just as good as the ones the publishers sent to him. Now he would have an opportunity to prove it.

Altogether, there were six titles in the *Tinker and Tanker* series that Richard Scarry created for Doubleday, starting with *Tinker and Tanker* (1960), and ending with *Tinker and Tanker in Africa* (1963). They were typical picture storybooks for toddlers, with simple plots and very little text. The characters were all animals, for the most part behaving very much like humans, and the drawings showed the strong sense of the absurd that would become a trademark of Richard Scarry books. Unfortunately, a tight budget didn't allow Doubleday to use full color throughout the books. Every other double-page spread was in black and white. This mixture of full

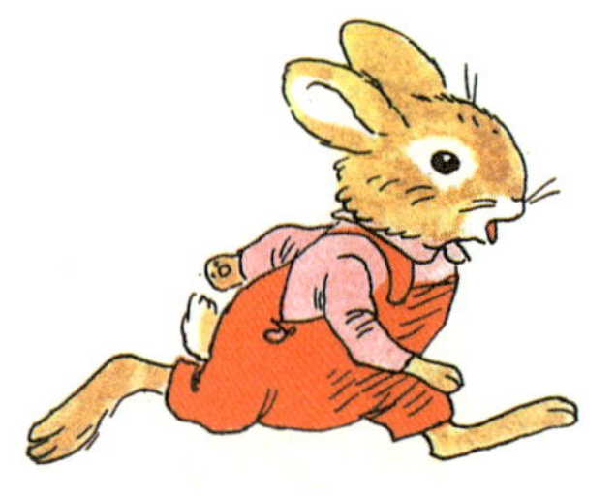

color with black and white was rather jarring, and probably worked against the series. The Tinker and Tanker books were popular, but sales were not phenomenal. The *Fables* of Jean de la Fontaine contained the same mixture of color and black and white. In addition, Scarry created a novelty book called *The Hickory Dickory Clock Book* (1961) and provided the illustrations for a special Doubleday edition of Edward Lear's *A Nonsense Alphabet* (1962).

While Scarry was finishing the artwork for all of these Doubleday projects, he was also working on sketches for a word book. He wanted to create a different kind of word book for children, one that would arrange words by categories instead of by the alphabet. He planned to have sections on the seasons, cars and trucks, boats and ships, numbers, the alphabet, country life, city life, and so on—forty-eight categories in all. When he was well along with his sketches, Dick took the rough sketches and text for the book to Bill Hall, who liked the idea very much but told Dick that Doubleday had decided not to continue with the sort of list he had been building up, and that the editorial director of children's books was not enthusiastic about publishing the word book. Hall explained that he himself would soon be leaving Doubleday for another job.

Illustration for "The Fox and the Stork" from Jean de La Fontaine's *Fables*

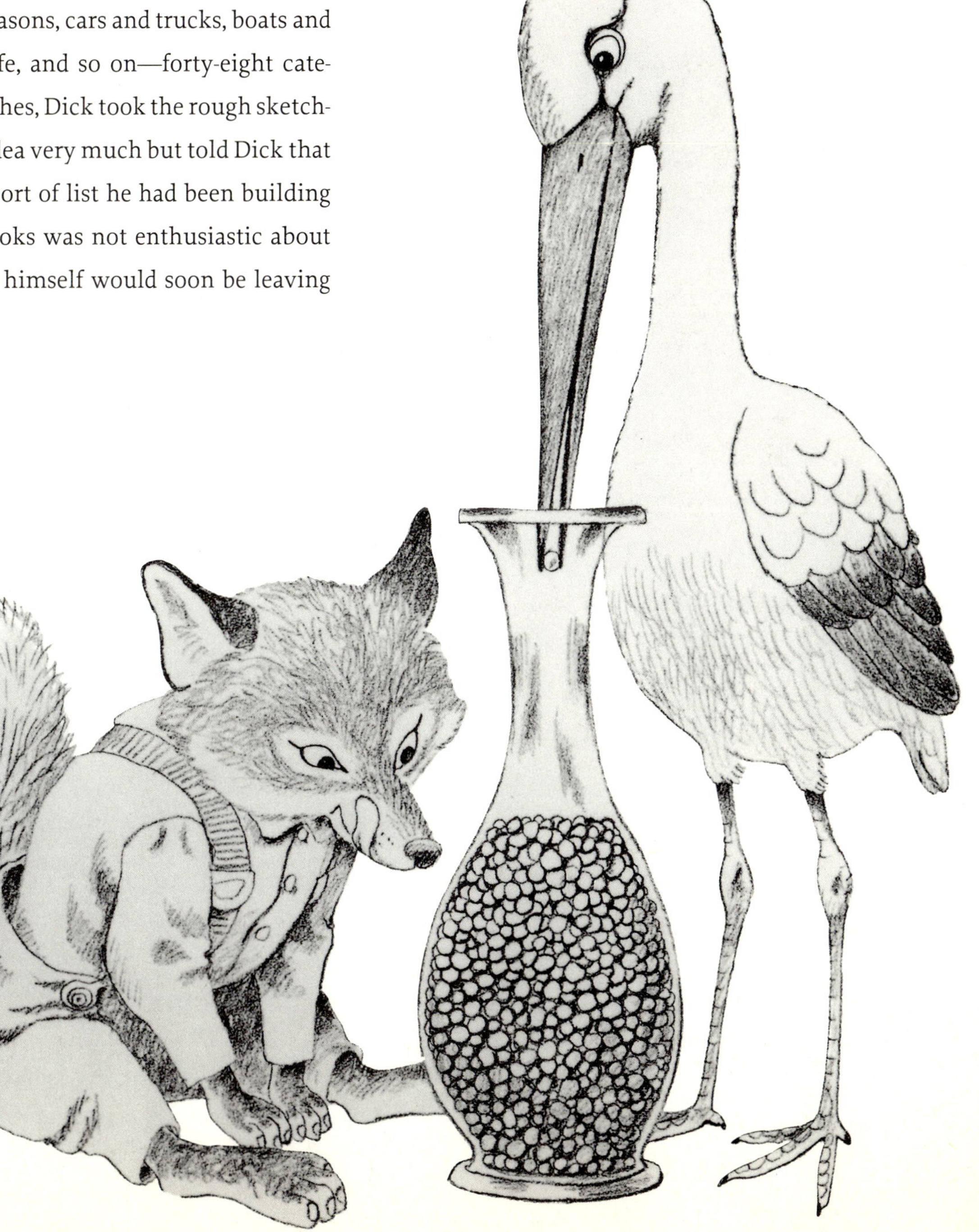

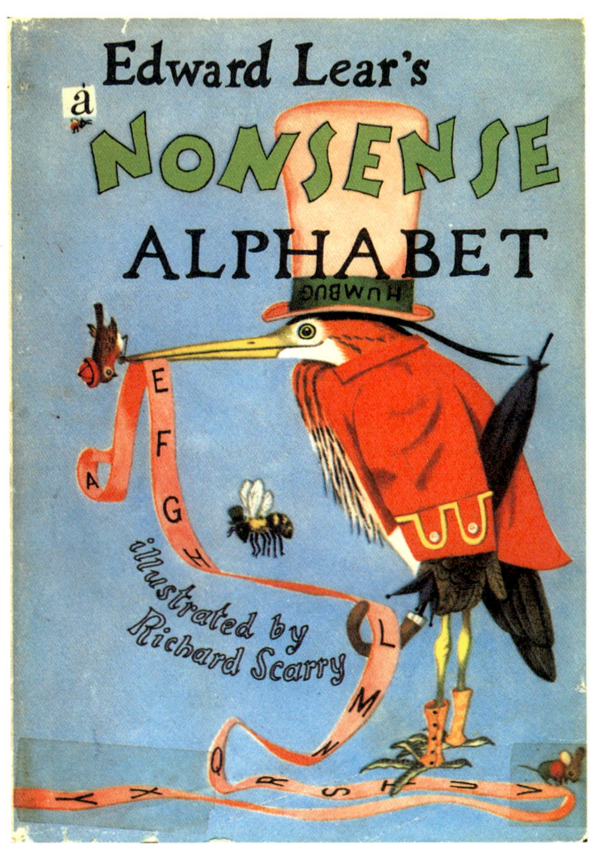

The back cover for a special edition of Edward Lear's *Nonsense Alphabet* that Scarry illustrated for Doubleday.

Disappointed, but not about to give up, Dick took the mock-up for the book to his old friends and publishers, Golden Press. Albert Leventhal loved it and, according to legend, exclaimed: "That's the best word book ever!" Whether or not he actually said it, the book was published in 1963 under the unforgettable title, *Richard Scarry's Best Word Book Ever.* It was the first Richard Scarry book to feature the artist's name as part of the title, and it was an immediate sensation. Illustrated in full color, in a nearly square (10¼ x 11⅞ inches) oversized format, it truly was a word book to dwarf all others. It contained more than 1,400 objects identified by labels. In addition, there were short amusing texts for each category, asking questions and pointing out details that would invite reader participation. Children everywhere loved it. So did their parents. They quickly discovered that it provided hours of fun and learning for their children, who wanted to browse through the colorful contents over and over again. There had never been a book quite like it. By the end of 1975, in only a dozen years, more than seven million copies had been sold.

During all his early years as an illustrator, Dick must have been learning his craft, while thinking—perhaps subconsciously—about what he would really like to do, and suddenly, with the *Best Word Book Ever,* the Scarry genius broke loose. In this one big volume he was able at last to incorporate all his ideas about just what a good children's book ought to be. It is ironic that for this book, destined to become one of the most popular, best-selling children's books ever, his contract provided a royalty of only 8 cents a copy on a tentative retail price of $2.99; his advance was just $7,000. Even at that low retail price, the royalty rate was little more than 2½ percent per copy. As the retail price gradually rose, the 8 cents per copy remained in effect, so that the royalty rate was even lower.

Before Scarry finished his work on the word book, Golden Press asked him to illustrate a short, oversized board book with a text by Ole Risom. It was called *I Am a Bunny.* The book, through its very appealing title character, takes small children through the four seasons, describing common seasonal activities and weather changes. The illustrations were very simple full-color paintings just right for young toddlers, and the text was equally simple. This book was also published in 1963, a few months earlier than the *Best Word Book Ever.* Both books have remained in print ever since they were published.

Opposite: For a revised edition of *Best Word Book Ever,* Scarry responded to criticism of gender bias by showing male and female animals in roles that reflected the new freedom from stereotyping.

Overleaf: A double spread from the innovative *Richard Scarry's Best Word Book Ever,* shows how the artist created situations to demonstrate word meanings rather than simply identifying objects.

Pages 54–55: Single pages from *Best Word Book Ever*

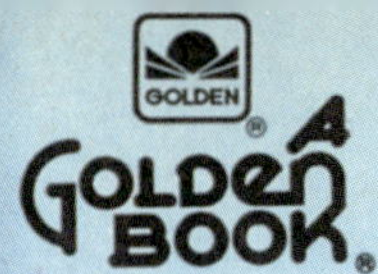

RICHARD SCARRY'S

BEST WORD BOOK EVER

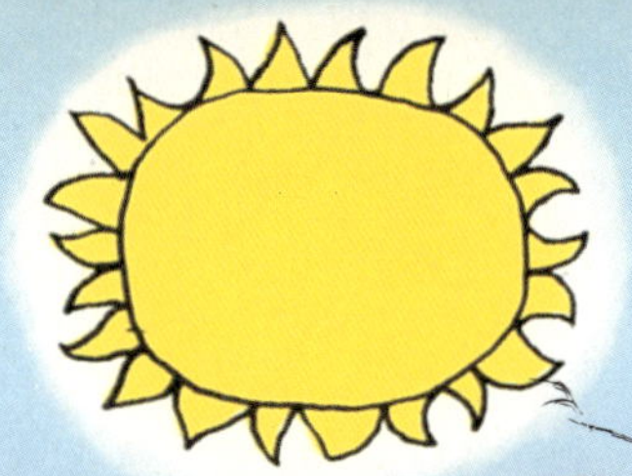

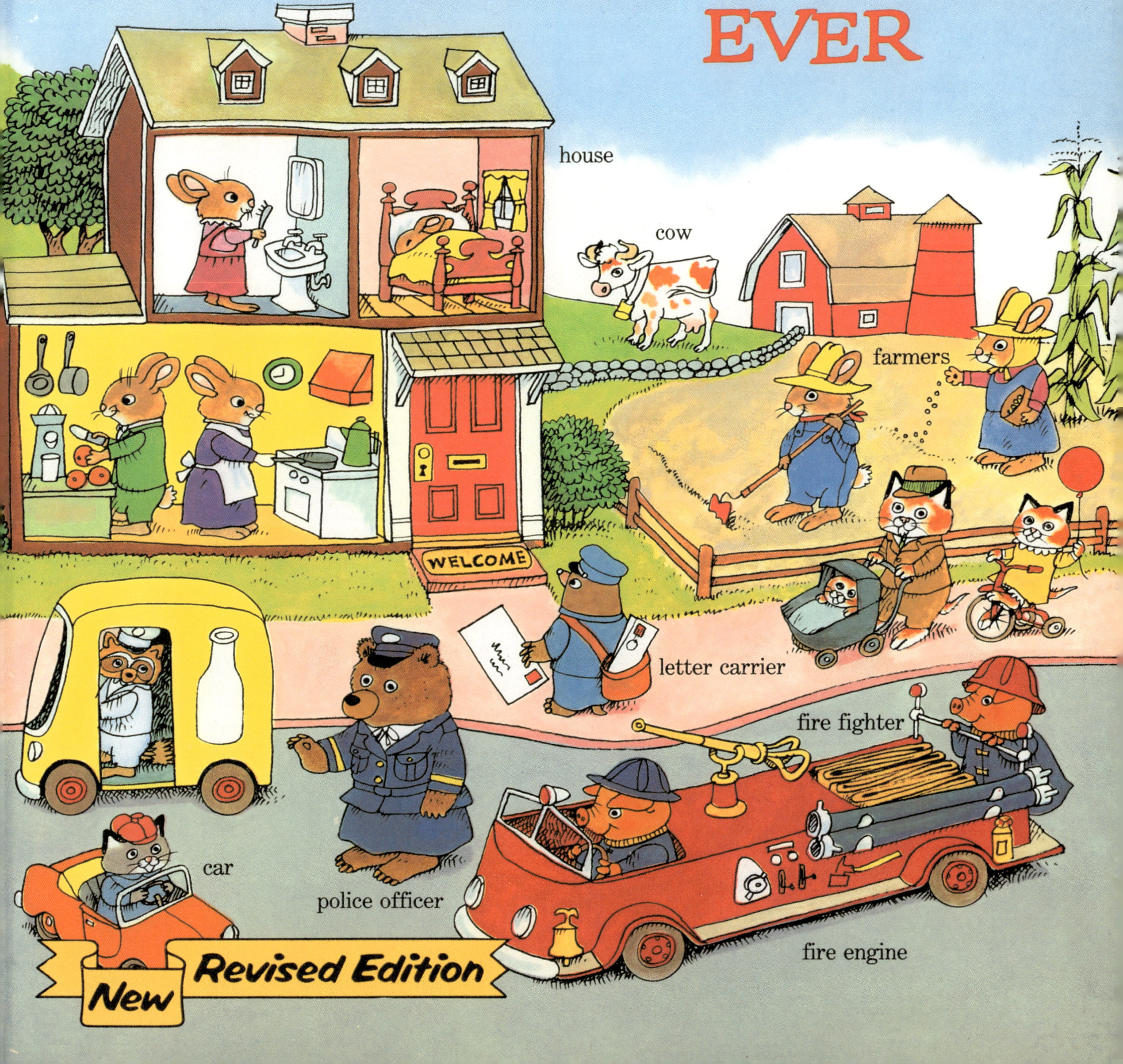

house

cow

farmers

WELCOME

letter carrier

fire fighter

car

police officer

fire engine

New Revised Edition

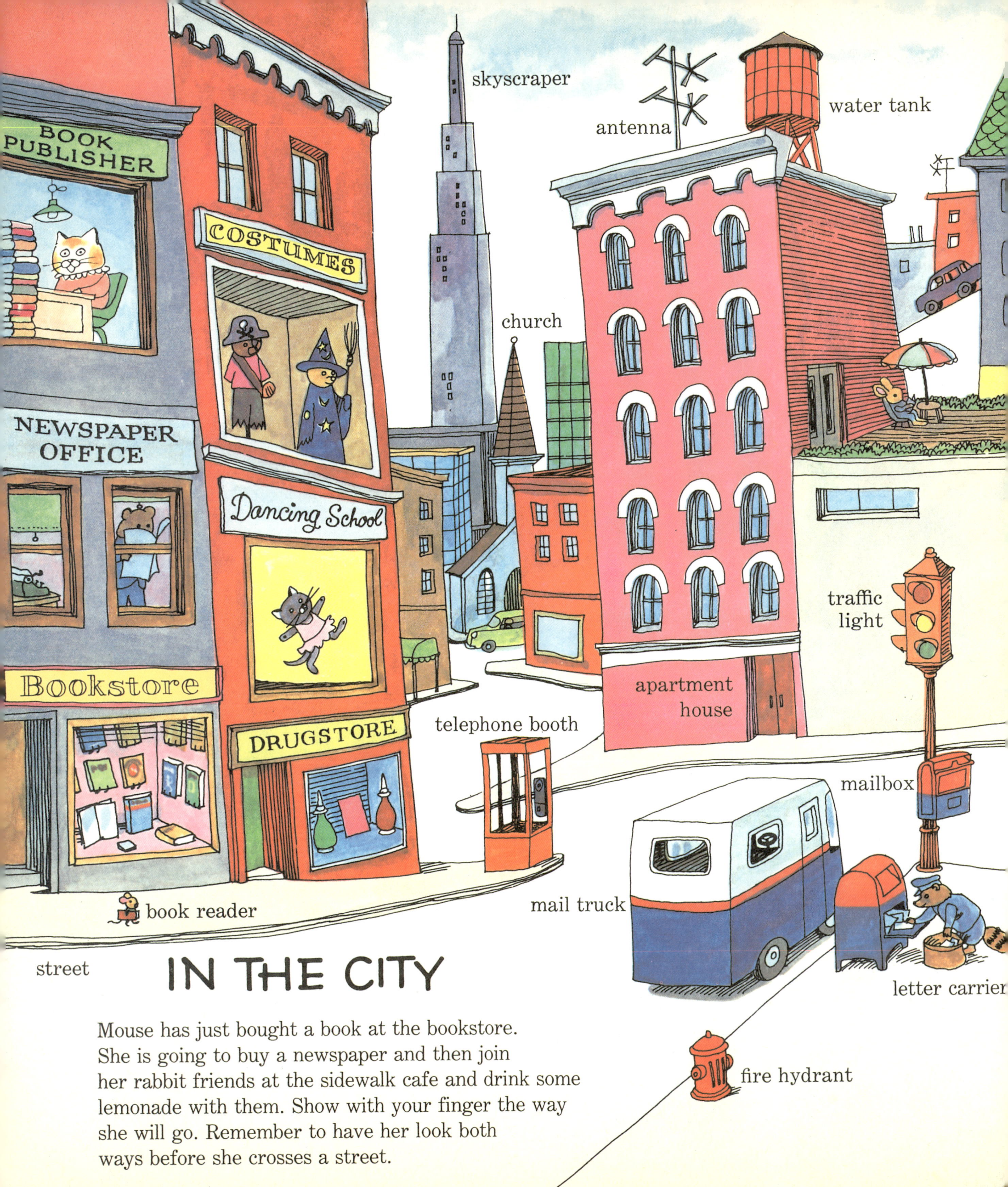

IN THE CITY

Mouse has just bought a book at the bookstore. She is going to buy a newspaper and then join her rabbit friends at the sidewalk cafe and drink some lemonade with them. Show with your finger the way she will go. Remember to have her look both ways before she crosses a street.

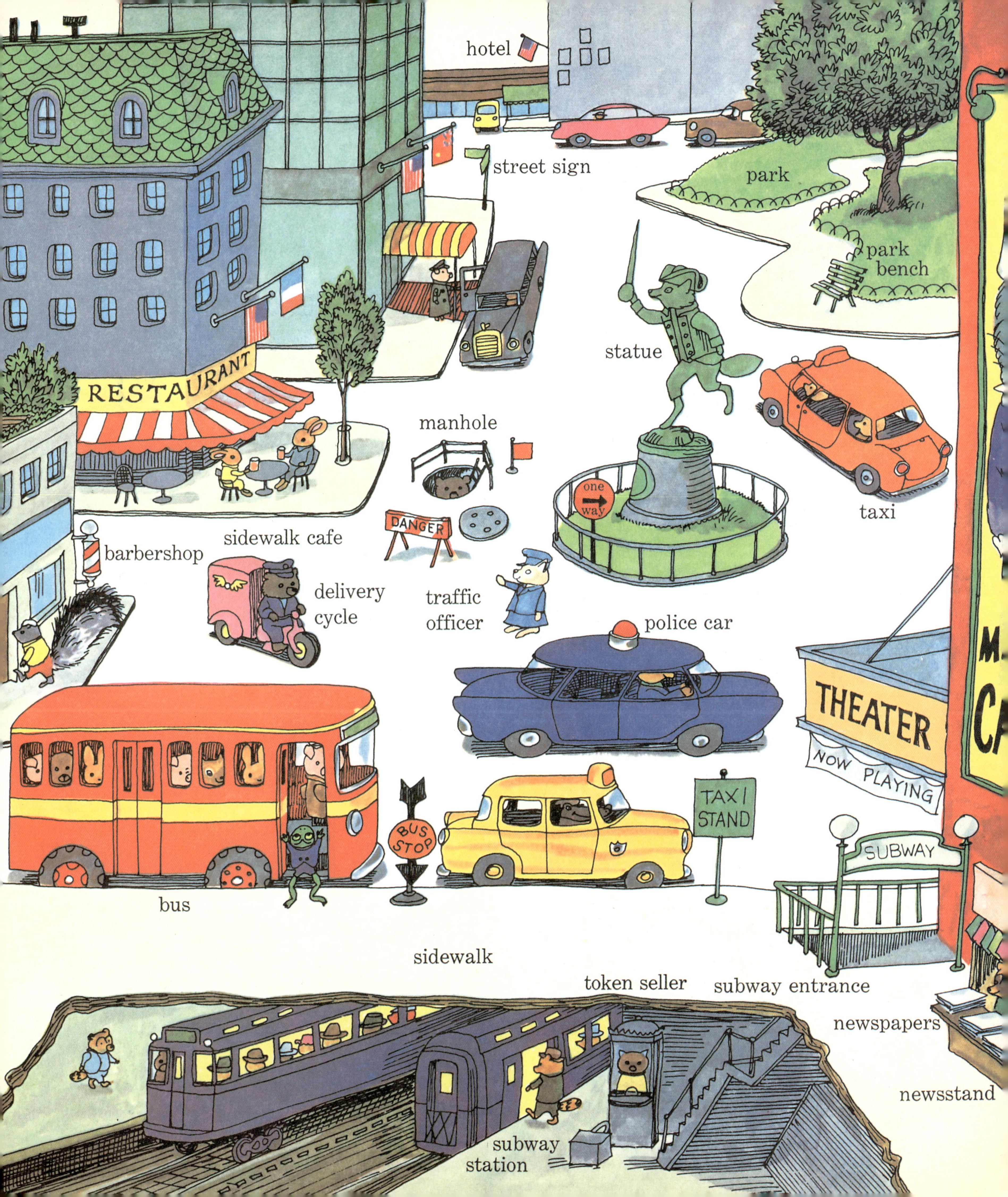
hotel
street sign
park
park bench
RESTAURANT
statue
manhole
DANGER
one way
taxi
sidewalk cafe
barbershop
delivery cycle
traffic officer
police car
THEATER
NOW PLAYING
TAXI STAND
BUS STOP
SUBWAY
bus
sidewalk
token seller
subway entrance
newspapers
newsstand
subway station

SUMMER

Do you like to go
on picnics in the summertime?
Ants just love to go to picnics.
Do you know why?

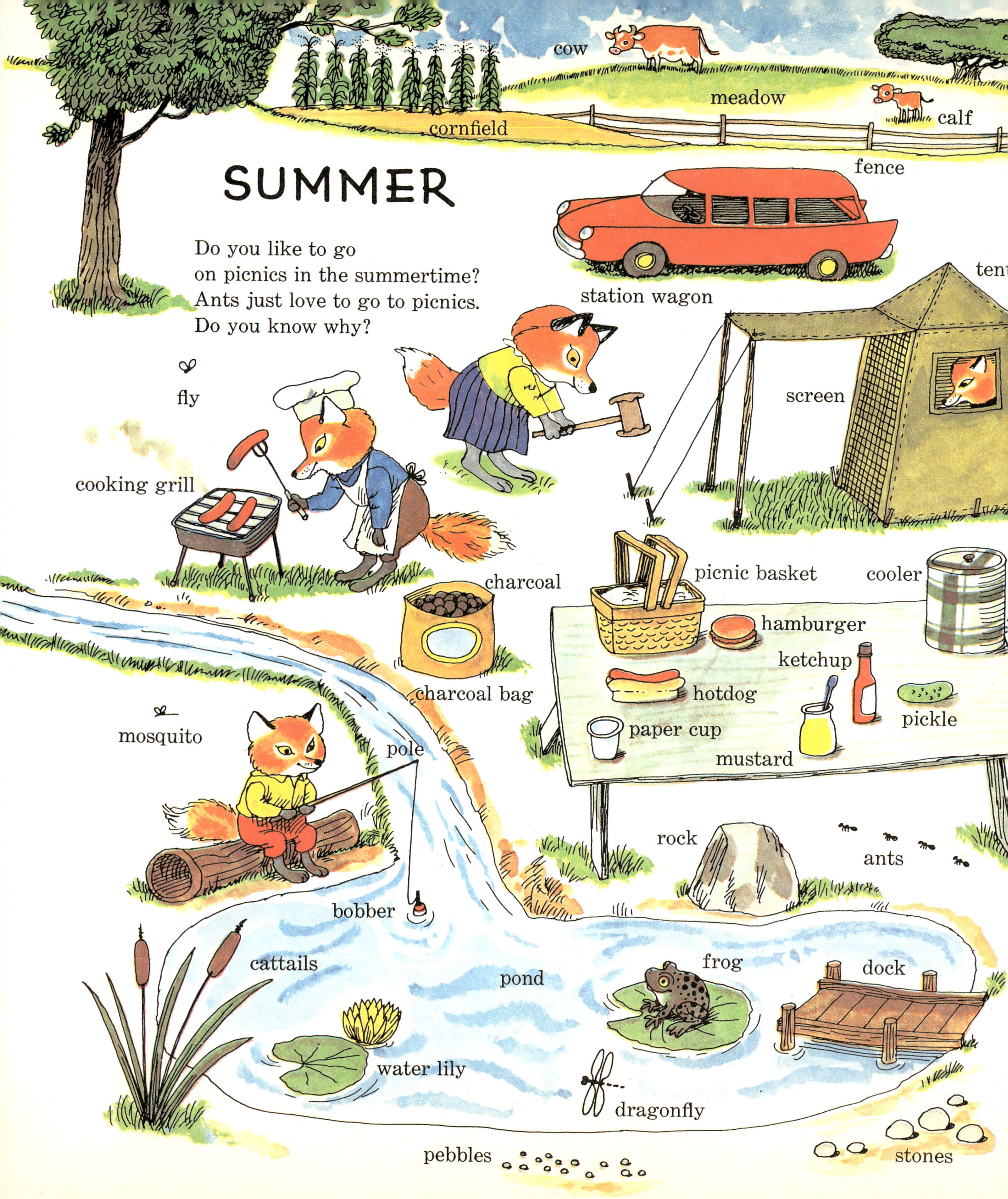

PARTS OF THE BODY

Bears use their paws to pick things up.
What do you use?

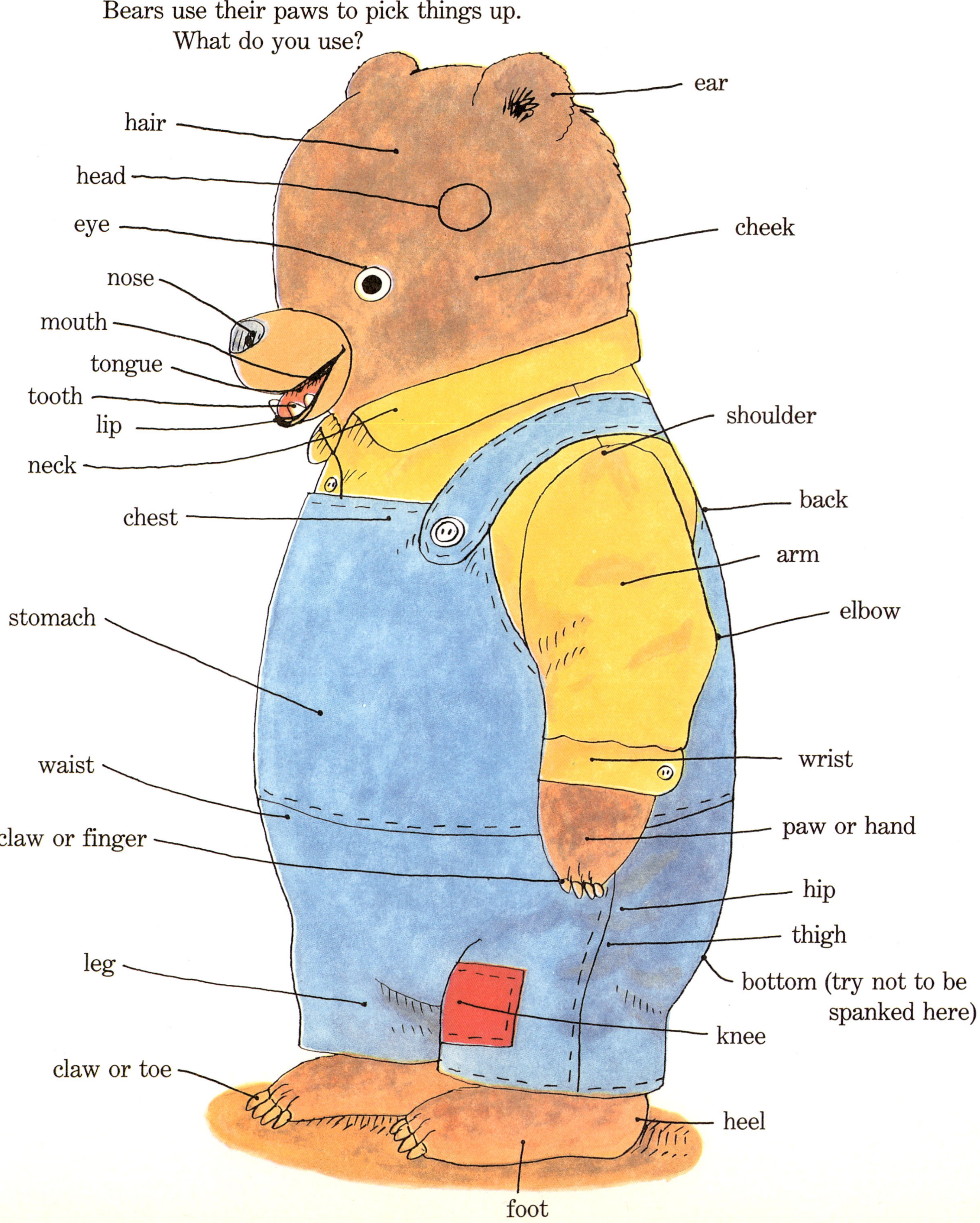

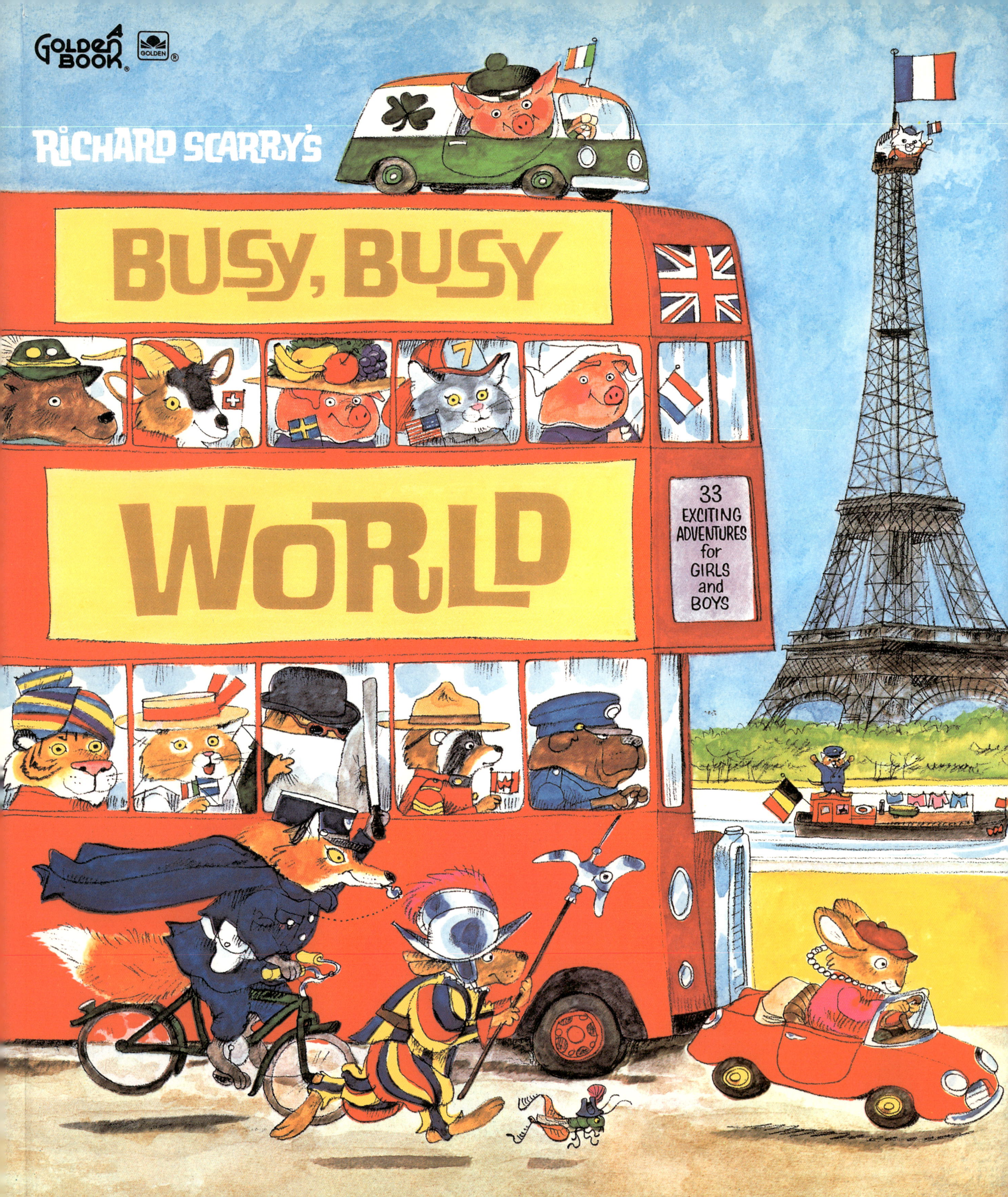
GOLDEN BOOK
GOLDEN
RICHARD SCARRY'S
BUSY, BUSY
WORLD
33
EXCITING
ADVENTURES
for
GIRLS
and
BOYS

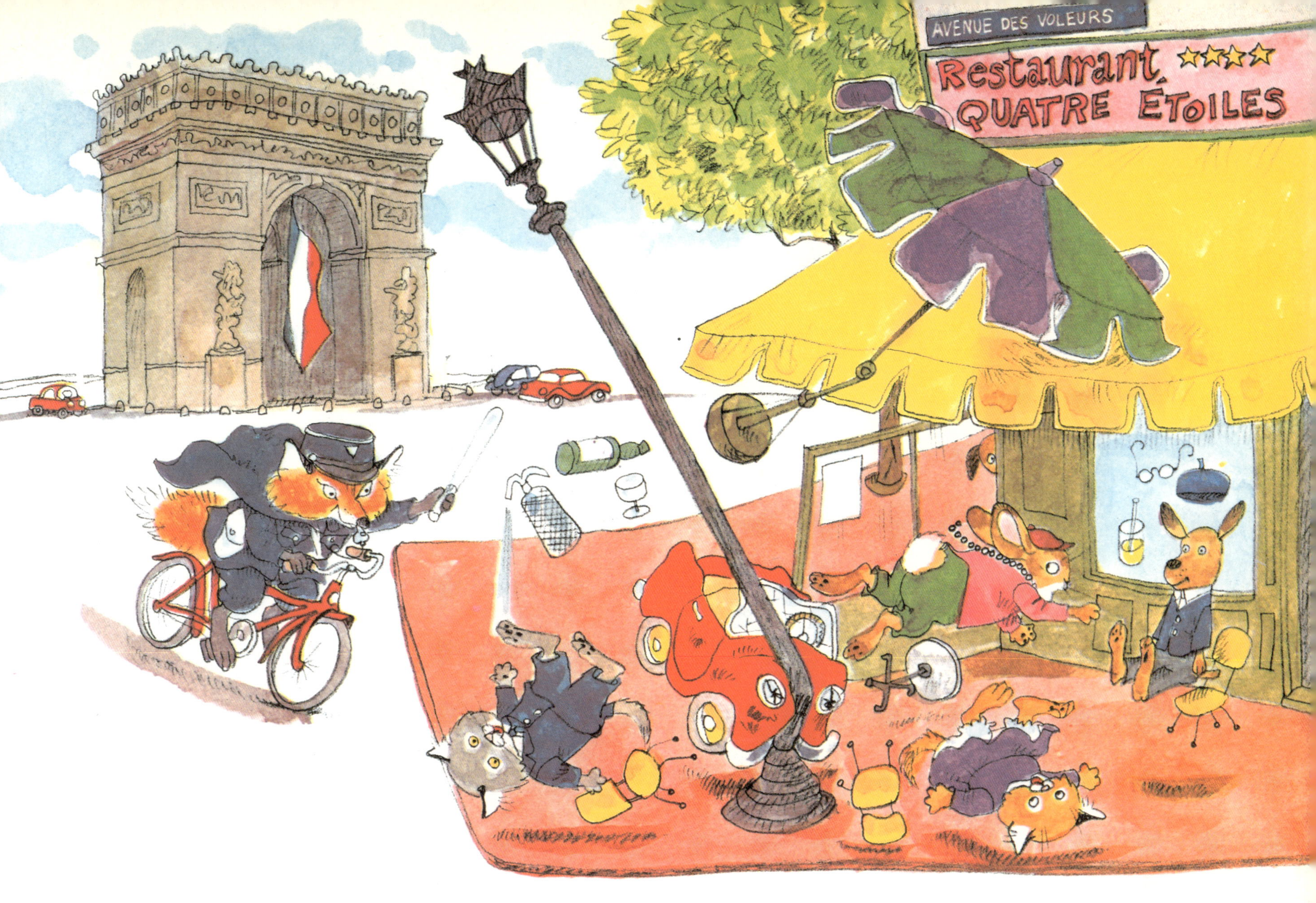

After the phenomenal success of his *Best Word Book Ever,* Scarry had no difficulty in interesting Golden Press in other ideas for large-format picture books. In August of 1965 they published *Richard Scarry's Busy, Busy World,* a collection of thirty-three funny stories set in countries and cities around the world. Although the Scarrys had made several trips abroad since their first honeymoon voyage, Dick hadn't actually been to all of the countries included in the book. For those, he had to do special research, using heavily illustrated encyclopedias, travel books, and his own file of pictures torn from old magazines, newspapers, travel brochures, and so forth. In *Busy, Busy World,* Scarry provided marvelously detailed, colorful paintings of some of his favorite cities such as Paris, Rome, Venice, London, and New York. He also included the first of his amazing double-page schematic drawings—this one showing the complicated interior of "A Castle in Denmark." It was accompanied by

Above: In this illustration from *Richard Scarry's Busy, Busy World,* Pierre the Parisian policeman chases a car thief near the Arc de Triomphe. The unfortunate thief has crashed into a lamp post and is trying to hide in a restaurant. Typical Scarry humor keeps the accident from seeming threatening to young readers.

Opposite: The cover for *Busy, Busy World*

Overleaf: A cutaway drawing of the Danish castle, Elsinore, also from *Busy, Busy World*

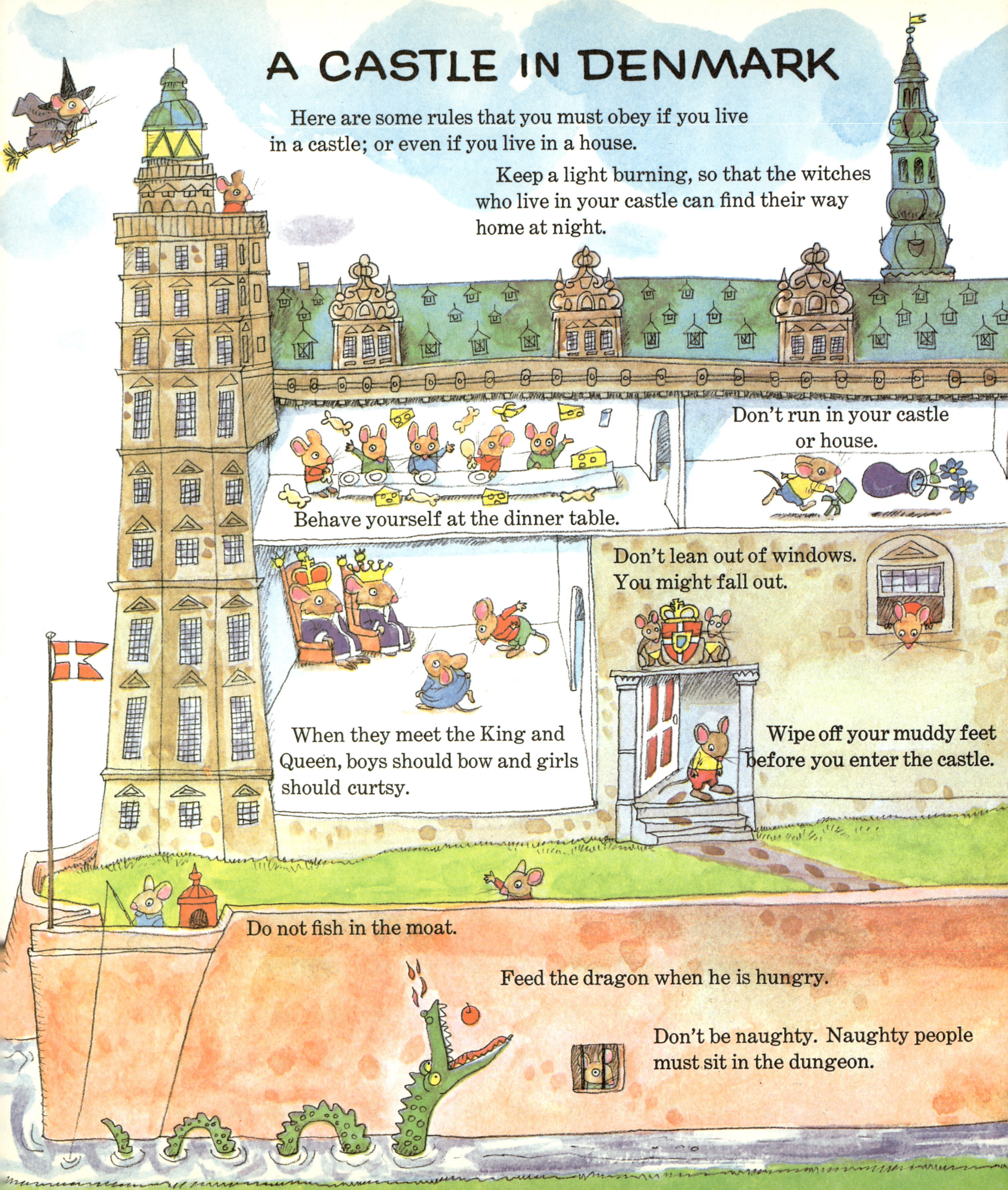
A CASTLE IN DENMARK
Here are some rules that you must obey if you live in a castle; or even if you live in a house.
Keep a light burning, so that the witches who live in your castle can find their way home at night.
Behave yourself at the dinner table.
Don't run in your castle or house.
Don't lean out of windows. You might fall out.
When they meet the King and Queen, boys should bow and girls should curtsy.
Wipe off your muddy feet before you enter the castle.
Do not fish in the moat.
Feed the dragon when he is hungry.
Don't be naughty. Naughty people must sit in the dungeon.

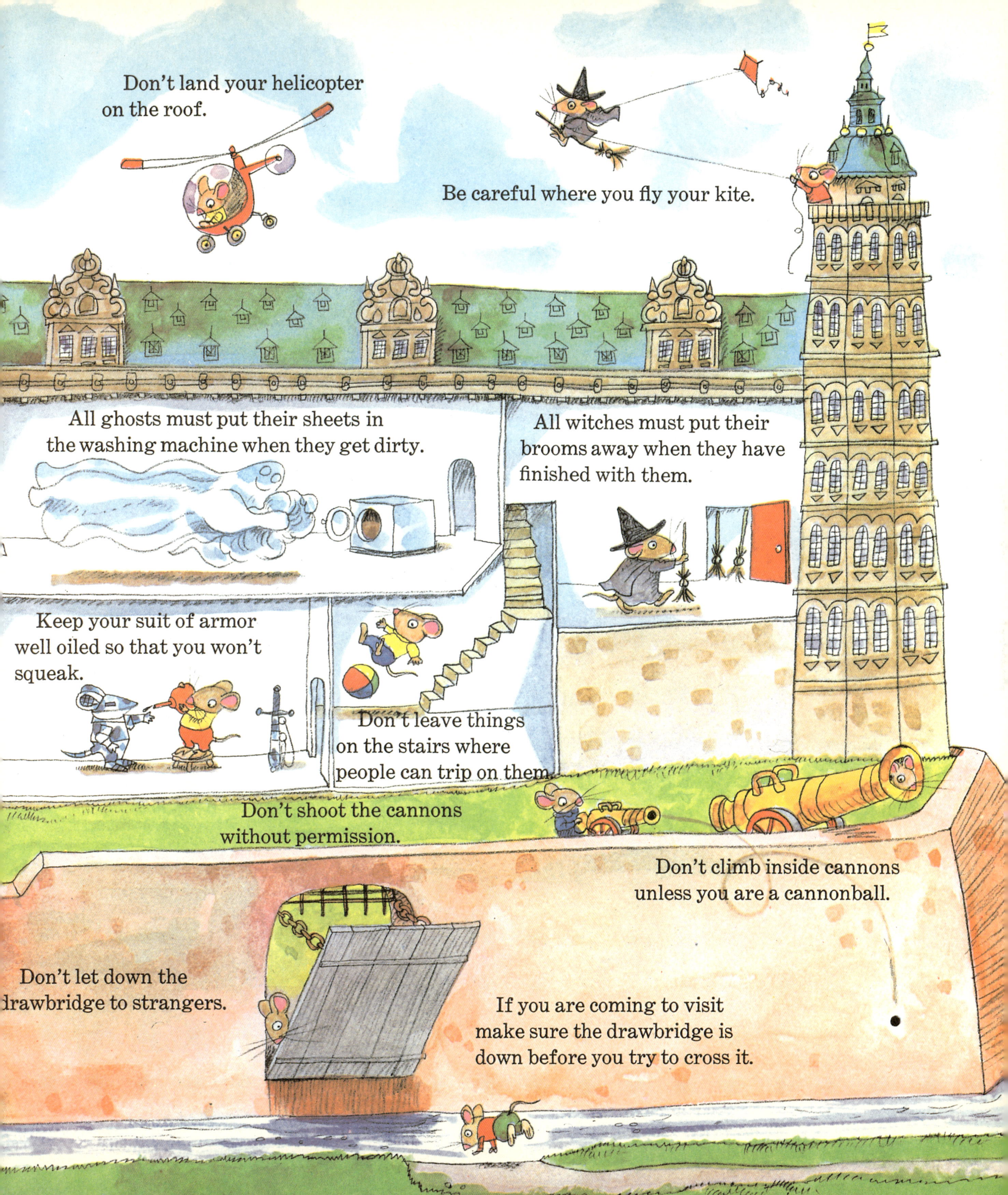
Don't land your helicopter
on the roof.
Be careful where you fly your kite.
All ghosts must put their sheets in
the washing machine when they get dirty.
All witches must put their
brooms away when they have
finished with them.
Keep your suit of armor
well oiled so that you won't
squeak.
Don't leave things
on the stairs where
people can trip on them.
Don't shoot the cannons
without permission.
Don't climb inside cannons
unless you are a cannonball.
Don't let down the
drawbridge to strangers.
If you are coming to visit
make sure the drawbridge is
down before you try to cross it.

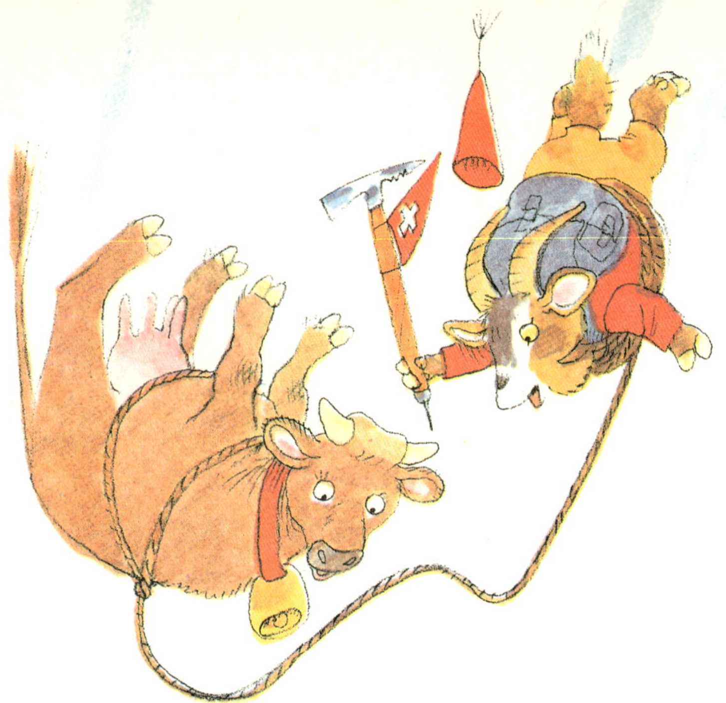

Six vignettes from *Richard Scarry's Busy, Busy World.*

Above: Ernest Goat, the Swiss Mountain Climber, tries to rescue Heidi Goat's cow. *Below:* Peter Pig catches a barge captain instead of a fish in *Busy, Busy World.*

Opposite Top: Professor Dig with his Egyptian mummy. *Upper Right:* Angus, the Scottish Bagpiper. *Lower Right:* Pip Pip Cat travels to London to serve the queen. *Bottom:* Rajah, a soldier from India.

Overleaf: In *Richard Scarry's Busy, Busy World* Mario takes his family for a ride through the canals of Venice in his melon boat. Scarry loved pigs and included them in most of his books. Perhaps for this reason, his work was never published in Muslim countries.

typical Scarry rules to obey if you live in a castle. There were sensible rules such as "Behave yourself at the dinner table" or "Wipe off your muddy feet before you enter the castle" mixed with typical Scarry absurdities like "All witches must put their brooms away when they have finished with them" or "Keep your suit of armor well oiled so that you won't squeak." He hadn't started to create any of his popular Scarry characters yet. Instead, there were many different characters typical of the country in which the story was set.

Busy, Busy World sold well, and it was always one of Dick's personal favorites, but it did not have the incredible success of most of his other big books. The reason is fairly obvious: toddlers of picture book age are more familiar with their neighborhoods than with foreign countries. Parents saw less reason to buy the book for them (though Scarry had thoughtfully provided many humorous asides for adults who had traveled abroad). Probably because his publisher anticipated smaller sales, his contract for the book called for a smaller royalty—only 5 cents a copy. The advance was $8,000, which was $1,000 more than he had received for *Best Word Book Ever.*

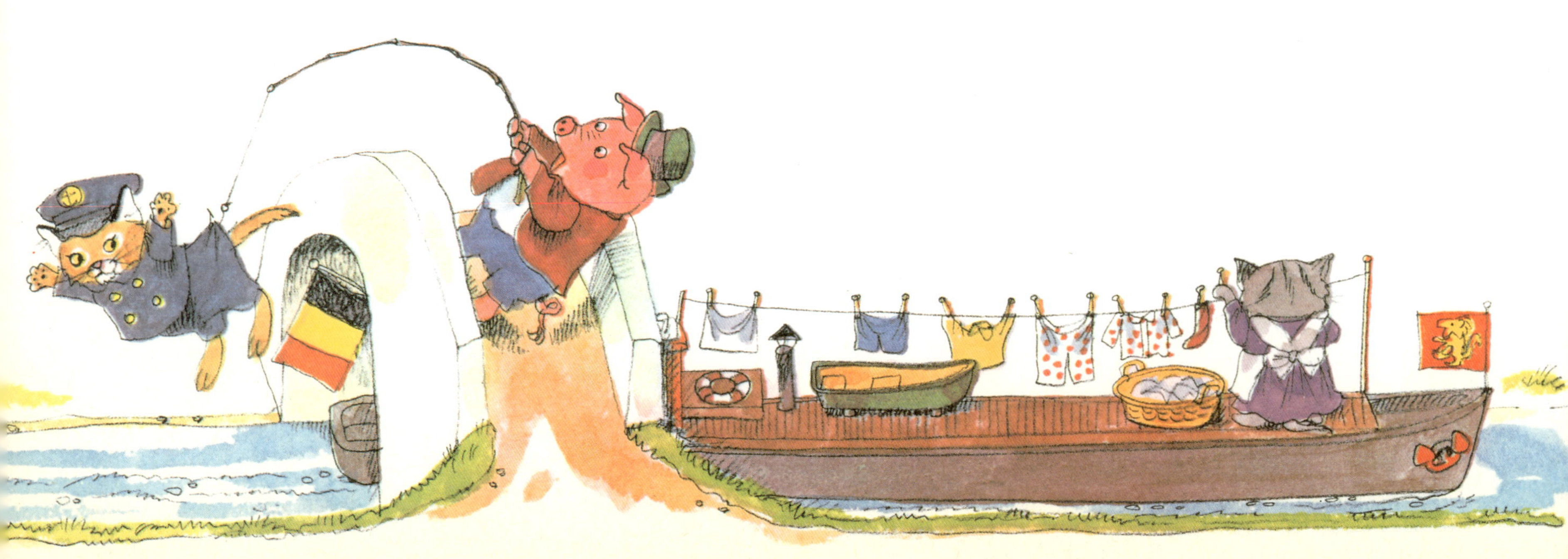

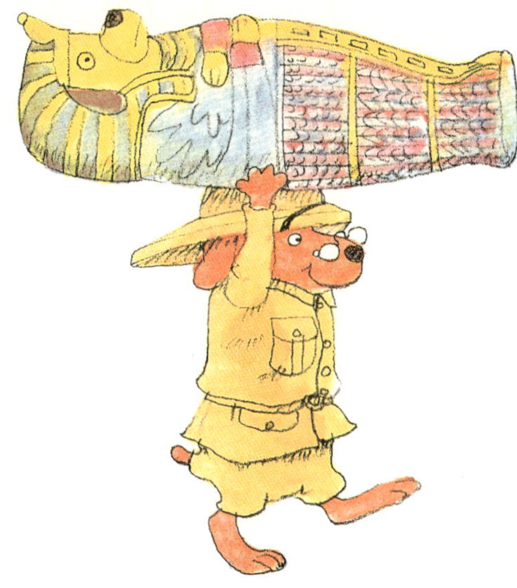

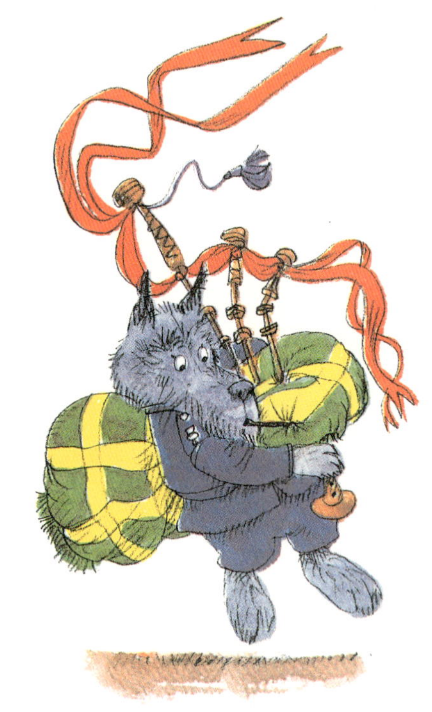

It's interesting to note that *Busy, Busy World* was one of the first new Golden Books to be sold by a Western sales staff. A year earlier, 1964, Western had acquired from Pocket Books their 50 percent interest in Golden Press. The company was now a wholly owned subsidiary, with all Golden Book sales and distribution in the hands of Western's own sales staff.

For his next big picture book Scarry came up with another surefire idea. He was going to create a brand-new kind of dictionary for beginners. Each separate word entry would be accompanied by just a snippet of a story illustrating the use of the word. In addition, there would be many other words used as labels alongside familiar objects included in the illustrations. Altogether the finished book contained more than 2,500 words.

The *Storybook Dictionary* required an enormous amount of work, so Dick and Patsy decided to rent a quiet cottage on the island of Nantucket for a three-month period during the summer of 1965. If they thought Dick was going to be able to work in peace and quiet, far from the distractions of Westport, they were mistaken. By now their famous hospitality had become legendary. Friends from New York flew

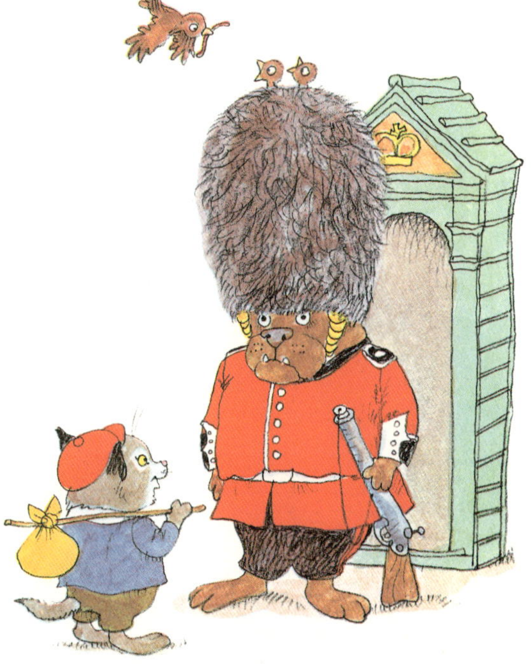

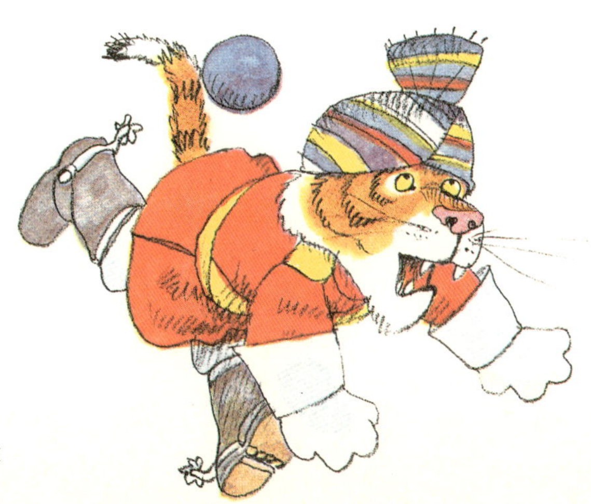

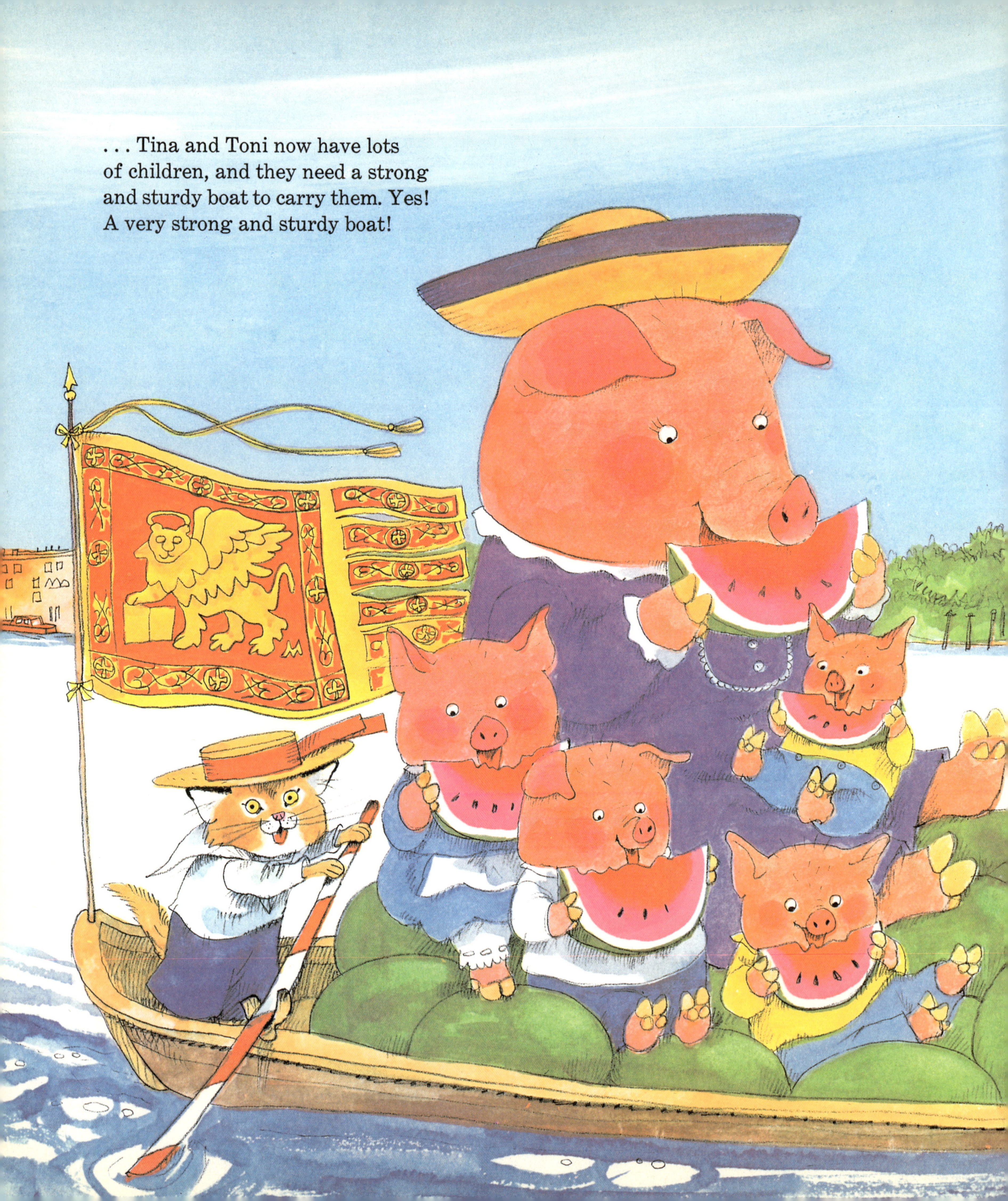

... Tina and Toni now have lots of children, and they need a strong and sturdy boat to carry them. Yes! A very strong and sturdy boat!

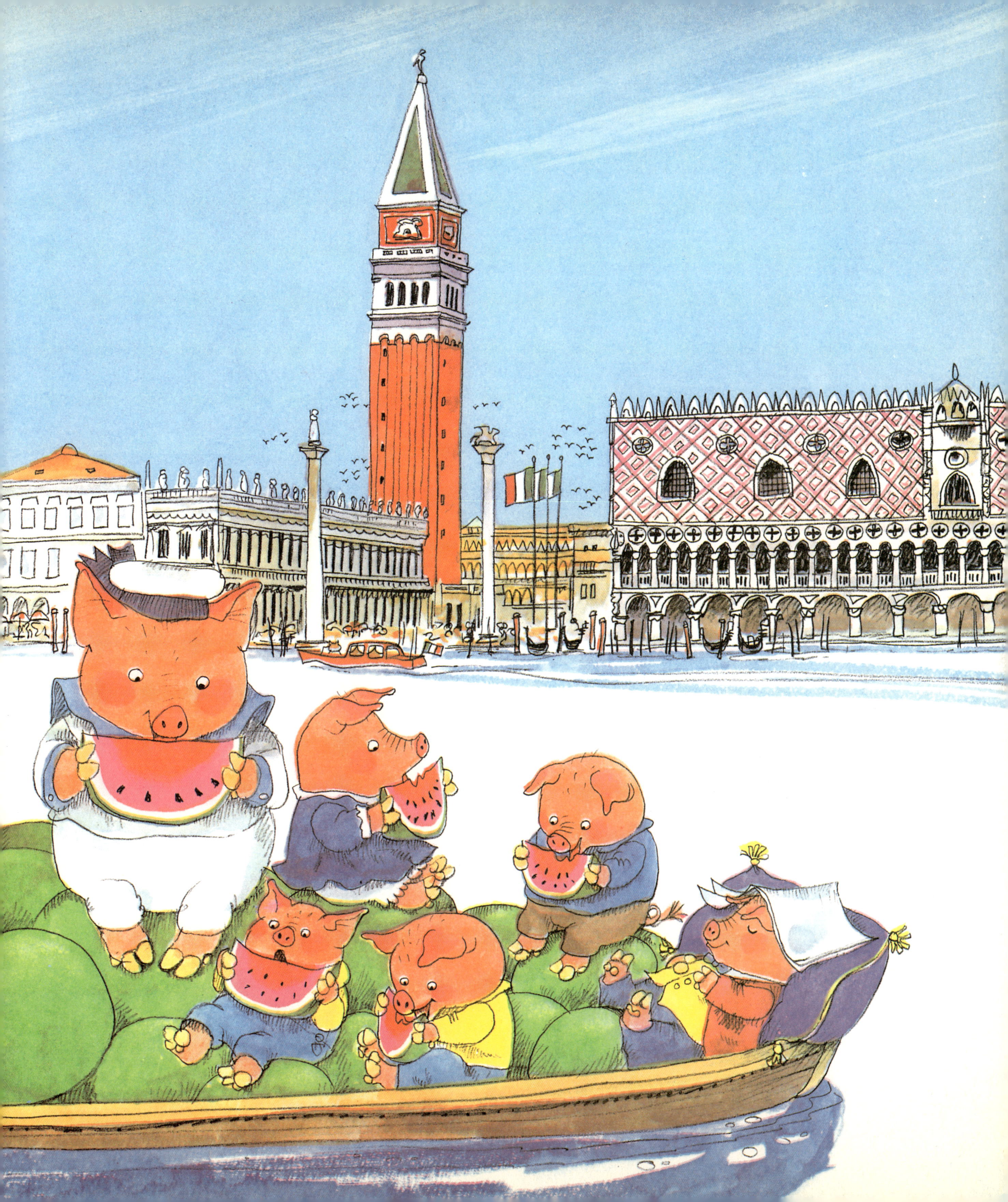

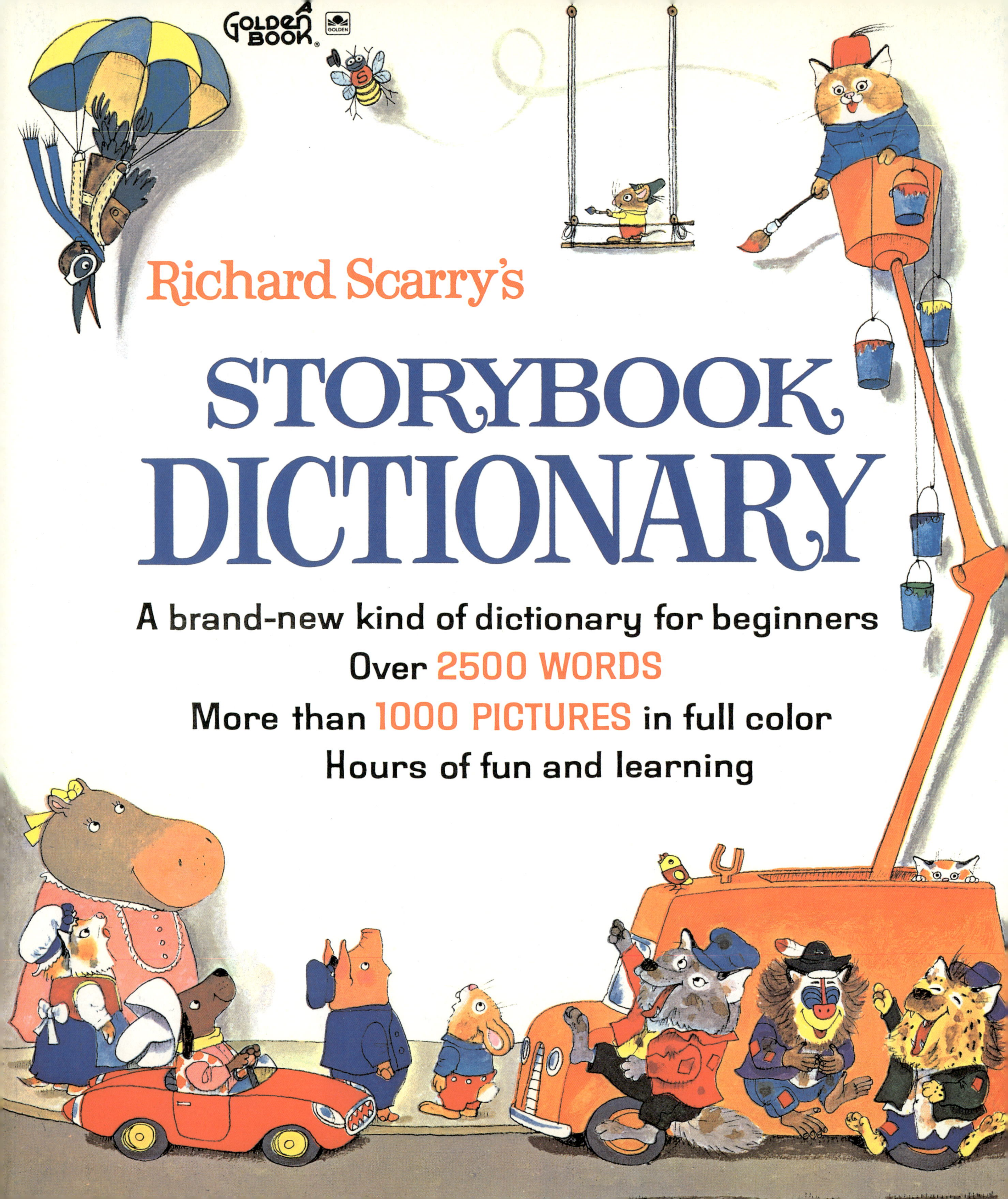
GOLDEN BOOK®
GOLDEN
Richard Scarry's
STORYBOOK DICTIONARY
A brand-new kind of dictionary for beginners
Over 2500 WORDS
More than 1000 PICTURES in full color
Hours of fun and learning

in for the weekend, and sometimes for a whole week. John Miller was with them for the entire summer.

In later years, Patsy reminisced about the time Kathleen Daly arrived for the weekend with a young man in tow. His name was George Nicholson, a new editorial employee at Golden Press (later to achieve considerable success as the creator of the Dell Yearling paperback line). To make sure of his welcome, George arrived loaded down with a case of champagne. Despite his wonderful hostess gift, Patsy had to tell him, somewhat ruefully, that there was absolutely no place for him to sleep except on the kitchen floor. That particular weekend there were twenty-three house guests. But the case of champagne ensured that everybody had a great time.

Even with the guests, the noise, and the confusion that reigned through most of the summer, Dick kept to his working schedule. In fact, he even found time to go sailing.

Dick wasn't the only Scarry drawing and painting that summer. His son, Huck, who had already become quite an accomplished artist, produced a number of watercolors, all of which he sold at a Nantucket art exhibition. Dick had never pushed his son into being an artist. Huck had just taken to it very naturally. As a small boy he would often lie on the floor, drawing or painting, while his father worked at the drafting table. If Huck asked for help or advice about how to draw something, Dick would make suggestions or give encouraging support, but he allowed his son's exceptional talent to emerge naturally.

At the end of the summer, the Scarrys returned to Westport, and Dick turned in the art and text for his new book. While the editorial and production departments worked out the final details for the manufacturing of the physical book, Dick busied himself with two or three smaller projects, including his *Egg in the Hole Book*, a boardbook with a hole for a child's finger die-cut right through the center.

On August 11, 1966, Golden Press officially published *Richard Scarry's Storybook Dictionary*. It was such a success that the printing plant had trouble keeping up with the orders. The blurb on the cover said "Hours of fun and learning," and for once a cover blurb was absolutely right. Young children loved the book with the same devotion they had bestowed on *Richard Scarry's Best Word Book Ever*. The looseness of his line, the multitude of details, and the sense of action and real characterization

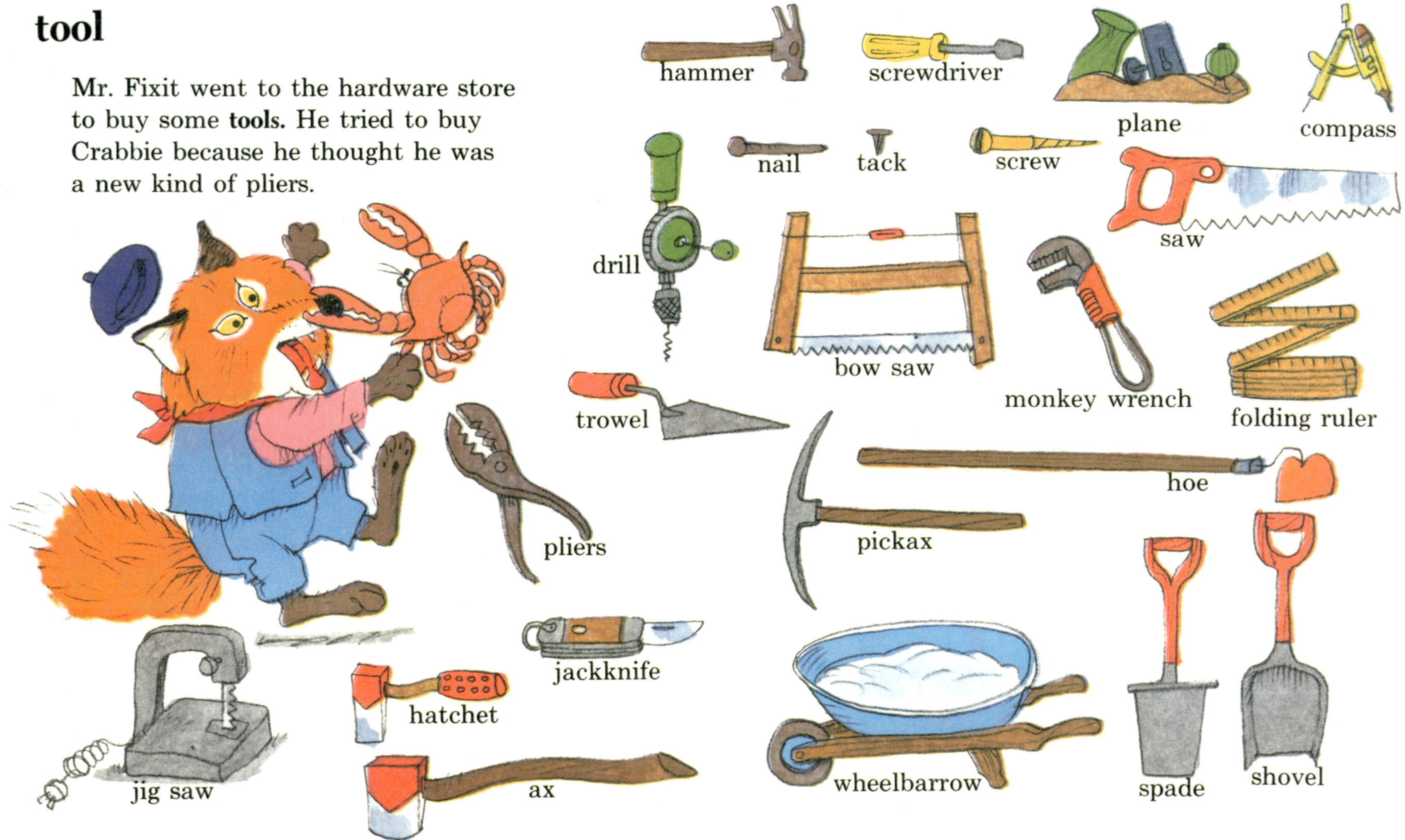

Above, and opposite: Word entries from *Storybook Dictionary*

all combined to make the book a perfect example of the ultimate Scarry style. He had abandoned completely the somewhat stiff, graphic painting style—accompanied by a good deal of white space—popularized by earlier Golden Book artists. His keen eye for absurd human behavior is evident throughout the book; at the same time there is a good deal of information combined with funny activities and characters to which a child can easily relate.

flatten flattens, flattened, flattening

flat

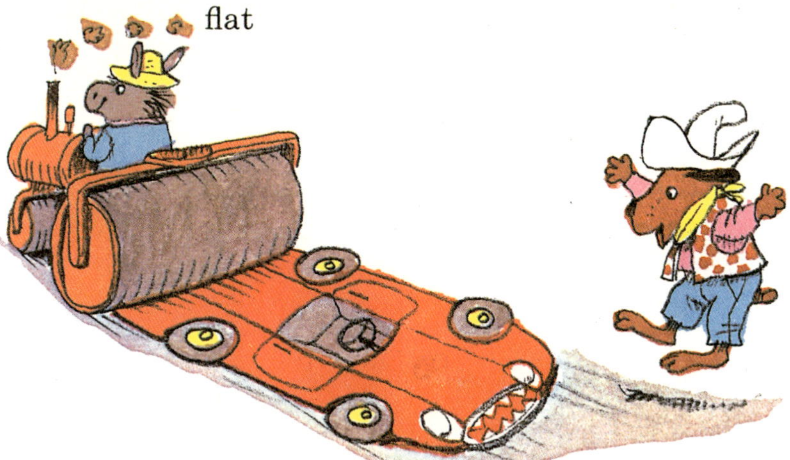

A steam-roller **flattened** Dingo's car.
That is certainly a **flat** car!

float floats, floated, floating

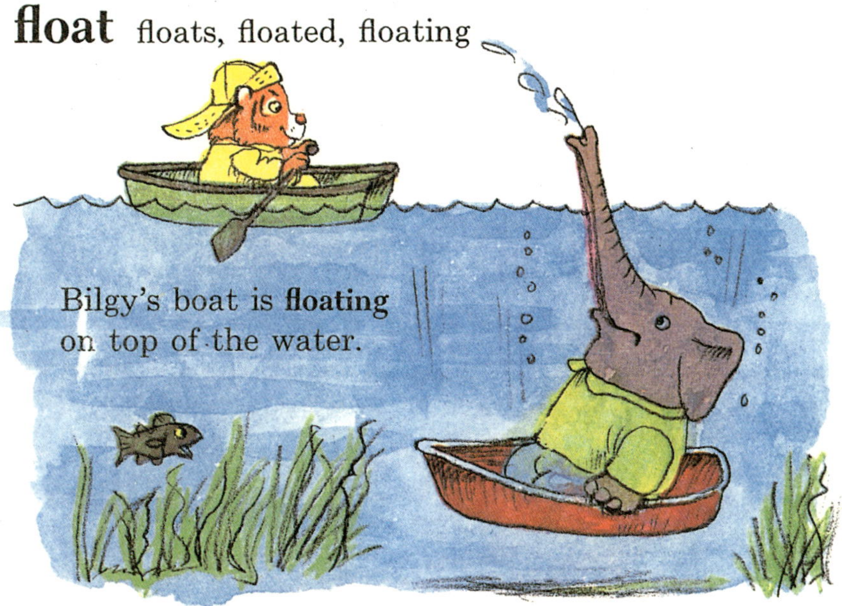

Bilgy's boat is **floating** on top of the water.

Hannibal's boat is sinking.

flow flows, flowed, flowing

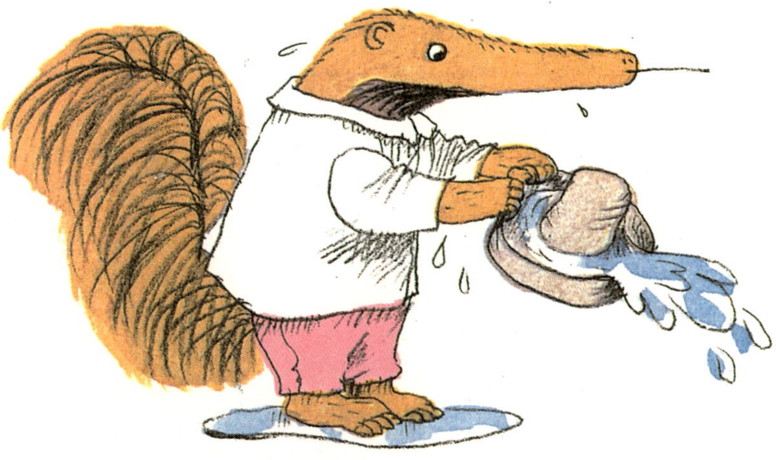

Andy came in out of the rain.
When he took off his hat, a stream of water **flowed** out of the brim.

flower

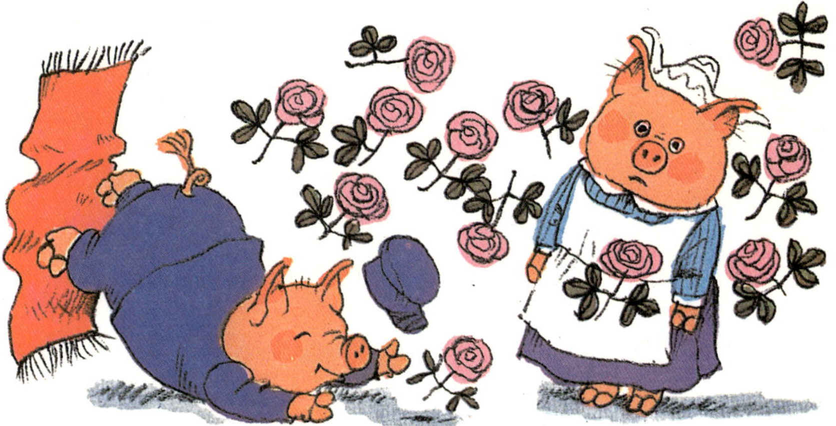

Pa Pig brought a bouquet of **flowers** home to Ma Pig.

fly flies, flew, flown, flying

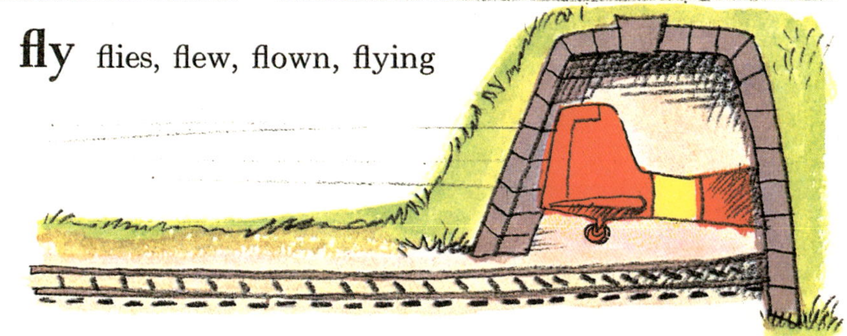

Baron von Crow **flew** into the railroad tunnel.

fold folds, folded, folding

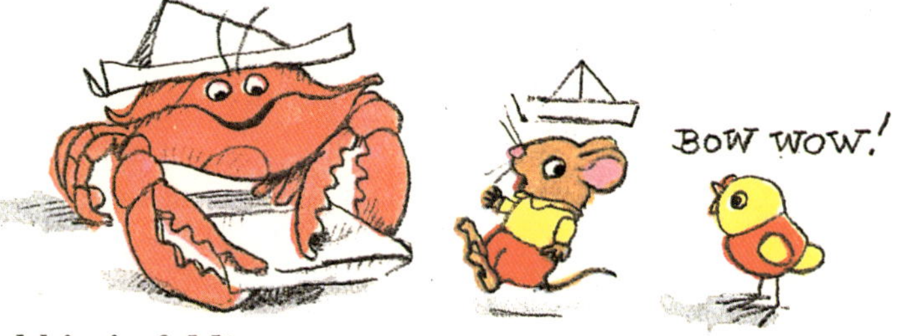

Crabbie is **folding** newspapers to make paper hats.

follow follows, followed, following

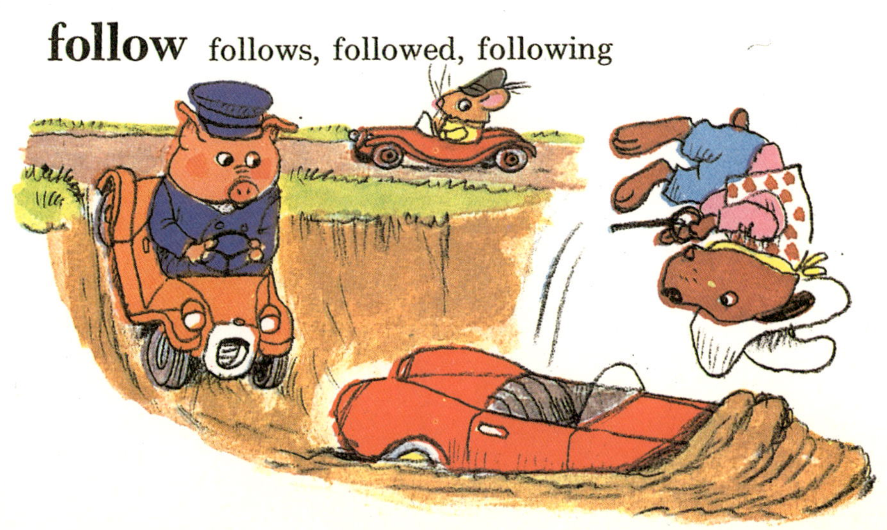

Pa Pig **followed** Dingo into the mud hole.

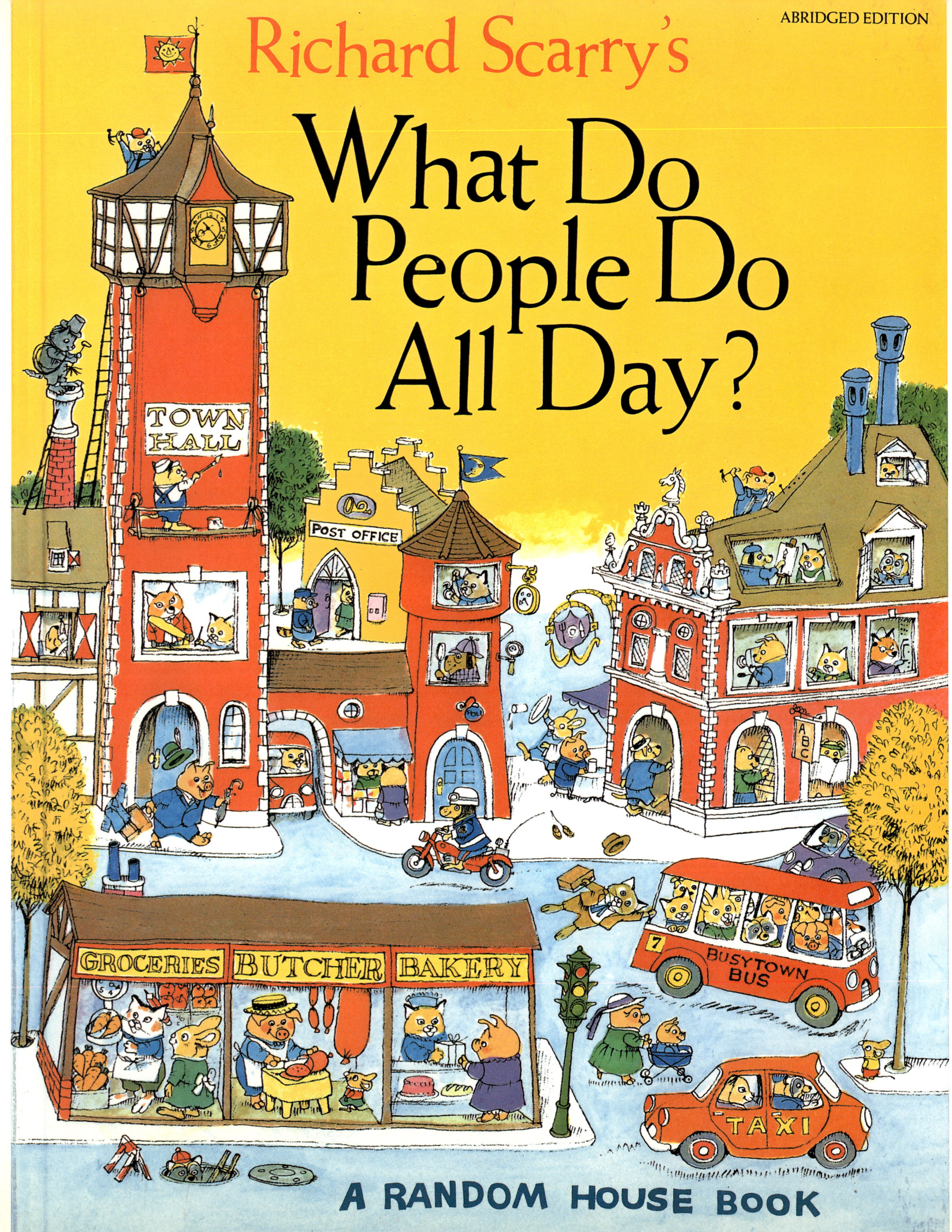
ABRIDGED EDITION
Richard Scarry's
What Do People Do All Day?
TOWN HALL
POST OFFICE
GROCERIES
BUTCHER
BAKERY
BUSYTOWN BUS
TAXI
A RANDOM HOUSE BOOK

A NEW PUBLISHER, A NEW COUNTRY

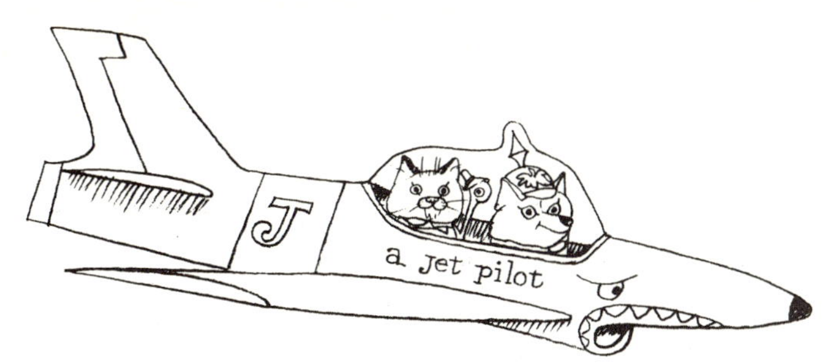

Above: From *Best Rainy Day Book Ever*

Even though his new books were such a success, Scarry was becoming restive. The *Storybook Dictionary* was his third oversized, best-selling picture book. This time the contract called for an advance of $15,000 against a royalty of 10.6 cents a copy. While that was an improvement over the two previous contracts, he still was earning only slightly more than 3½ percent on a $2.95 book. Because Dick found it difficult to stick up for himself in the matter of royalties, he began to realize that he needed help in negotiating new terms. He had recently met a lawyer living in Westport, whose wife owned The Remarkable Bookshop. The lawyer's name was Sidney Kramer, a former publishing executive himself. Dick asked Kramer to represent him in placing the publication rights for his next book, *What Do People Do All Day?*

Scarry had finished the rough pencil sketches and text but he hadn't made any formal commitment yet. Sidney Kramer took the manuscript to Albert Leventhal, president of Golden Press, for his inspection; then he showed it to Robert Bernstein, president of Random House. Kramer asked each publisher to make a bid for the book with special emphasis on royalty rates and advances, plus rights to be retained by the author. Both executives showed the manuscript to appropriate members of their staff and discussed with them its potential, as well as the importance of having Scarry on their list.

Random House, which badly wanted to add Scarry to its very successful juvenile list, offered a multi-book contract with royalty rates that were significantly higher than what he had been getting at Western. In return, Random asked for his exclusive services during the period of the contract.

Albert Leventhal refused to consider improving Golden's terms. He resented having to deal through Kramer; in fact, he initially refused to have any-

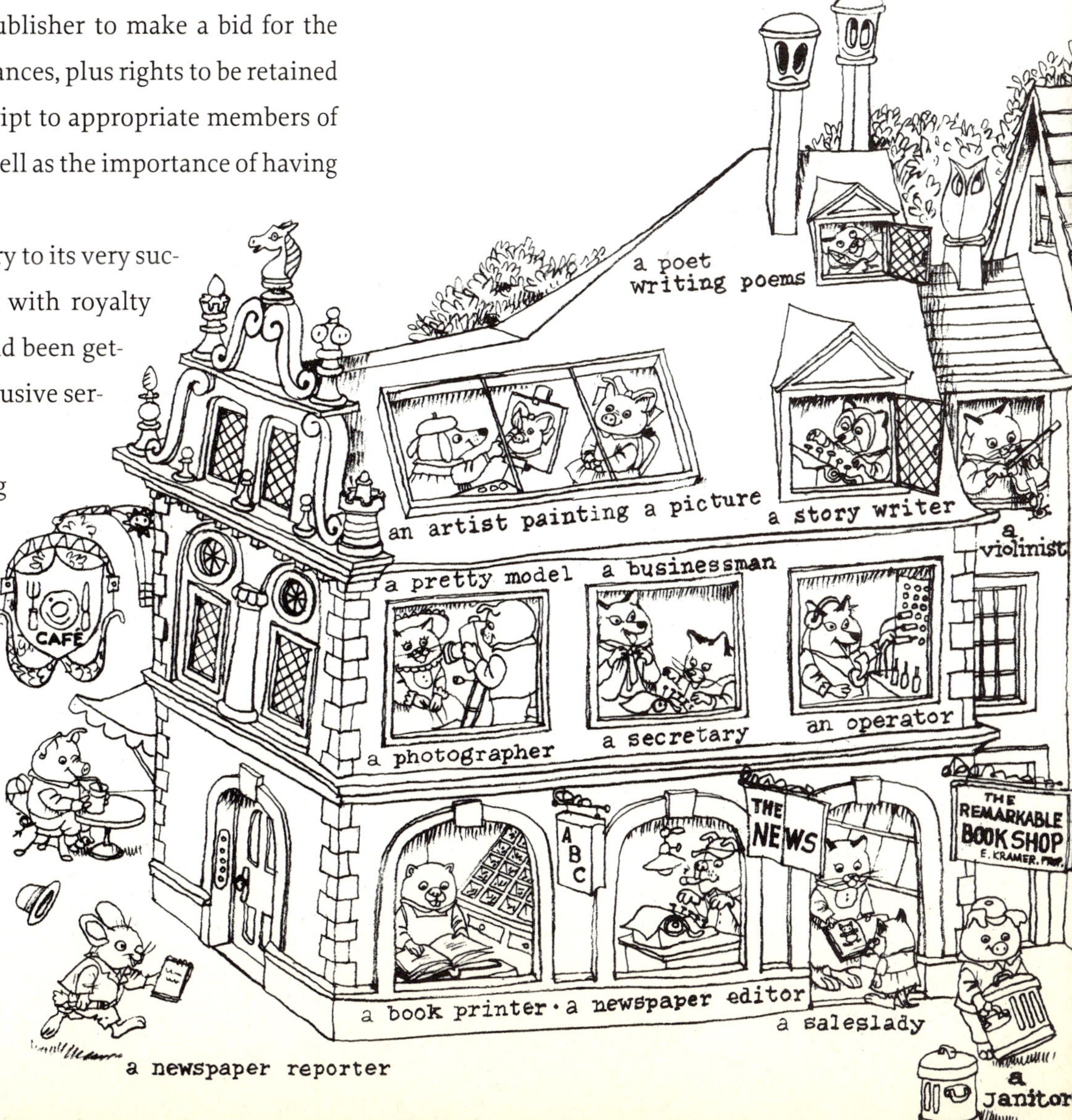

Below: This pencil drawing is the rough sketch for the painted title page illustration from *Richard Scarry's What Do People Do All Day?* It was later published with a collection of other early pencil drawings in an activity book, *Best Rainy Day Book Ever.*

thing to do with him. He felt that he had been betrayed by an author who had benefited enormously from his association with Golden Books. He also conveyed to Dick the impression that he was rather lukewarm about *What Do People Do All Day?*

As various Golden Press staff members began to argue with him, urging him not to be so hasty, Leventhal decided that perhaps he was wrong and offered to improve the Western terms. Unfortunately he was too late. Richard had decided to sign the multi-book agreement with Random House. Because such an agreement would take considerable time to negotiate with Scarry's agent, Random House prepared a separate contract for *What Do People Do All Day?* This allowed them to put the book into production without a big delay. Scarry signed the contract on April 28, 1967.

The multi-book contract was signed nearly six months later on October 18, 1967. It provided for a total advance of $105,000 against the delivery of twelve books in various price ranges and sizes. This was an almost unheard of amount of money in those days for a children's book author/artist. For books with a price range of

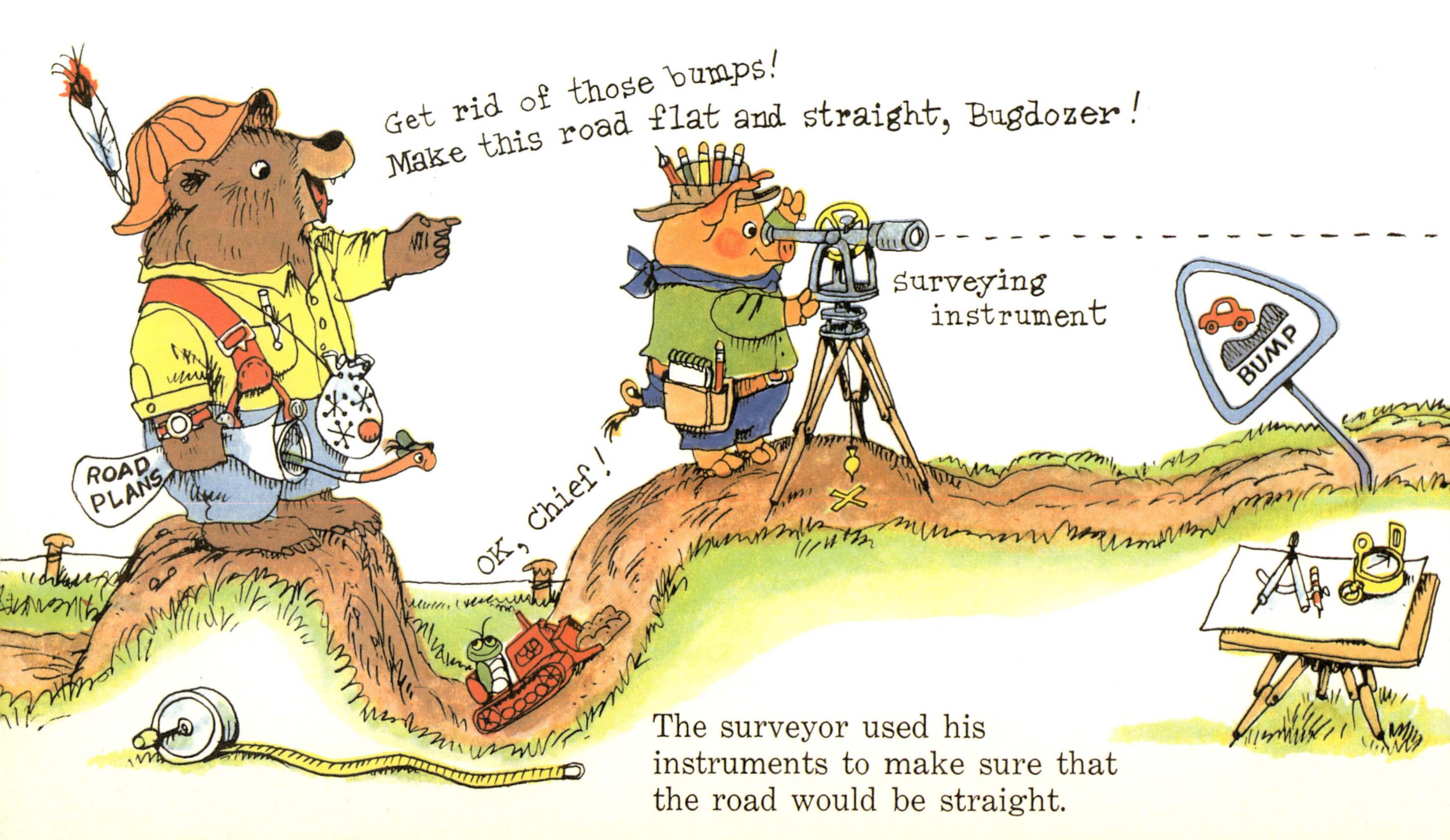

The surveyor used his instruments to make sure that the road would be straight.

$3.50 to $5.95, he would receive a royalty of 5 percent of the retail price up to the sale of 75,000 copies. From 75,000 copies to 150,000 copies he would earn 6 percent, and on all sales after that he would receive 7.5 percent. This was a great deal more than the 8 cents a copy he had earned on *Best Word Book Ever.*

After twenty years with Golden Books, Richard Scarry moved across Madison Avenue to his new publisher. Everybody at Random House was delighted by their new acquisition, even though their children's book list already included a number of stars: Dr. Seuss, the de Brunhoff Babar books, Stan and Jan Berenstain with their Berenstain Bear books, and Walter Farley, author of the Black Stallion novels. But there was always room for one more, particularly when the star was of Richard Scarry's stature. The transfer of a best-selling author from one house to another is always a bit delicate; there has to be a period of getting acquainted, of learning one another's working habits, and building trust. Walter Retan was division vice president and editor-in-chief of children's books when Scarry arrived at Random House. Below is his recollection of their first meeting:

A scene from "Building a New Road" in *What Do People Do All Day?*

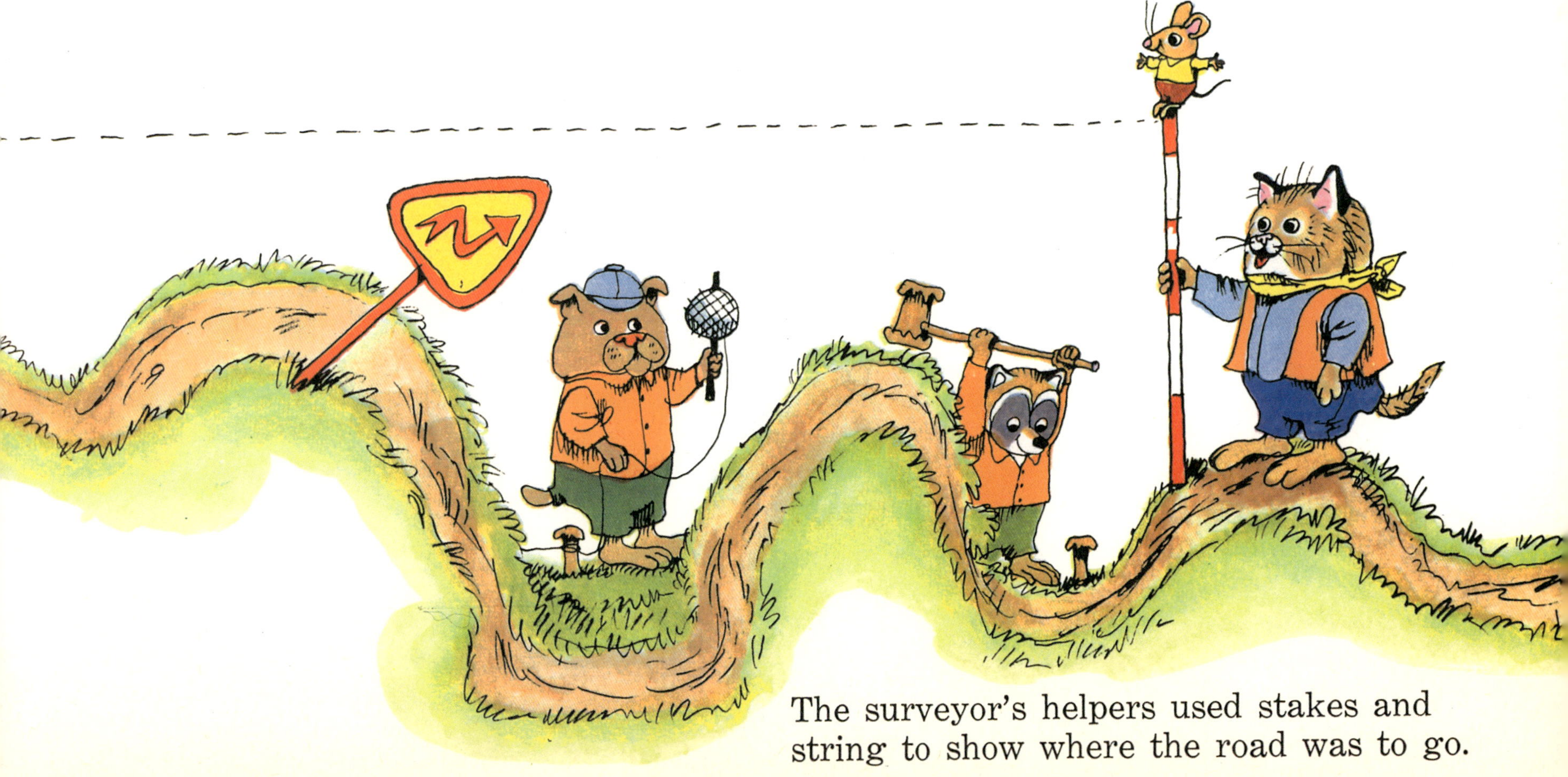

Up until the time that Richard Scarry decided to move to Random House, I had never met him. I was thoroughly familiar with his books, of course, and admired them very much.

I remember well the day that Bob Bernstein brought Scarry into my office for our first meeting. Dick was wearing a blue blazer, a striped rep tie and light blue shirt, and gray flannels, all of which looked like pure Brooks Brothers. He had brought in the rough pencil sketches for What Do People Do All Day? *with typed patches of text pasted onto them, and I quickly realized that he wanted me to look at them right away. (Usually I tried not to read texts or look at artwork while the creators were hovering over me, but in Dick's case I realized it was essential that I look immediately.)*

From the very first doublespread, I knew he had created an absolutely wonderful book. I read very slowly, studying the myriad of detail in all the illustrations and apologizing to Dick for taking so long. I explained that when I read a children's book I tended to read like a child. The book was chock-full of fascinating information about people's activities and professions. There were sections on how a house is built, how a fire department operates, where electricity comes from, what happens on an ocean liner and many, many other subjects. Obviously he had done a prodigious amount of research, yet he had managed to present this material in such a clear, simple, visual way that it could be understood by very young children. Most important of all, there were all kinds of typical Scarry funny characters and situations scattered across the pages. I immediately found myself laughing almost constantly. Every time I laughed, Dick would lean over my

Below and opposite: Two illustrations from "Building a New House" in *What Do People Do All Day?* Notice that Scarry offers cautionary advice to children in scenes such as the one opposite with the electrician standing next to the fuse box.

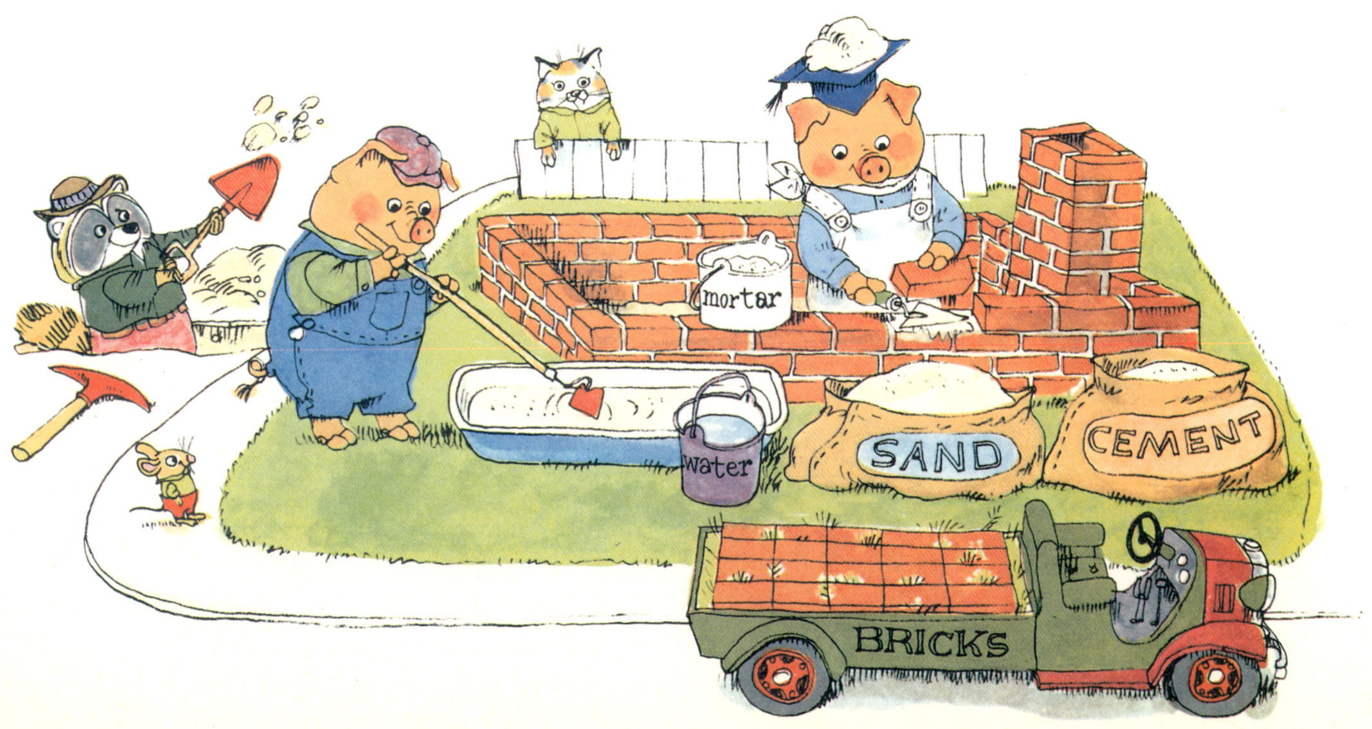

Jason finished making the chimney.
Be careful you don't fall, Jason!

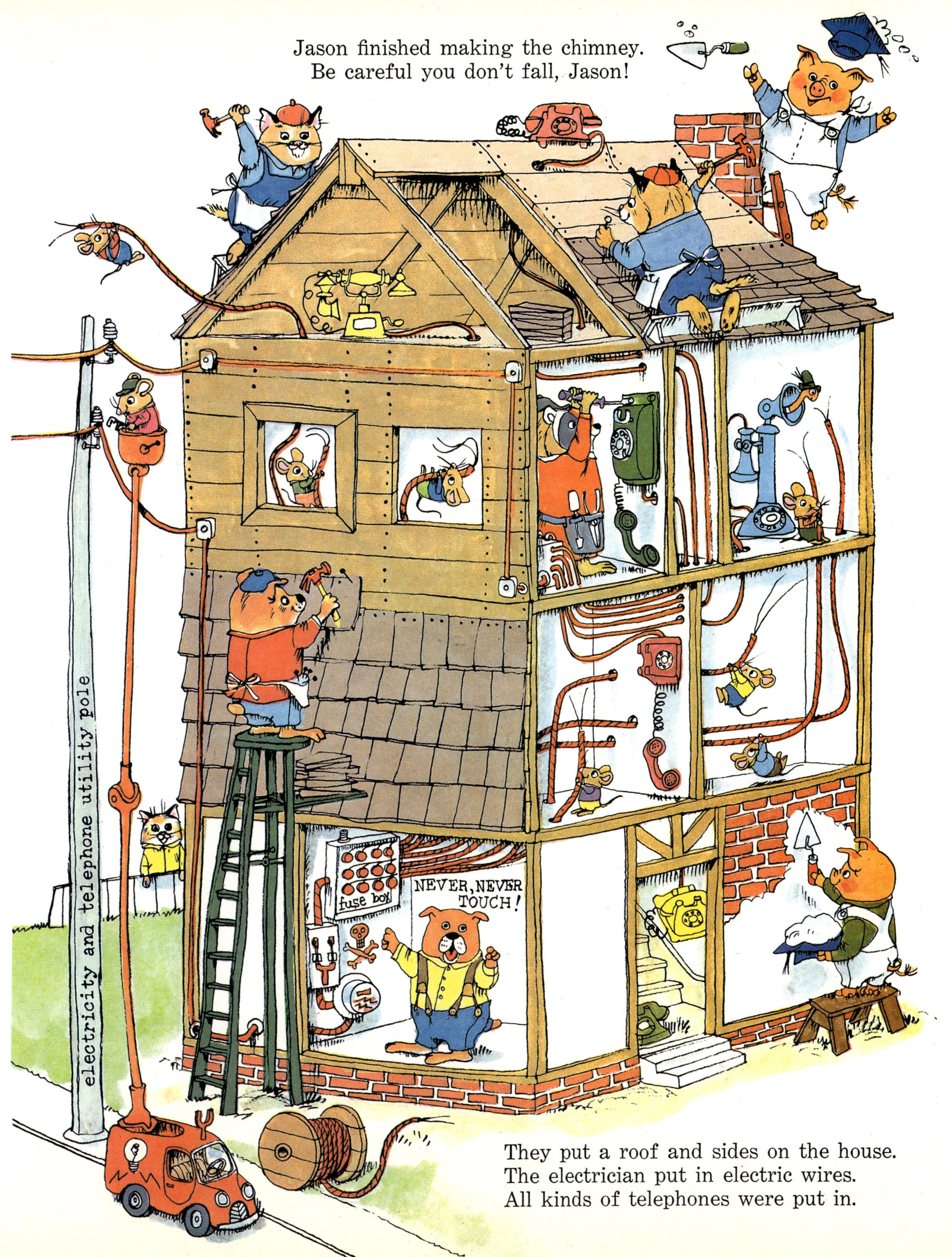

They put a roof and sides on the house.
The electrician put in electric wires.
All kinds of telephones were put in.

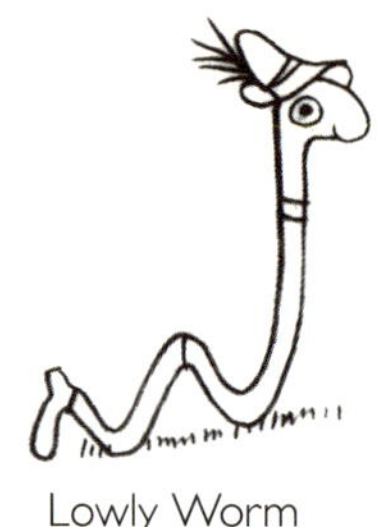

shoulder to see what I was laughing at. Then he would laugh, too, sometimes quite boisterously. He was particularly pleased whenever I spotted Lowly Worm, who was to become Dick's most popular character. Lowly appeared on nearly every spread, usually in some comical place or situation, but he wasn't named until the very end of the book, where Dick drew and named the whole cast of characters.

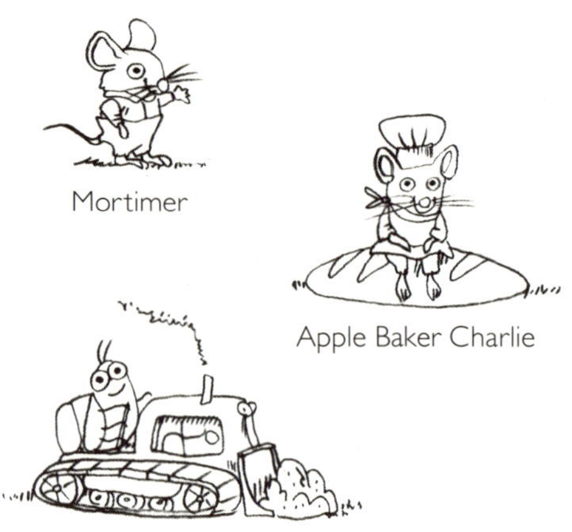

This mutual reading of the book was probably the best possible way to start an author/editor relationship. Dick couldn't help but know from my reactions that I was extremely enthusiastic about it. He explained that he always had his books set in the same type face and type size because it matched the old portable typewriter on which he wrote his texts. I called in the production manager to discuss this and several other concerns. We had discovered that no bindery in the country other than Western could handle the large, almost square format that Golden Press used for Dick's books. For obvious reasons we didn't want to have his books printed by our biggest competitor, so we asked Dick if he could adapt his illustrations to a 9¼ by a 12½ inch size, a popular Random House format. Dick agreed. He was always very practical and accommodating in such matters, though he could be stubborn when something really didn't please him.

Before he left my office that day, he gave me a typed version of the text, saying that he knew his spelling and syntax weren't always perfect and giving me a free hand at making any necessary corrections. He typed by the hunt-and-peck method, using just two fingers. I found that most of his spelling errors were actually typos. I never tried to rewrite his texts; I always felt that he knew exactly what he was doing, even when his writing style was somewhat unconventional.

Drawings for some of the cast of characters shown on the front endsheet of *What Do People Do All Day?*

Overleaf: A doublespread from "Wood and How We Use It" in *What Do People Do All Day?* Note the headline on the newspaper covering the face of the workman sleeping under the apple tree.

Dick left his sketches on the big table where we had been looking through them, and we parted on the best of terms. The sketches were still on the table the next day when Ted Geisel (Dr. Seuss) unexpectedly appeared in my office. While we talked about the new

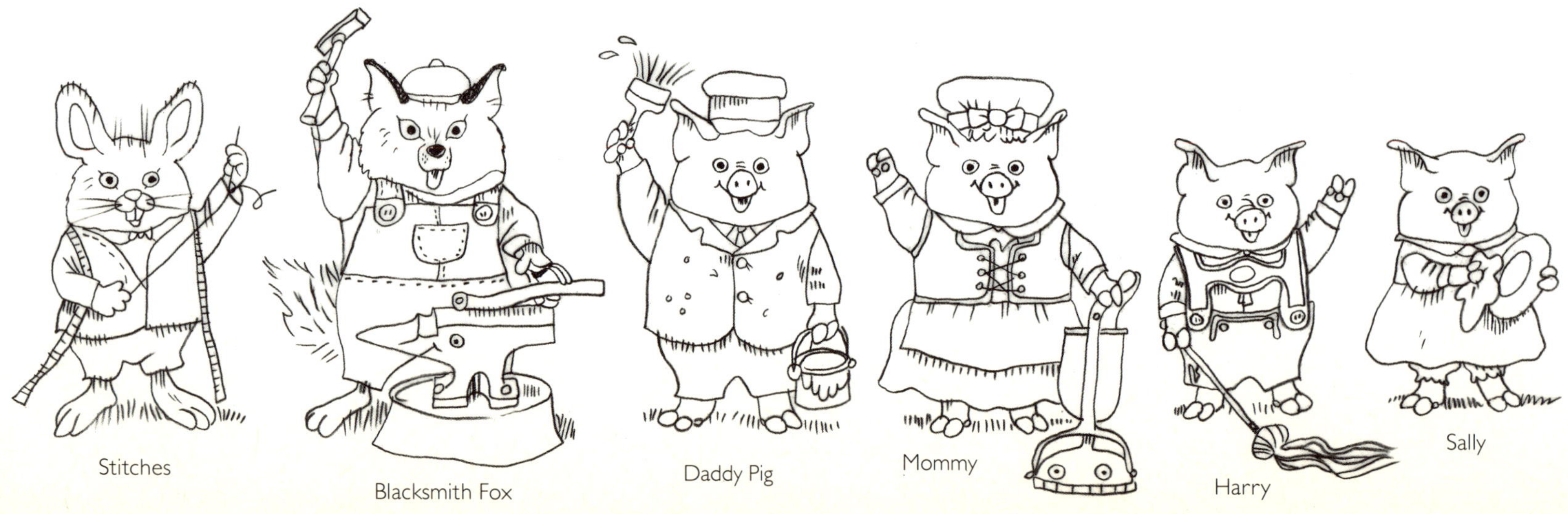

Sergeant Murphy

Seuss book, Ted wandered over to the table and began idly leafing through Dick Scarry's drawings. (He didn't ask whose work it was; I suspected that he knew.) Suddenly he asked, "Does this sort of thing sell?" I assured him that it sold very well indeed. I didn't tell him that at the moment Scarry books were outselling Seuss books: editors have to be good diplomats. The two men couldn't have been more different; Scarry was almost totally visual, while Ted was extremely verbal. It was interesting to work with the two of them and note the differences.

The only objection to the new Scarry book came from the sales department. When I showed them the sketches, they immediately started to question the title, What Do People Do All Day? *After all, they argued, the characters are animals. Shouldn't we call it* What Do Animals Do All Day?

"They're not animals, they're people," I argued, "If you use the word animals, *readers will expect a book of true facts about animal activities." Eventually they agreed, and the title remained unchanged. Nobody else ever quarreled with the title, though a few reviewers made amused references to the apparent paradox.*

Shortly before Dick joined Random House, my wife and I had purchased a brownstone in Park Slope, Brooklyn. It was a beautiful old house, but needed considerable work. I recall that the second time I saw Dick, he brought Patsy and Huck along, and we all had lunch together. I spent quite a lot of time talking about the leaky pipes and the heating problems in our house. When the finished art for the new book arrived a few months later, I suddenly discovered on page sixty-nine that Father Pig was lying under an apple tree with a newspaper over his face so he could take a nap. The headline on the newspaper read: GREAT HEATING AND PLUMBING PROBLEMS AT THE RETAN HOUSE. That was a typical Scarry touch. He often included the names of friends in his books, sometimes in store names or signs on trucks.

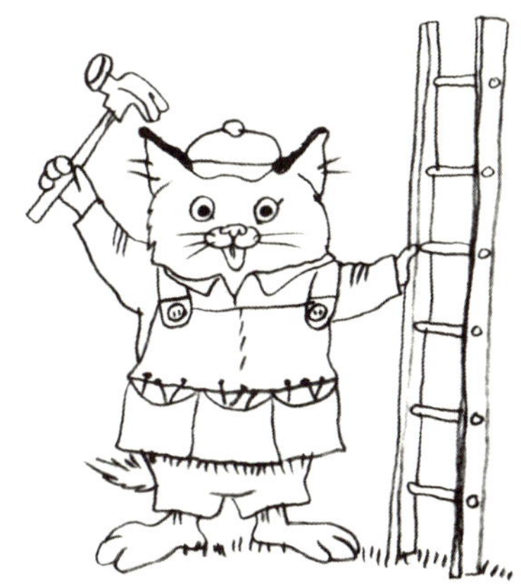

Sawdust the carpenter

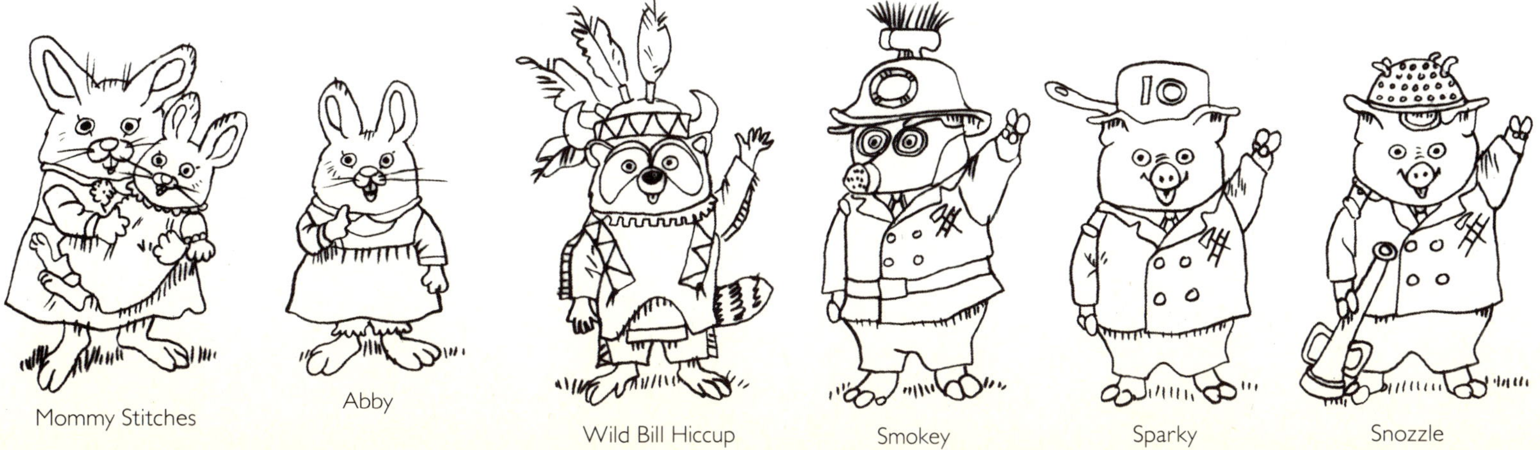

Mommy Stitches Abby Wild Bill Hiccup Smokey Sparky Snozzle

The paper makers use scraps of wood to make paper.

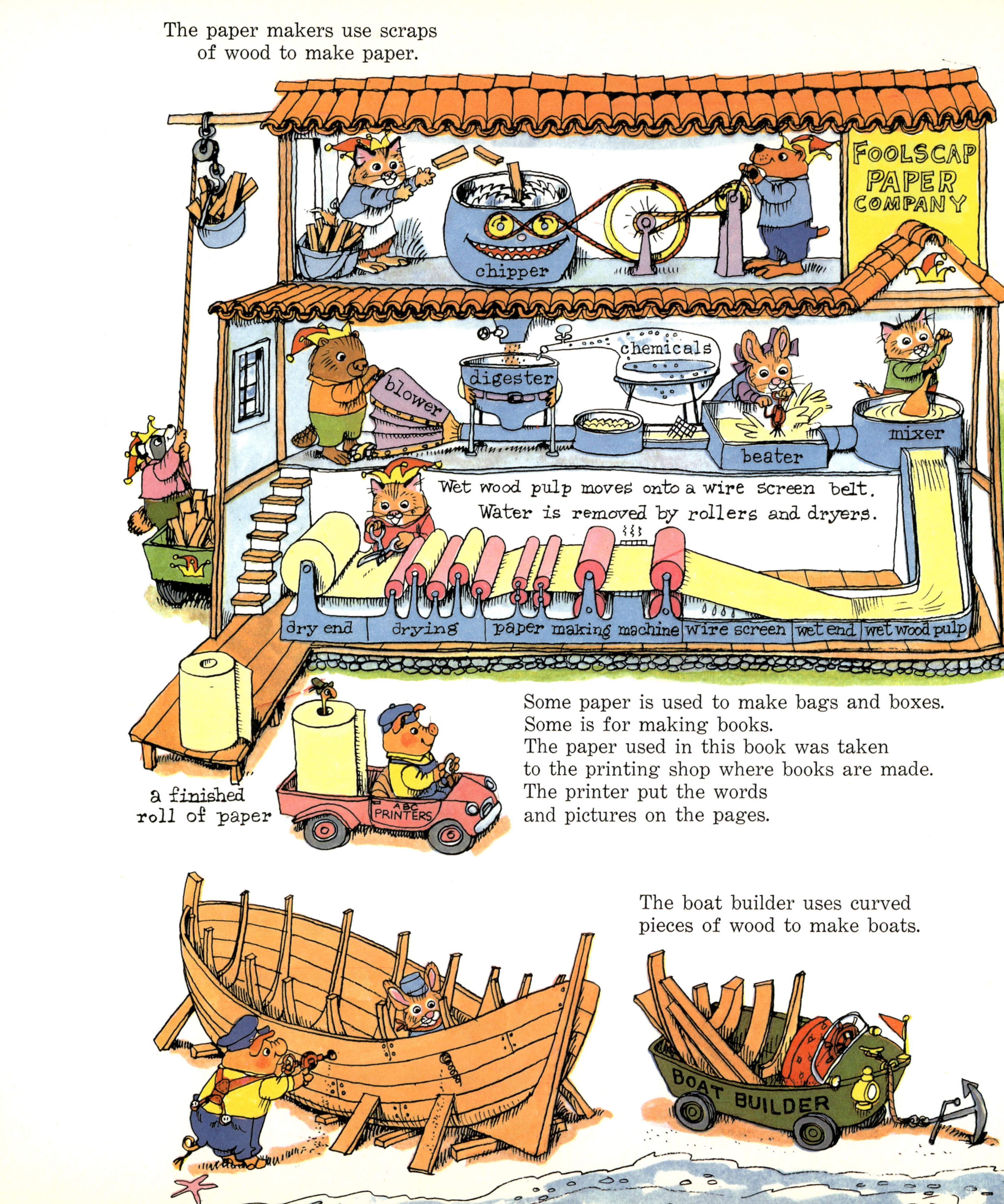

Some paper is used to make bags and boxes. Some is for making books. The paper used in this book was taken to the printing shop where books are made. The printer put the words and pictures on the pages.

The boat builder uses curved pieces of wood to make boats.

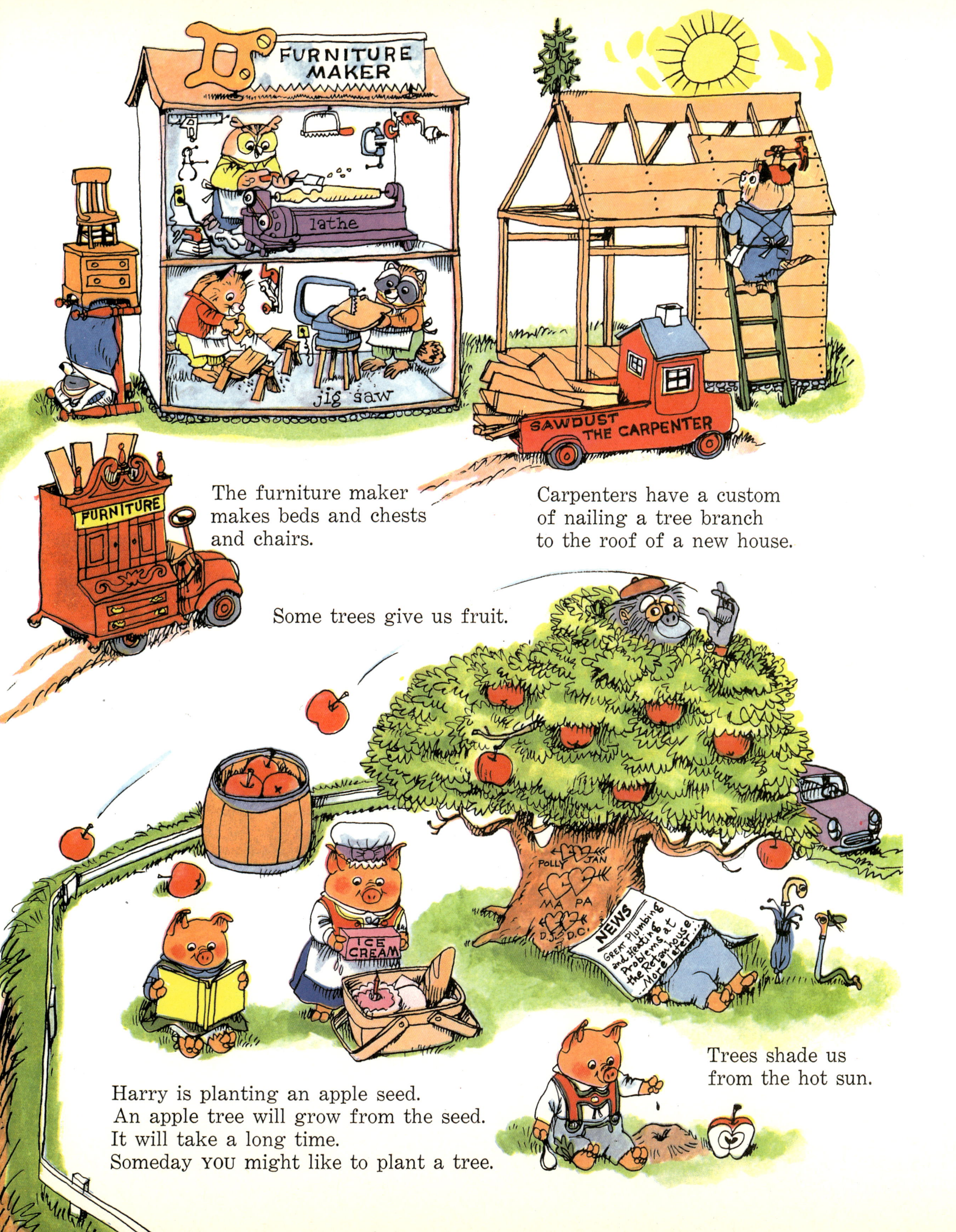

The furniture maker makes beds and chests and chairs.

Carpenters have a custom of nailing a tree branch to the roof of a new house.

Some trees give us fruit.

Trees shade us from the hot sun.

Harry is planting an apple seed.
An apple tree will grow from the seed.
It will take a long time.
Someday YOU might like to plant a tree.

As soon as the first contract was signed, Dick began to prepare the finished art for *What Do People Do All Day?* Working steadily though the summer, he turned in the line drawings first, then painted in the color on a production preparation material called blueboards. (See page 137.) Random House scheduled the book for publication in spring, 1968; they wanted to get a big Scarry book on their list as soon as possible. While spring is seldom as good a time as fall to publish an important book, the Random House staff felt that they could resell it with fresh promotion and advertising at the start of the big Christmas season.

Meanwhile, during the winter of 1967, Dick decided to take Huck to Switzerland on a skiing trip. Patsy was going to spend the Christmas holidays in Canada with her father, who had not been well recently. As a native Canadian, she had skied as a girl and loved it, and had introduced Dick and Huck to the sport. Soon her husband and son shared her enthusiasm. They often drove up to Manchester, Vermont, for weekends, skiing at Stratton Mountain.

According to Dick, the 1967 trip to Switzerland "was the usual twenty-one-day excursion. But coming home," he later explained, "we had to pass through Lausanne in order to catch our plane from Geneva. From the train window I caught a glimpse of a child throwing a snowball—just that, nothing more—and I thought, 'Now is the time to move to Switzerland.'

"The move was not a political one. We had always hoped at some time to live in Europe, but couldn't make plans because of Huck's being in school. But Huck was fifteen, and Switzerland was magnificent, and suddenly the time seemed right."

His new friends at Random House could scarcely believe him when he dropped the bombshell. They hadn't really had time to develop a solid author/publisher relationship. What would it be like to try to work with him if he moved to Switzerland? There was no point in arguing, however; he had obviously made up his mind, and Patsy shared his enthusiasm. There were many reasons for his decision, but the most important one was probably the reason he didn't mention at the time: he and Patsy were both tired of the hectic life they had been leading in Westport. They were weary of the constant parties, the steady flow of house guests, the drinking, and the endless interruptions. If they moved to Switzerland, they could leave all that behind.

In the spring of 1968, the first printing of *What Do People Do All Day?* came off the press. When the first copies arrived at the Random House offices, everyone was

Opposite: Dick and Huck Scarry hike in the Alps near Switzerland's Matterhorn. Dick loved hiking in the mountains and, as Huck has written, "each Saturday morning he would drive us up to a new valley to hike and eat fondue. My father and I literally drove to the end of every valley in Canton Valais—and a few in Val d'Aosta."

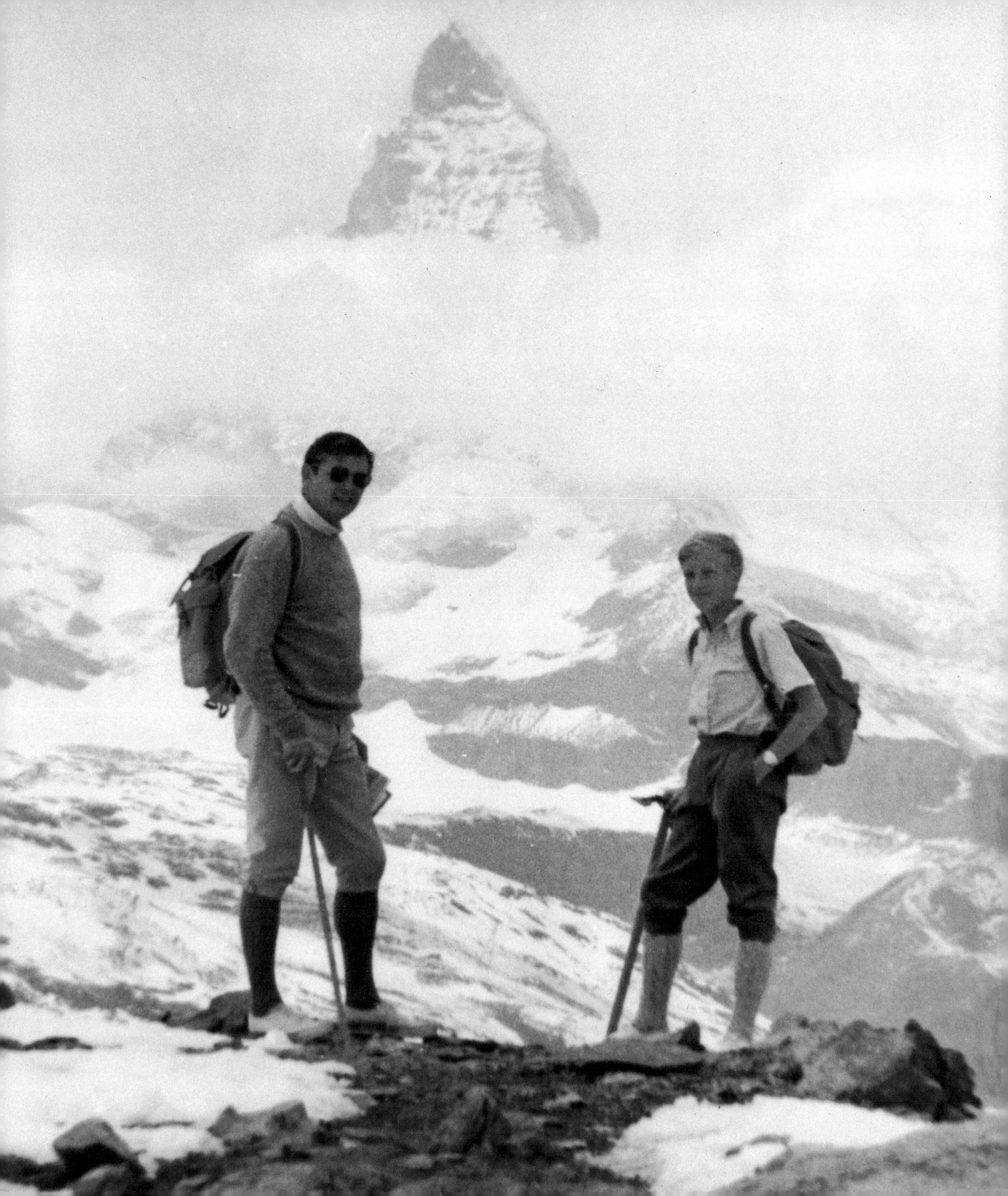

shocked. The black line was much too weak. It just barely held its own with the other colors. The manufacturing department should have stopped the run when the first proofs came off the press: instead, they okay'd it. This was a dreadful blunder to have happen with an important new author. After considerable discussion, Random House executives decided to order a new, corrected printing right away. They would wait until they had properly printed books before sending copies to reviewers, buyers at book outlets, and librarians. They advised Scarry about the mishap and told him what steps were being taken to correct it.

The book received some excellent reviews. Critics were really beginning to appreciate the hours of painstaking research and the inimitable humor that Scarry was able to bring to his books. They were also impressed by his amazing ability to make complex material understandable to children.

Meanwhile, throughout May, the Scarry family was making feverish preparations for their move to Lausanne. First they had to make arrangements to lease their house in Westport for one year. Then they had to figure out what they wanted to take with them. Dick had given strict instructions that no one would be allowed to take more than one suitcase. This meant that there were many difficult decisions about what to pack and what to store. Dick wanted to have a car in Switzerland, but not the old station wagon they had been using. He went to a Mercedes dealer in Greenwich, Connecticut, and ordered a black Mercedes-Benz coupé, which he could pick up directly from the factory in Stuttgart. He had never owned such a beautiful car before, and he was extremely proud of it. Woe to any passenger who slammed the door too hard.

Official records show that the Scarry family entered Switzerland on June 2, 1968, and headed directly for Lausanne. They temporarily booked into a hotel while they searched for more permanent living quarters. Lausanne, a beautiful old city, which now has some 124,000 inhabitants, rises up from Lake Geneva on a series of hills, with the magnificent thirteenth-century Cathedral of Notre Dame at the top. The Scarrys were enchanted and did a great deal of sightseeing while they began to look for a place to live. They wanted to find a studio for Richard and an apartment for the family, but they soon realized it would not be easy to get just what they wanted. Nevertheless, they were having a wonderful time, beginning to feel quite at home, when they suddenly received a summons to report by the end of the week to the police chief in charge of foreign residents. It seemed that unless they applied for

Opposite: Dick and Patsy hurry to board their ship to Europe from a New York City pier.

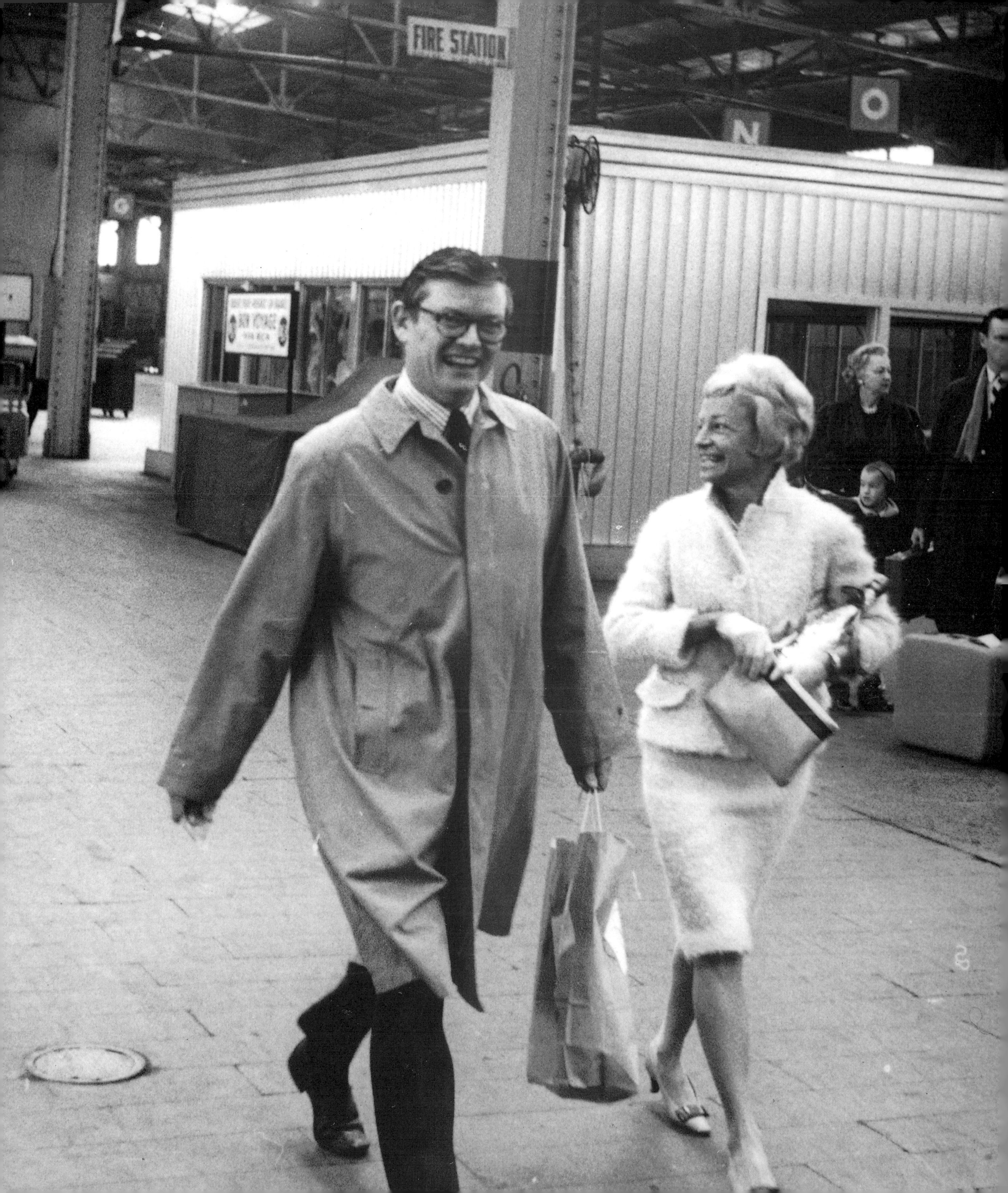
FIRE STATION
N
O
BON VOYAGE

and received a residency permit, they would have to leave in three months.

Dick was stunned. Had they come all the way to Switzerland only to be told that they must leave at the end of three months? Remembering some of the know-how he had acquired in the army, Dick packed a selection of his books in a knapsack, and together he and Patsy started off to police headquarters. Although it was a stiflingly hot August day, they dressed very formally. Eventually they found the official they were looking for in a tiny boxed-in office that felt like a baker's oven.

At first the police official was quite austere. He explained that Swiss law prevented anyone from renting an apartment, or even living in Switzerland for more than three months without a residency permit. Since they had not applied for one, what were they planning to do? Their time had just about run out. Dick explained that he hadn't known about the residency permit.

As he began to tell the official that he was a children's book author and hoped to spend a year in Switzerland working on his books, he noted that the man became more and more interested. "Do you like children's books?" Dick asked. "Oh yes," said the man, "and so do my children." Whereupon Dick stood up and poured out the contents of his knapsack, uttering one of the few French words he had learned. "*Un cadeau* [a gift]!" he exclaimed, pointing at the array of books that had spilled all over the desk and even onto the floor. The official burst out laughing. As he began leafing through the books with intense excitement, he explained that he collected paintings as well as children's books and had a keen interest in art. Soon all formality vanished. Dick tore off his tie, opened up his shirt, and for a long time they chattered with great enthusiasm about art.

Drawings from *Best Rainy Day Book Ever*

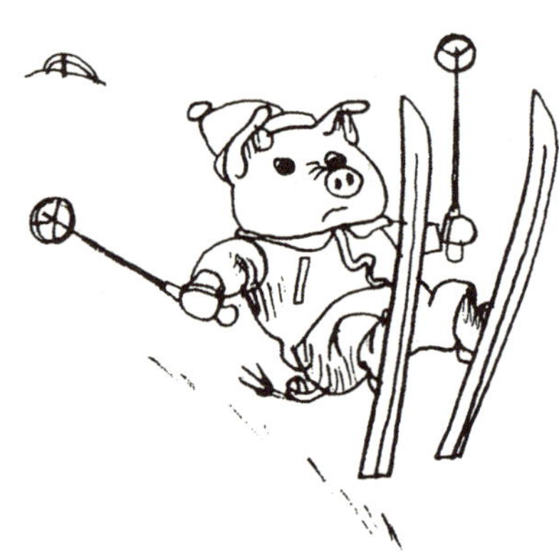

At the end of their interview, the police chief said, "Just go to the office right around the corner, and they will give you your residency permit right away." Dick and Patsy returned to their hotel with great relief. Now they could safely continue their search for proper quarters.

First they found a small rooftop studio high on a hill in the old quarter of Lausanne, with a leg-killing flight of stairs, but a romantic view of the cathedral. This they rented as a studio for Dick. Soon they also found a sunny apartment within walking distance of the port, down in Ouchy. The large living room windows provided a view of the fabulous snow-peaked French Alps six miles away. Patsy set to work furnishing the new apartment, while Dick worked at his studio. Needless to say, Patsy found the furniture in Lausanne stores rather traditional and heavy-looking. It was also very expensive, so she began to haunt the secondhand shops, decorating their new home with her usual flair.

She painted an old dining-room table bright green, sewed slipcovers of mill-end chintz for the furniture she had picked up, and bought inexpensive but smart looking glass and china at variety shops. There were also a couple of small round tables draped with colorful cloths. Dick had his intricate hi-fi system installed. (He loved classical music and owned an extensive library of records which he enjoyed listening to in the evenings.) On the tops of bookcases and cabinets he arranged displays of his wildly assorted collection of Chinese birdcages, Swiss chronometers, Napoleon figures, rocks, coins, and early Sumerian figurines. Some of the latter were quite valuable. On the walls, there were some amusing illustrations painted by Huck when he was six. In one corner of the living room hung a huge gold-painted pretzel Dick had bought in Denmark. (It was a baker's shop sign commonly found all over Denmark.) With very little money and a great deal of imagination and hard work, Patsy created a marvelously warm and appealing living space.

Gradually the family settled into a regular routine. At eight o'clock each morning, Dick would set off for his studio with a rather elegant-looking traveling bag over his shoulder. The bag contained his lunch, which usually consisted of a ham sandwich and a small plastic bag of pickles. To get to his studio, he took what he called the shortest metro [subway] in the world. It started near the shore of the lake and climbed steadily uphill (mostly above ground) until it reached the center of the city. There were only three stops along the way.

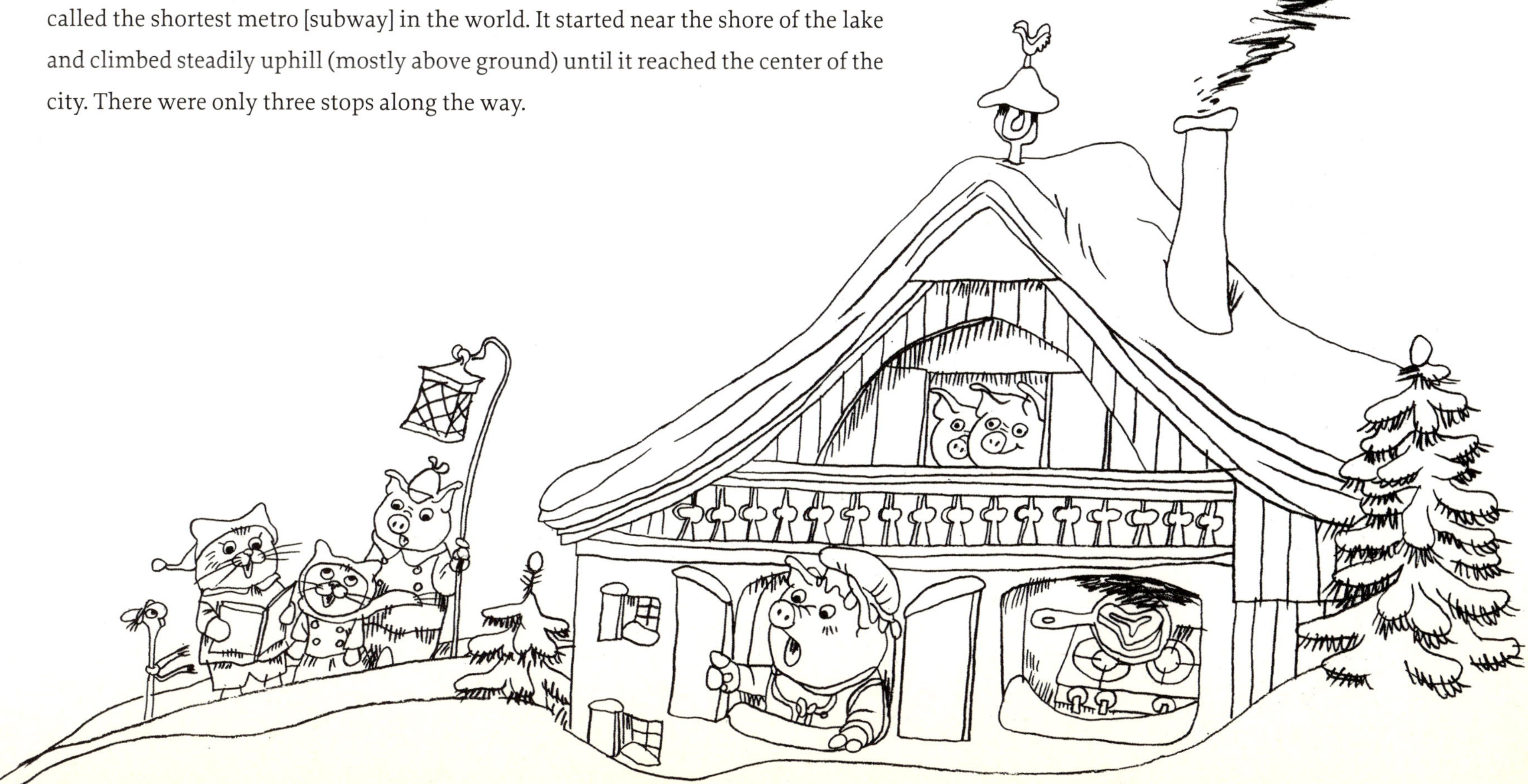

Drawing for the *ABC Word Book*

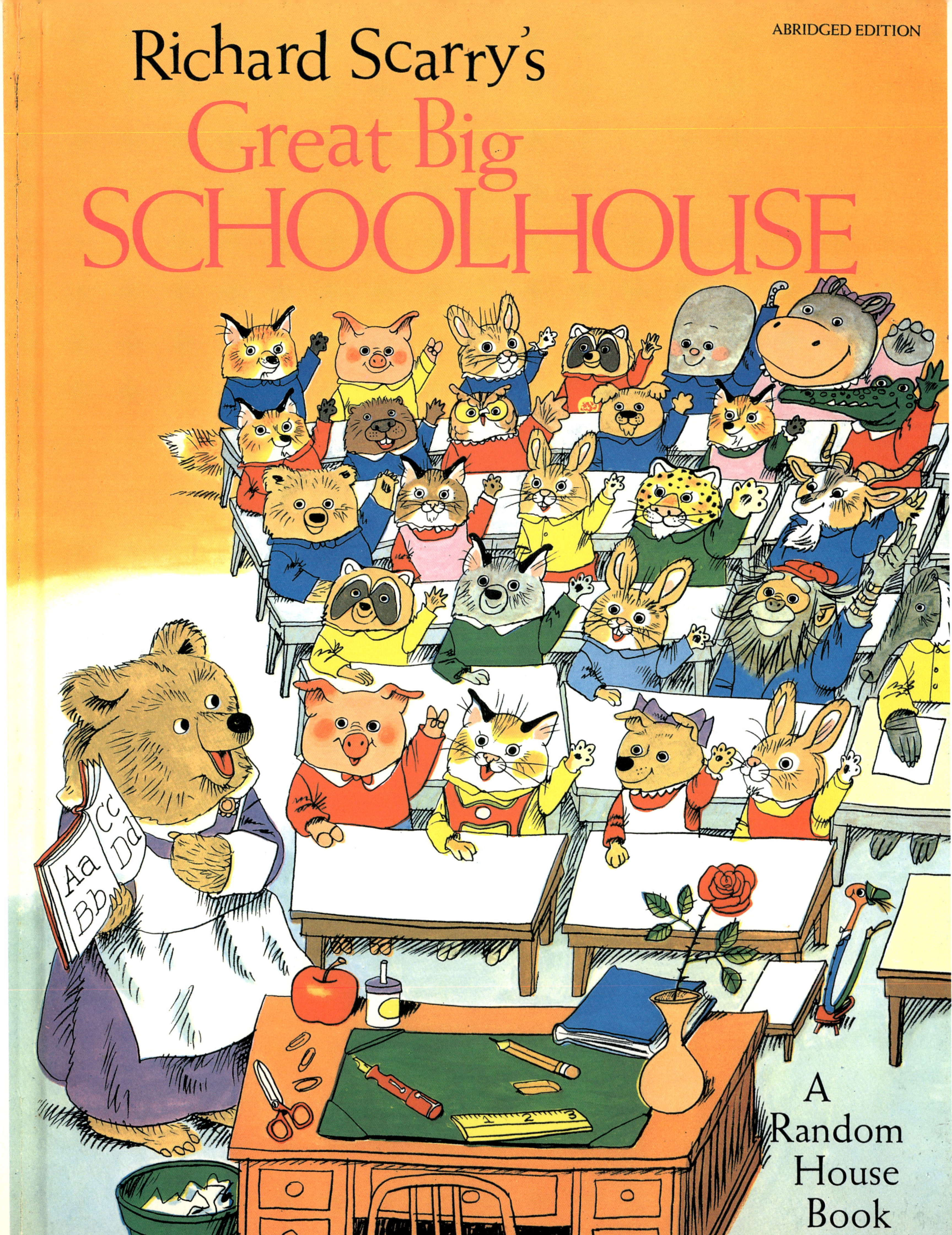
ABRIDGED EDITION
Richard Scarry's
Great Big
SCHOOLHOUSE
Aa Bb Cc Dd
A Random House Book

Dick was starting work on a new book for Random House, which he called *Richard Scarry's Great Big Schoolhouse.* His publisher had suggested the project because of the increasing interest back in the States in Head Start, a federally sponsored program intended to provide preschool education for children from culturally and economically disadvantaged backgrounds. He planned the contents of the book to include all the things that children might encounter during their first experience in a classroom, and he created a lovable teacher in the shape of a bear called Miss Honey.

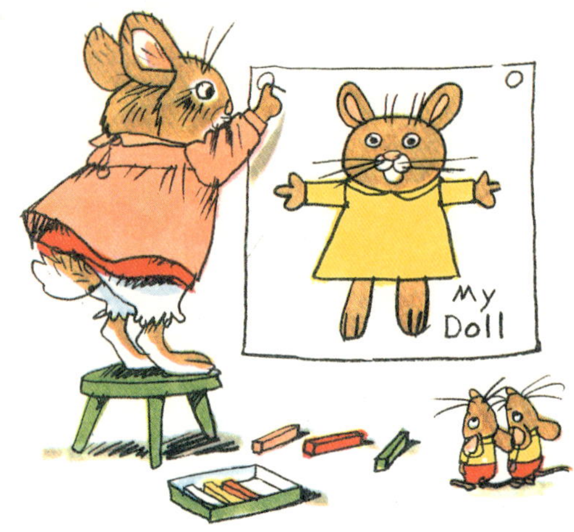

While Dick worked on the book, Patsy finished furnishing the apartment, familiarizing herself with the shops and the layout of the city. She and Dick decided to enter Huck in an international school for foreign-language-speaking students in Lausanne. At the same time, both Dick and Patsy enrolled in French language courses at the Berlitz School since Lausanne was located in the French-speaking section of Switzerland. Neither of them took very readily to learning a new language. Patsy wrote to her friends, telling them how she had seen a pickpocket at work in a Swiss store. She wanted to alert everyone to what was happening so she began shouting: "Voyeur! Voyeur!" What she meant to shout, of course, was *"Voleur! Voleur!"* the French word for thief. She later said that everyone looked at her as if she were crazy.

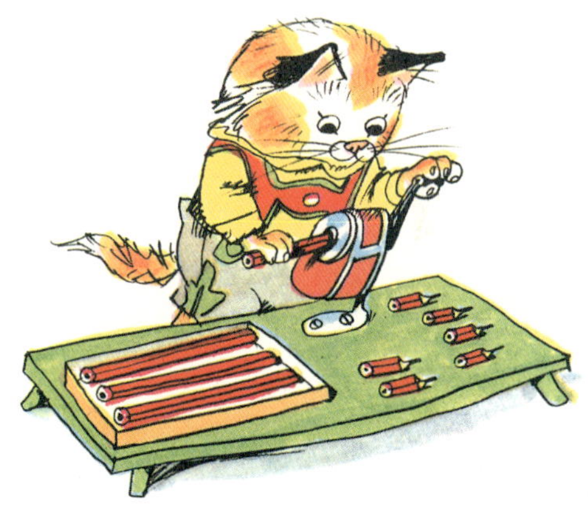

Because of the language barrier, Dick and Patsy at first had difficulty making friends. The Swiss were friendly but shy, and, contrary to reports, a large number of them did not speak English. Huck also had trouble making friends at his school. He was only a day student, while many of the others lived there. Most of the pupils seemed to be children of rich parents who had dumped them at the school in order to avoid taking care of them. The majority weren't at all interested in intellectual achievements, and the course work was far below the educational level of his

The cover *(opposite)* and three vignettes from *Richard Scarry's Great Big Schoolhouse*:

Top: Elizabeth Rabbit tacks her pastel drawing on the wall.

Center: Huckle Cat has enthusiastically sharpened the pencils.

Bottom: Some orange things that Huckle painted.

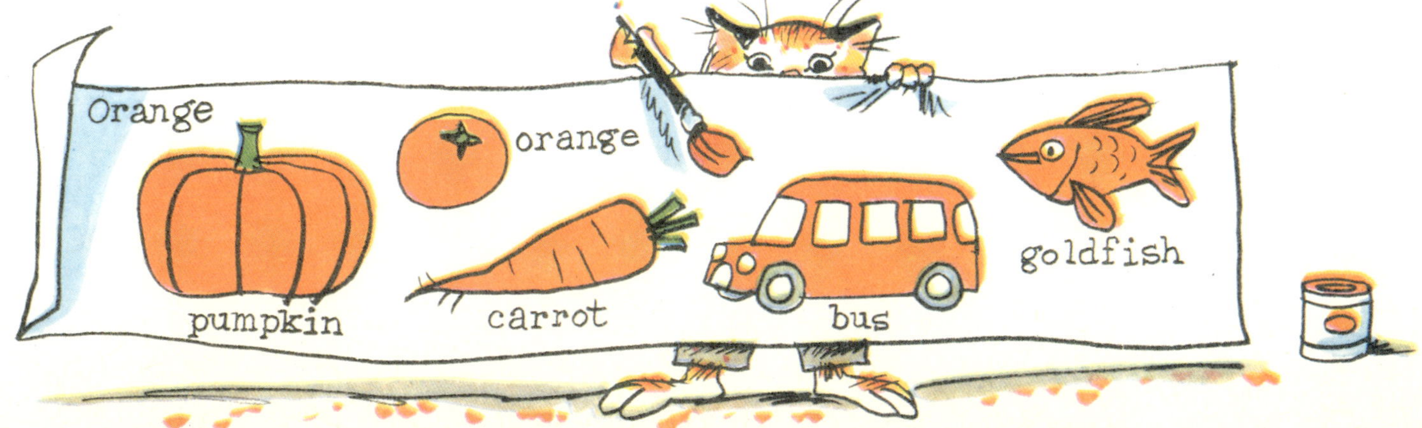

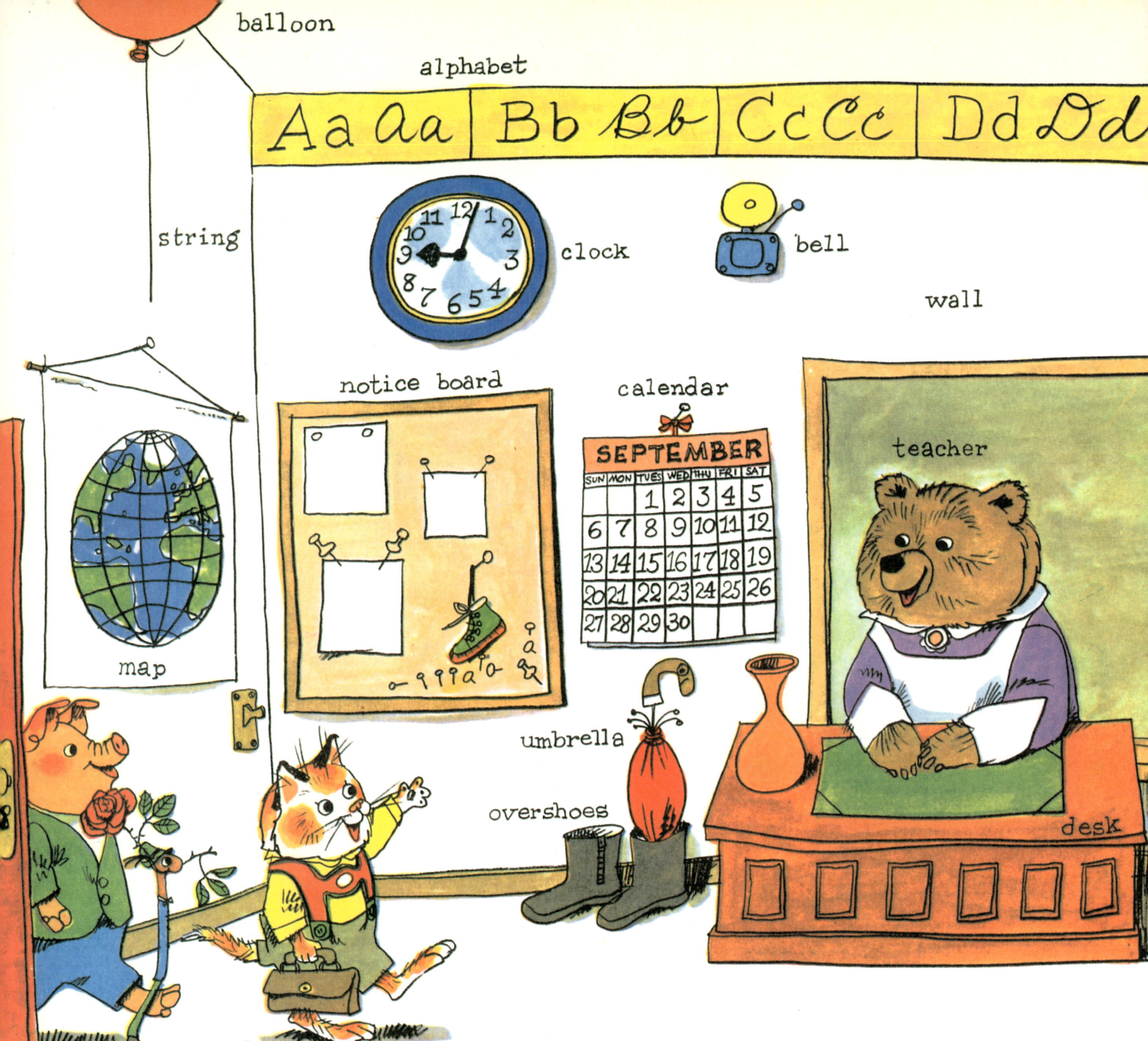

Lovable Miss Honey greets her students in *Great Big Schoolhouse*. Scarry always added words to his pictures of things, so that a young child would learn by reading as well as by looking.

preparatory school, St. Luke's School, in New Canaan, Connecticut. A couple of the boys who were over age for their class placement were unpleasant bullies. They enjoyed making life difficult for other, younger students, including Huck.

For Christmas of 1968, the Scarrys decided to go on a skiing expedition to Zermatt in the southwestern section of the country. Dick took his paints and drawing

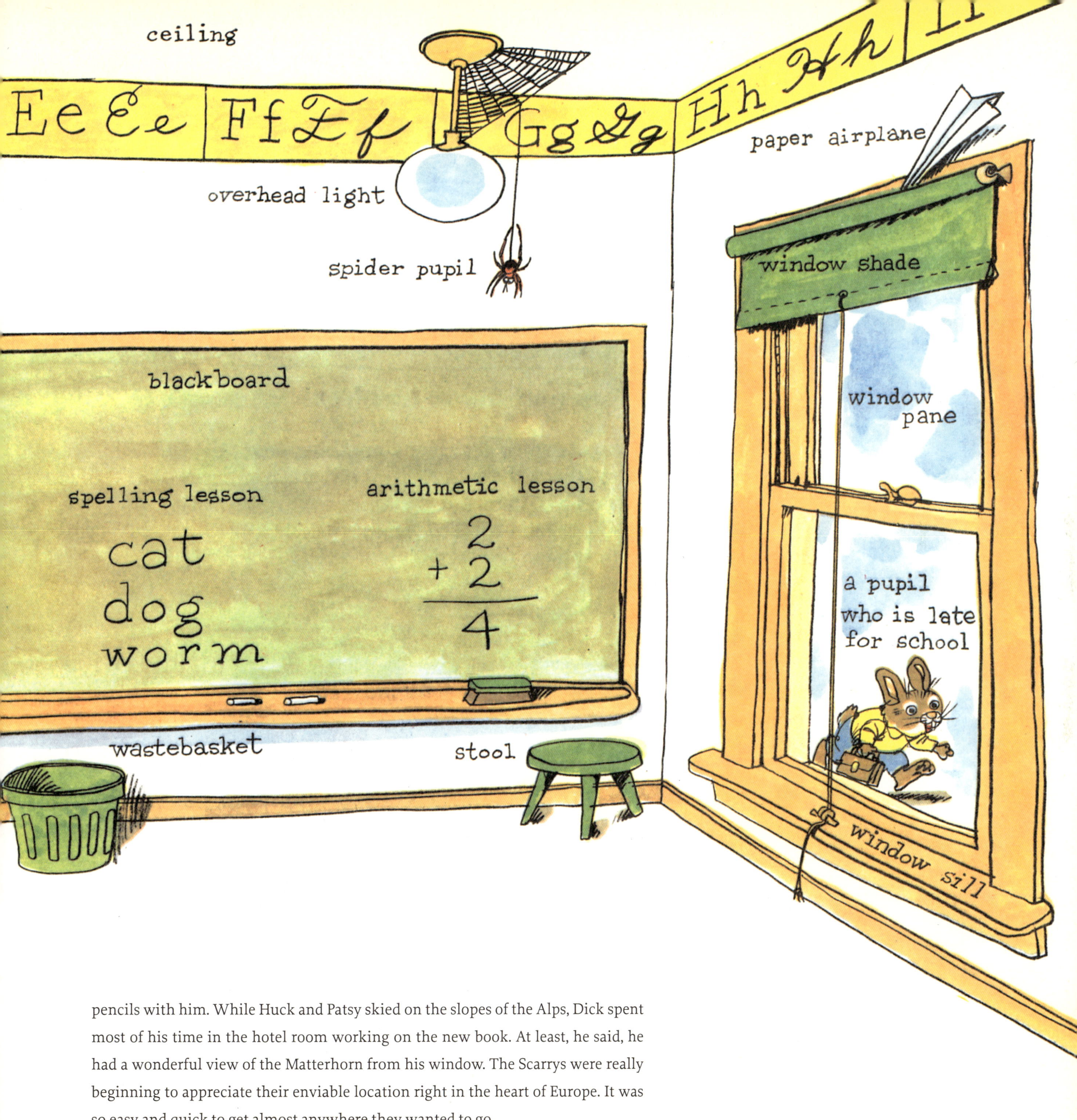

pencils with him. While Huck and Patsy skied on the slopes of the Alps, Dick spent most of his time in the hotel room working on the new book. At least, he said, he had a wonderful view of the Matterhorn from his window. The Scarrys were really beginning to appreciate their enviable location right in the heart of Europe. It was so easy and quick to get almost anywhere they wanted to go.

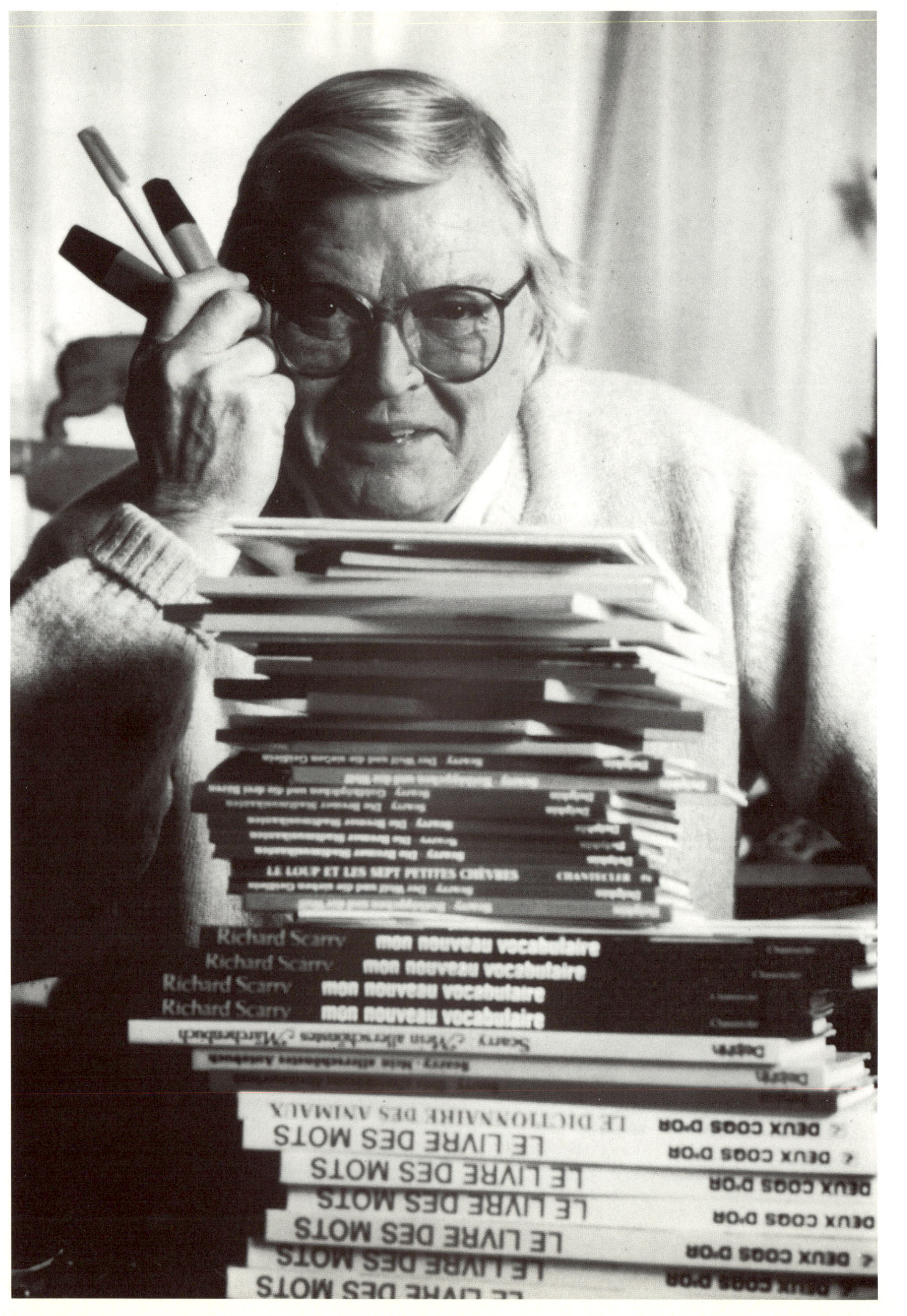
LE LOUP ET LES SEPT PETITES CHÈVRES
CHANTECLER
Richard Scarry
mon nouveau vocabulaire
Richard Scarry
mon nouveau vocabulaire
Richard Scarry
mon nouveau vocabulaire
Richard Scarry
mon nouveau vocabulaire
LE DICTIONNAIRE DES ANIMAUX
DEUX COQS D'OR
LE LIVRE DES MOTS
DEUX COQS D'OR
LE LIVRE DES MOTS
DEUX COQS D'OR
LE LIVRE DES MOTS
DEUX COQS D'OR
LE LIVRE DES MOTS
DEUX COQS D'OR
LE LIVRE DES MOTS
DEUX COQS D'OR

THE BEST AUTHOR EVER

Gradually Dick and Patsy began to accumulate an interesting group of friends in Lausanne. Many were English or Irish, working in Switzerland at diplomatic or public relations jobs. Others worked for the Swiss branch of an overseas firm, and a few were journalists. Naturally Patsy couldn't resist giving a party now and then. She discovered that she could get waiters from the famous hotel school in Lausanne to help with the serving and the preparation of food. She and Dick were supposed to rate them for the school; she said that they always gave the students the highest possible rating, so the young people were always eager to help out whenever they could.

Dick began to be a familiar figure in Ouchy, the port area where they lived. Though he usually dressed rather formally when he went to work at the studio, in the summer he would walk along the lakeshore in a pair of khaki shorts, a short-sleeved button-down shirt, and white Top-Sider sneakers. The Swiss weren't used to this kind of informality, and at first they were a little shocked, but they soon grew accustomed to his casual dress. The small gift and souvenir shops in the lakeshore area even began to put Richard Scarry books in their display windows; the regular bookstores in the center of the city all stocked many Scarry titles, often in several different languages.

One of Dick's favorite restaurants in Lausanne was at the Hotel d'Angleterre next to the lake, just around the corner from the apartment. On warm, sunny days practically all the customers ate on the outdoor terrace overlooking the sparkling blue water. Dick's order never varied. He always asked for a *tournedos saignant* (very rare fillet steak), *pommes frites*, and a bottle of Dole (a local red wine). This was where Dick often took guests for lunch, or ate with Patsy and Huck on weekends, when he wasn't working.

When Dick liked something, he tended to go overboard. Just as he always ordered a *tournedos saignant* at every restaurant he visited in Switzerland or France, he also bought his favorite clothes in large quantities. It wasn't at all unusual for him to have at least twenty pairs of chino shorts, specially made for him at Brooks Brothers, hanging in his closet alongside a dozen pairs of dark gray flannel pants made in Switzerland by the same tailor who clothed Georges Simenon, the famous French novelist, who also lived in Lausanne. Scarry also had at least twenty-five

Opposite: Scarry poses behind a stack of French editions of his books.

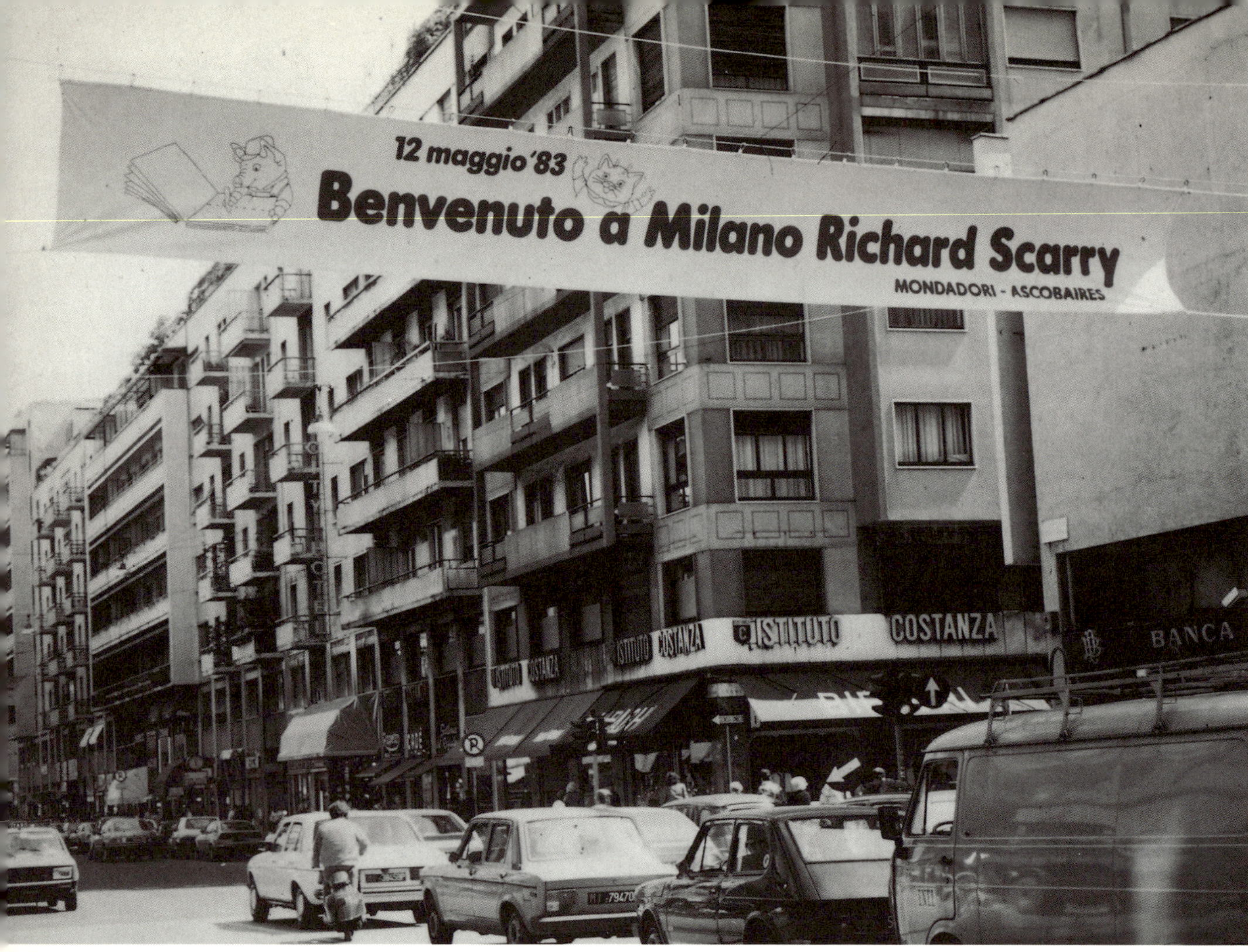

Scarry's books were so popular in Italy that his Italian publisher, Mondadori, declared May 12, 1983, "Richard Scarry Day" and hung banners over certain streets in Milan, the publisher's headquarters location, to welcome Dick to the city.

The mouse-drawn banner at the top of the opposite page reveals that Lowly Worm was translated as Zigo-Zago in Italy.

Pages 92–93
A display of some of the many foreign language editions of Scarry's popular books

pairs of white sneakers (Top-Siders) stored in his closet, and stacks of plain blue or pink oxford-cloth, button-down Brooks Brothers shirts in a chest drawer. He hoarded clothes in this way because he had found that the ones he liked were always going out of stock just when he needed a new supply. He was never a wasteful shopper, throwing his money around. Quite the opposite.

Now that Scarry was located in Switzerland, he was more readily available for consultation with his foreign publishers. Western's international sales unit had done a good job of licensing Scarry books for foreign language editions in Europe. They were helped in their effort by the fact that Dick's books avoided most of the ethnic traits that make licensing American books difficult in other cultures. His animal characters, buildings, vehicles, and settings had a charm that appealed to young readers in any country.

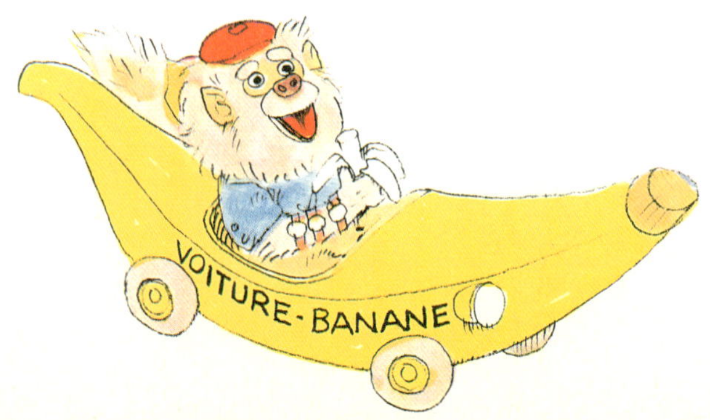

i passatempi di Zigo-Zago

Unlike so many previously published word books, *Richard Scarry's Best Word Book Ever* arranged the words by subject matter instead of by the alphabet. This made the book easily translatable into any foreign language because it didn't matter if the foreign equivalent of the English word started with a different letter. In England, Western had licensed most of its Scarry books to Paul Hamlyn. In France, they finally settled on Deux Coqs d'Or. The German language editions were distributed by Delphin Verlag, located in Zurich, Switzerland. The printing for most of these editions was done by Mondadori in Italy, which also published the Scarry books in Italian.

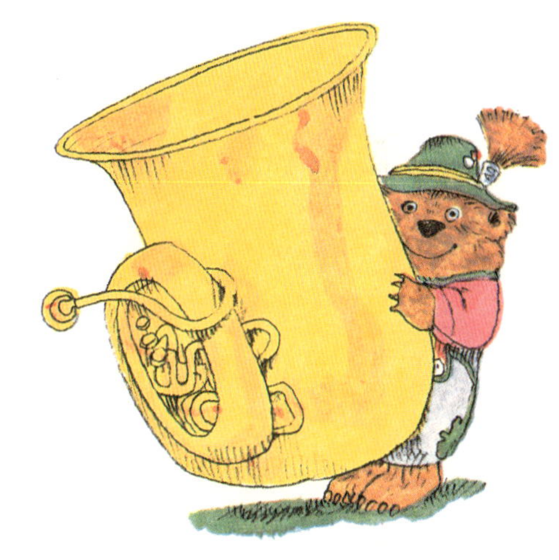

Western's contracts with Scarry gave the publisher all licensing rights for foreign editions. They could make any deal they wished without Dick's approval. Worse yet, Scarry received only 25 percent of the income from foreign editions. This went counter to the usual publisher/author split of 50/50 where no agent was involved.

The Random House contracts, in contrast, gave all translation rights to the author, although the publisher got one-third of the income received. Random House retained control only of the British or English-speaking rights (again receiving just

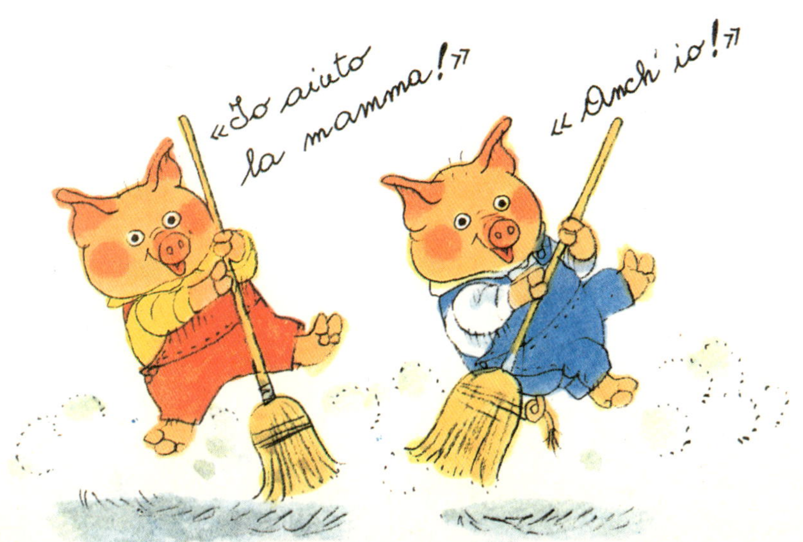

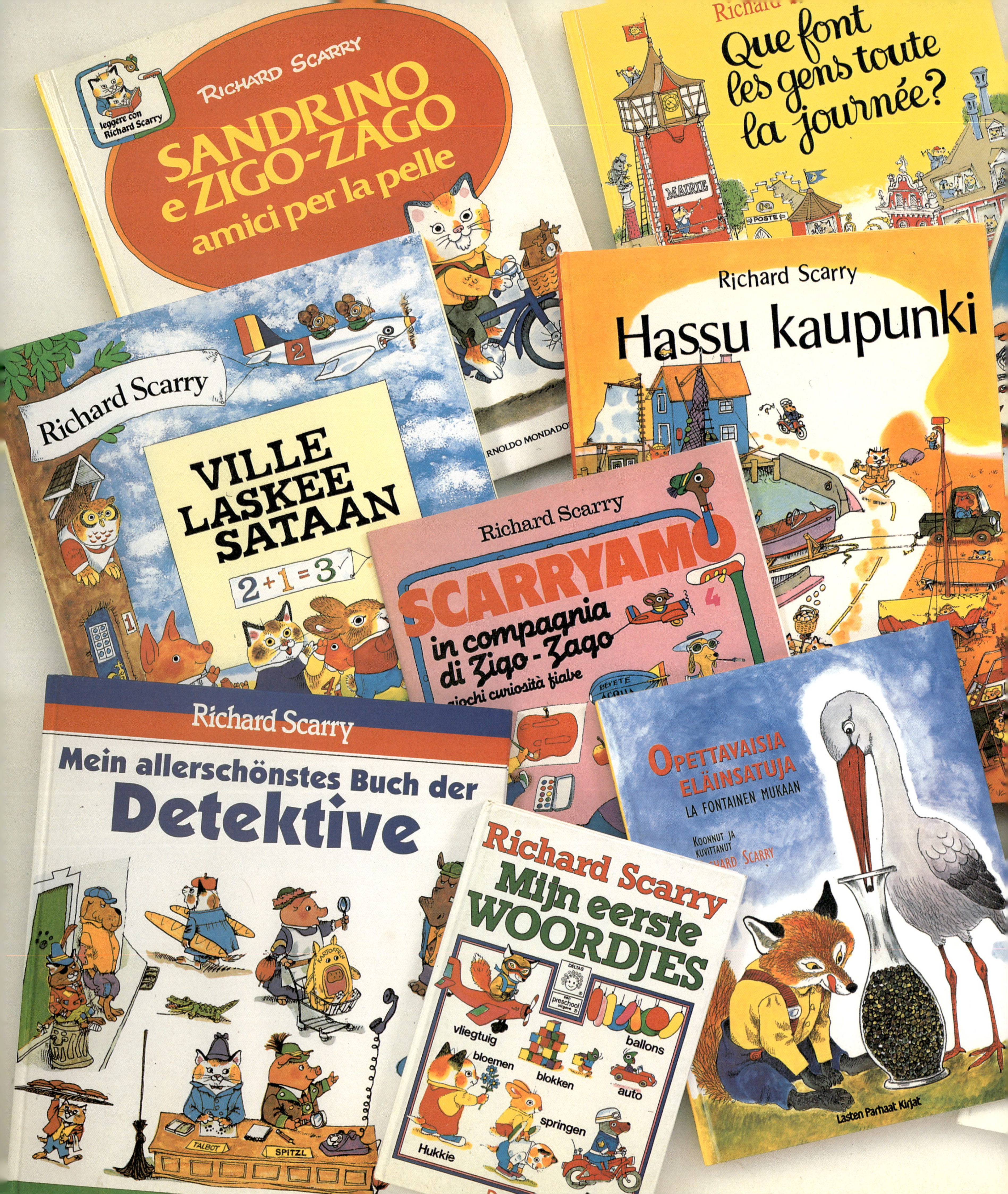

Richard Scarry
SANDRINO e ZIGO-ZAGO amici per la pelle
leggere con Richard Scarry
Que font les gens toute la journée?
MAIRIE
POSTE
Richard Scarry
Hassu kaupunki
Richard Scarry
VILLE LASKEE SATAAN
2+1=3
Richard Scarry
SCARRYAMO
in compagnia di Zigo-Zago
giochi curiosità fiabe
Richard Scarry
Mein allerschönstes Buch der
Detektive
TALBOT
SPITZL
OPETTAVAISIA ELÄINSATUJA
LA FONTAINEN MUKAAN
KOONNUT JA KUVITTANUT
Lasten Parhaat Kirjat
Richard Scarry
Mijn eerste WOORDJES
vliegtuig
bloemen
blokken
ballons
auto
springen
Hukkie

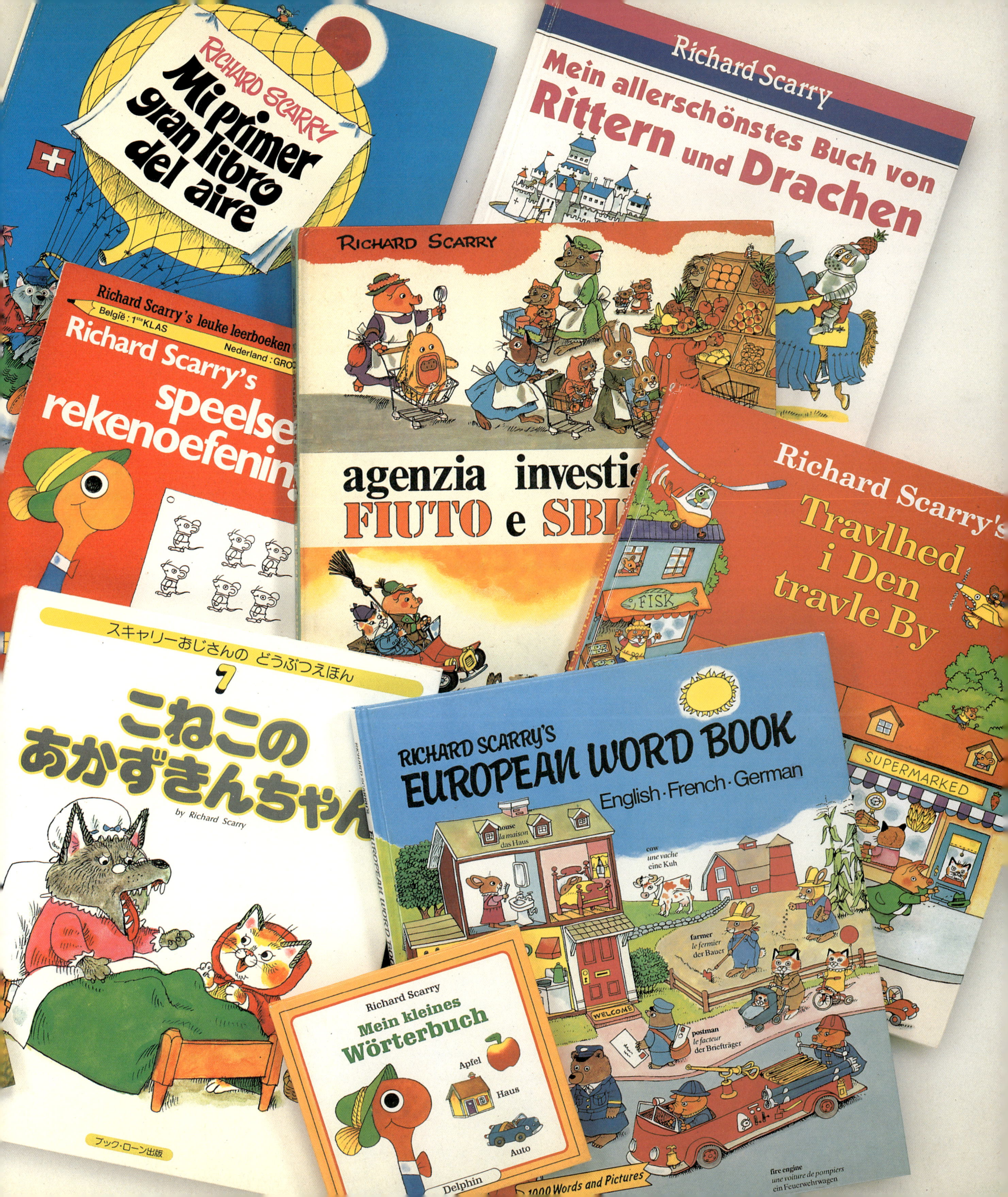
RICHARD SCARRY
Mi primer gran libro del aire
Richard Scarry
Mein allerschönstes Buch von Rittern und Drachen
RICHARD SCARRY
agenzia investi
FIUTO e SB
Richard Scarry's leuke leerboeken
België: 1ste KLAS
Nederland: GRO
Richard Scarry's
speelse rekenoefenin
Richard Scarry's
Travlhed i Den travle By
FISK
SUPERMARKED
スキャリーおじさんの どうぶつえほん
7
こねこのあかずきんちゃん
by Richard Scarry
ブック・ローン出版
RICHARD SCARRY'S
EUROPEAN WORD BOOK
English · French · German
house
la maison
das Haus
cow
une vache
eine Kuh
farmer
le fermier
der Bauer
WELCOME
postman
le facteur
der Briefträger
fire engine
une voiture de pompiers
ein Feuerwehrwagen
1000 Words and Pictures
Richard Scarry
Mein kleines Wörterbuch
Apfel
Haus
Auto
Delphin

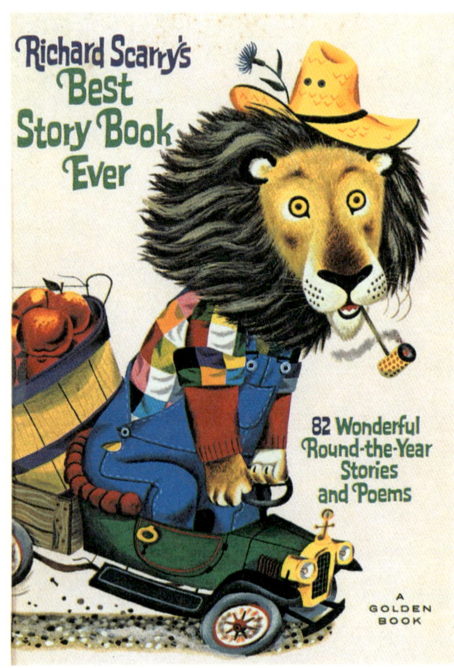

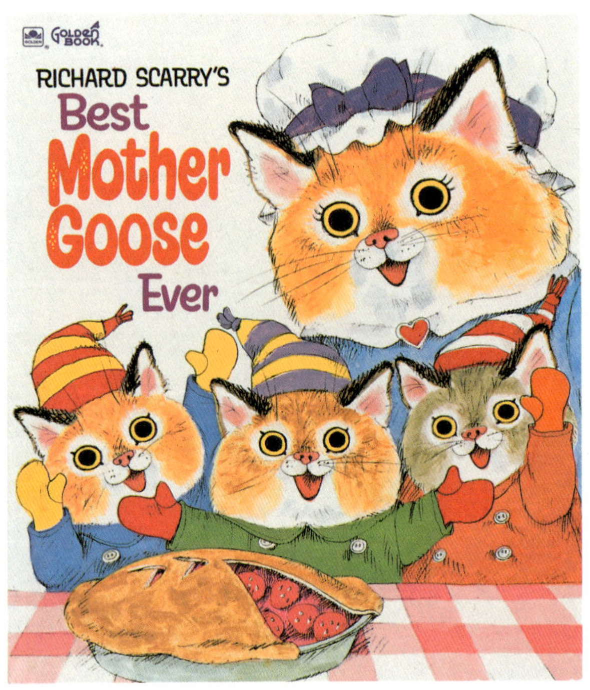

Overleaf: This illustration from *Richard Scarry's Great Big Air Book* is a good example of the Scarry genius for making a complicated subject simple, accurate, and fun.

one-third of the income). Deals for foreign language editions were negotiated by Scarry's agent, Sidney Kramer. Random House licensed the British rights to William Collins & Sons. Collins had already proved remarkably successful selling Dr. Seuss books in the United Kingdom, especially in Australia, where sales were even greater than in Great Britain. For obvious reasons, the British publisher was extremely eager to add Richard Scarry to its list.

Back in the States, Western Publishing was beginning to understand what a blunder it had made in letting Dick go. Without any new Scarry books to promote, they realized that it would soon be difficult to persuade bookstores to keep reordering the old titles. Sales of already published books were bound to fall off. But what could they do to prevent this? One solution was to repackage old material in new formats. In a process more fully described in Part Two of this book, they resized and reformatted previously published material to look like new.

Where possible, they sought permission from Random House for Dick to design and prepare new artwork for the covers of these conversions. Although Random House realized that this repackaging of old material would confuse the book-buying public and compete with Random's new product, they were sympathetic to Dick's desire to keep the old titles selling so that he would continue to receive royalties from Western. Thus they granted permission for him to do a very limited amount of such work. In 1968 Golden Press published *Richard Scarry's Best Storybook Ever,* and in 1970 they brought out *Richard Scarry's Best Mother Goose Ever.* Both books contained old material put together in a new format with a new title.

In an effort to repair the relationship between Scarry and Western, John Worrell, vice president of publishing at Western, and Ray Butman, the director of rights and royalties, arranged to meet with Dick in the fall of 1969 at the Frankfurt International Book Fair. In the words of Ray Butman, the meeting was "tense, but it was the beginning of an effort to heal the breach between Western and Scarry." Sidney Kramer, Scarry's lawyer and agent, began to work with Butman to resolve the problem issues. "Scarry," according to Butman, "felt abused by Western, and Western was embarrassed in the book trade to admit that it had lost an author/artist as valuable as Scarry."

In the fall of 1969, Random House published *Richard Scarry's Great Big Schoolhouse.* It proved to be another very popular book, in both the United States and the foreign market. For his next big picture book, Dick proposed a book about the

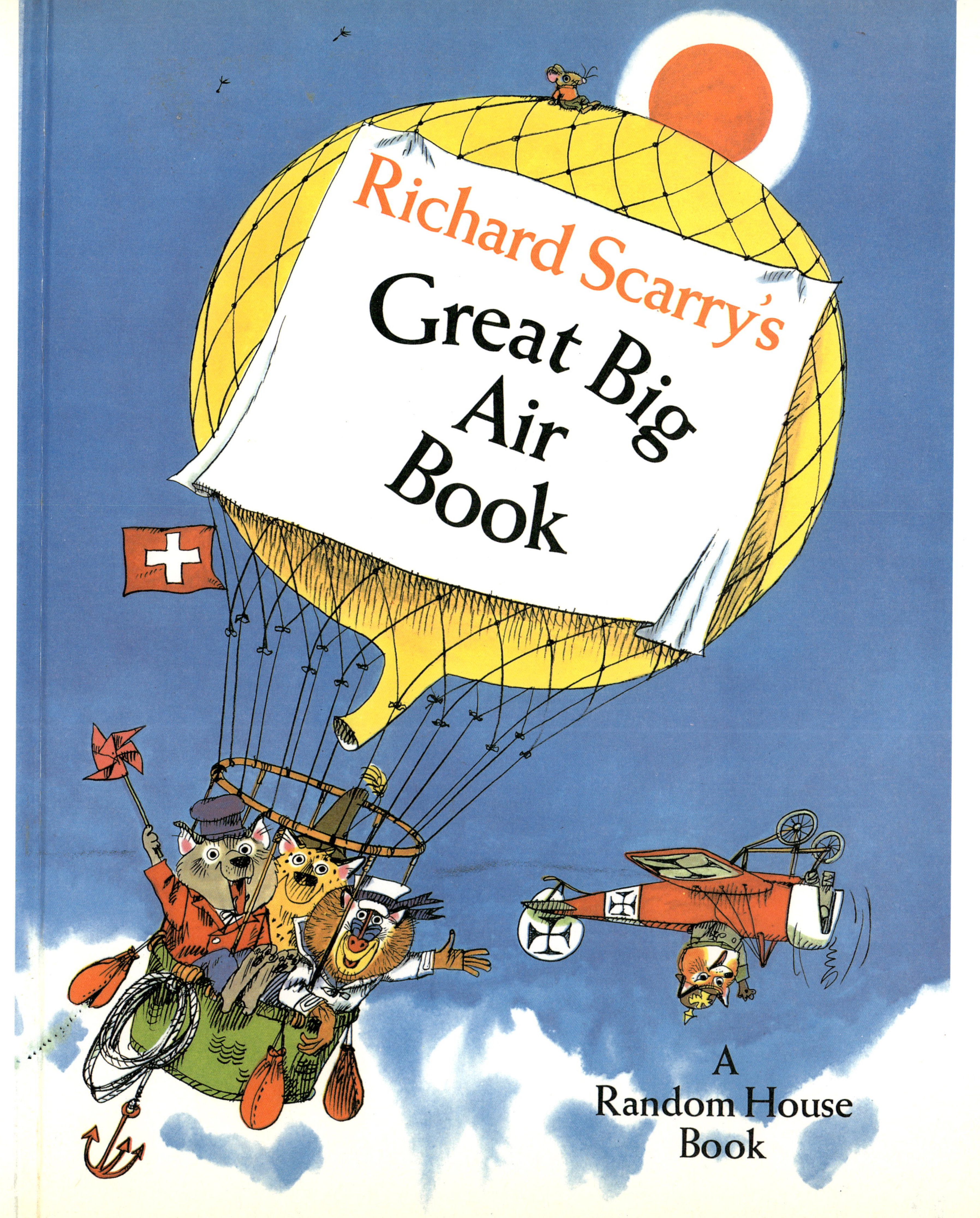
Richard Scarry's
Great Big
Air
Book
A
Random House
Book

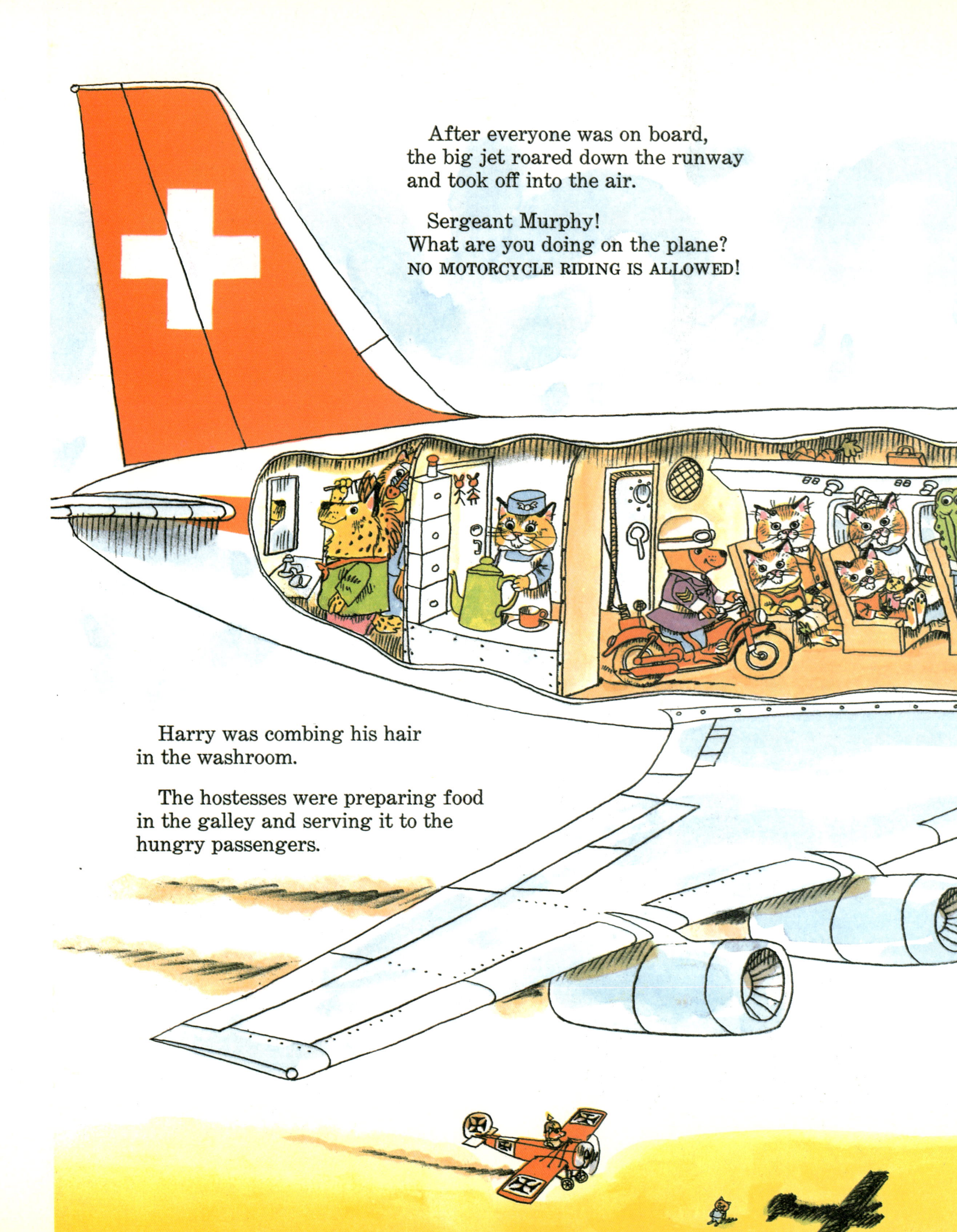

After everyone was on board, the big jet roared down the runway and took off into the air.

Sergeant Murphy! What are you doing on the plane? NO MOTORCYCLE RIDING IS ALLOWED!

Harry was combing his hair in the washroom.

The hostesses were preparing food in the galley and serving it to the hungry passengers.

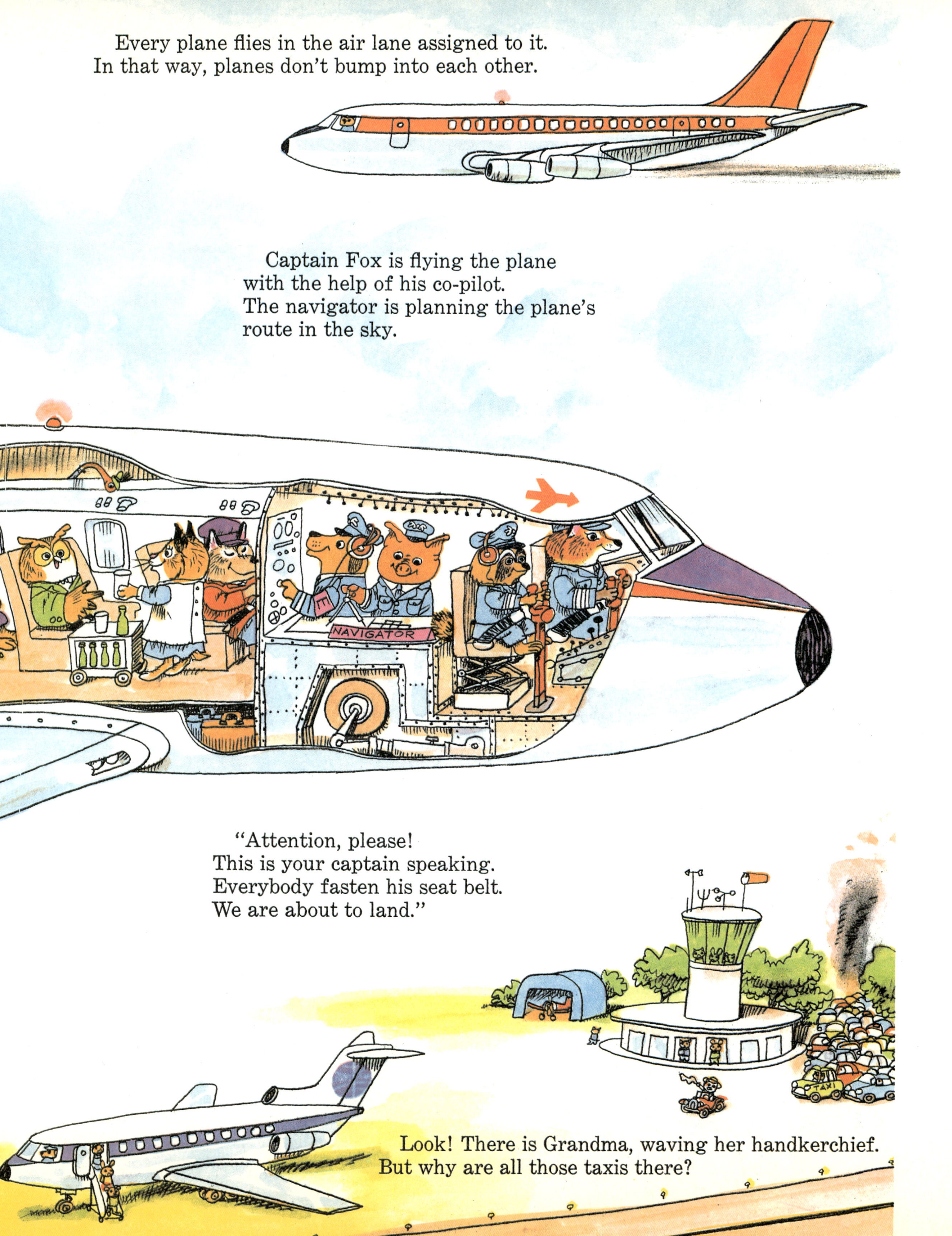

Every plane flies in the air lane assigned to it. In that way, planes don't bump into each other.

Captain Fox is flying the plane with the help of his co-pilot. The navigator is planning the plane's route in the sky.

"Attention, please! This is your captain speaking. Everybody fasten his seat belt. We are about to land."

Look! There is Grandma, waving her handkerchief. But why are all those taxis there?

importance of air. He planned to focus on the part that air plays in weather, flight, sailing, cooking, pollution, and so on. The subject sounded a bit formidable, and Scarry mentioned in one of his letters that he had done an enormous amount of research. The sales department at Random House was worried about the appeal of such a book for children, so in the spring of 1970 Walter Retan stopped in Lausanne on his way to the annual International Children's Book Fair in Bologna, Italy. Dick showed him the early sketches and rough text for his *Great Big Air Book.* As usual, he had done a masterful job of simplifying a complex subject so that children would have no difficulty understanding the material. He had also included his usual generous amounts of humor, excitement, and appealing characters.

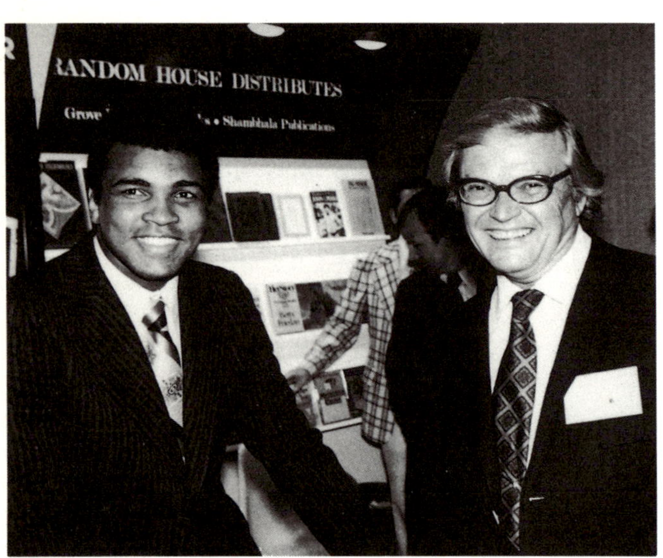

At one meeting of the annual international book fair in Frankfurt, Germany, Scarry met Muhammad Ali, former world heavyweight boxing champion. Both were at the Random House booth to promote new books. When the boxer heard the artist's name, he said, "Hmm, you don't look very scary to me."

Dick and Walter had planned their schedules so they could go together to the Bologna fair, which Dick had never attended before. They caught an early morning express train from Lausanne to Milan, where they had to change to a local train that would take them to Bologna. On the station platform at Milan they spotted Ole Risom of Western Publishing. The day was unbearably hot, and the train was absolutely jam-packed. The three men had to stand in the vestibule of an old passenger car all the way to Bologna, a four-hour journey on the slow-moving local. To add to the torture, the train carried no dining car, and none of them had eaten since an early breakfast. Finally, the train drew in to the Bologna station.

At the book fair the next day Dick met all of his foreign publishers. Some he knew quite well, others were new to him, all were most enthusiastic about his books. It was a truly gratifying experience. The following year, Sidney Kramer began attending the Bologna fair every year, meeting with foreign publishers and arranging for the publication of Dick's Random House books in many foreign countries. In addition to licenses to European publishers, both Western and Random House began, during the next ten years, to sell rights in such unusual countries as Japan, Hungary, Lithuania, Finland, China, and South Africa. Western, of course, still handled the foreign rights for the books Dick had published with them.

When Dick went to Switzerland he had said that the family would probably stay for just one year. Now the first year was up, but it was clear that Dick had no thought of returning to the States for some time. In fact he was talking about possibly selling the house in Westport. The family had settled in quite happily, thoroughly enjoying their new life in Switzerland. They had begun to take advantage of their proximity to all kinds of interesting cities and countries. In the late spring of

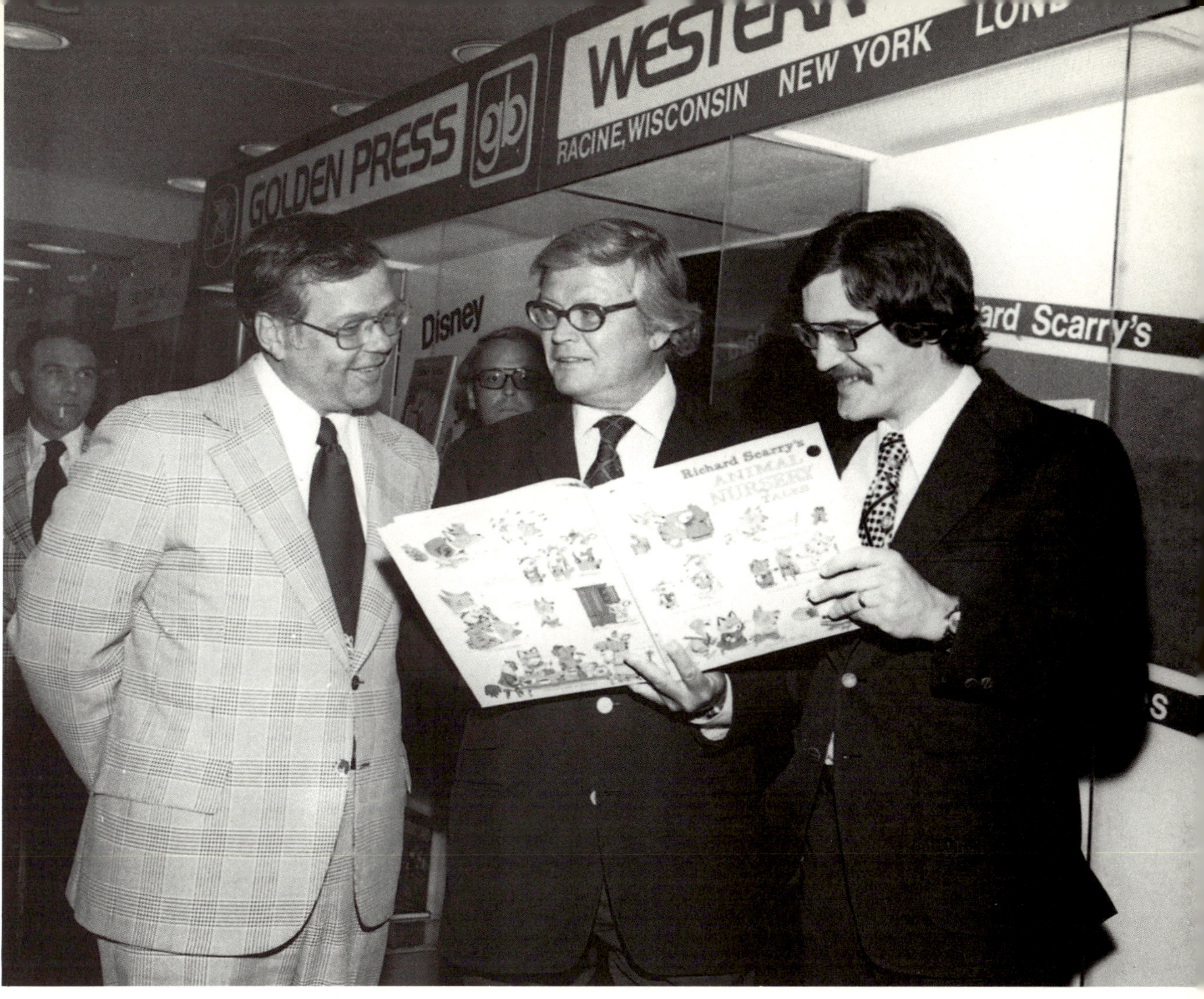

At the Western Publishing Company's booth in Frankfurt, Scarry shows his new Golden Press book, *Animal Nursery Tales*, to Dick Sadlon, sales manager *(left)*, and Josh Gaspero, marketing director *(right)* with Ray Butman, director of rights and permissions in the background *(far left)*.

1969 they decided to spend a few weeks at one of their favorite spots, St. Jean Cap Ferrat. Booking rooms at the Hotel Brise Marine, they packed their bags in the Mercedes and headed for the French Riviera.

This early-summer, three-month visit to St. Jean Cap Ferrat became an annual trek, as Huck Scarry describes:

> *Every summer at the beginning of May or so, my parents would pack up the Mercedes with all their stuff, put their little Sailfish on top of the car, and start their annual exodus to the south of France. During their later years, they never used the car except to go between Gstaad and St. Jean Cap Ferrat and from St. Jean to Gstaad. That was all the car ever did all year long.*
>
> *Because my father lived in Switzerland, he thought his car should have snow tires on it. And he never took the snow tires off, summer or winter, because even if he only took this one trip in the summertime he always wanted to know that if he ever had to go out in the snow, he would have snow tires on.*
>
> *One time, as he was getting ready to leave, I said, "Don't you think you ought to put ordinary tires on your car?" "Oh, no, no, no, no, no," he said. "Well," I warned, "you*

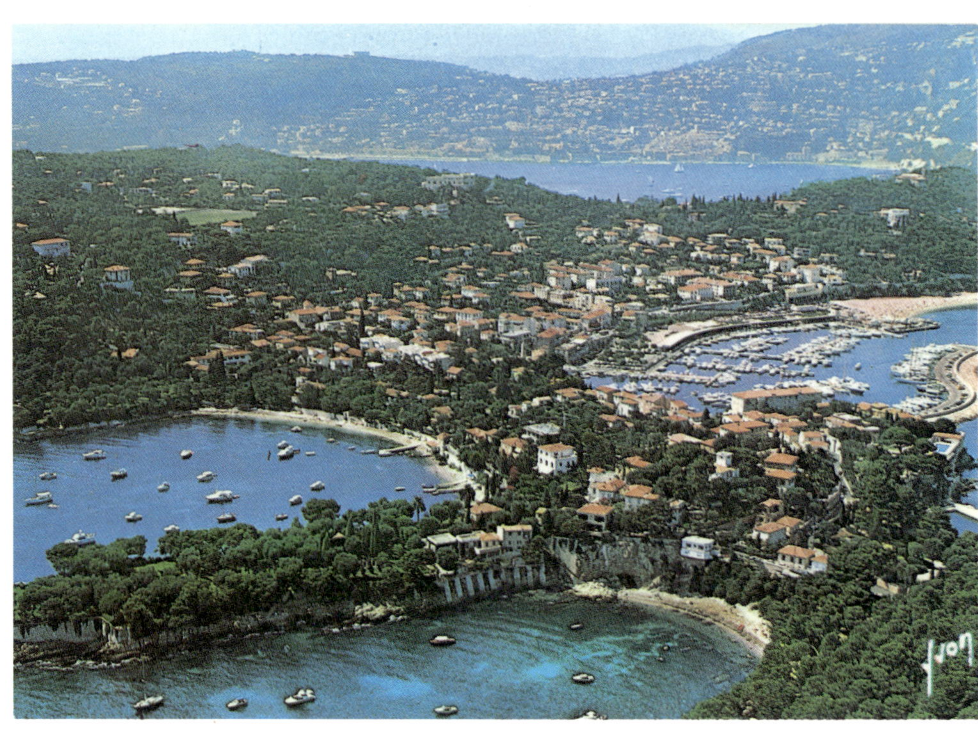

Right: A postcard view of Cap Ferrat from the air. The Scarrys' villa can be seen in the lower right-hand corner.

Below: The small white house cantilevered over the rocky cliff is the villa the Scarrys rented every summer at St. Jean Cap Ferrat on the French Riviera.

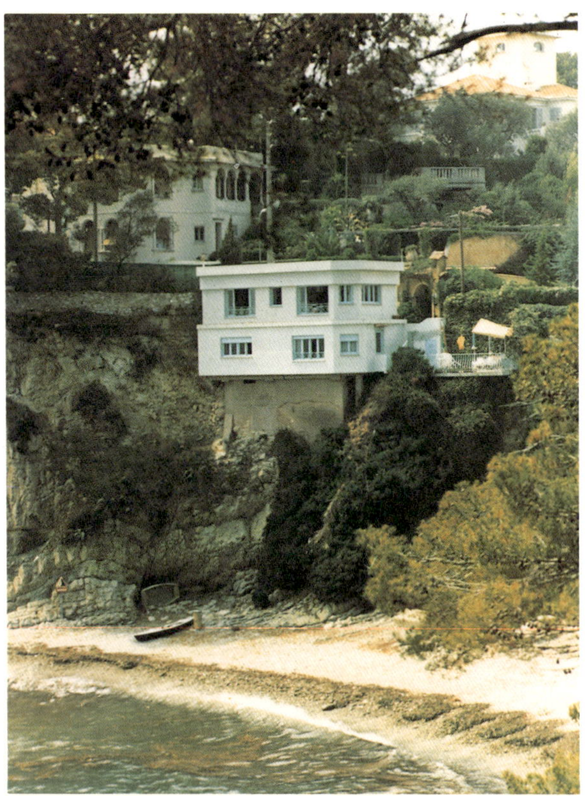

know you shouldn't really drive at high speed in the summertime with snow tires on."

"Why not?" he asked.

"They get hot. They explode!"

"Oh, no, no, no, no, no," he repeated.

Well, anyway, they started off on this trip, driving down as far as Geneva—I was living in Geneva at the time. They thought that would break up the trip. They used to do it in one go, but as they were getting older they thought they would do it gently and enjoy the trip. So they spent the night at the Hotel le Richemond, and we had dinner together.

They took off next morning, arriving at the French border, where they went through French Customs. They had gone a few kilometers farther when they were suddenly stopped by the French customs officers, who told them to get out of the car. The men then started to take everything out of the Mercedes.

On that trip my father was carrying down to the south of France a photocopy machine he had bought in Gstaad. He hadn't declared it. "Aha!" they said, "a smuggler!" So then they started going through all his papers. My father, because he liked to draw pictures instead of making lists of things, had drawn pictures of everything he wanted to take to St. Jean, and one of the pictures he had was of a Scotch tape dispenser. A customs policeman picked up this paper with the Scotch tape dispenser drawing on it and said, "Aha! A gun!"

So right there on the roadside they went through the contents of the entire car. They looked under the seats, they pried open the doors to see if there was anything inside. They even telephoned Paris to find out the value of the photocopying machine. My father was stuck there for three or four hours on the side of the road while they did all this.

By the time the men were finally finished, my parents realized that they weren't going to make it to the south of France that day. They decided to go as far as they could and spend the night in a hotel, continuing on the next day. They drove and they drove down the auto route until my father noticed that gas was getting low. So he pulled off at the next filling station, got out of the car, and waited and waited, but nobody came to fill up his tank. Then he noticed that other people were helping themselves, and he realized that he was in a place where he had never been before in his life—something called a self-service filling station! So he reached for the nearest hose and filled up his car. After paying his bill, he drove off.

Well, my parents were tired—they had a bad day behind them—but they continued on their way until a short while later the Mercedes started to act up. My father pressed down harder and harder on the pedal, but the car just went slower and slower

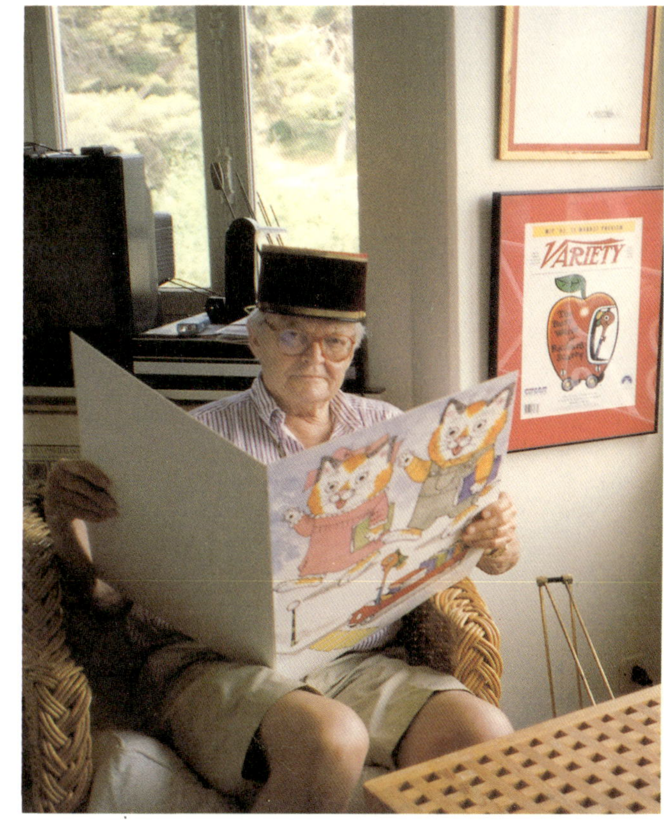

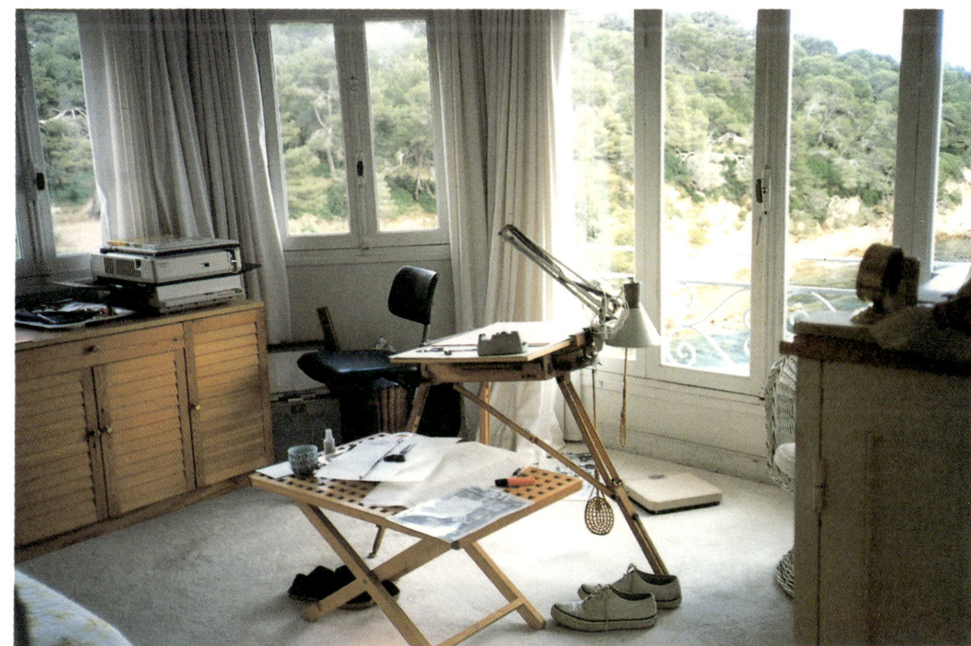

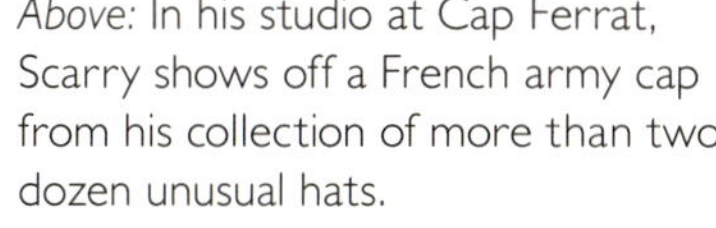

Above: In his studio at Cap Ferrat, Scarry shows off a French army cap from his collection of more than two dozen unusual hats.

Below: When he was working at his drawing board, Dick had a spectacular view of the bay.

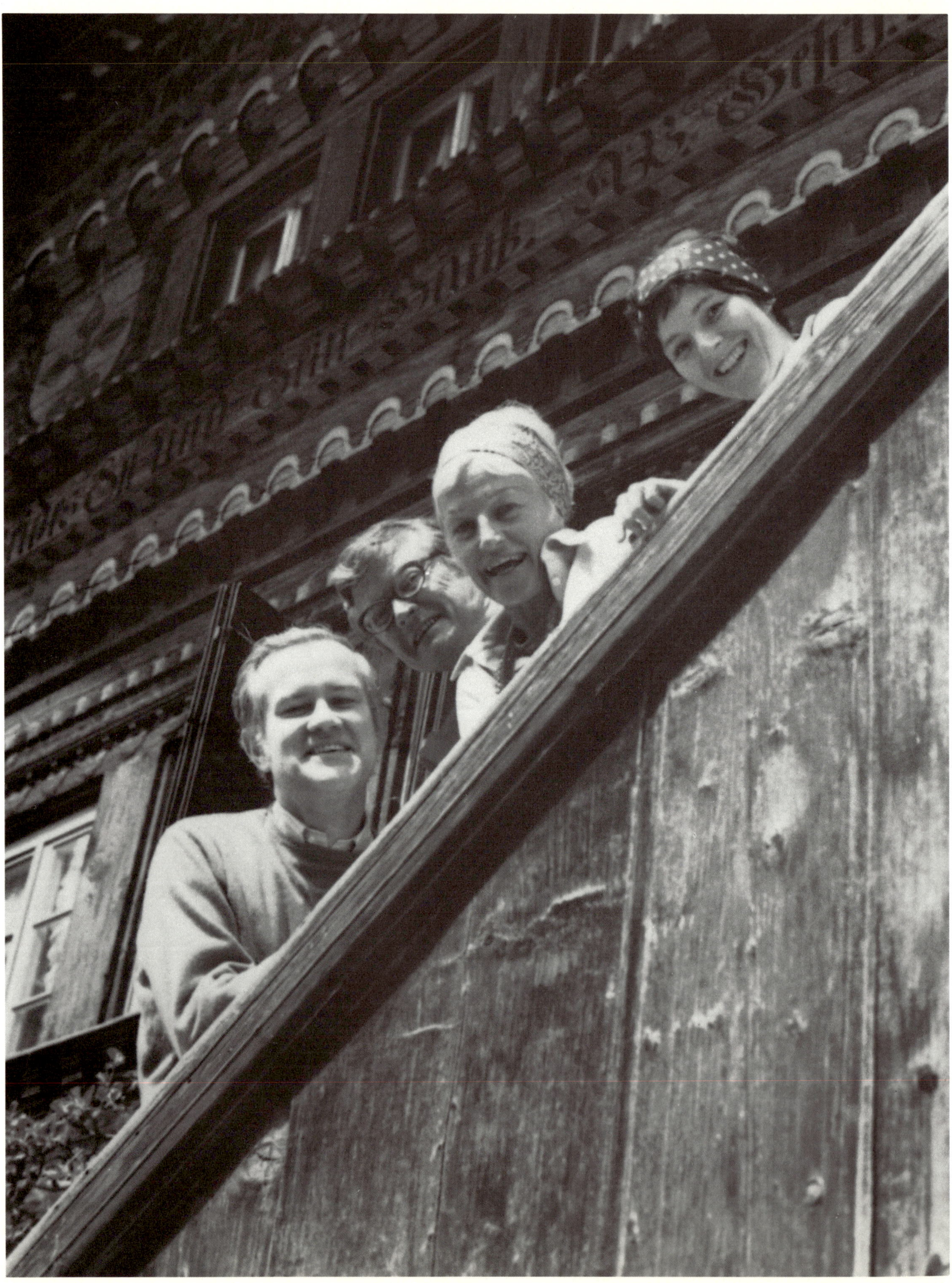

until finally it didn't go at all. He pulled over to the side of the road to investigate, but he just couldn't figure out what was wrong. So he walked and walked until he came to a phone and telephoned for help. Finally a tow truck arrived and towed him off to a small village in Provence, where they stopped at a garage. The mechanic looked here and he looked there, but everything in the car was perfect. He couldn't figure out what could possibly be wrong. My father said, "I don't understand it. All I did was fill it up with gasoline a while ago."

"Aha!" the mechanic said, "and what did you put in it?"

"Oh, I don't know—just some gasoline."

When the mechanic heard that, he checked the tank, and of course it was diesel fuel. He drained the tank, refilled it with proper gasoline, and my parents were able to drive away again. But they couldn't go much farther; it was nighttime by now. They decided to stay at a hotel in Arles. They didn't get much sleep, however, because the townspeople were electing a new Miss Arles that evening. There was a big parade and a tremendous amount of noise.

The next morning was very hot, and they were driving along in the heat when suddenly they heard a tremendous BANG! *The car began to swerve this way and that way while my father grasped the wheel tightly. Finally he was able to bring it to a stop at the side of the road.*

What had happened?... One of the snow tires had exploded, of course. A nice Belgian man who happened to be a Mercedes dealer stopped and helped my father put on the spare tire.

As soon as my parents got to St. Jean, my father took his car to the local garage and what did he order?... A new snow tire!

After staying in hotels the first two years, they found a delightful little villa perched on a cliff just above the sea. The windows gave a wide view over the rocky cliffs and the Mediterranean Sea, which Patsy always called the "Big Blue." Dick rigged up a big wicker basket with a chamois skin lid to use as a mailbox. He also fastened a sign on the door which read, BEWARE OF THE DOG. It was accompanied by a suitably fierce-looking drawing of a dog. The Sailfish was anchored in the bay, so Dick could scramble down the cliff, dive into the water, swim out to his boat, and crawl aboard. When there were guests, Dick preferred to be the skipper, but occasionally he would let an old friend like Ole Risom take the helm. He always laughed heartily

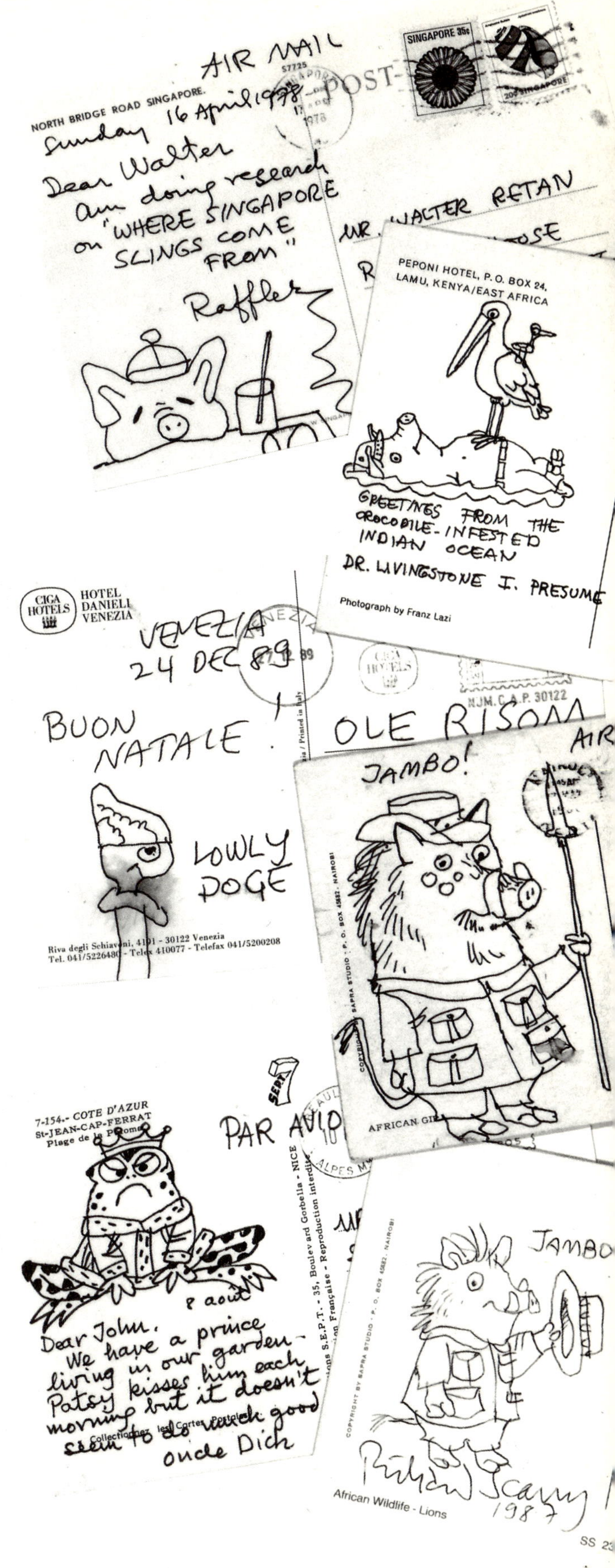

Above: An assortment of the funny drawings and messages on postcards that Dick sent to friends

Opposite: Walter Retan, Dick Scarry, Patsy Scarry, and Elizabeth Retan on the steps of a chalet in Gstaad. The Scarrys were then thinking about buying a chalet in the Swiss village.

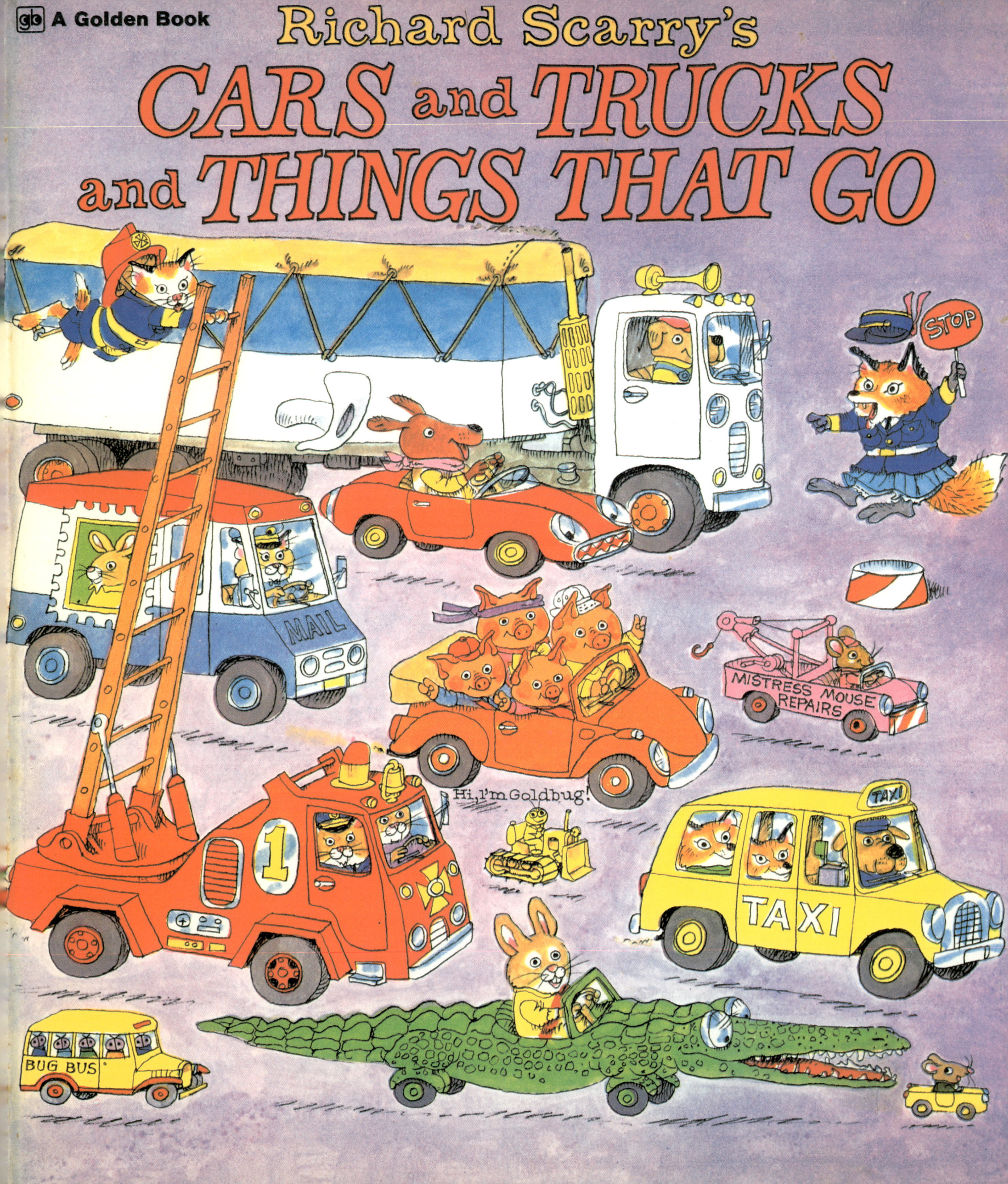
A Golden Book
Richard Scarry's
CARS and TRUCKS and THINGS THAT GO
STOP
MAIL
MISTRESS MOUSE REPAIRS
Hi, I'm Goldbug!
TAXI
TAXI
1
BUG BUS

when he saw someone hacking about, handling his boat badly but trying to look important because he had a bigger, fancier craft. Once he and Ole laughed so hard at one of these amateur sailors that they capsized their own boat; the more they laughed, the more difficult it became to struggle back into the boat.

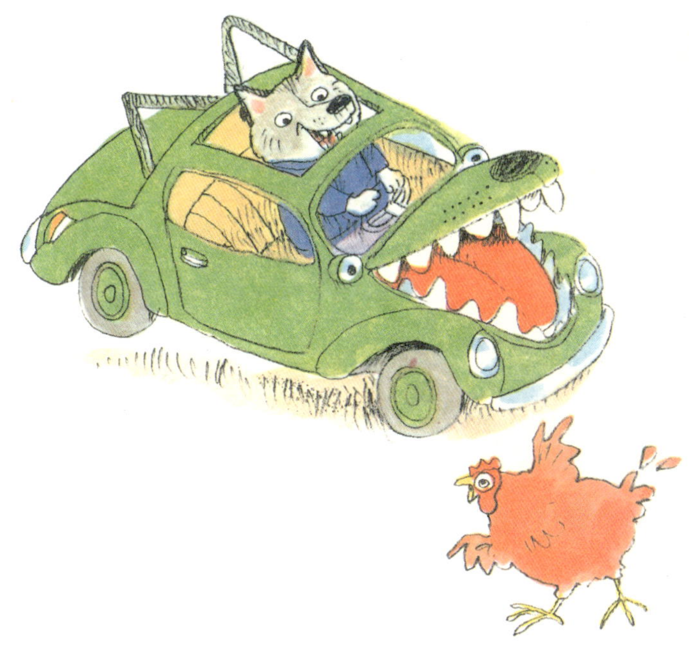

Although Dick loved a lot of rigorous activity while he was on the Riviera, he always found time to work. There never ceased to be deadlines to meet, new books to create; yet he never disappointed his publishers. Wherever he was living he stuck to a rigid work schedule.

Dick and Patsy also made frequent short trips to London, where they liked to stay at the Hotel Connaught and enjoy the shopping they couldn't find in Switzerland. Sometimes Collins, his new British publisher, would invite him to address a sales conference, or Jan Collins and his wife, Lady Sally, would invite the Scarrys to their home as weekend guests. Venice was another favorite city. They often took the sleeping train for a few days at the Lido, and for the hamburgers Dick could have at Harry's Bar, for, as he would say, "only fifty dollars."

Cover and interior illustrations from *Richard Scarry's Cars and Trucks and Things That Go.* In this book, Scarry introduced a tiny goldbug as a character that young readers had to find in each drawing. Goldbug appears on the cover as well as in each double spread, including the one on the following pages.

Once, while in Venice, Ole Risom was sitting with Dick and Patsy at an outdoor café, drinking coffee. Dick doodled on a sketch pad, while Ole read a newspaper and Patsy watched the passing crowd. Suddenly a tremendous racket shattered the morning quiet. Everybody turned to see what could be producing so much noise. Three wild-looking musicians were marching by. One was making ear-splitting squawks by drawing an old bow over the strings of a violin. Another had a drum

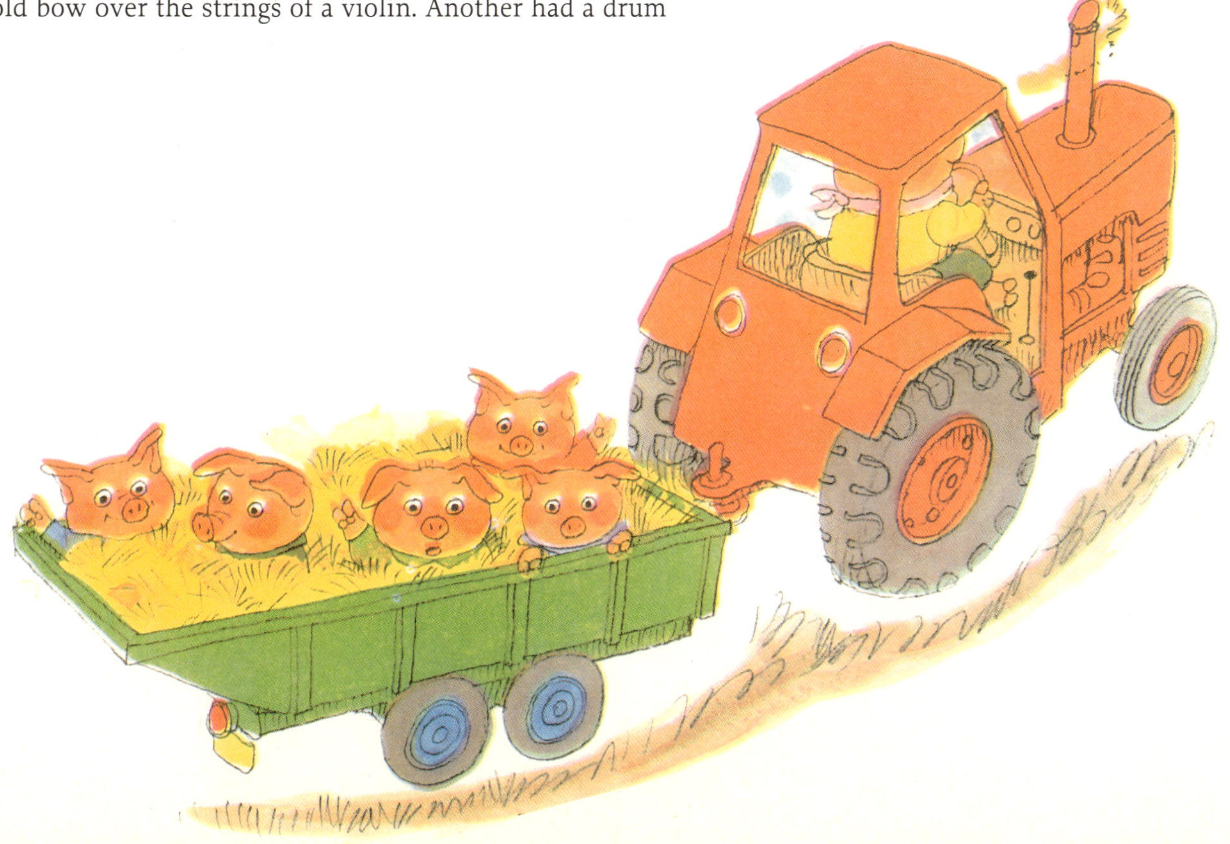

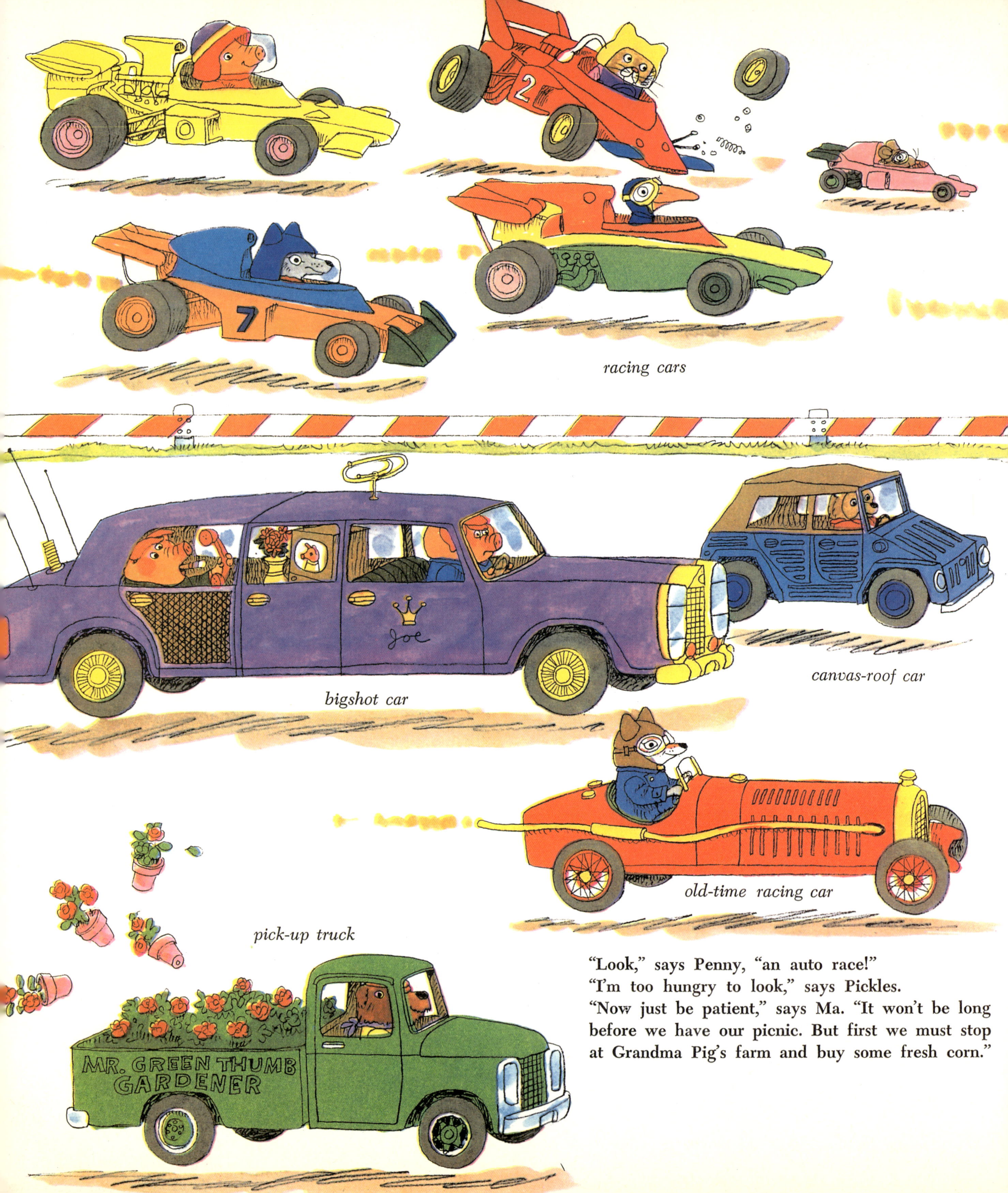

racing cars

bigshot car

canvas-roof car

old-time racing car

pick-up truck

"Look," says Penny, "an auto race!"
"I'm too hungry to look," says Pickles.
"Now just be patient," says Ma. "It won't be long before we have our picnic. But first we must stop at Grandma Pig's farm and buy some fresh corn."

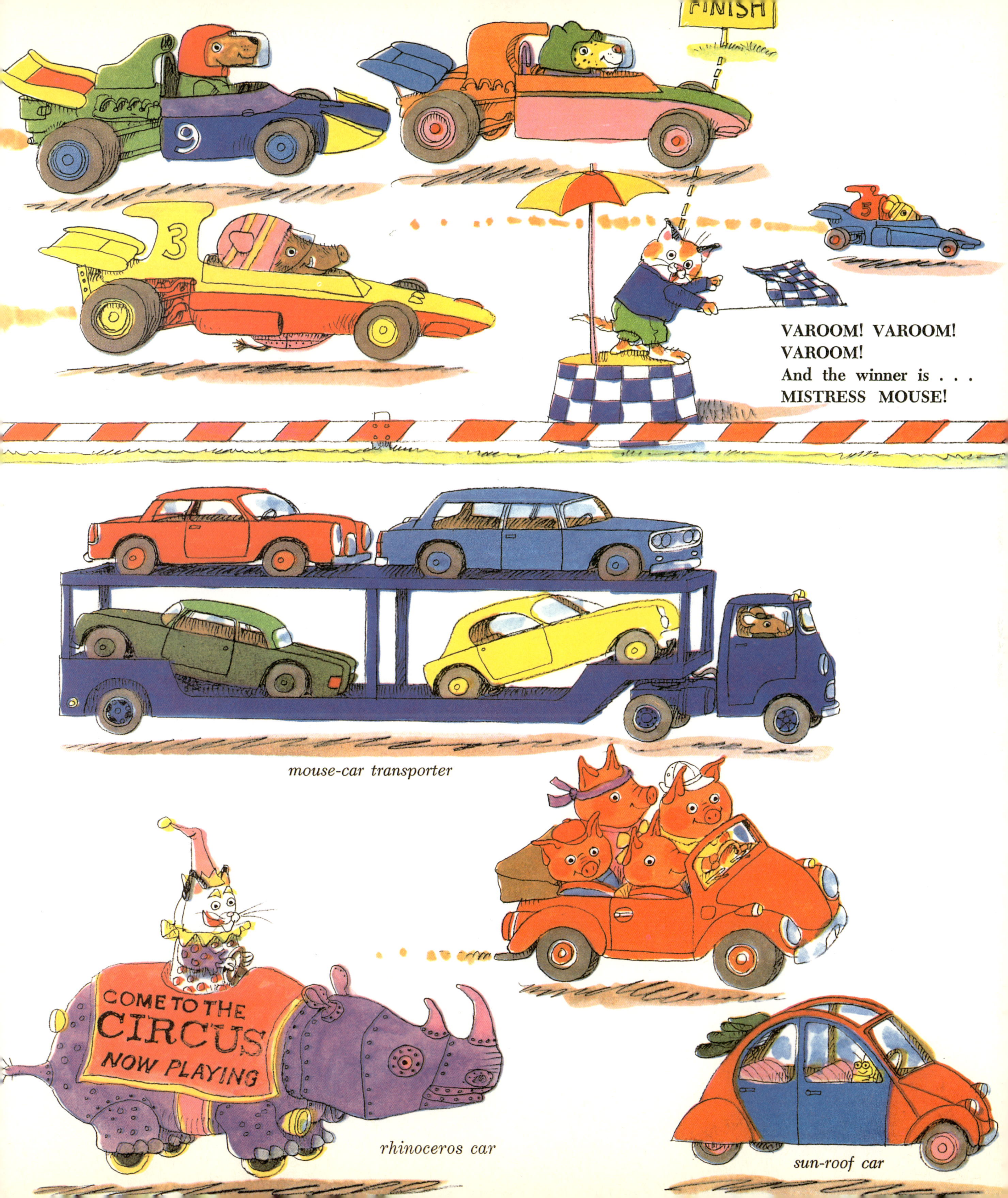

VAROOM! VAROOM! VAROOM!
And the winner is . . . MISTRESS MOUSE!

mouse-car transporter

rhinoceros car

sun-roof car

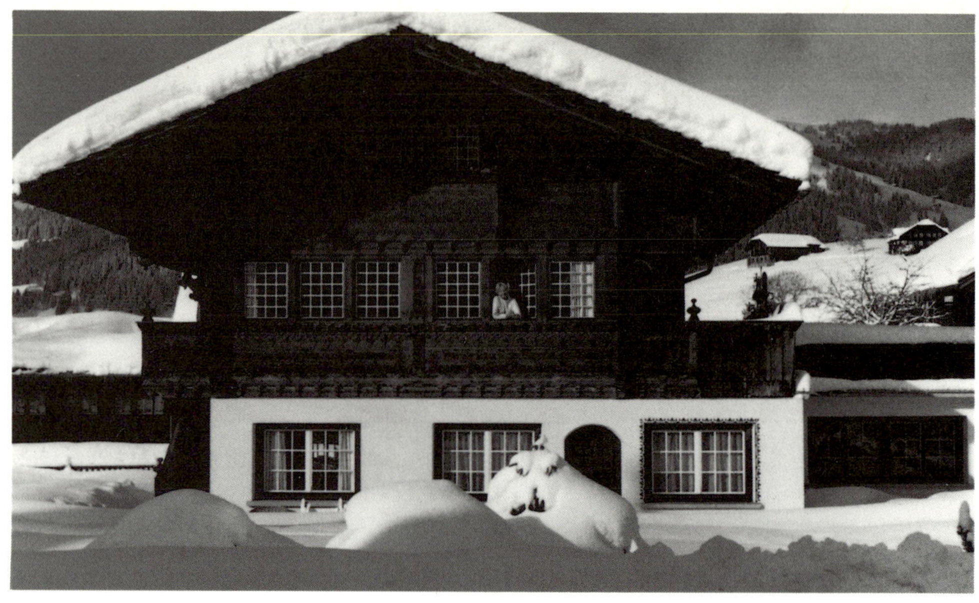

attached to his head, which he regularly reached up to hit with a drumstick. Every so often he punctuated his drumbeats by blowing on a shrill whistle. The third had an instrument none of them could identify, but it made an unearthly sound. Dick was enchanted. Grabbing his sketch pad and pencil, he rushed down the street. As he walked along behind the musicians, he was sketching them on his pad. They later turned up as a trio of rough-looking beggar gorillas in several of his books.

Above: The small chalet that the Scarrys finally purchased in Gstaad. Living quarters were on the upper floor; Dick's studio was below.

Opposite, above: The cover from *Richard Scarry's Animal Nursery Tales* and an illustration *(below)* from "Little Red Riding Hood" that appears inside the book.

Although the Scarrys were living a very pleasant life in Europe, Huck continued to be unhappy at his school. His parents decided to take him out of the school at the end of the year. He was learning very little, though he had already become quite fluent in French. They enrolled him in an art and graphics school (l'Atelier Ecole de Graphisme) in Lausanne. He liked the work and was much happier there.

By this time, Dick and Patsy had made the big decision to sell the house in Westport. Sidney Kramer helped with the business details, and Dick made a brief trip back to the States to attend the closing. Having sold one house, however, the Scarrys were already thinking about buying another, this time in Switzerland. They were

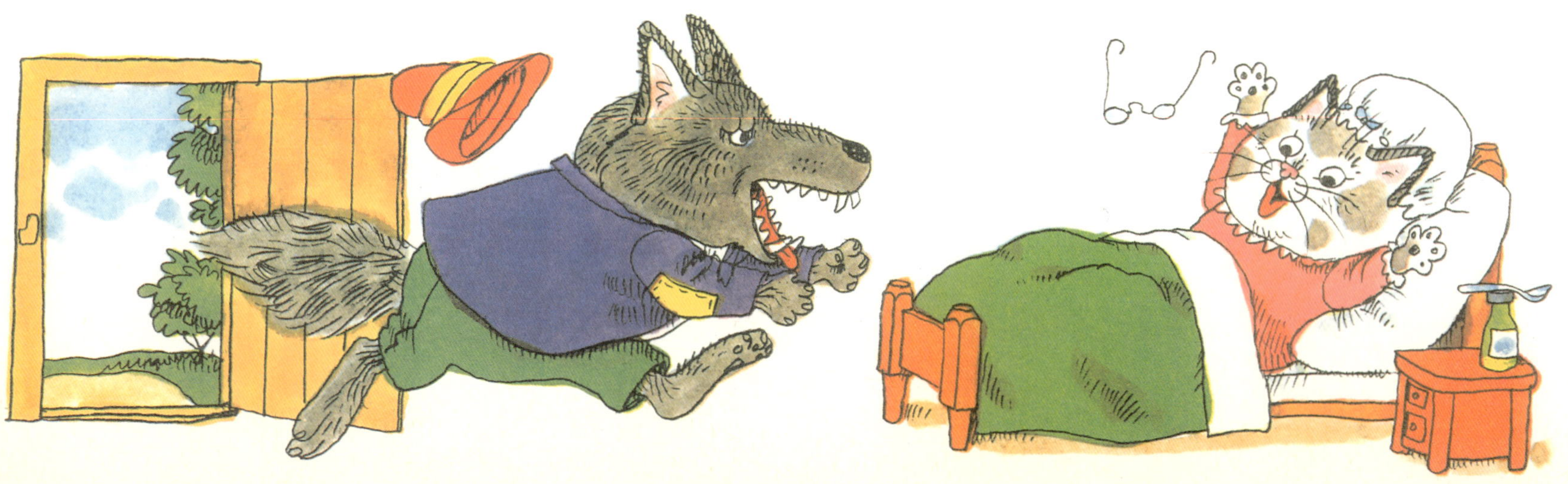

intrigued by the picturesque little village of Gstaad up in the mountains. When Walter Retan and his wife, Elizabeth, visited the Scarrys in the spring of 1971, Dick and Patsy drove them, along with Huck, up to Gstaad to show them a beautiful little chalet, decorated outside with wood carvings that they particularly admired. It was a warm, sunny day in May, and the cows in the fields were all decorated with wreathes of flowers, an old Swiss custom. When they stopped at a local inn for lunch, they could hear some Swiss men yodeling out behind the café.

Dick explained that it was very difficult for a foreigner to buy property in Switzerland, and there were many details to be ironed out before the purchase could be made. A little house in Gstaad would be perfect for skiing expeditions and weekend trips. Dick found much inspiration here in the farming life, the solid, well-proportioned Swiss barns, and an atmosphere of hard work and respectfulness among the local people. He loved to walk in the mountains and made a number of good friends. In the winter Gstaad was filled with skiers and tourists, including many of the so-called beautiful people, such as movie actors David Niven, Roger Moore, and Elizabeth Taylor and Richard Burton.

While visiting Dick in Gstaad, Walter Retan learned that Western Publishing was still wooing him with considerable urgency. In their desperation to get some new books, they offered to rewrite the old contracts to allow for higher royalties. Though the rates were still not equal to those offered by Random House, they were a great improvement. But the real incentive for Dick came from Western's offer to make the new rates retroactive to a certain cutoff date. It would mean an enormously increased amount of income, an increase that Dick certainly deserved. His publishers at Random House were naturally not happy at the prospect of such a deal but realized what it could mean to Dick. Feeling they could not in good conscience stand in his way, they granted formal permission for him to create two new books for Western.

In February of 1971, Dick signed a series of agreements with Western. One provided for his creating the two new books. Another agreed to pay him additional money for his services as a consultant; then there was a separate agreement providing for increased royalty rates. The two new titles that resulted from these agreements were *Cars and Trucks and Things That Go* (1974) and *Animal Nursery Tales* (1975). But Random House remained his principal publisher, and Scarry never created any more large-sized picture books for Western.

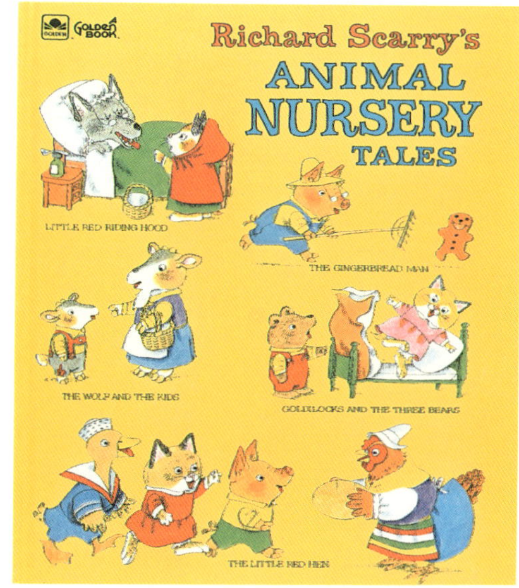

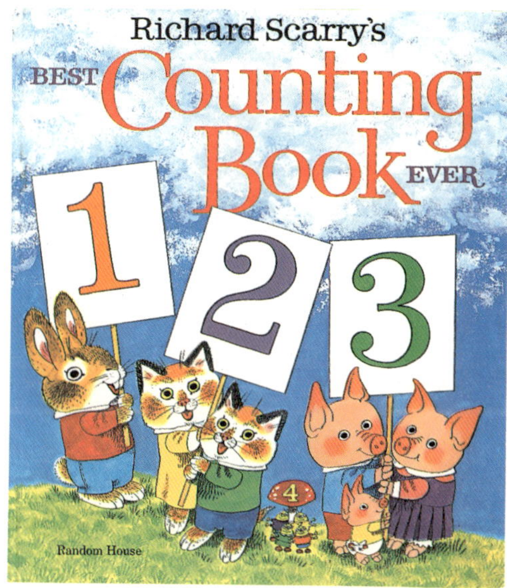

Above: The cover for the counting book that Scarry created for Random House to publish in 1975.

Overleaf: In illustrating the number 100 for his counting book, Dick meticulously drew 100 fireflies to make sure that his readers had fun while learning. Several Random House editors painstakingly counted the fireflies to be sure he had painted the correct number.

100 one hundred

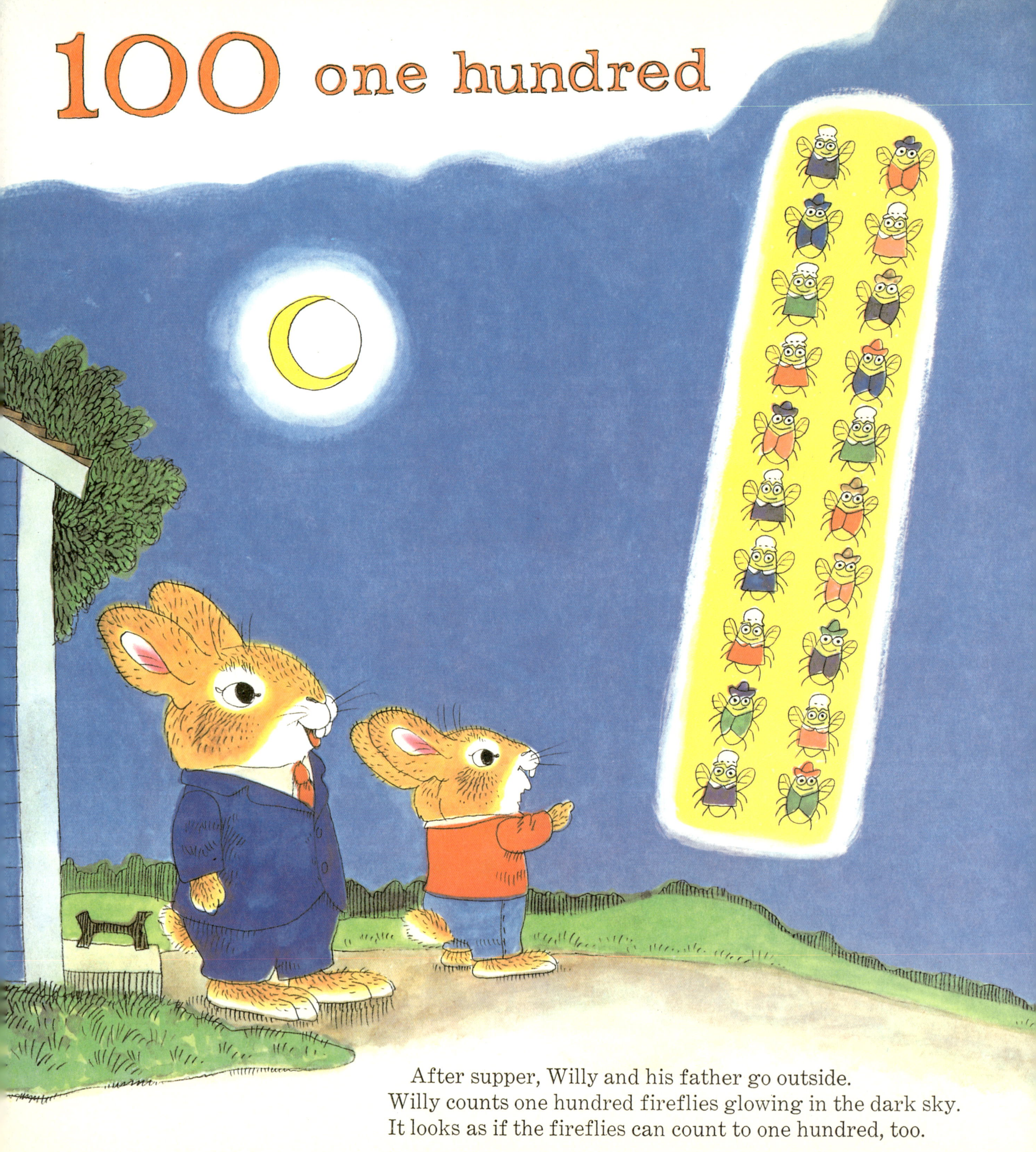

After supper, Willy and his father go outside. Willy counts one hundred fireflies glowing in the dark sky. It looks as if the fireflies can count to one hundred, too.

And so can you!

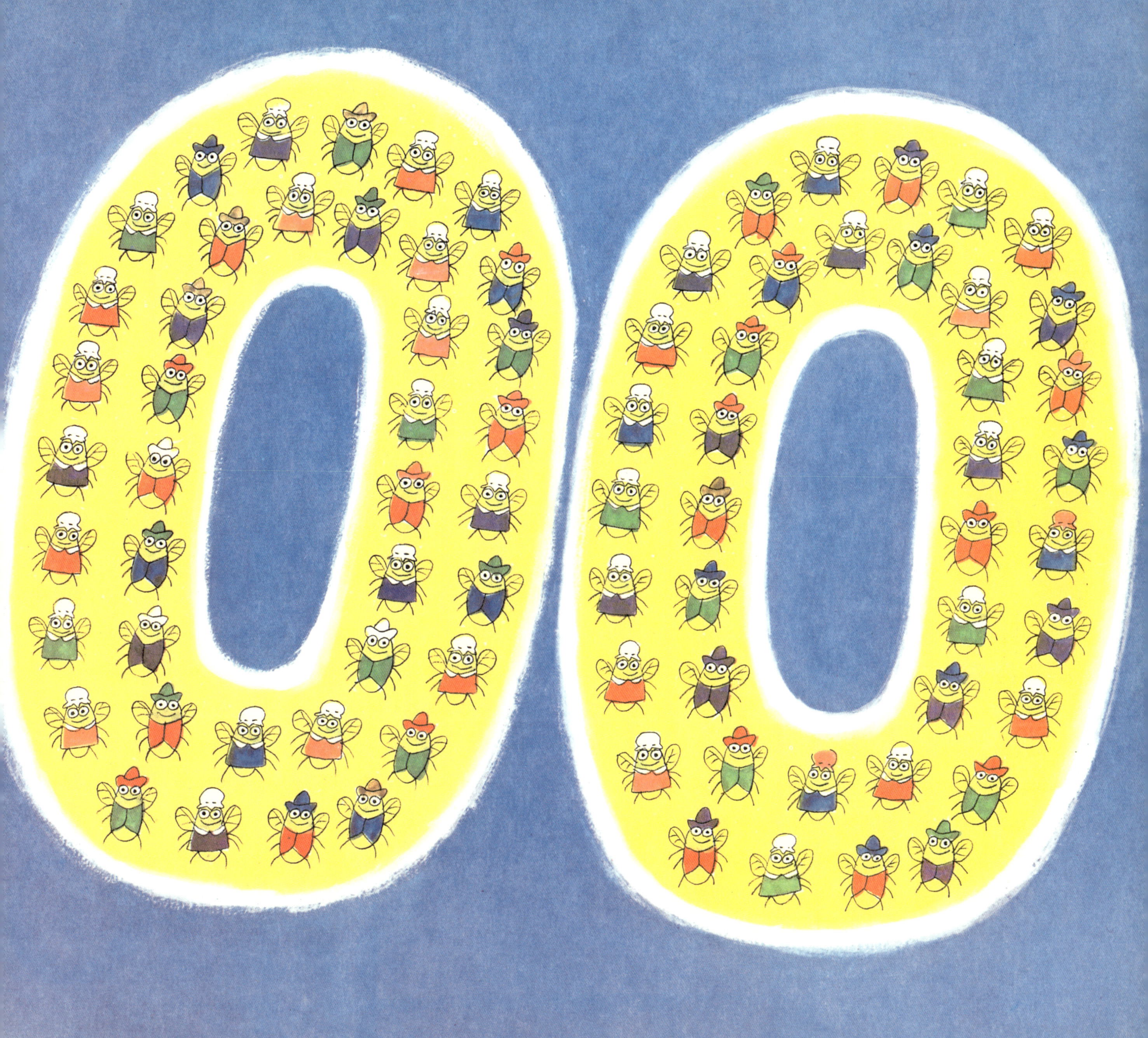

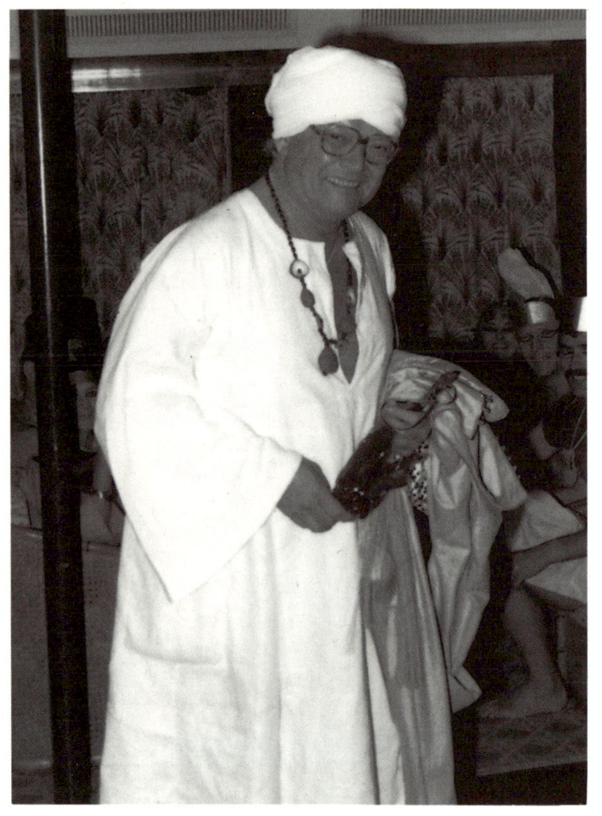

In 1972, Richard finally bought the chalet in Gstaad. At the same time he gave up the studio he had been renting in Lausanne; he felt that it would not be economical to keep both. At first the family used the chalet mainly for short visits, but after a while, Dick got tired of trying to keep a set of art supplies in both the Lausanne apartment and the chalet at Gstaad. He also found that it was a nuisance to carry his artwork back and forth. Eventually he gave up the apartment and the family used the chalet as their home base.

The following year, 1973, produced another important change. Ole Risom moved from Western Publishing to Random House. The move brought about a very happy reunion for the two old friends. Now Ole could once again work with Dick on his books. Walter Retan continued to edit them, while Ole worked with Dick on creating new projects and new formats, often within the framework of a new line of books being developed for the Random House list. The first new large-format picture book on which they worked together was *Richard Scarry's Best Counting Book Ever.* This was an ideal project since Random House had no other counting book on its list. In his usual enterprising fashion, Dick invented all sorts of novel and absurd situations to teach numbers to young children, including nineteen very hungry

Above: During a holiday visit to Egypt, Scarry dressed as a sheik for a costume party he and Patsy attended on a Nile River steamboat.

Below: Like most tourists, Patsy and Dick tried their hand at riding camelback.

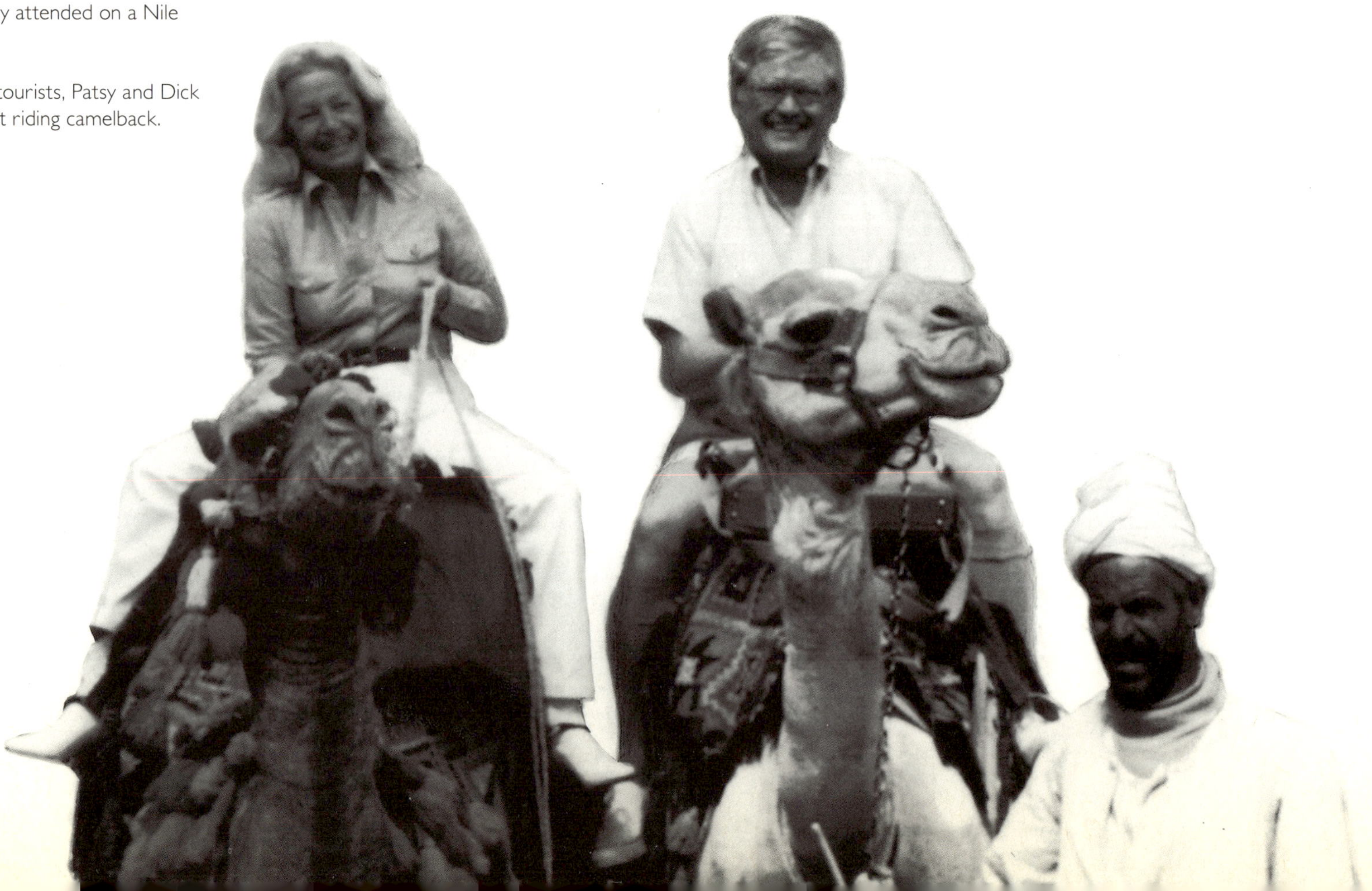

pigs having a picnic out of just one unbelievably long hot dog. Coincidentally, the Random House manufacturing department found a printer who had just acquired the kind of press and bindery equipment that could handle the square type of format Western had used for Dick's books. This was really good news for Dick, who much preferred working with the large, oversized doublespread that resulted from the format.

But Richard was not the only Scarry whose life was changing during the seventies. Huck graduated from art school and in 1975 decided to go to New York City. He was trying to make up his mind about his future and wanted to see if he could obtain work in New York as a free-lance artist. On the basis of his excellent portfolio he received several commissions, including one from Random House to design and illustrate a picture dictionary for very young children.

For living quarters, Huck found a small apartment in a building on Madison Avenue, where an attractive young German woman named Marlis was also residing. She worked for Pan American Airlines, and had recently broken her leg in an accident in Rio de Janeiro. Because her leg was in a cast, she had difficulty getting about. Huck offered to help, and gradually they became close friends.

After several months in New York, however, Huck decided to return to Switzerland, where he secured a job as a designer in the Lucerne branch of McGraw-Hill, Inc., an American publishing giant. In 1977, he and Marlis were married. They settled in Switzerland, where they eventually found an attractive apartment in the old section of the city of Geneva. On July 12, 1979, their first child, a daughter named Fiona, was born; about three and a half years later, on January 25, 1983, they had a second daughter, Olympia. Dick and Patsy enjoyed their new role as grandparents, making frequent trips to Geneva to see their granddaughters. Huck continued to illustrate, and often write, his own beautiful picture books in a style quite different from his father's.

Even though Dick was still pursuing a very rigorous working schedule, he and Patsy began to add new and exotic destinations to their annual travels. Almost every winter they spent some time in Africa. Patsy loved Morocco and Egypt, and Dick wanted to retrace some of his army haunts in Algeria. But most of all they came to love Kenya, where they went on safari every year to see all the animals native to Africa, including elephants, lions, giraffes, zebras, and hippopotamuses. Riding through the game preserves in a four-wheel drive van, Dick would make drawings

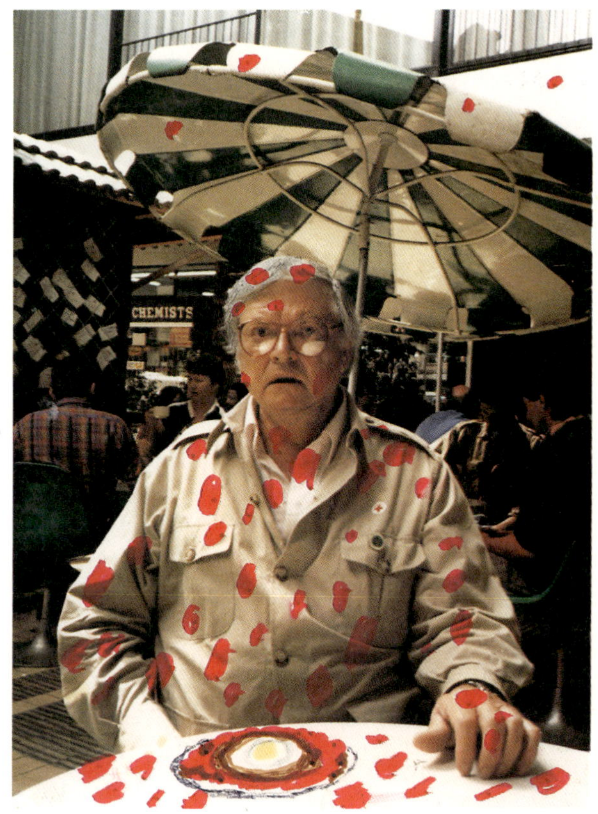

After one of their several safari trips to Africa, Dick painted red spots on this photo taken at the New Stanley Hotel in Nairobi, Kenya. He sent it to John Miller with the comment: "When will they ever design a ketchup bottle that works?"

Below: Drawing from *Best Rainy Day Book Ever*

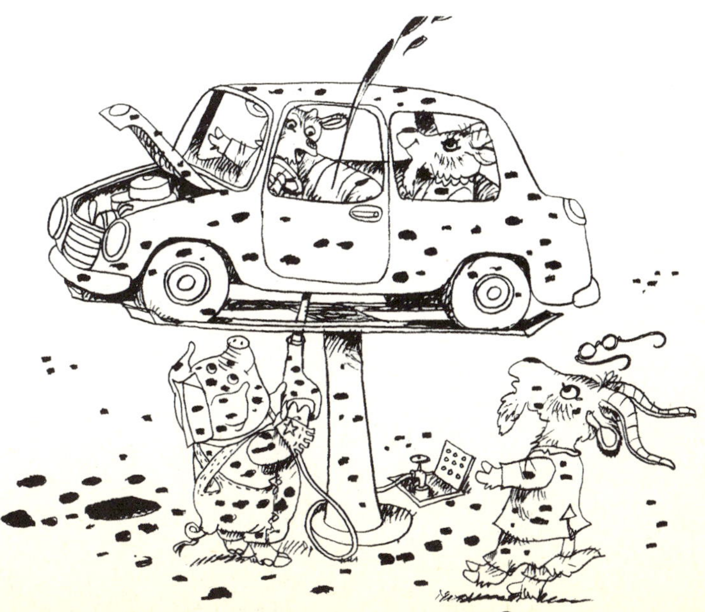

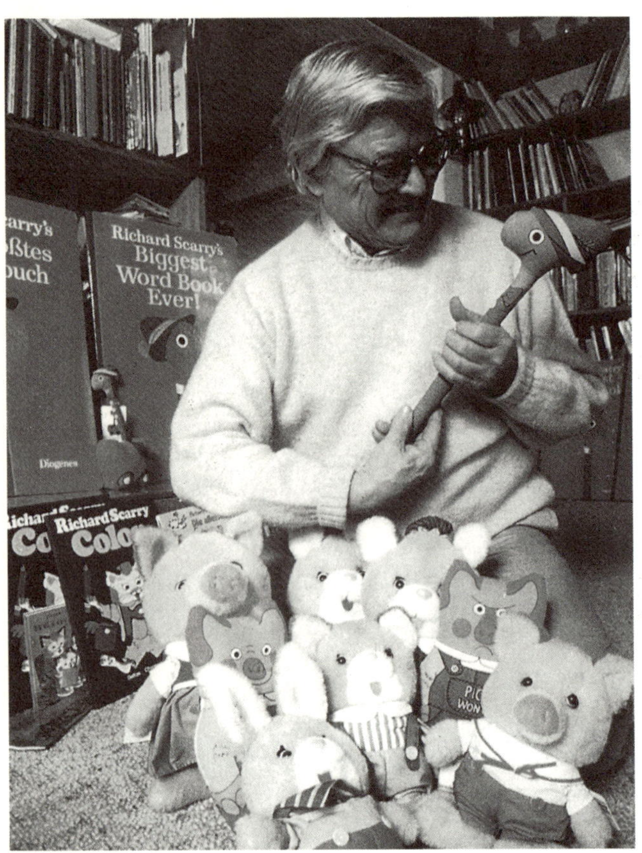

Dick looks at a variety of samples of stuffed toys based on his characters. Merchandise and other licenses resulting from Scarry's enormous international popularity added considerably to his income.

and take photos of the animals in their natural habitat. He and Patsy frequently stayed at Little Governors Camp in the Masai Mara on the border of Tanzania, where the guests slept in tents. During the night they could often hear elephants or hippos snorting and rustling around in the darkness. Dick had a special fondness for hippopotamuses, and used them as characters in many of his books.

Sometimes the Scarrys made reservations at a larger camp with permanent dwellings such as the Keekorok Game Lodge farther west in the Masai Mara Game Reserve, where they once invited Ole and Agnes Risom to join them as their guests. Ole later reported that the big sport among guests at the hotel was to list in a special register all the different kinds of animals they had seen that day while on safari. When Dick stepped up to the desk to give his own accounting, he wrote: 32 MOSQUITOES, 50 FLIES, 3 BEES, AND 1 ANGRY SPIDER. Beside them, he drew careful pictures of the insects. The man who kept the register was not amused. How could anyone show such a lack of seriousness toward this very important list?

In 1978, in one of those ironic switches that occur so frequently in book publishing, Walter Retan left Random House to accept the position of vice president and publisher of Golden Books, Richard Scarry's old publisher. One of his first tasks there was to oversee a revision of *Richard Scarry's Best Word Book Ever.* During the previous few years, with the increasing importance and acceptance of the feminist movement in the States, both Western and Random House had received many letters of complaint about the roles played by women in Richard Scarry picture books. A very large percentage of the female characters were depicted as housewives, cooking, cleaning, and washing dishes. At first Dick didn't take the complaints too seriously. He maintained that because his characters were animals and because most wore trousers, it was difficult to tell whether a worker was a man or woman. Most of the women characters were dressed just like the men. But the complaints continued to roll in, and the publishers went to work to convince Dick that he must change with the times.

Dick was not too difficult to persuade once he realized that sales were being affected. Because his *Best Word Book Ever* was still his bestseller and one of the worst offenders, he agreed (with the permission of Random House) to make a considerable revision in the book. He drew a great deal of new art, using women workers on the job, and he showed men taking a more active role in household duties and activities.

By this time, Dick and Patsy had been to just about all of the countries Dick had

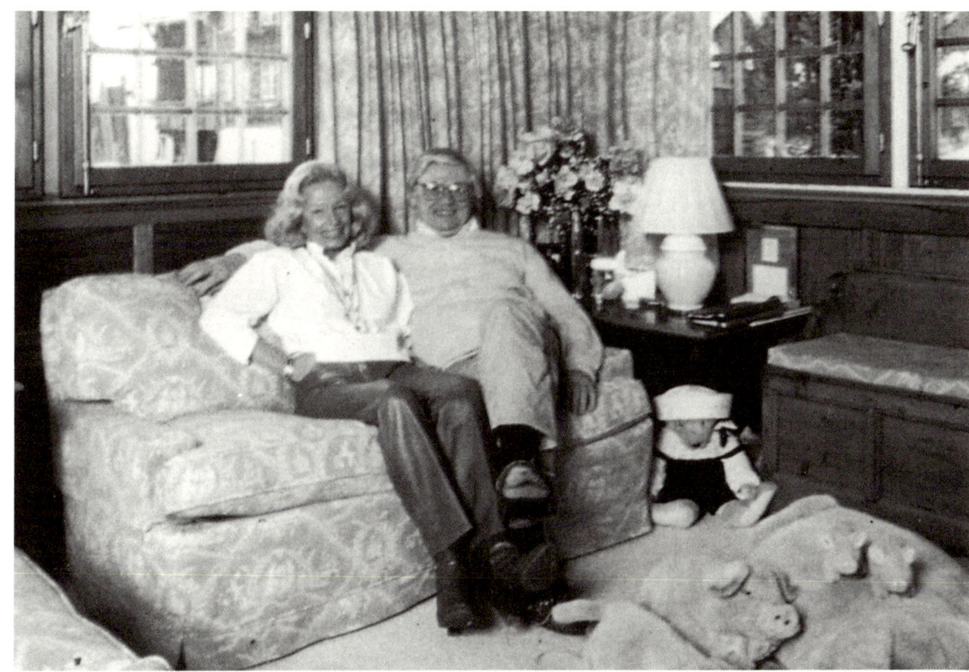

Dick and Patsy relax in the living room at Gstaad. Some of their collection of stuffed animals lies on the rug in front of them.

portrayed in *Busy, Busy World*, including a "grand tour" of the Far East, where they visited Japan, Australia, China, India, Indonesia, and many other countries they had never seen before. But Dick began to long for one of his favorite spots when he was young—the coast of Massachusetts. About 1980, he decided to rent a house on Nantucket for the late summer months. That, too, became an annual pilgrimage, although Patsy often grumbled about the fog and the rain.

While they were on the island, they usually flew to New York City at least once. Patsy loved that part of the trip, especially shopping at Bloomingale's and staying at the Plaza Hotel in a suite overlooking the park. Whenever Dick traveled anywhere, he carried a hunting bag that he had purchased from Abercrombie & Fitch. In it, he kept his meticulous royalty records enclosed in beautiful leather books from Hermes. In addition there were always a few small gold bars "in case of emergency," as well as a plentiful supply of cash separated into individual stacks of pounds, dollars, francs, etc. He never carried a credit card. Early in his career Western had helped him get a credit card, but he discovered what he thought to be an error on one of the bills and never used it again.

On what turned out to be his final visit to New York, he and Patsy invited Ole and Agnes Risom to have dinner with them at the Oak Room of the Plaza Hotel. As

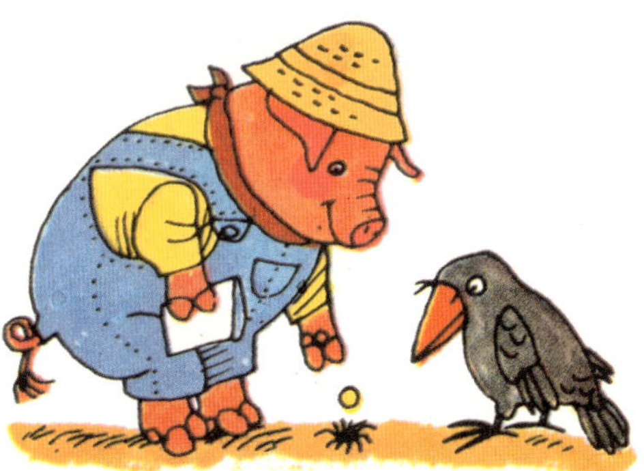

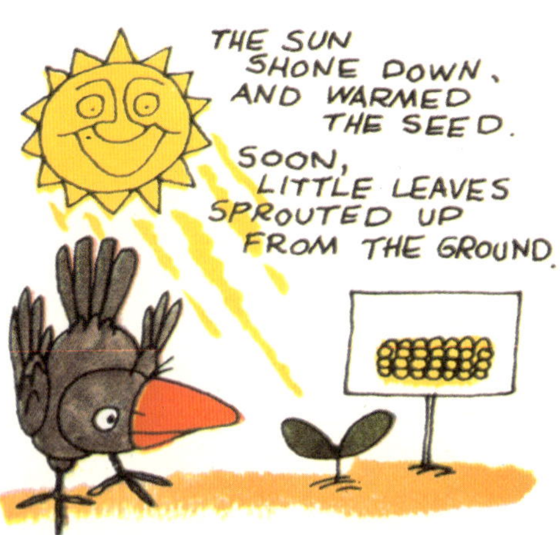

usual, Dick had his cherished bag with him, and he set it on the floor while they ate dinner. At the end of the meal, when he reached down to pick it up, he discovered that the bag was gone. Someone had stolen it: his cash, his gold bars, his royalty records, their passports, everything. The Plaza never found the bag for him or gave him any kind of restitution, and he never again returned to New York City.

Dick continued to create all kinds of successful books, at the same time becoming more and more popular all around the world. Mondadori, the famous Italian publisher, celebrated a Richard Scarry Day in Milan with big welcoming banners draped above the streets. Random House produced film strips based on his books, and toy makers began to create Richard Scarry character dolls and other toys. There was an elaborate Richard Scarry's Busytown display that traveled around the country to various science museums. Paramount Pictures began to make animated films based on Scarry books and characters, and the films became a popular television series on the Nickelodeon channel.

All of this required Dick's approval and took up a good deal of his time, especially since Sidney Kramer no longer represented him. (In early 1985 Stanley Garrett, who was by then Scarry's lawyer, had helped Dick to work out an appropriate severance arrangement with Sidney.) As far as Scarry was concerned, however, his books remained his first love.

During the 1980s Richard Scarry's eyesight began to be affected by macular degeneration, a progressive disorder that attacks the central part of the retina, causing gradual loss of vision. Despite this problem, however, he finished in 1985 the drawings for one last big book, called *Richard Scarry's Biggest Word Book Ever.* Not only was it Dick's biggest word book ever; it must surely have been the biggest one ever published, with dimensions of 15¾ x 24 inches. Although Random House had to charge $29, the entire printing sold out, and the book was licensed for publication in England, Italy, France, and Germany, as well as for a special Book-of-the-Month Club edition.

In addition to his vision problem, Dick developed cancer of the esophagus, and the operation to remove the tumor, along with follow-up chemotherapy, proved successful. Recovery was not easy, however, and he had to have excess fluid drained from his lungs every so often. He and Patsy lived quietly in Gstaad, playing their beloved game of chess every evening.

Finally, on April 30, 1994, the sad news reached New York. Richard Scarry had died of a heart attack in his home at Gstaad. He was 74 years old. Peter E. Spier, a gifted artist and illustrator himself, has written for this book a very fitting final note about Scarry:

It must have been twenty years ago that I met Dick Scarry for the first and last time, and I do not think that meeting lasted more than a few minutes. I remember Scarry from that short meeting as a friendly, courteous gentleman, tall and lean, but cannot recall a single word of what we talked about.

It did not make much difference, for I knew Dick Scarry well. He was a constant presence in our home through his wonderful books, which we had read and reread with our small children. I believe we had all of his books, but there were no favorites among them because they were, without exception, all favorites.

Of course my children were very familiar with my own books, but they were books they had seen me work on at home, day after day. Old hat! Boring stuff!!

Scarry's books were far more fun. Things were happening everywhere, and something new could be discovered again and again. To many people Dick's books may superficially have looked alike. The same cats, pigs, geese, and dogs over and over again, albeit in different clothes and settings. But to the serious observer there was far more to it than that: small, sometimes whimsical, philosophical gems, simple lessons or parables.

One I remember well (Farmer Pig) *consisted of a few very small drawings of a pig/farmer planting a seed of corn in the ground. The rain came down, the sun shone, and soon little leaves sprouted. The plant grew and grew until finally there were three ears of corn waiting to be picked. Farmer Pig gave one ear to Mr. Crow. He gave another to his wife, who loved corn, and then with his knife Farmer Pig made his third ear into a pipe. "Isn't it wonderful," the text read, "to think of what you can do with* one *little seed."*

Scarry's books were beautifully drawn, humorous, teeming with life. Every detail well observed and technically always correct. He knew how a tractor, a drag line and road scraper were put together, and the same was true of everything else he put into his books. He was a consummate craftsman, and the quality never varied.

We all know the immense, worldwide success his books enjoyed, and I never ceased to wonder why Dick Scarry never even received a single one of the countless awards

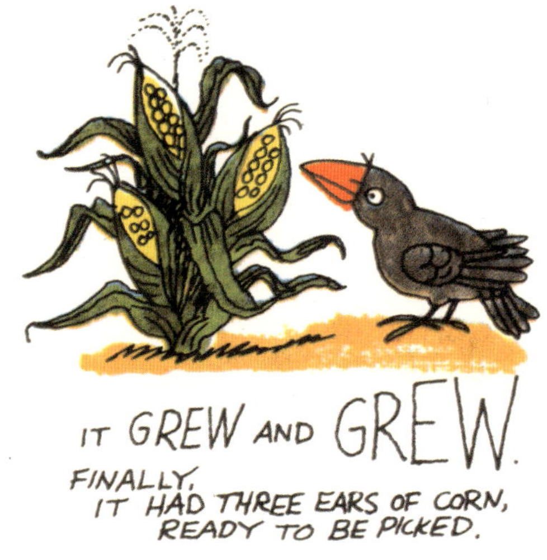

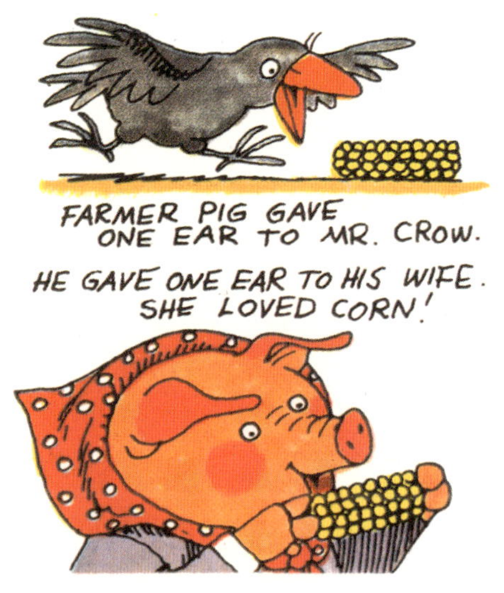

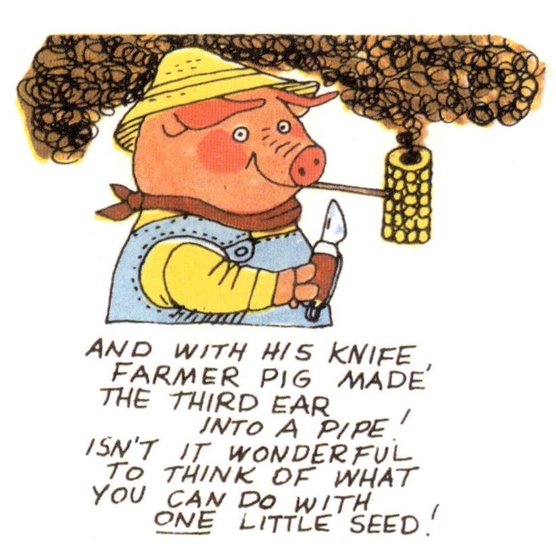

handed out year after year. I could not understand why none of his drawings were ever selected by the New York Times *as among the "Best of the Year," or why he never received a Caldecott Honor Book award. He so richly deserved it, and his contribution to the world of children's book was enormous.*

Some years ago at one of the large children's book conferences I sat at dinner next to someone serving on an important awards committee, and I asked her why Richard Scarry had never won any award, or, as far as I knew, had never even been considered. "Oh," was the answer, "he is too popular; he sells too many books. The millions he is earning are his reward!"

I could not believe my ears.

Once in awhile I later asked the same question again, and the answers were invariably variants of the first answer. The sad truth is that Richard Scarry's great success disqualified him from being eligible for awards.

It is comforting to assume that, if given the choice between the highest awards and accolades for modestly successful books, or the unimaginable success he did have, Dick would have chosen the latter. (I would have!)

Three months ago my wife and I became grandparents for the first time, and I cannot tell you how much I look forward to getting some of the tattered, well-loved books stored in our basement back upstairs, putting our grandson in my lap and starting to read.

And Richard Scarry's Best Word Book Ever *is going to be the first one!*

Peter Spier has said it well. Nothing need be added except that Patsy Scarry died in their home at Gstaad on December 31, 1995. Now only Huck is left to carry on the Scarry creative tradition, though Dick frequently observed in his last years that he thought at least one, and perhaps both, of his granddaughters showed signs of a promising talent.

Scarry's studio at Gstaad. The Danish baker's pretzel sign that formerly decorated the living room in Lausanne hangs over his drawing table.

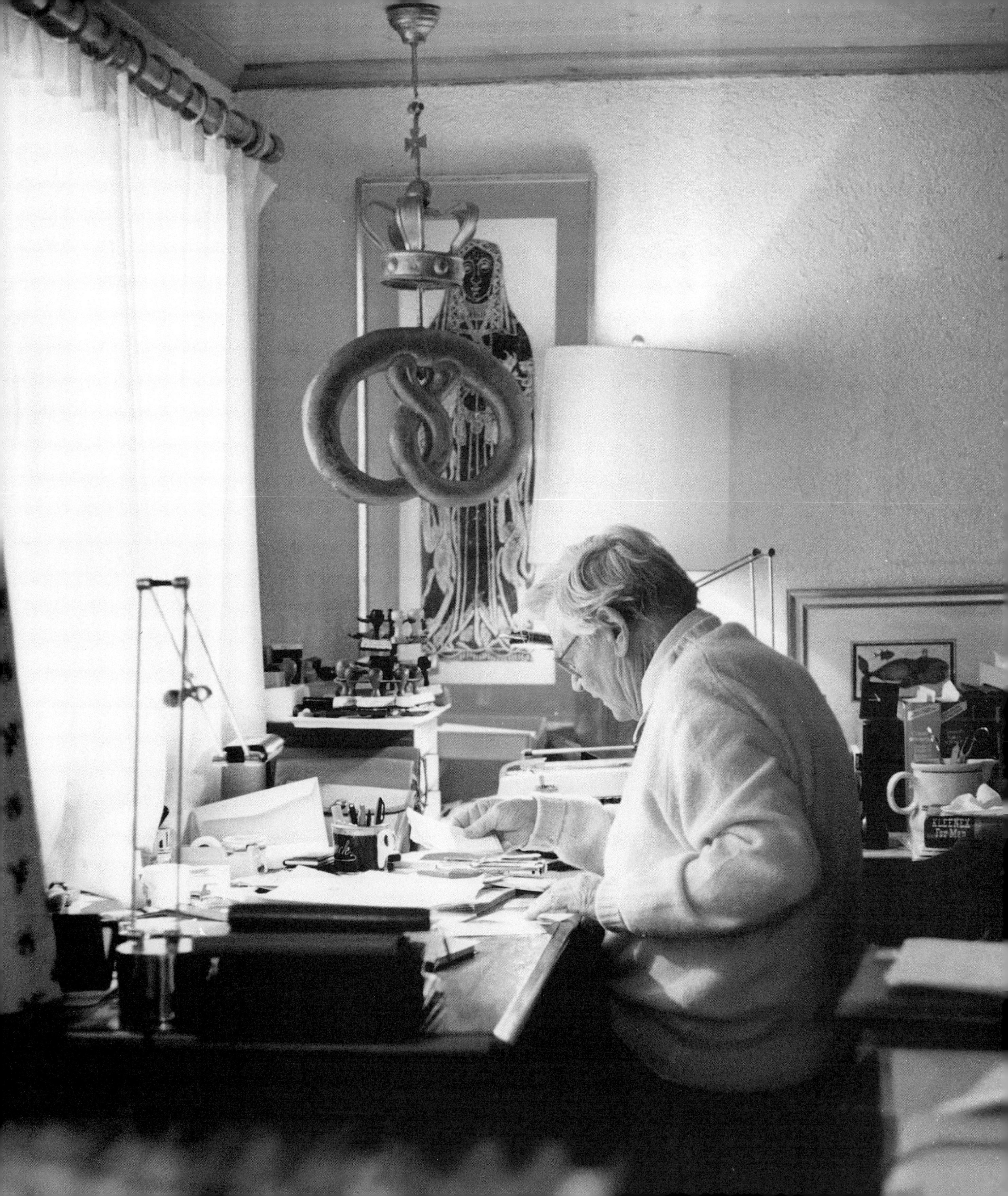
KLEENEX
For Men

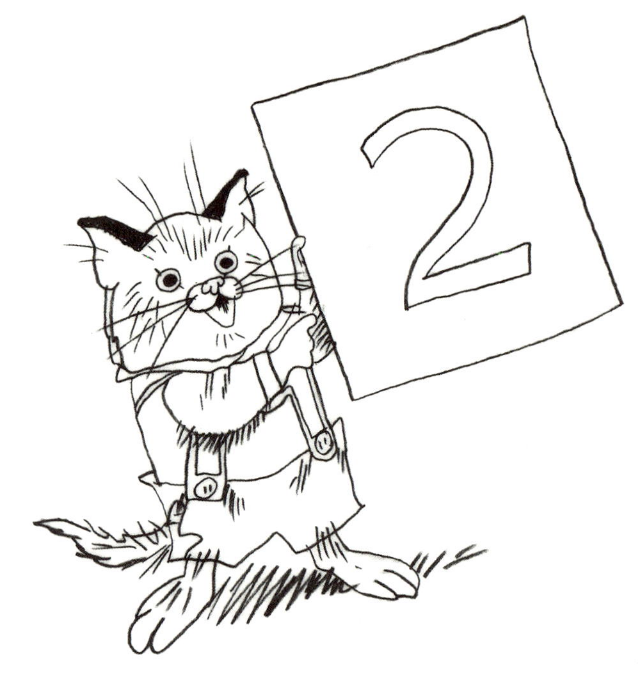

AN ARTIST'S WORK

DRAWING A STORY

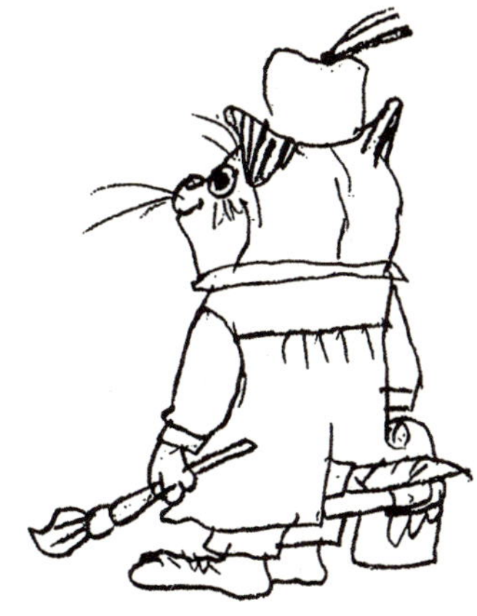

Richard Scarry didn't write his stories; he drew them. Because he was such a visual person, he created a story as a series of images in his head, which he then turned into pencil sketches. When these were finished, he wrote a text to fit the pictures. Frequently his illustrations told a much more complicated story than his text, which he always kept very simple. He deliberately tried to fill each page with as much pictorial material as possible; he didn't like to see a lot of white space. He felt it was a waste. Scarry seemed to know intuitively that, if he filled the pictures with as much detail and activity as possible, young readers would want to look at his books over and over again. And with each reading they would always find something new.

He also seemed to understand that many adults don't really know how to read a book to a child. They read straight through the text, never stopping to comment on the details in the illustrations or extraneous activities not mentioned in the printed words. They don't give the child an opportunity to participate actively in the experience. To guide parents in this process, Dick would point out in his text a few special details in the illustrations, or ask a few questions that would stimulate a dialogue between the reader and the listener. Through this device, children realized that there were all kinds of interesting and funny things to find in the pictures, things that the text never mentioned. Every time they looked at the book they found something new and entertaining. And adults learned that it was important to "read" the pictures as well as the words.

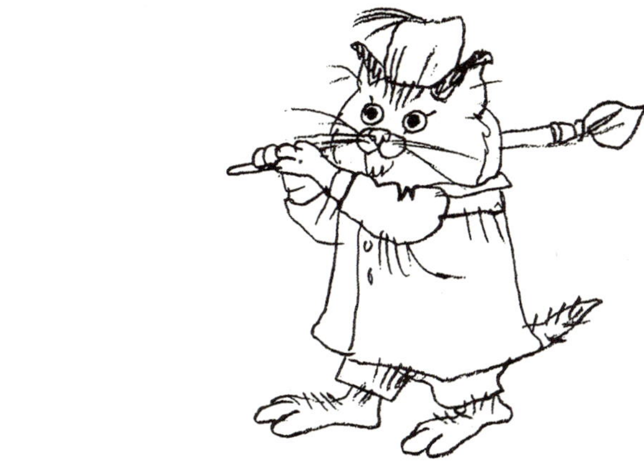

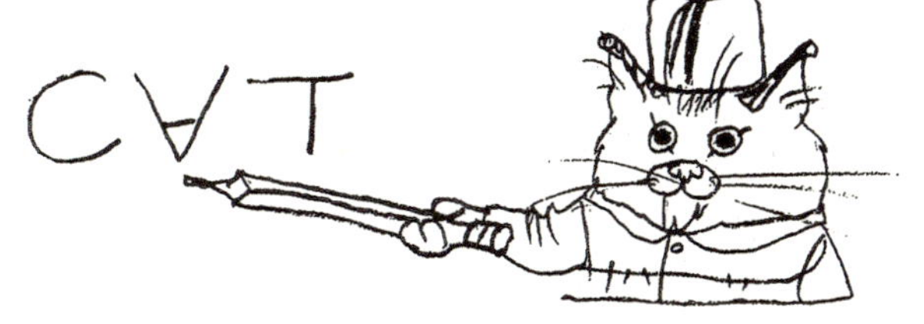

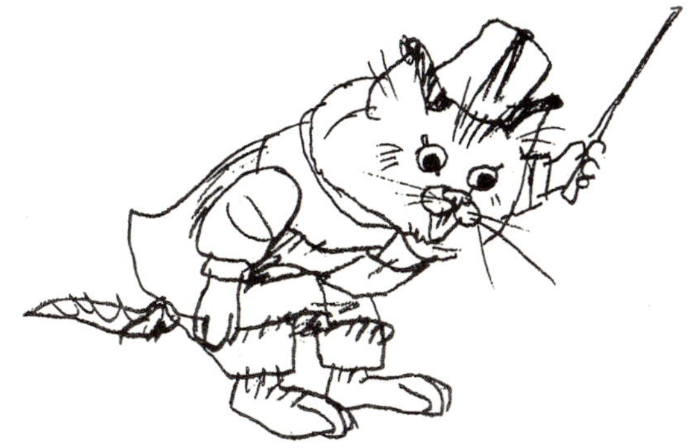

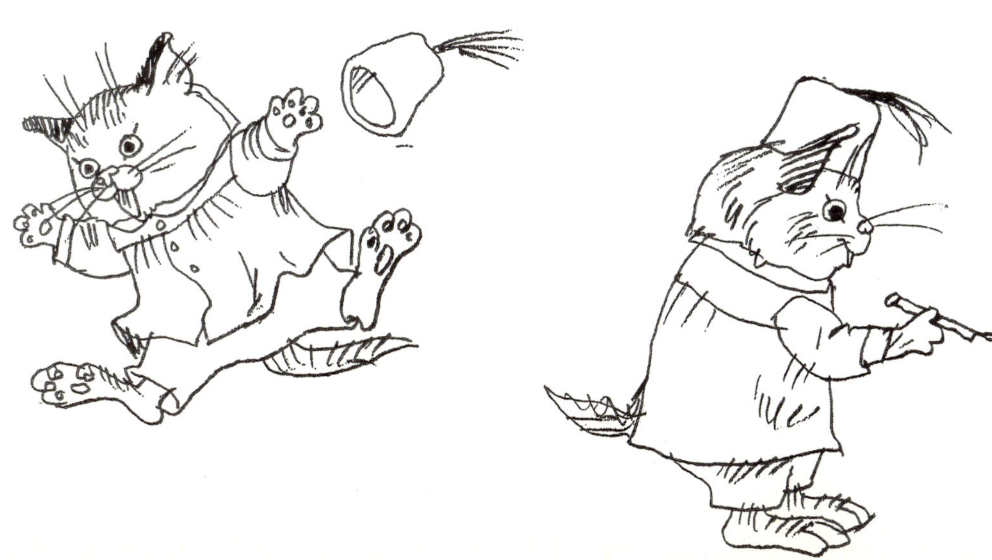

Some unpublished drawings from Dick Scarry's sketchbook

Overleaf: In this double spread from *Richard Scarry's Funniest Storybook Ever,* the artist combines familiar buildings and trucks with wonderfully absurd activities, and in four short paragraphs he manages to direct a young reader's attention to many different details.

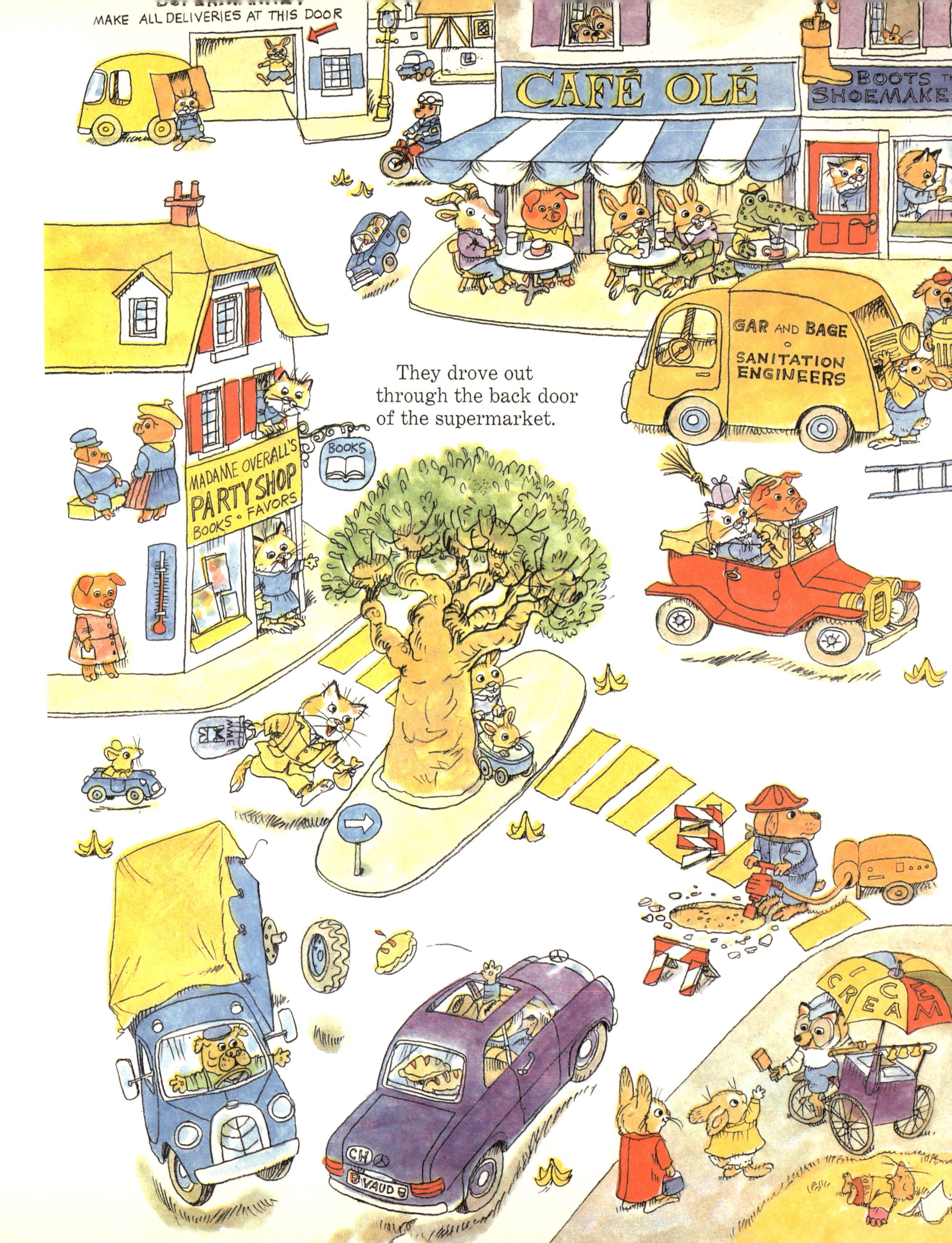

They drove out
through the back door
of the supermarket.

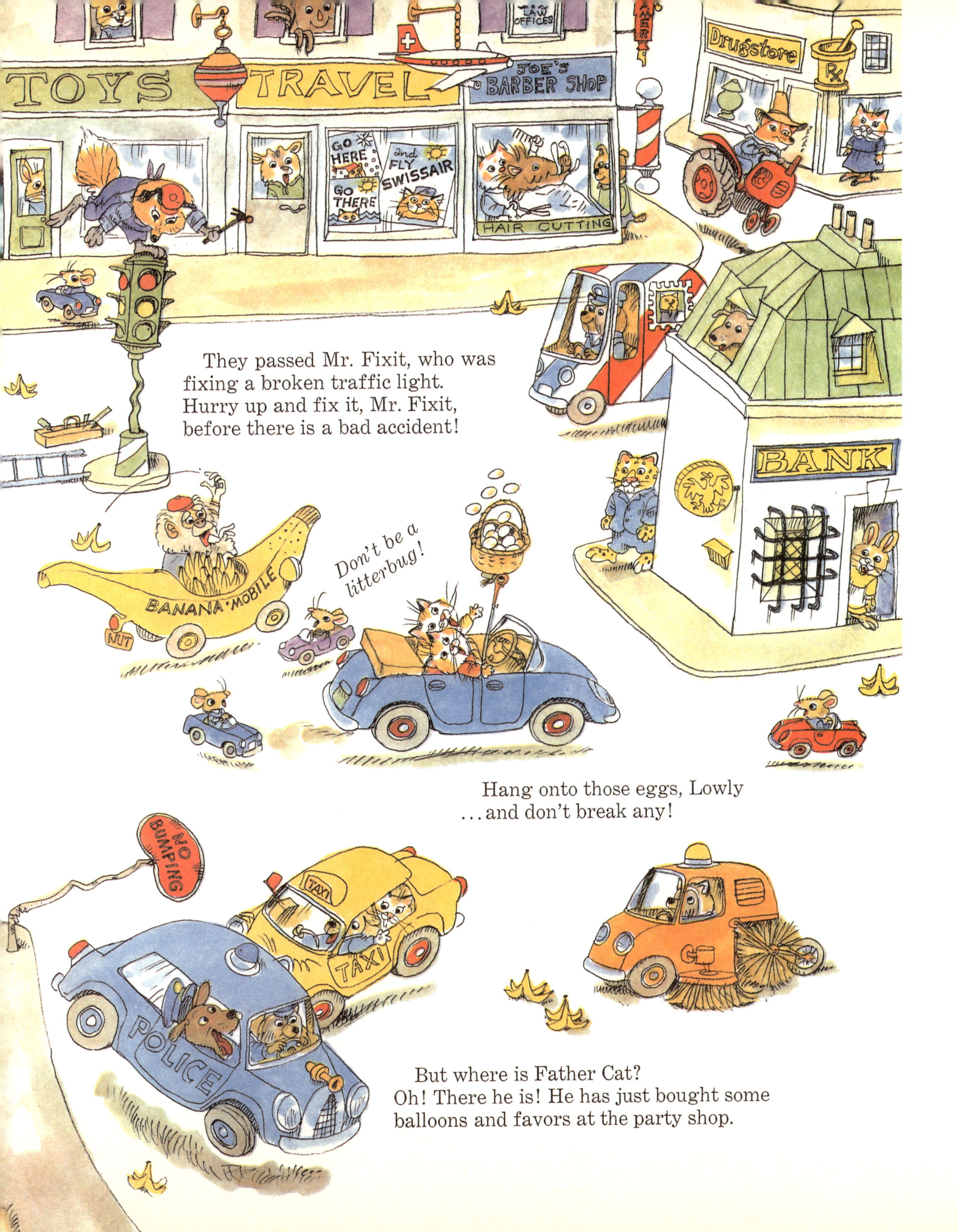

They passed Mr. Fixit, who was fixing a broken traffic light. Hurry up and fix it, Mr. Fixit, before there is a bad accident!

Hang onto those eggs, Lowly ... and don't break any!

But where is Father Cat? Oh! There he is! He has just bought some balloons and favors at the party shop.

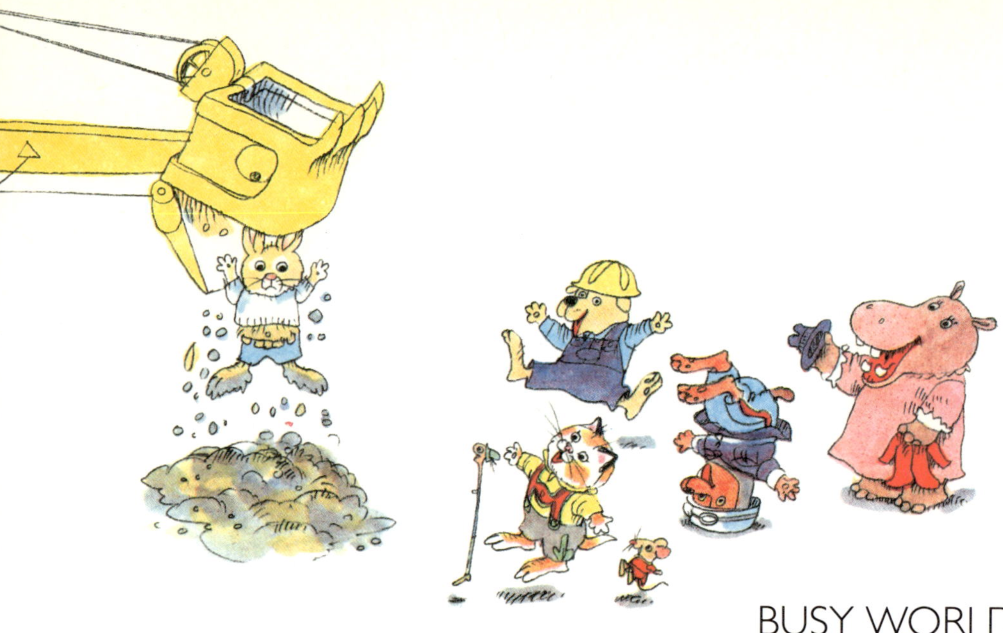

BUSY WORLD, BUSY PEOPLE

Two vignettes from *Richard Scarry's Funniest Storybook Ever*

Opposite: Scarry often laughed about the funny scenes he witnessed during the years he and Patsy ate in Greenwich Village restaurants. This page from *Richard Scarry's Busiest People Ever* might have been inspired by those memories.

Scarry wrote and illustrated to please himself. He felt no need to try things out on children because, as he frequently said, there was still a great big child in him. He was one of those lucky souls who retain a strong feeling of childhood with all its delights and problems. He had an enormous appreciation for the absurd, comical things that humans do in their everyday lives.

"Wherever I go," he was fond of saying, "I'm watching. Even on vacation when I'm in an airport or a railroad station, I look around, snap pictures and find out how people do things. Someday it will all show up in a book." Anyone who ever watched him sketch could observe the funny little smile that lighted his face when he drew something that especially amused or pleased him. Sometimes he would laugh out loud with his typical boisterous guffaw.

He once wrote to an interviewer in San Francisco: "I cannot explain how I get all my ideas, but I observe the world around me, and my books, with a few absurd situations, truthfully reflect that world. For example, in Nantucket last year a person drove through a stop sign without stopping, and whom did he collide with but the police chief! In Morocco a woman was dragging her daughter through the crowded streets at the same time a baker's boy was delivering a huge tray of rolls on his head. Mamma dragged her child into the baker's boy, knocking the tray of rolls onto the dirty street. Mamma gave the child a tongue-lashing for doing that to the baker's boy, who picked up all the dirty rolls and continued his deliveries. I could go on and on."

Richard Scarry was very aware of the need children have to know and understand the world around them, and he excelled in bringing that world to life. A child's world begins with the home, then extends to the surrounding neighborhood. In books like *Richard Scarry's Busiest People Ever* and *Postman Pig and His Busy Neighbors*, Dick brought that world vividly to life.

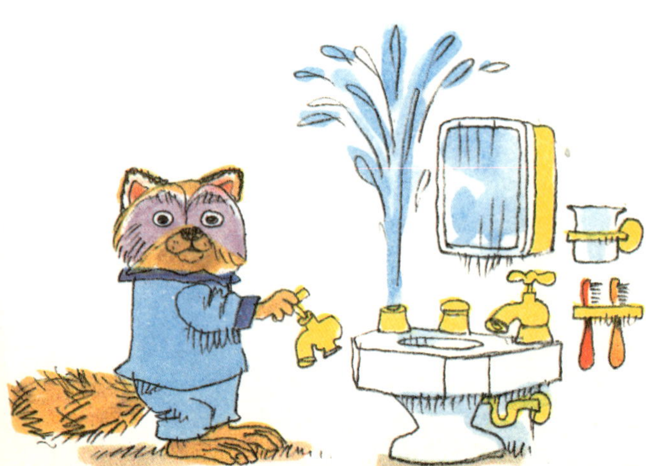

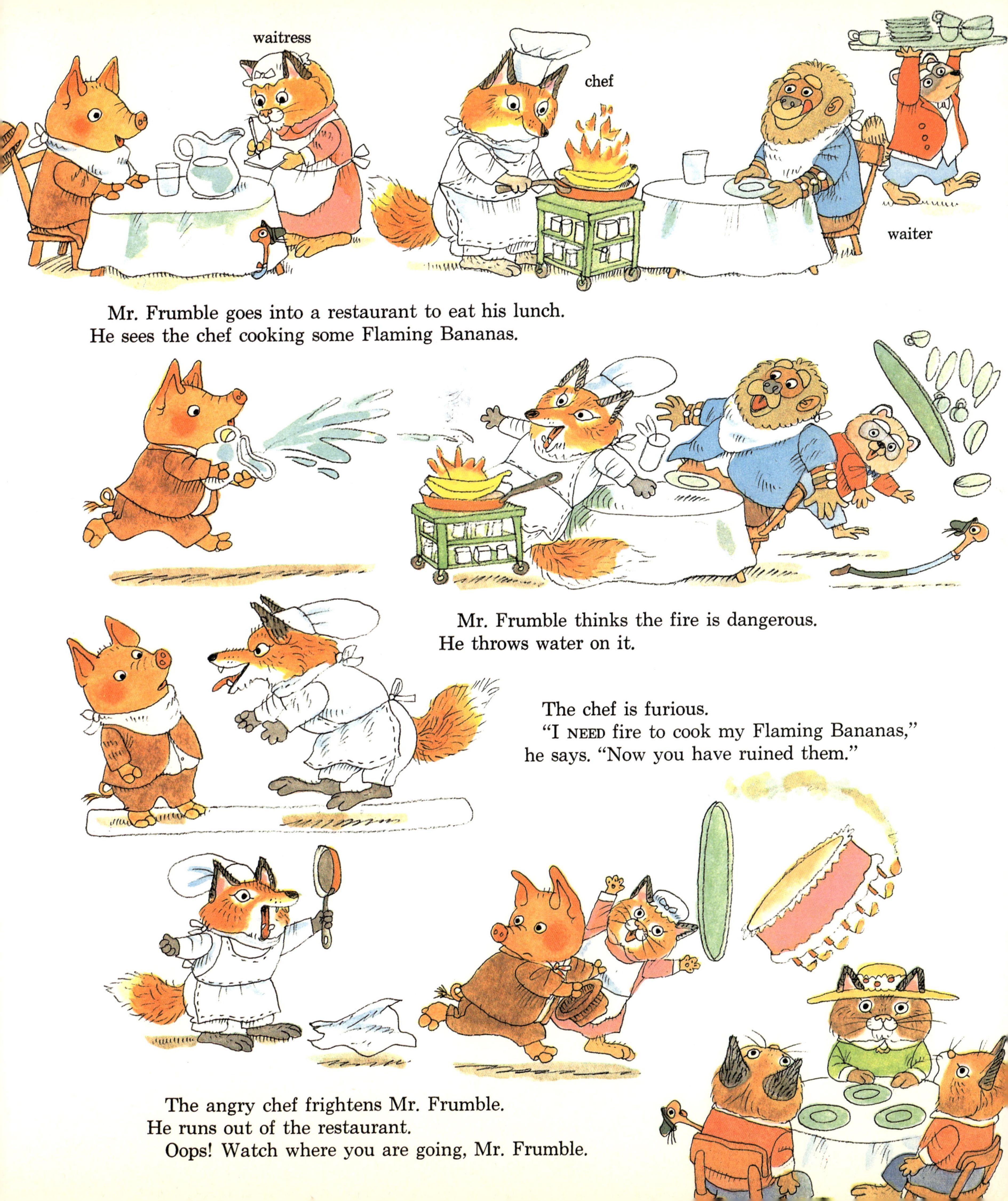

Mr. Frumble goes into a restaurant to eat his lunch.
He sees the chef cooking some Flaming Bananas.

Mr. Frumble thinks the fire is dangerous.
He throws water on it.

The chef is furious.
"I NEED fire to cook my Flaming Bananas," he says. "Now you have ruined them."

The angry chef frightens Mr. Frumble.
He runs out of the restaurant.
Oops! Watch where you are going, Mr. Frumble.

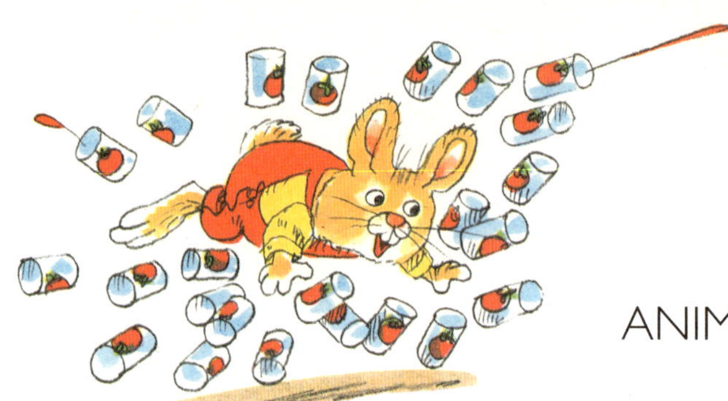

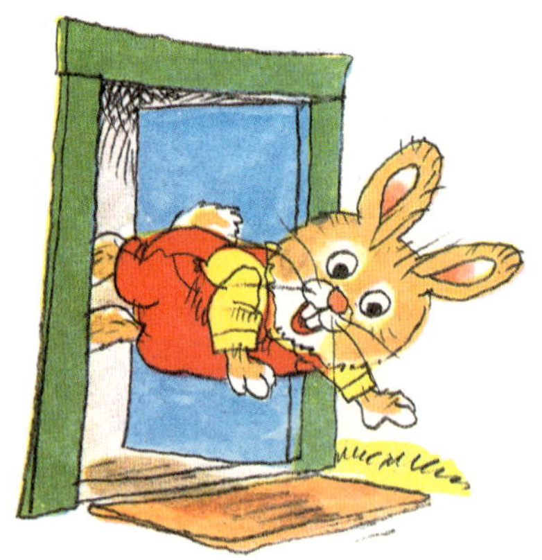

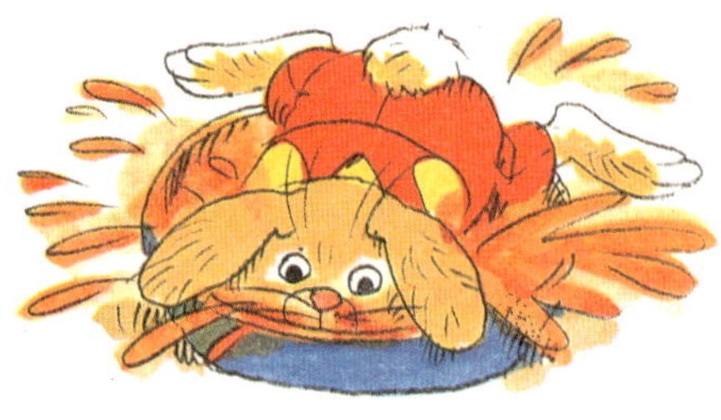

ANIMALS AS HUMANS

Interviewers were forever asking Dick why the characters in his books were always animals dressed as people instead of real human beings. Probably the truest answer he ever gave to this question was a paragraph in a "Dear Reader" letter written for his many fans: "I have often been asked why I use animals dressed and acting like humans in my books rather than humans. The answer is that it is more fun. Fun for me, fun for kids, and fun for adults who have to read and reread these book for non-readers. If I show a human father falling off a ladder or getting into a monstrous auto crash, it suggests danger and someone getting hurt. If I show Father Pig in the same situation nothing more is hurt than his dignity. Also a chocolate cake can explode out of Mother Bear's oven—something that is not possible in a realistic human mother's oven."

To their creator, the pigs, cats, bears, and other characters in Scarry books were not animals. They were real people living normal lives. He showed these busy folks doing all sorts of everyday tasks—from cleaning house to building a building to attending school or visiting the doctor. Although he never claimed to have done any scientific research on the subject, Scarry strongly believed that his animal characters were easier for children to identify with. "If you have a picture of a little girl with long blond hair," he said, "a dark-haired girl won't relate to it as well as to a picture of, say, a young girl bunny rabbit." The use of animal characters also solved the problem of children of one race relating to the activities of children of another race. In fact, it minimized all sorts of cultural and ethnic differences. Librarians and teachers particularly welcomed Scarry books as a way of appealing to all kinds of children.

Six scenes from *Funniest Storybook Ever* show Scarry's animal characters carrying human behavior to absurd extremes, but the accidents and mishaps are always funny, never threatening.

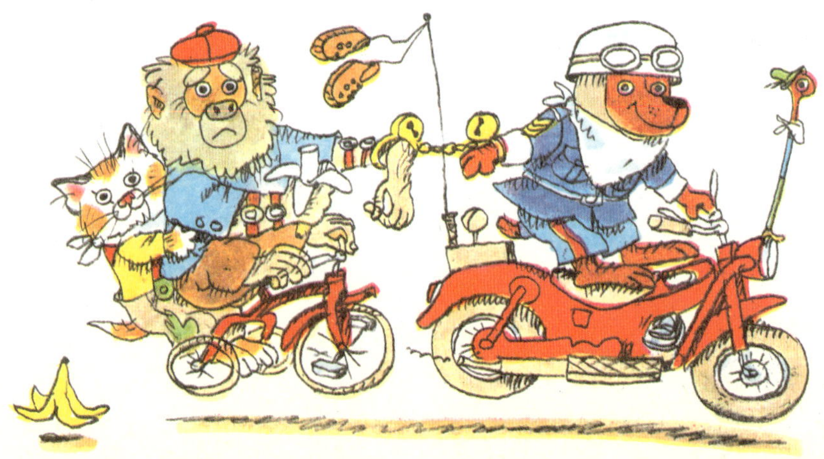

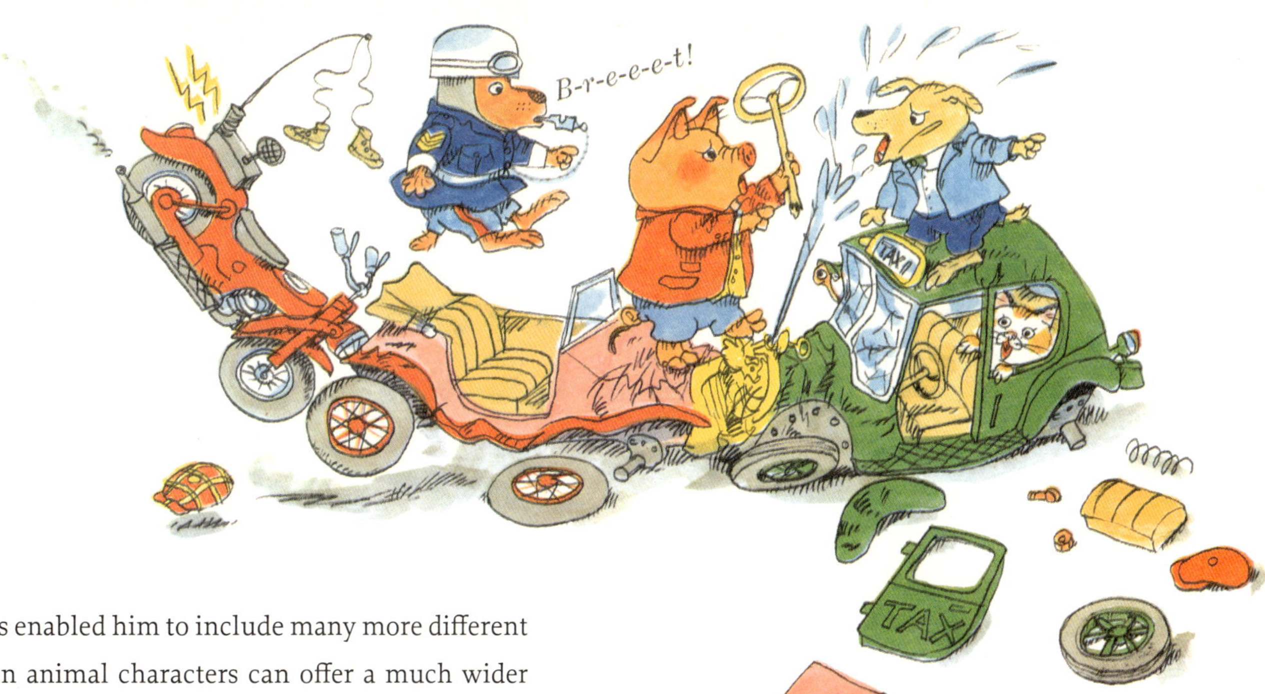

Scarry said that the use of animals enabled him to include many more different kinds of characters in his books. "Ten animal characters can offer a much wider range of types than ten human characters." His animals dressed like humans, acted like humans, and engaged in all kinds of human activities. As Scarry himself once put it: "The birds don't use their wings to fly around, they take planes; my ducks don't swim, they go sailing in boats." He understood that fantasy has to be consistent to be believable.

Dick admired the books of Beatrix Potter, but he didn't try to copy her style. Miss Potter sometimes put a few articles of clothing on her animal characters, but basically she was interested in animals as animals. She spent countless hours studying them and making very realistic drawings. The reader never thinks of her characters as humans. Occasionally Scarry emphasizes a particular animal habit or trait for one of his characters. For instance, Bananas Gorilla loves bananas and gets into frequent trouble when he tries to steal them. Lowly Worm likes to eat his way through apples. There is always a hole in the roof of the bus to accommodate a giraffe's long neck. But Scarry uses these little characteristics as a source of incidental humor, not as a means of establishing a figure's identity as an animal.

Overleaf: In this busy scene of village life from *What Do People Do All Day?*, Scarry's animal characters behave in ways that any child from any background can identify.

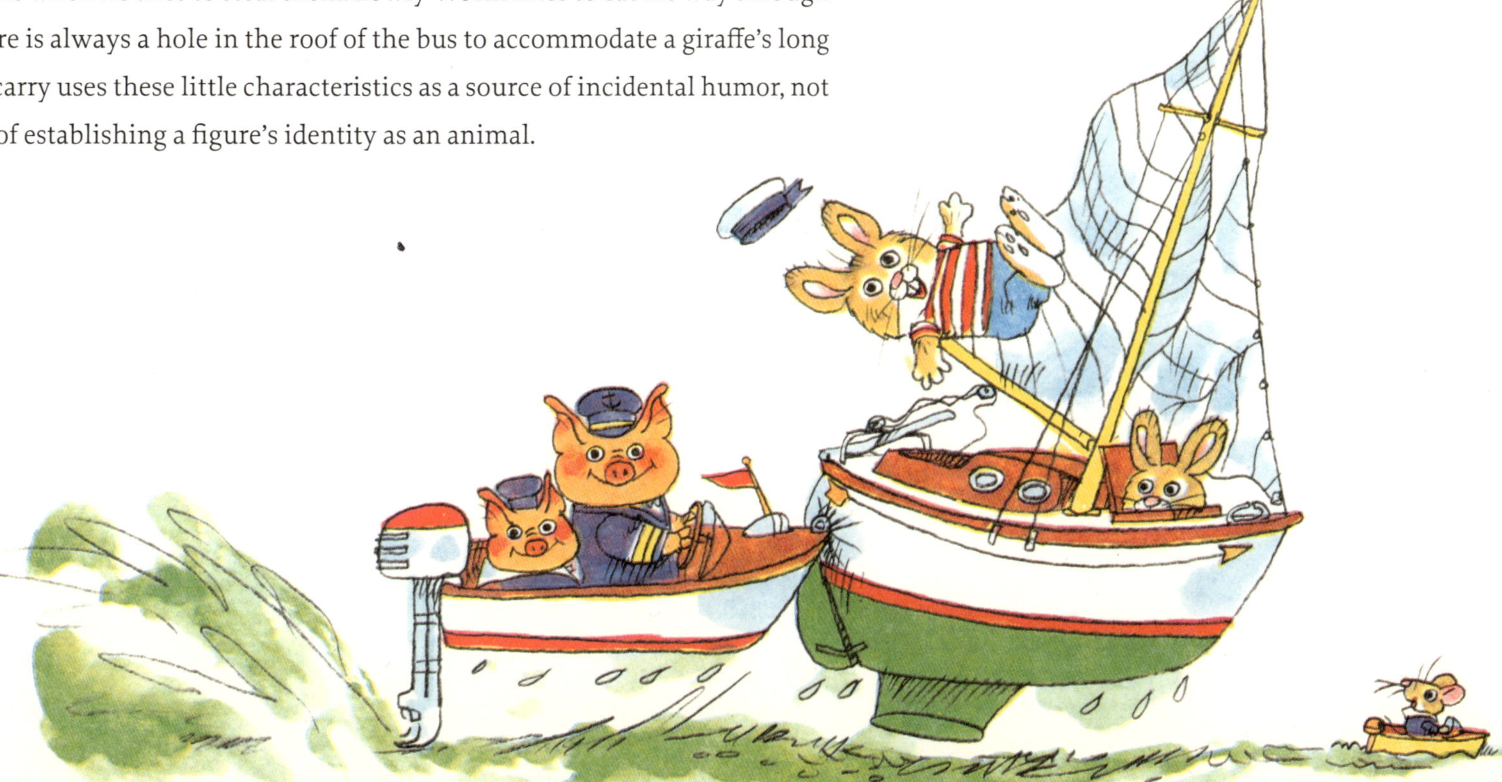

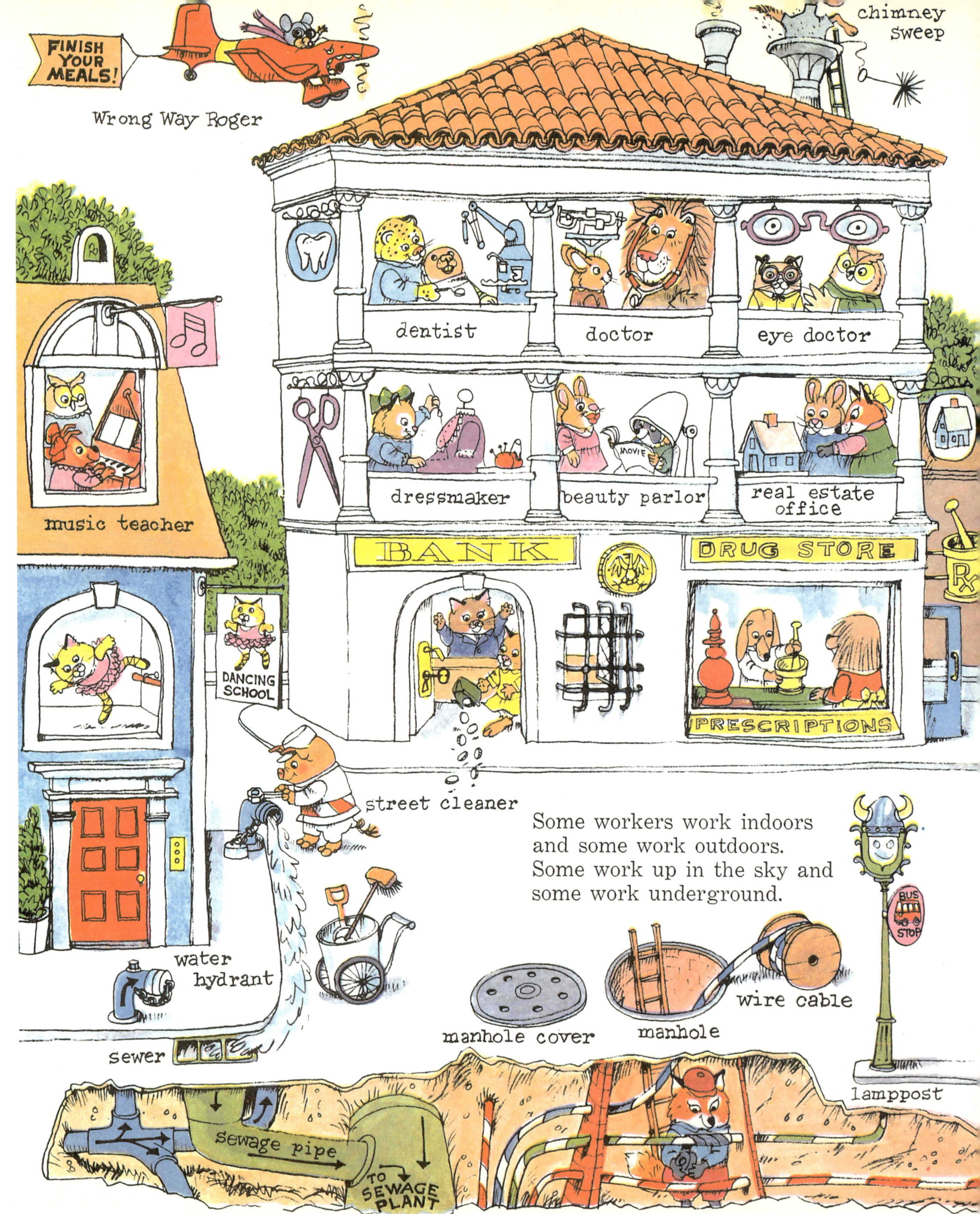

Some workers work indoors and some work outdoors. Some work up in the sky and some work underground.

All kinds of pipes and wires are buried underground

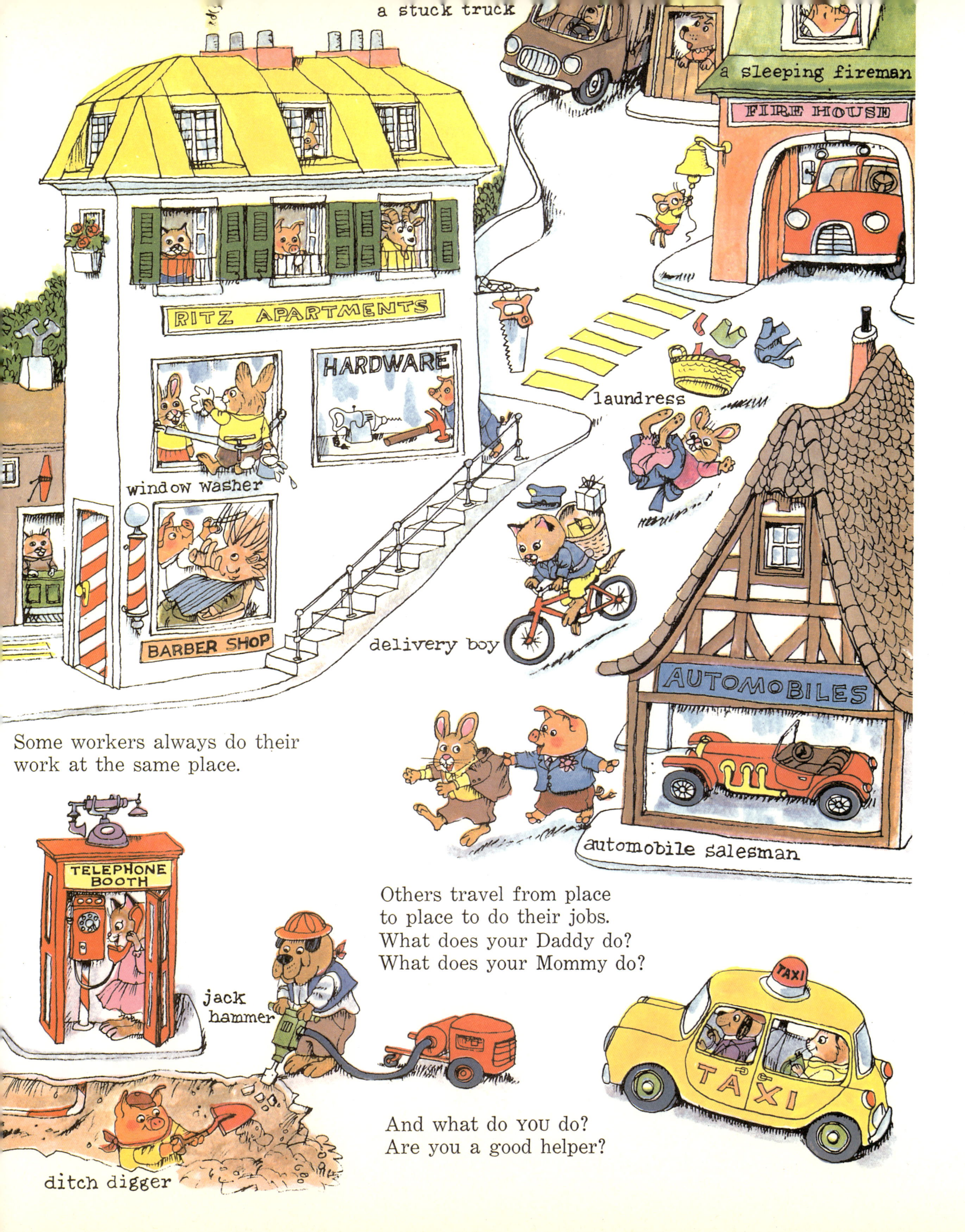

Some workers always do their work at the same place.

Others travel from place to place to do their jobs. What does your Daddy do? What does your Mommy do?

And what do YOU do? Are you a good helper?

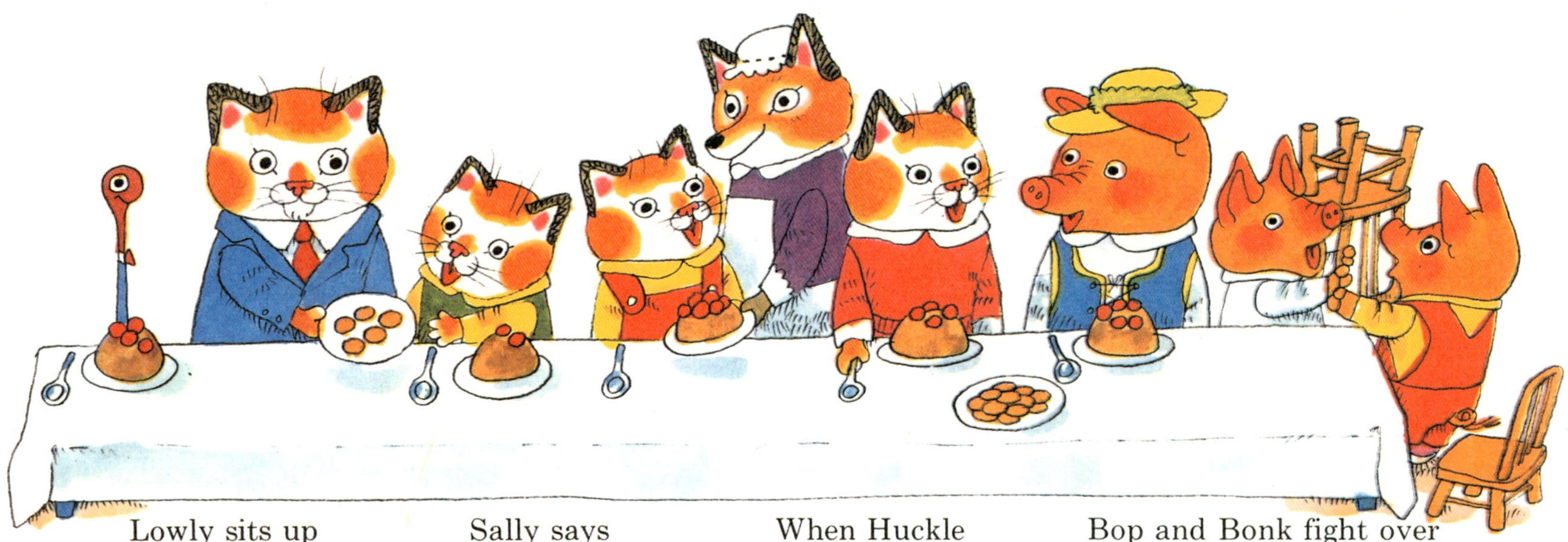

Lowly sits up straight in his chair like a good worm.

Sally says politely, "Please pass the cookies."

When Huckle is served, he says, "Thank you."

Bop and Bonk fight over who is going to have which chair. *Naughty boys!*

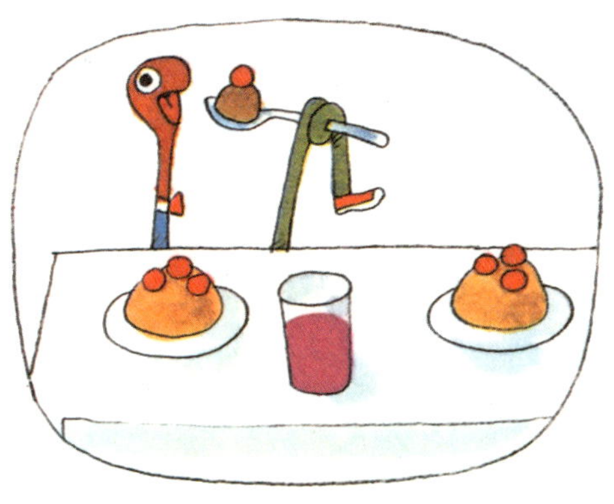

Lowly eats slowly and quietly.

Following pages: In these illustrations, from *Richard Scarry's Best First Book Ever*, and *What Do People Do All Day?*, the author shows that learning doesn't have to be dull.

FUN WITH LEARNING

Richard Scarry was once asked if he was basically an educational writer disguised as a fun-man, or a fun-man disguised as an educator. He answered, "I would say a fun-man disguised as an educator. . . . Everything has an educational value if you look for it. But it's the fun I want to get across."

His stories, for example, usually contain many reminders that children should be polite and well-behaved, wipe their feet, say please and thank you, and in general observe the rules of courteous conduct. Scarry said, "I try not to be pedantic, but I feel that children—like adults—should be well-behaved. Good manners mean more than opening doors. Isn't respect for somebody else's opinion one of the most important things in life?" One of the most appealing aspects of Scarry's picture book world is the respect and dignity with which his characters treat each other. But the fun inherent in the characters and situations always keeps the books from being didactic or pedantic. The fun-man cleverly disguises the educator. He never talked down to his readers. Although he wrote simply and clearly, he didn't hesitate to use scientific words where necessary, and he was a stickler for complete accuracy.

Sometimes several months of research were necessary before Scarry started work on a book. He was particularly influenced by the German Dudan Encyclopedia with its clear-cut schematic drawings and labels, and he employed this technique in many of his books. His account of "A Voyage on a Ship" in *What Do People Do All Day?*, with the amazingly detailed cut-out of a ship's interior, is an excellent example of Scarry's genius for making an extremely complicated subject understandable and fascinating for a very young child.

In another lively spread, this one from *Busiest People Ever*, he tells the story of "Mr. Frumble's Bad Day." Mr. Frumble, who never looks where he is going, has run into a water hydrant, and the escaping gush of water extinguishes the fire on a restaurant chef's flaming banana. (It also knocks off Lowly Worm's hat.) All over the double-page spread, drawn in careful detail, are the kinds of businesses and stores that a child would find in his own town. The different workers are identified with labels, including the schoolteacher and her pupils. Once again Scarry has combined his typical slapstick humor with accurate neighborhood information.

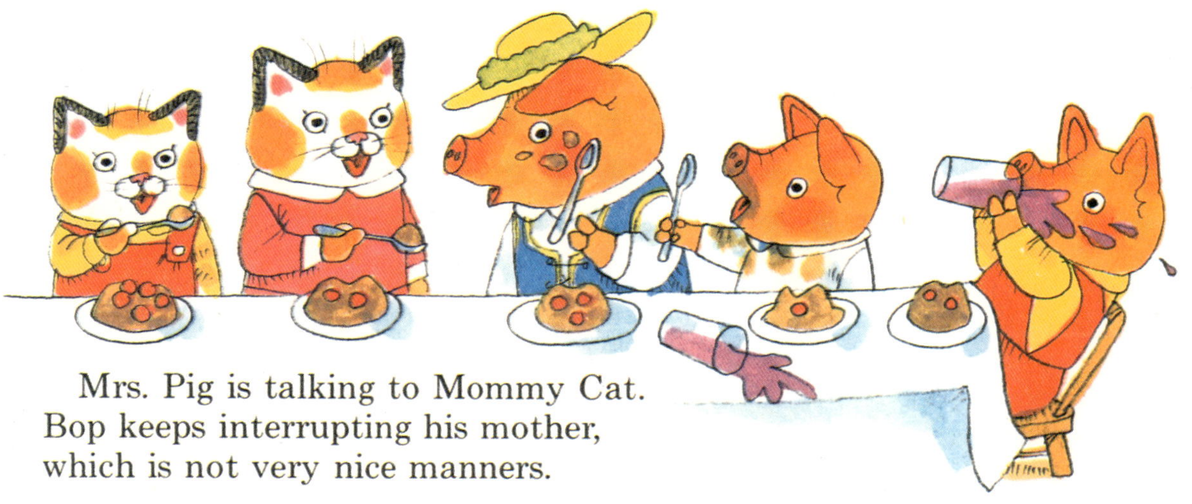

Bonk guzzles his juice and spills it all over his shirt. You should take smaller sips, Bonk!

Mrs. Pig is talking to Mommy Cat. Bop keeps interrupting his mother, which is not very nice manners.

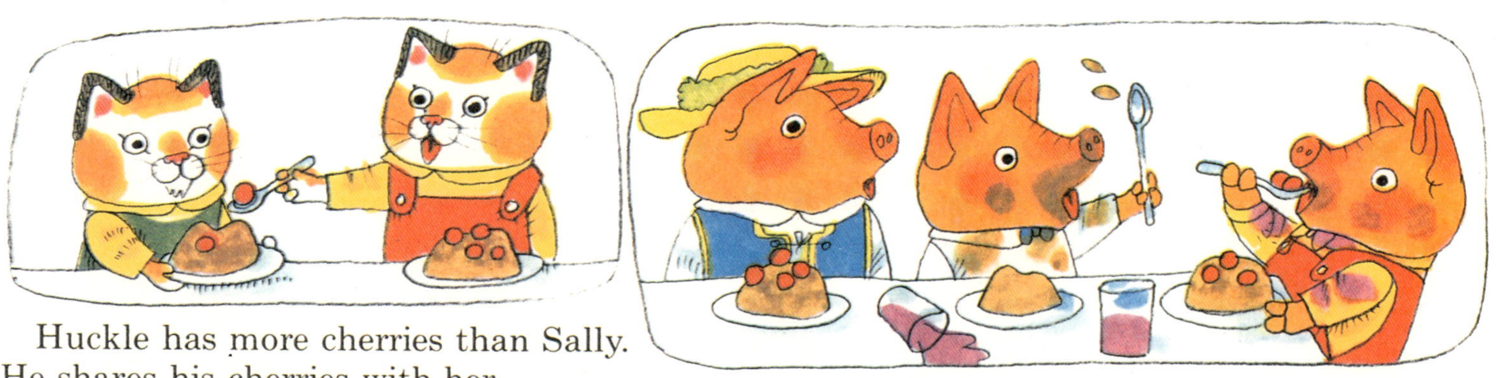

Huckle has more cherries than Sally. He shares his cherries with her.

Bonk steals the cherries from Bop's ice cream. What an awful thing to do!

Action Words

Farmer and Mrs. Pig certainly have a lot of children. And they are all doing something.

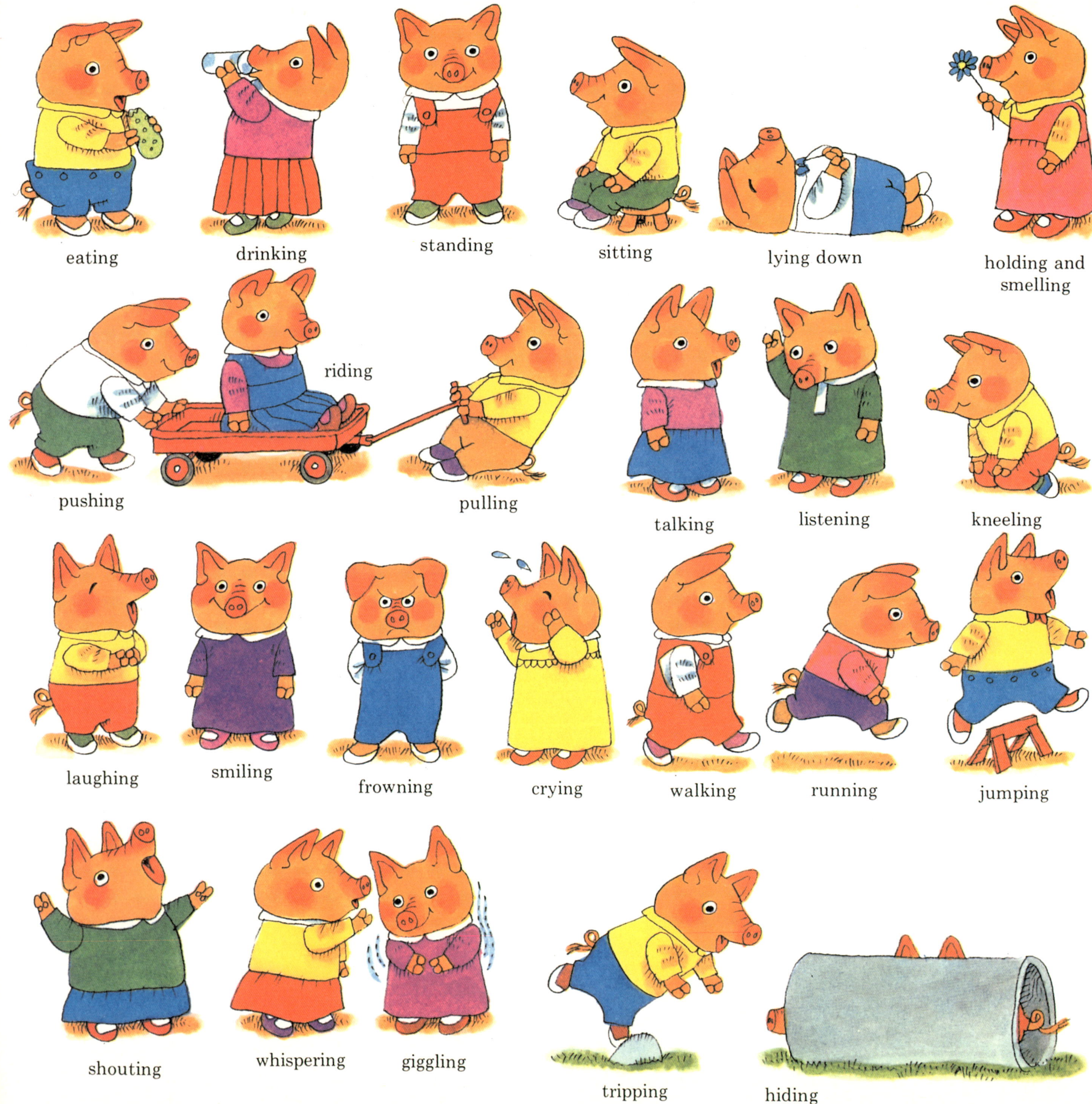

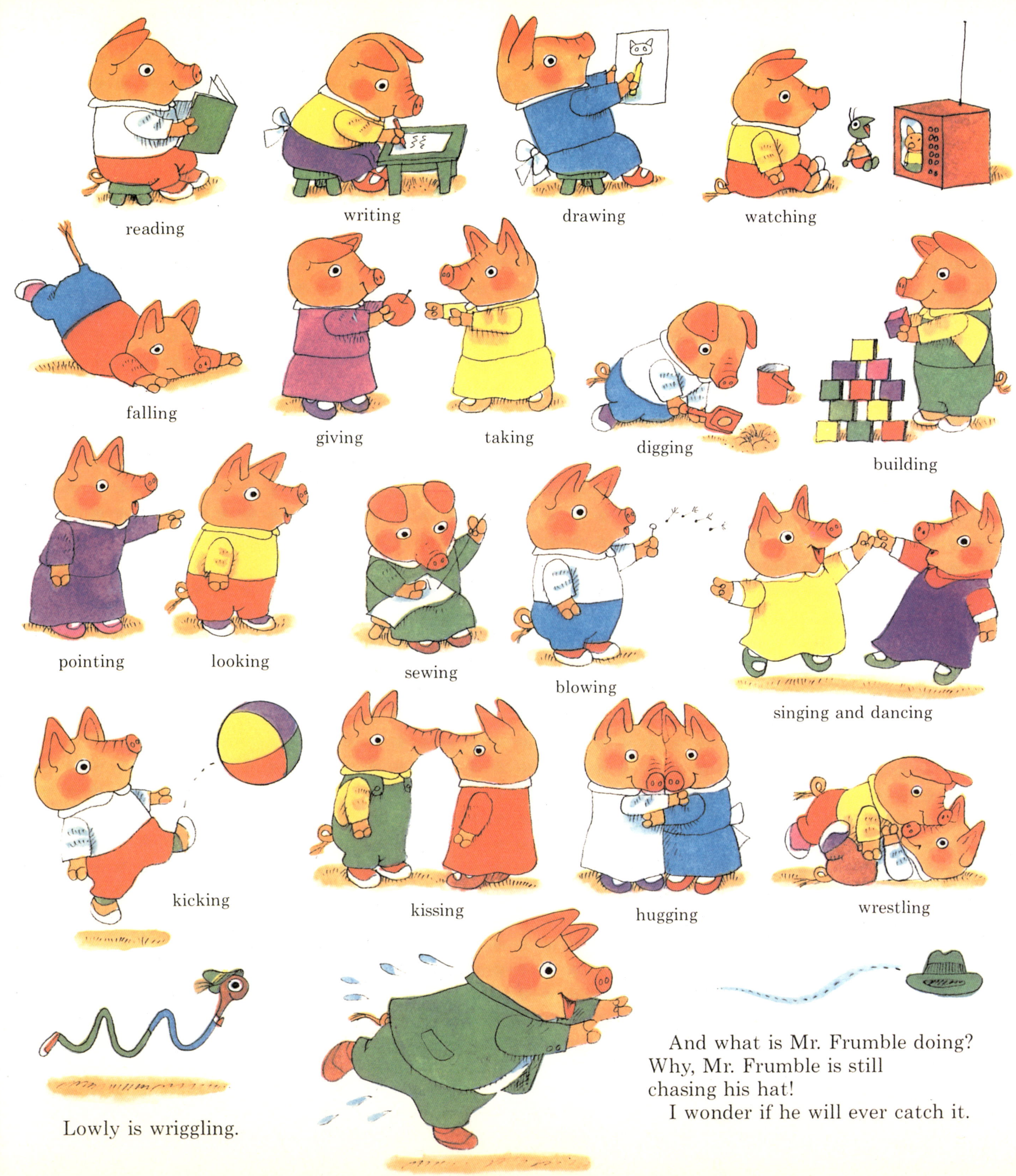

Lowly is wriggling.

And what is Mr. Frumble doing? Why, Mr. Frumble is still chasing his hat!
I wonder if he will ever catch it.

Soon it is crossing the wide ocean.
There is no land in sight.
Just look at all the things that
happen on an ocean-going ship!

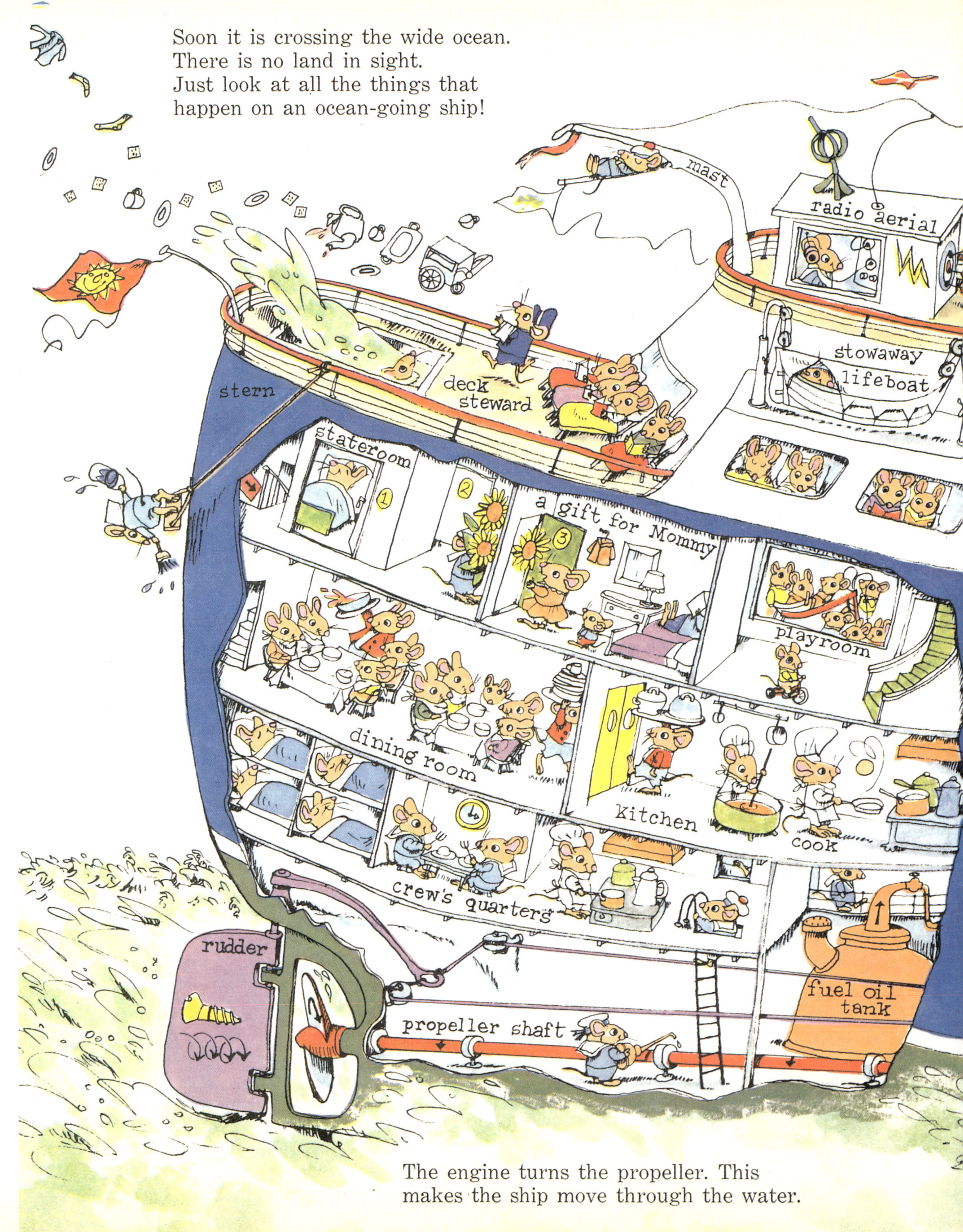

The engine turns the propeller. This
makes the ship move through the water.

Captain Salty and the crew work hard. They want all the passengers to have a safe and pleasant journey.

Captain Salty lets the engineer in the engine room know when he wants the ship to go fast
—or go slow
—or stop.

The helmsman steers the ship from the wheelhouse.

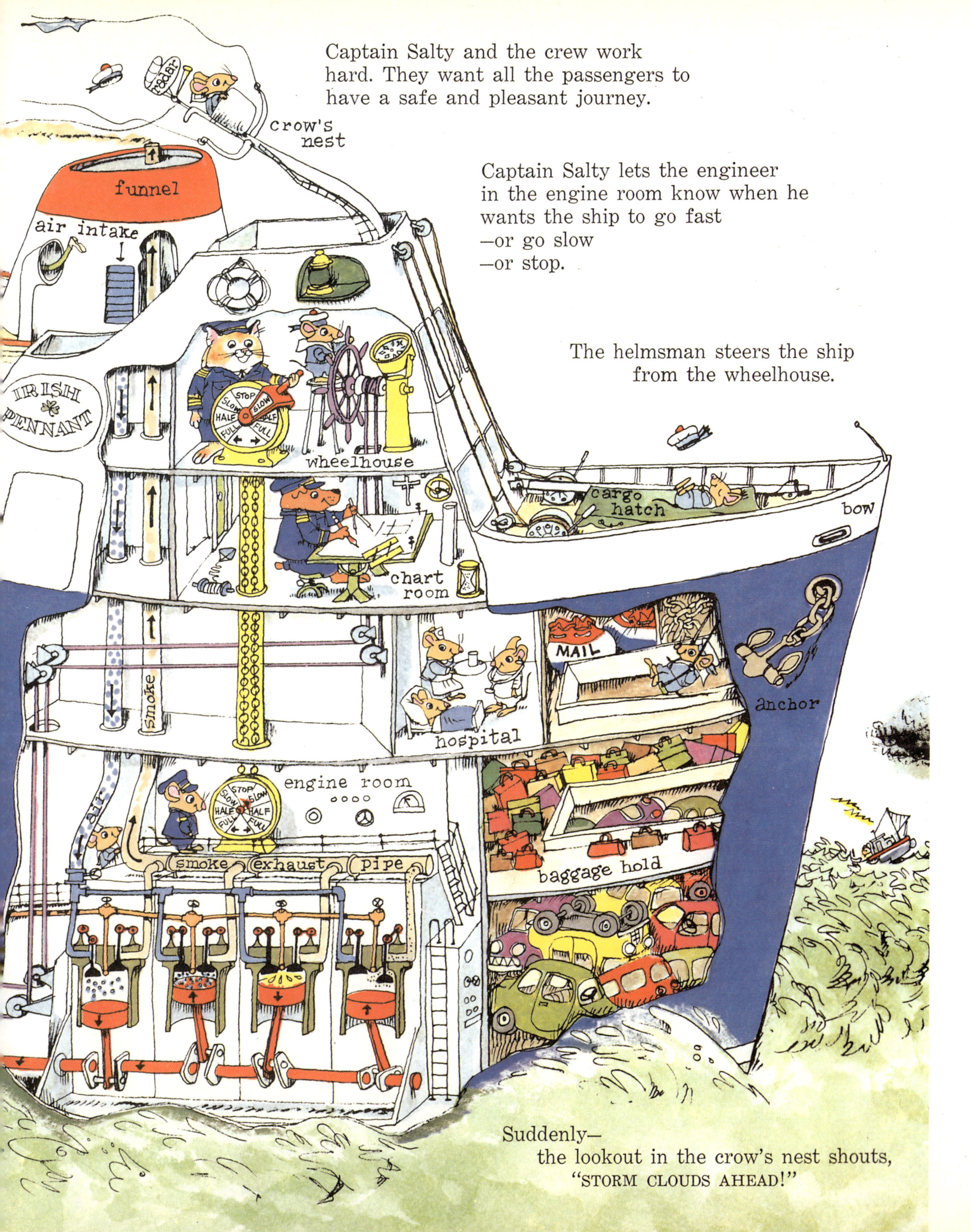

Suddenly—
the lookout in the crow's nest shouts,
"STORM CLOUDS AHEAD!"

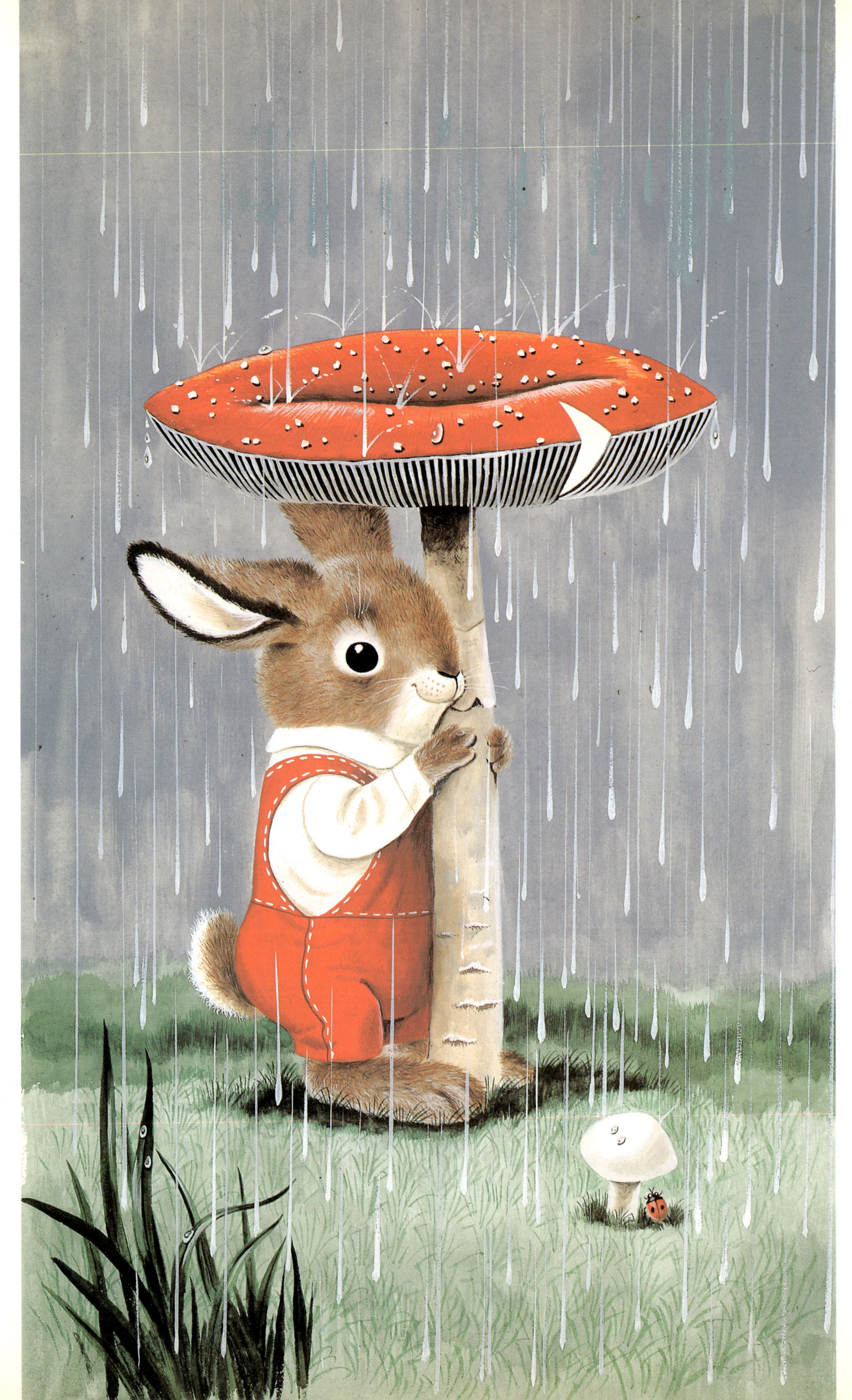

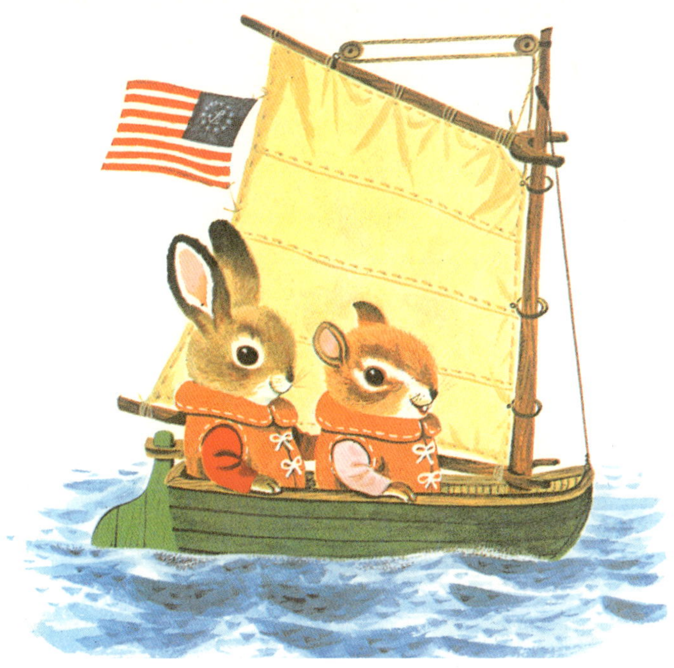

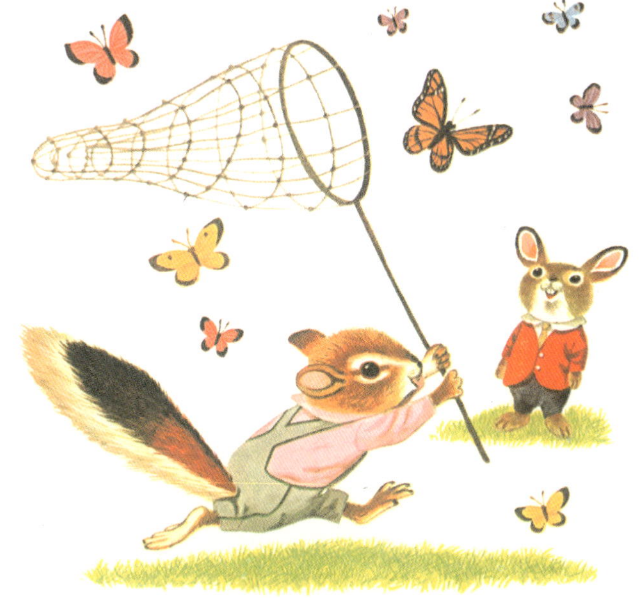

Scarry painted the art for *I Am a Bunny* (opposite), and the two illustrations above from *Chipmunk's ABC,* in full color, a different technique from that used in most of his later, big books, which were drawn in line with the color filled in later.

THE SCARRY TECHNIQUE: FROM FULL-COLOR PAINTING TO BLUEBOARDS

In the first books Richard Scarry illustrated for Artists and Writers, he painted in full color. However, by the time he created his first big book, *Richard Scarry's Best Word Book Ever,* Western Printing had devised another method for creating what looked to be full-color art. It was called blueboarding. In using this technique, the artist first draws the black line art for the whole book on sheets of acetate large enough to contain two facing pages. In Dick's case, he drew the line for *Best Word Boook Ever* with a pen, but in his later books he drew with a pencil on frosted acetate. He felt that a pen created a stiff, scratchy line, whereas a pencil allowed for more shading, and it didn't slip on the acetate. He said he could model either delicately or darkly with a pencil. The engraver photographed the black-line drawings on transparent acetate and produced a film positive. Then, by a chemical process, the film positive was used to print the black line drawings in blue on an illustration board. The result was called a blueboard.

As soon as Dick received the blueboards, he would start painting in the colors, using a water-based paint. He painted through the entire book, color by color. That is, first he would paint in everything that was to be red. Then the blue, and so on. This method made for more consistent color, and it also saved a great deal of time because the artist didn't have to mix up a lot of different colors at the same time. Because the blue lines on the boards would be picked up along with the other colors when the boards were photographed for printing, Dick painted over them. When-

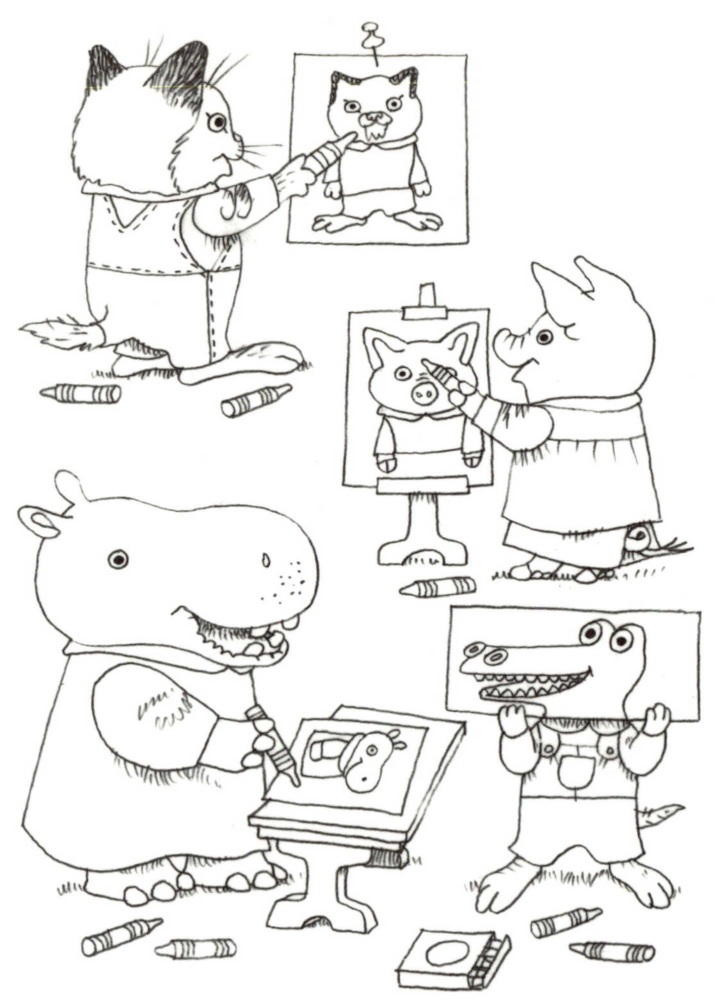

Original black line drawing

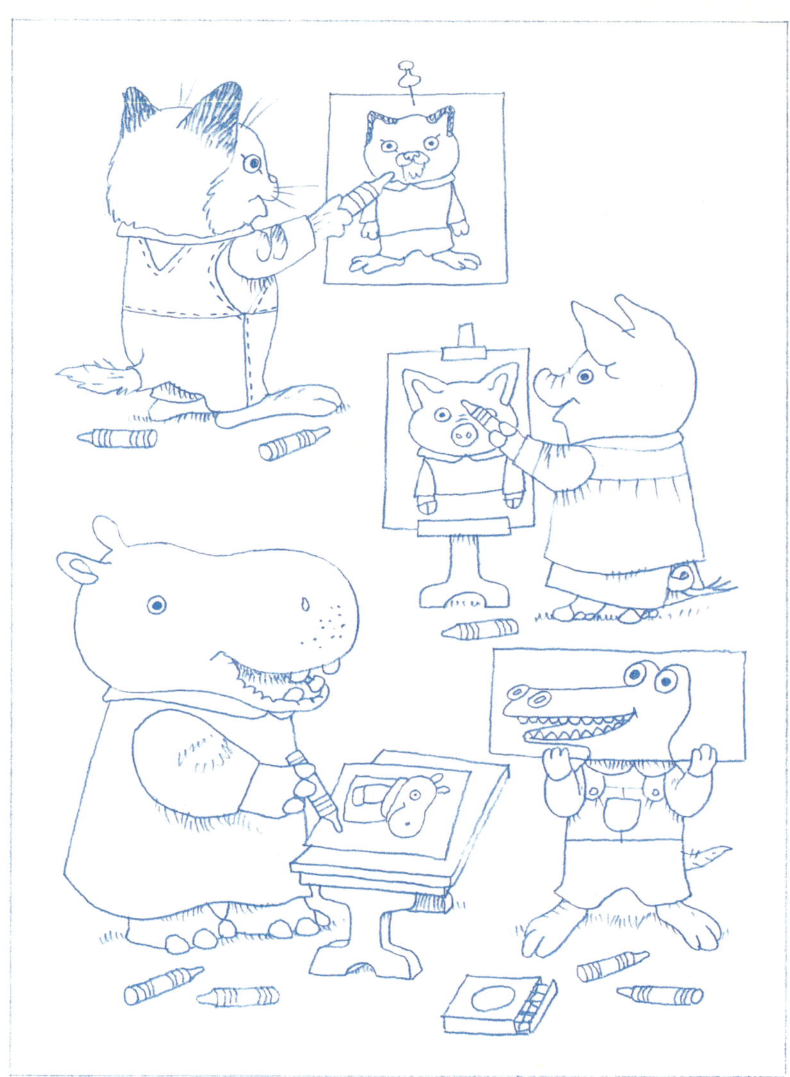

Blueboard

ever he wanted to see what the printed color would look like when combined with the black line, he put the film positive containing the black line over the colored-in blueboard. Immediately he could see how the printed art would look in the book.

Western Printing originally devised this technique in order to save money. They could prepare three-color camera separations for printing rather than using four colors. This saved time and materials in preparation for printing, and simplified the printing itself. Dick liked the technique for a different reason. He felt that it kept his black lines clean in the printed versions because the lines were always laid down as a pure black, not, as was usual in printing, a mixture of four colors. Dick also preferred a special red ink when the book was actually being printed. The publisher's production department had to make sure that before the book went on press the printer had an adequate supply of this special ink, which everyone called "Scarry red."

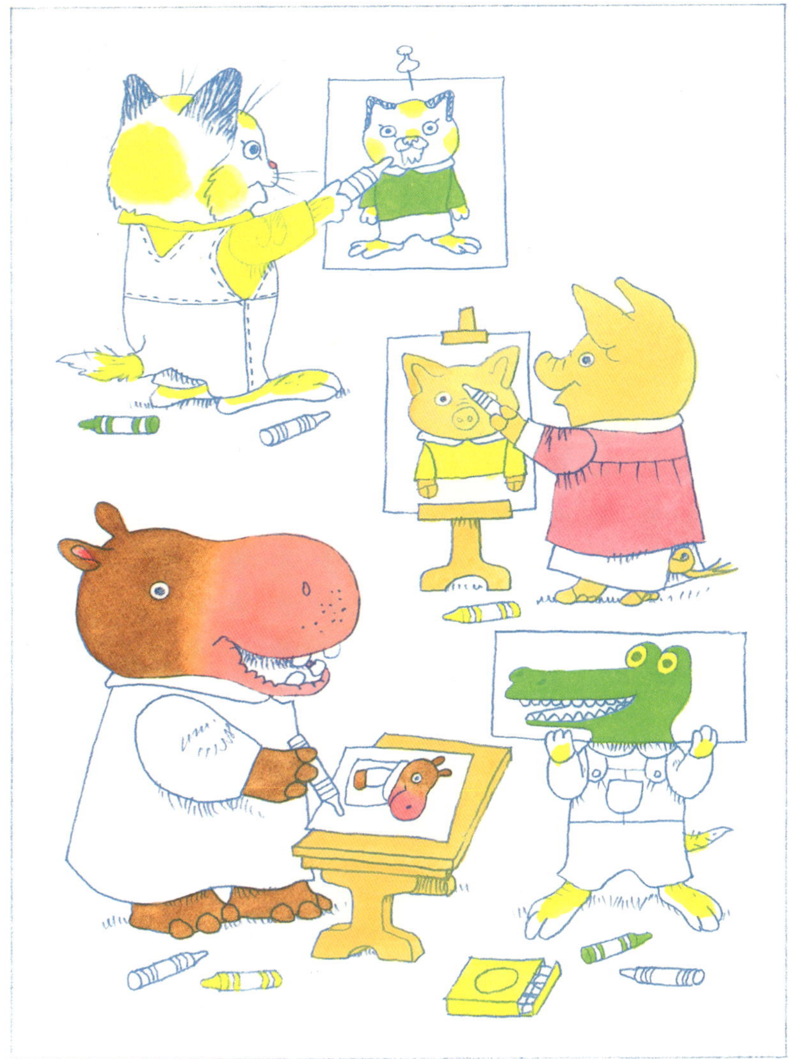

Blueboard with color partly painted in

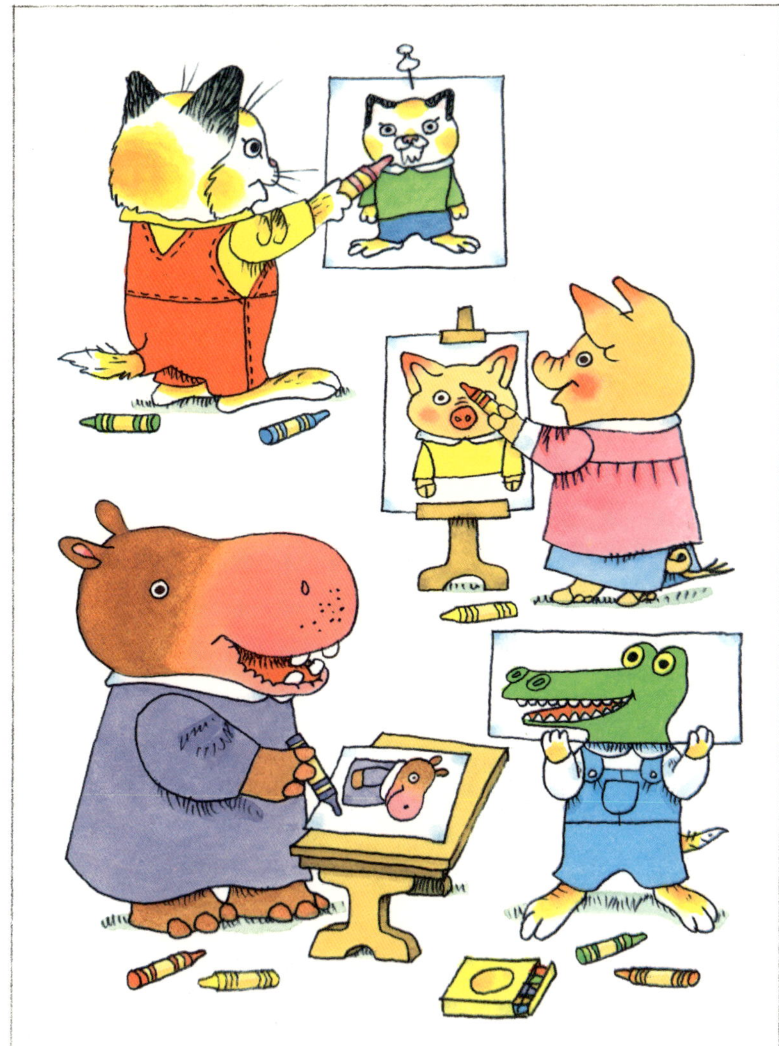

Blueboard with black line overlay

This sequence shows Scarry's technique for producing finished art for publication. He once wrote some notes on how he worked, and listed the colors he preferred:

"I use Winsor & Newton Designers Colors, this is a simple palette and bright. The method I use is to paint all the objects I know will be red, and go through the book with red. Then I do all the yellow objects, then blue, etc. Then all the pigs, cats, dogs, etc. I then return and paint those objects that couldn't be decided on as to color. This method elminiates switching from one color to another and hence is a great time saver.

No modelling is necessary except in the case of pig's cheeks and some animals' fur. Of course in some instances it might be desirable to add a touch of darker color for a fold in clothing, or leaves in trees.

The colors are as follows:

Flame Red
Carthamus Pink
Cadmium Orange
Cadmium Primrose (Yellow)
Golden Yellow
Linden Green
Permanent Green Middle
Permanent Green Deep
Winsor Green
Sky Blue
Winsor Blue
Burnt Sienna
Raw Umber
Burnt Umber
Chinese Orange
Spektrum Violet

teeny tiny TALES

$1.00
10670

16 tiny Golden Shape Books • 128 pages all in full color • by Richard Scarry

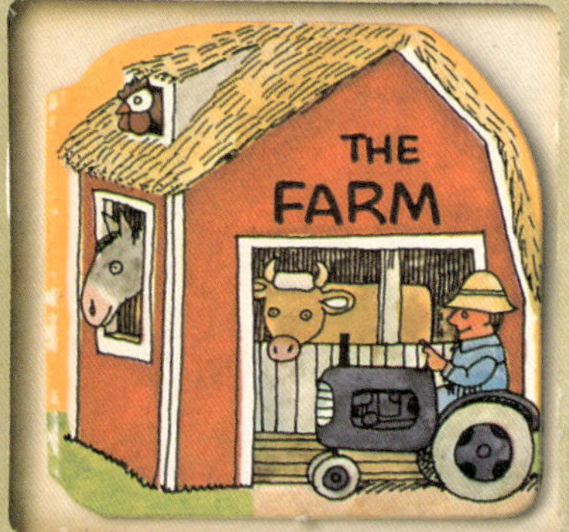

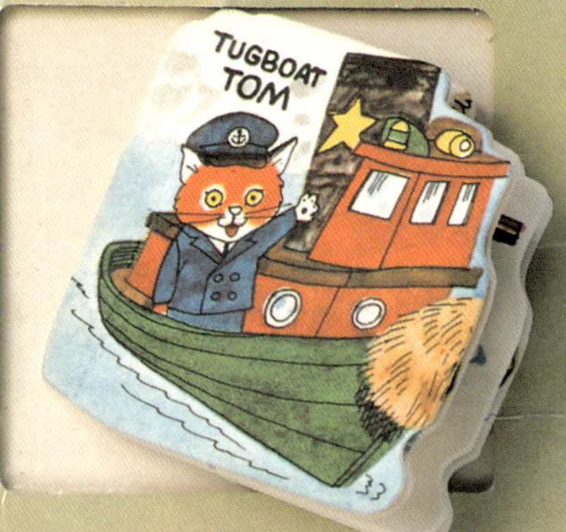

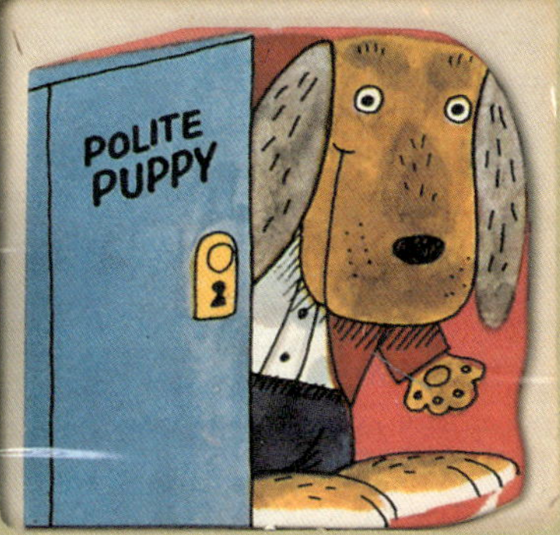

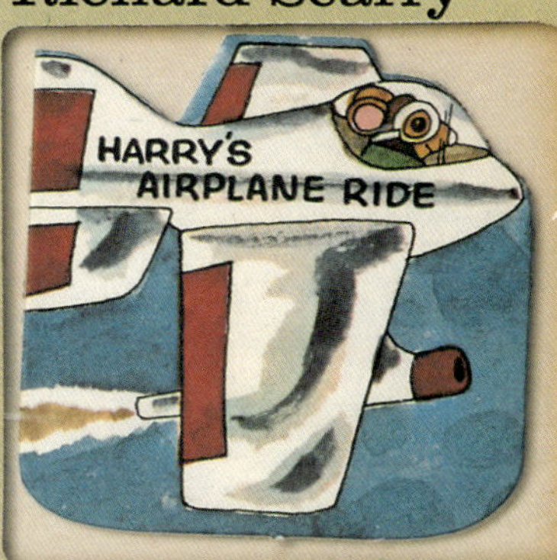

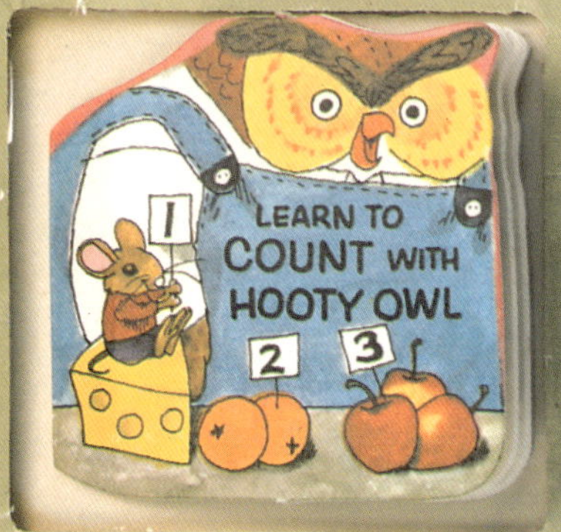

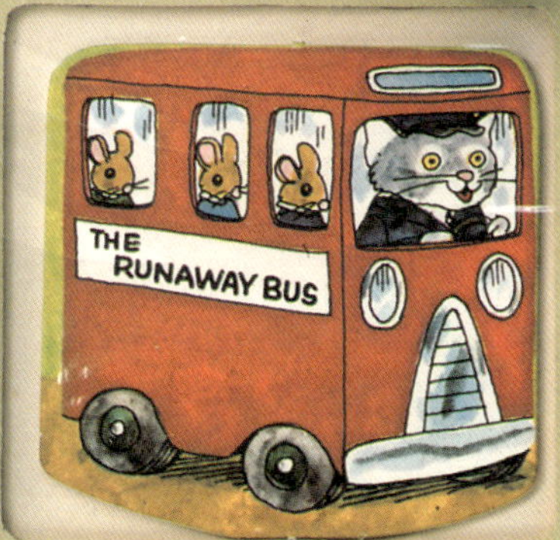

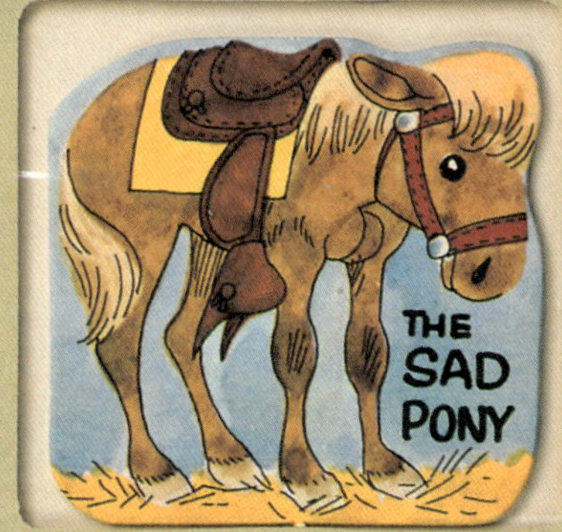

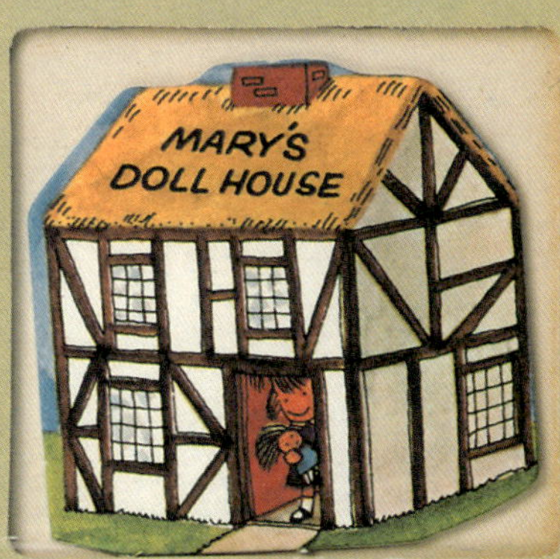

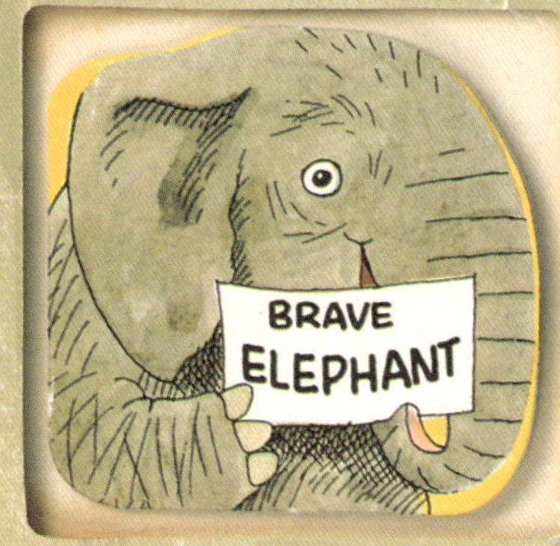

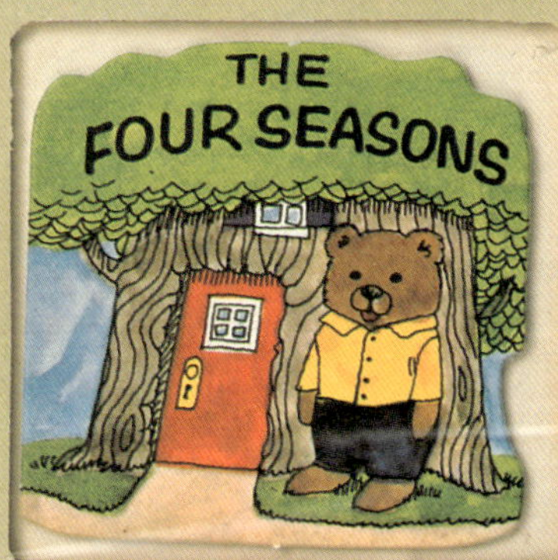

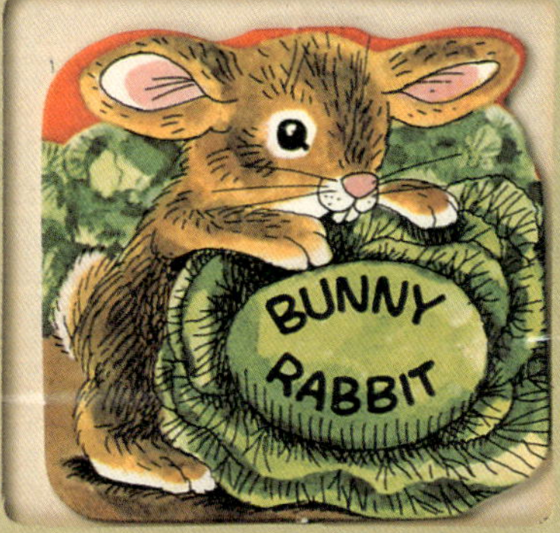

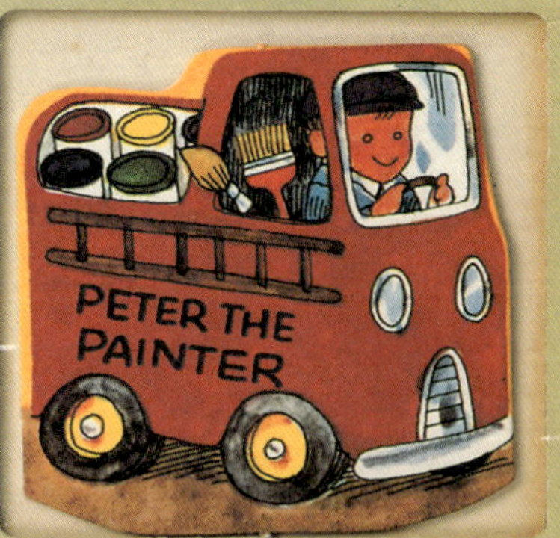

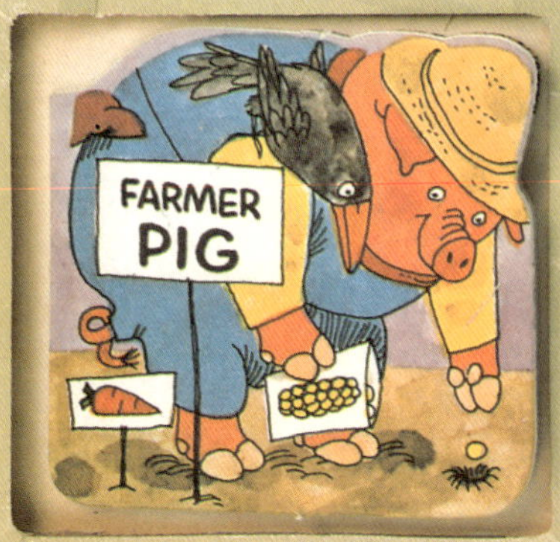

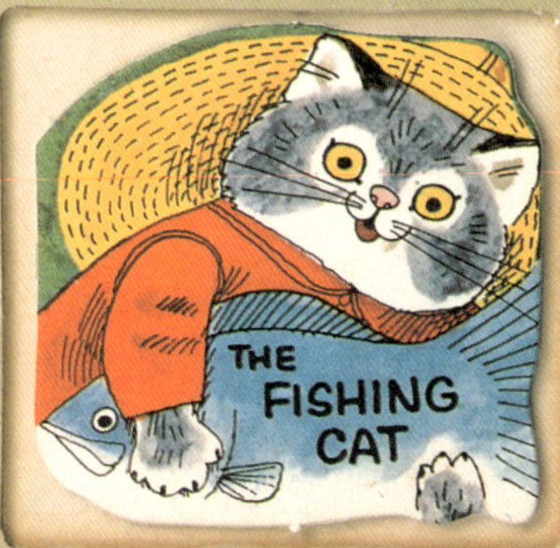

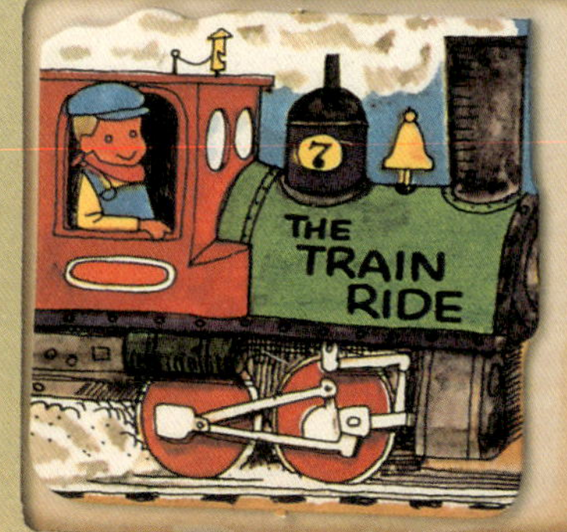

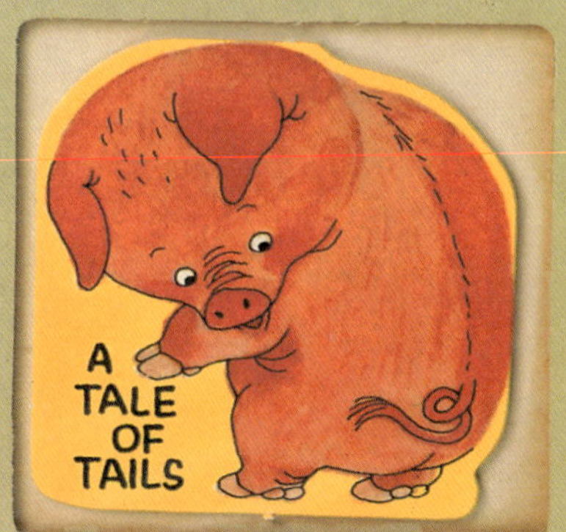

GOLDEN PRESS 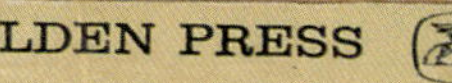

Published by Golden Press, Inc., New York. Printed in U.S.A.

SPECIAL FORMATS & NOVELTY BOOKS

Because Dick loved creating new books so much and, because he was such a disciplined, hard-working author-artist, publishers sometimes found it difficult to keep him busy with book projects that wouldn't compete with one another in book stores. A single big oversized picture book was usually enough to publish in any one year. But this would not have kept Scarry busy or creatively satisfied. As a result, his publishers were constantly searching for other kinds of formats for him to work with.

In the early sixties, Western Printing came up with a scheme for publishing sixteen tiny full-color picture books placed in sixteen small slots on a heavy cardboard backing. (This was called a frame tray.) The package was tightly shrink-wrapped in plastic so that the books would stay in place. The books themselves were printed on heavy stock and contained six pages with a short, short story, plus a front and back cover. The books measured approximately 2½ x 2½ inches and were die-cut in different decorative shapes to match the art on the cover. Golden Press published the books and the frame tray under the title of *Teeny Tiny Tales.* (Later, the frame tray was split in half to create two frame trays, each one containing eight titles. These were sold separately.) Dick was the kind of artist who could take an idea like this and make it completely his own. The books were charming and the stories, though brief, all made their point.

When Random House started a new line, called Picturebacks, they asked Dick to create two new titles for the very first list. The Picturebacks were thirty-two page, full-color paperback picture books eight inches square in format. Dick went right to work and created the *Please and Thank You Book* and *Find Your ABC's*, two of the best-selling titles in the series. At the publisher's request, he also designed a very clever series colophon, an identifying symbol, to go in the upper right-hand corner of the cover of each of the books. This was the sort of thing he could do with seemingly little effort.

Because Random House had had great success with its pop-up books, they asked Dick to create one featuring his familiar characters from Busytown. Working with designs given to him by a paper engineer, Dick worked out a story that would make use of the three-dimensional effects of a pop-up book with movable parts, including

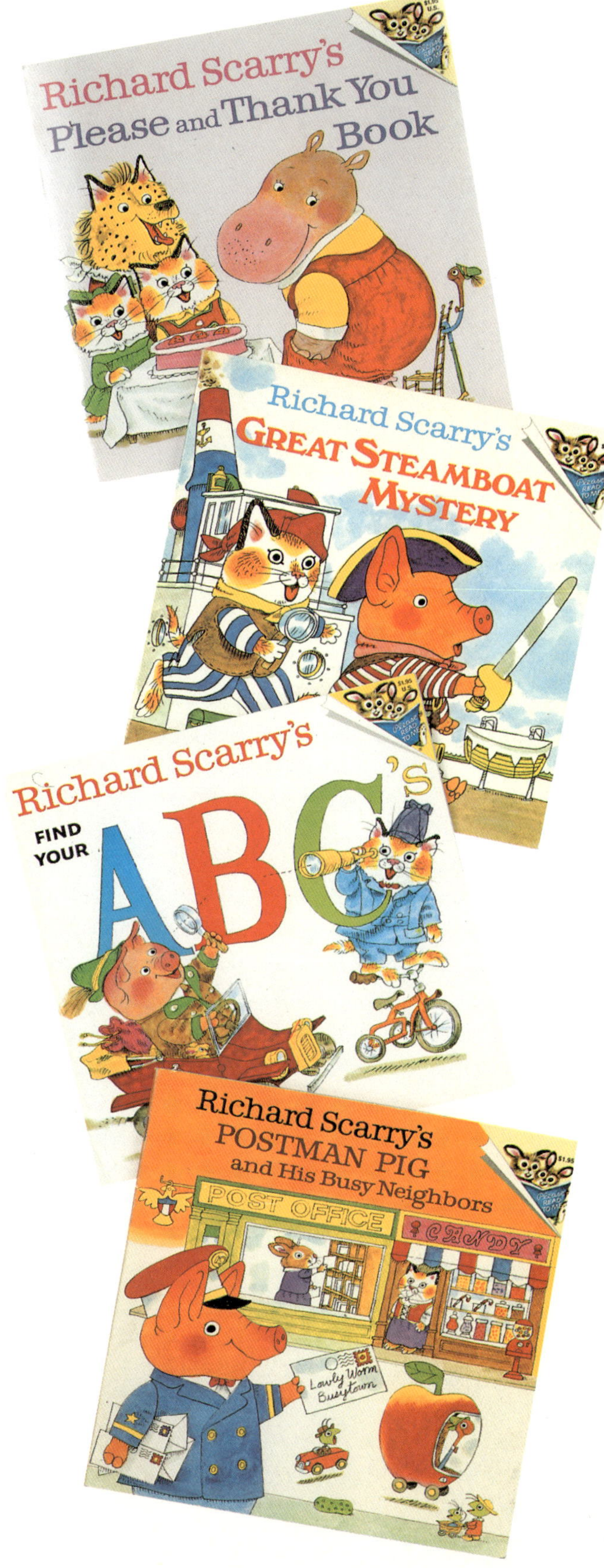

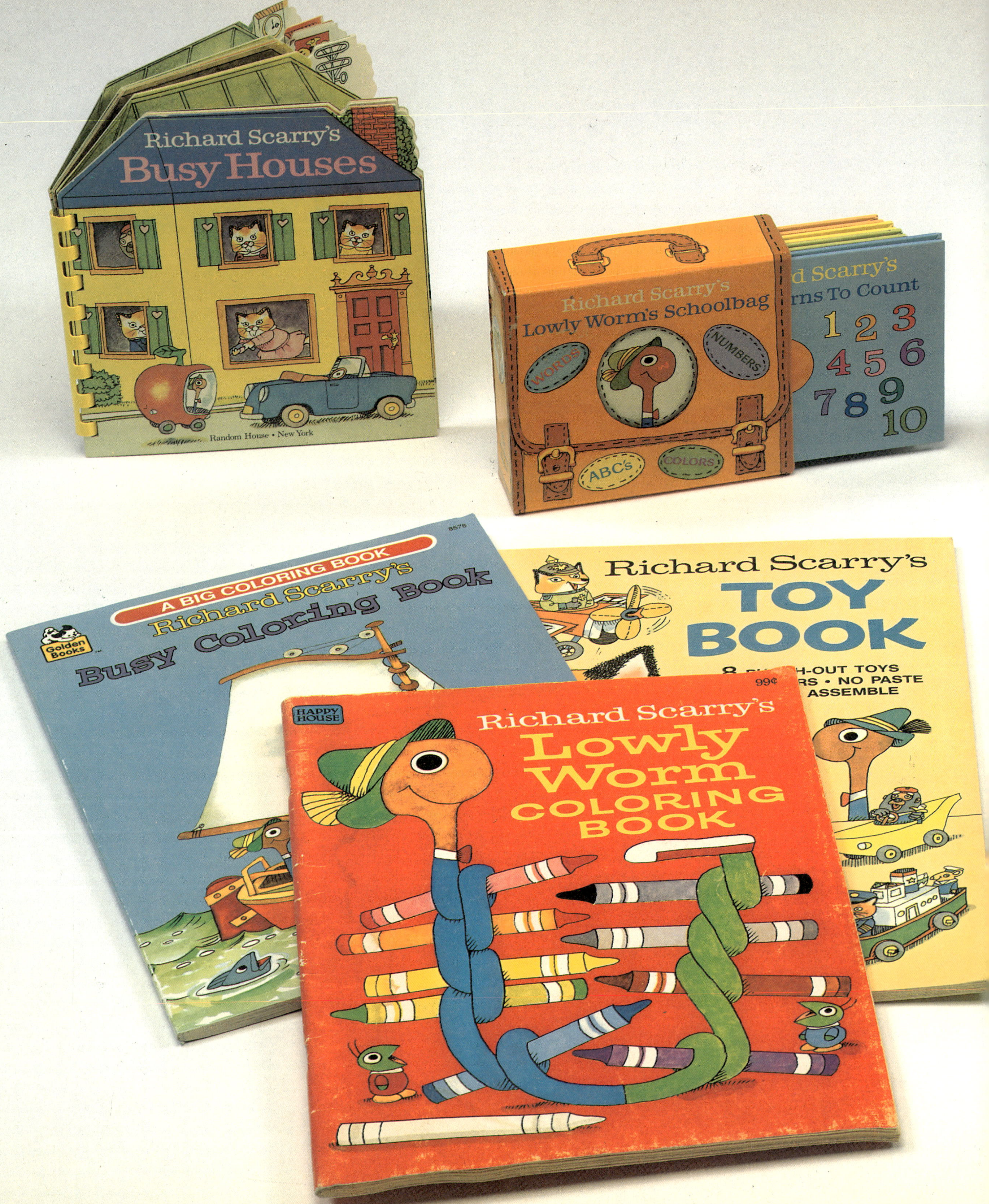

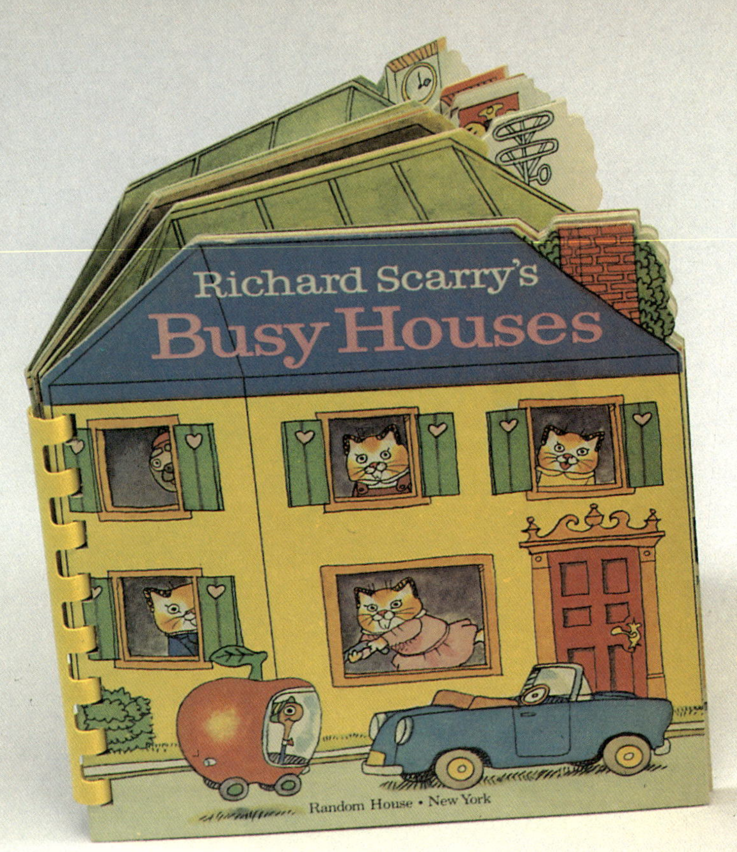
Richard Scarry's
Busy Houses
Random House • New York

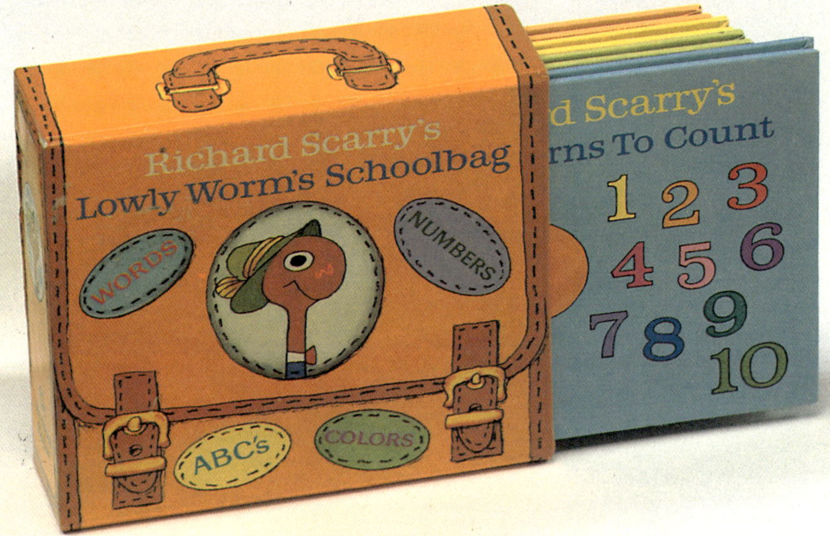
Richard Scarry's
Lowly Worm's Schoolbag
WORDS
NUMBERS
ABC's
COLORS
1 2 3
4 5 6
7 8 9
10

8578
A BIG COLORING BOOK
Richard Scarry's
Busy Coloring Book
Golden Books
Richard Scarry's
TOY
BOOK
ASSEMBLE
HAPPY HOUSE
99¢
Richard Scarry's
Lowly
Worm
COLORING
BOOK

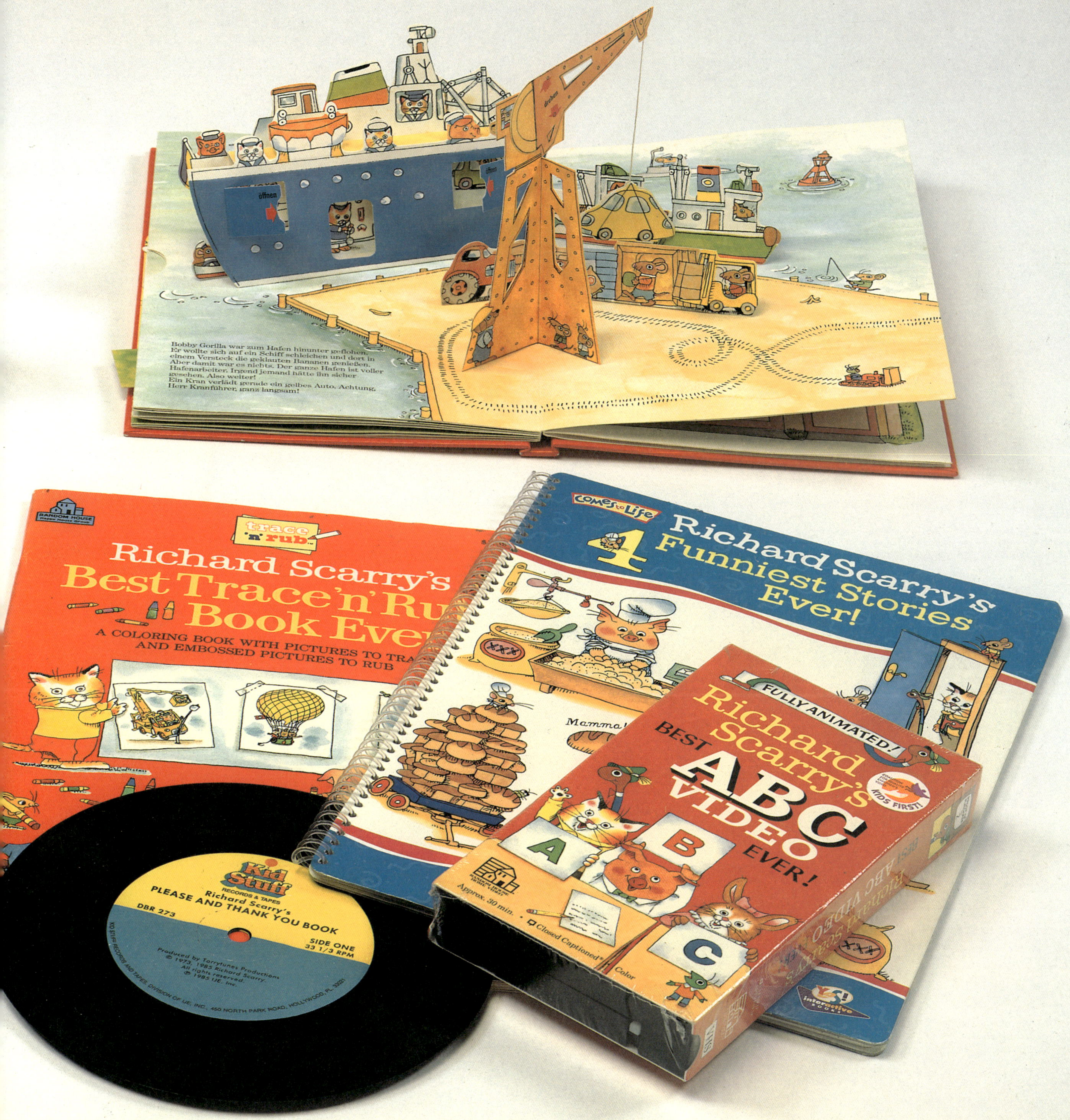

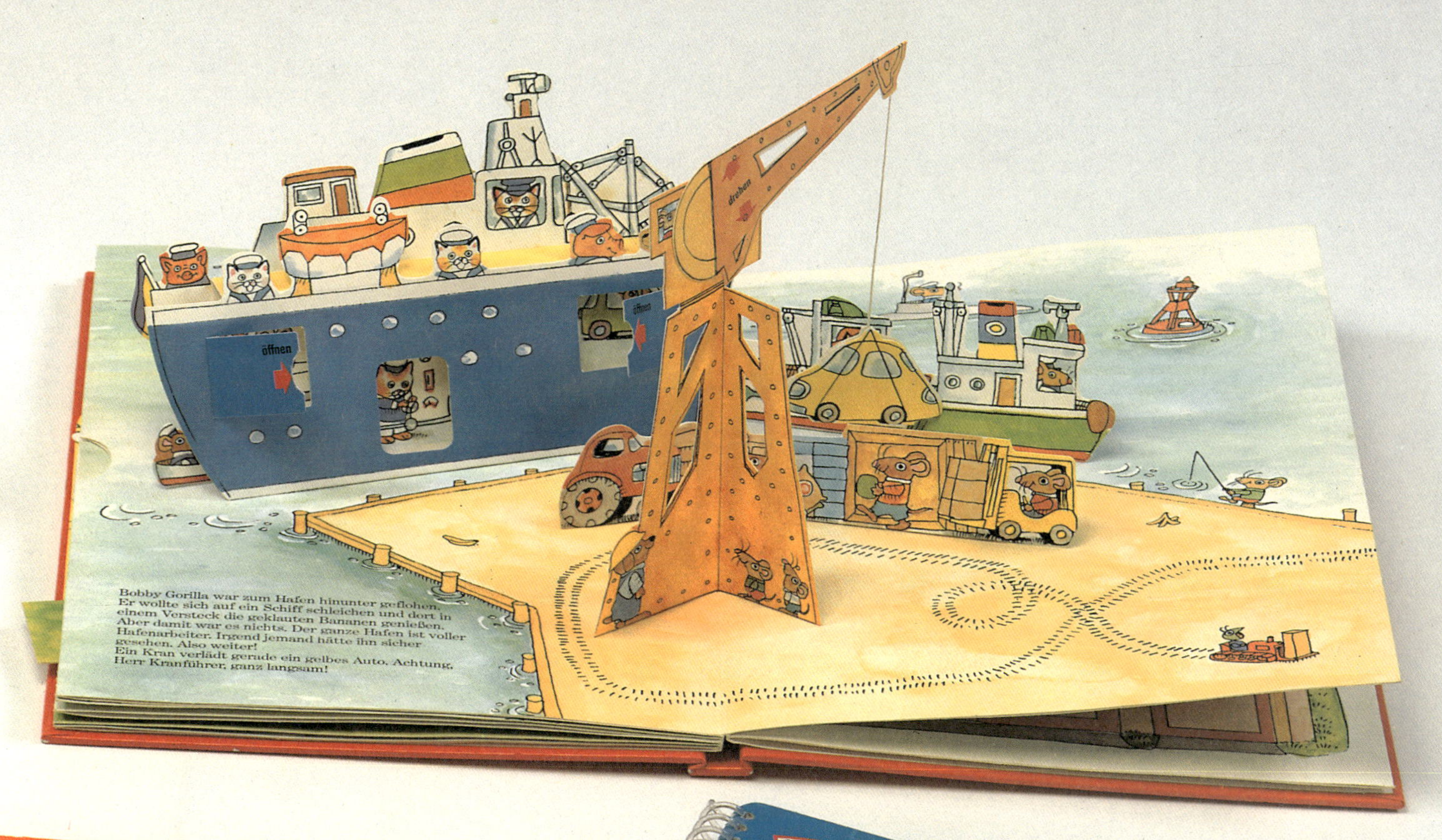
öffnen
Bobby Gorilla war zum Hafen hinunter geflohen.
Er wollte sich auf ein Schiff schleichen und dort in
einem Versteck die geklauten Bananen genießen.
Aber damit war es nichts. Der ganze Hafen ist voller
Hafenarbeiter. Irgend jemand hätte ihn sicher
gesehen. Also weiter!
Ein Kran verlädt gerade ein gelbes Auto. Achtung,
Herr Kranführer, ganz langsam!

trace 'n' rub
Richard Scarry's
Best Trace'n'Ru
Book Eve
A COLORING BOOK WITH PICTURES TO TRA
AND EMBOSSED PICTURES TO RUB
Comes to Life
Richard Scarry's
4 Funniest Stories
Ever!
Mamma
FULLY ANIMATED!
Richard
Scarry's
BEST
ABC
VIDEO
EVER!
KIDS FIRST!
A
B
C
Approx. 30 min.
Closed Captioned
Color
Kid Stuff
RECORDS & TAPES
Richard Scarry's
PLEASE AND THANK YOU BOOK
DBR 273
SIDE ONE
33 1/3 RPM

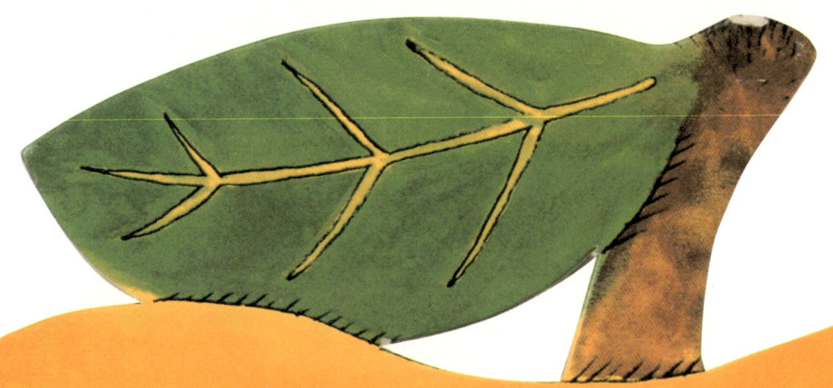

Richard Scarry's

LOWLY WORM

Car and Truck Book

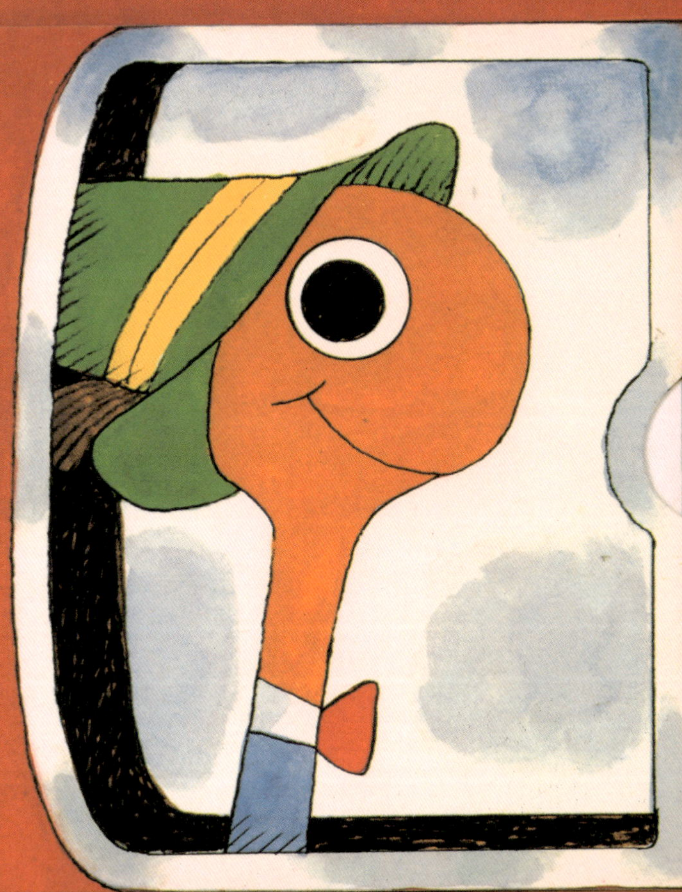

Random House

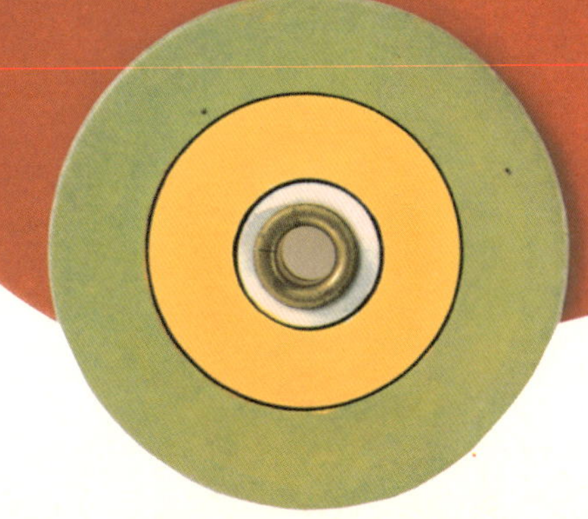

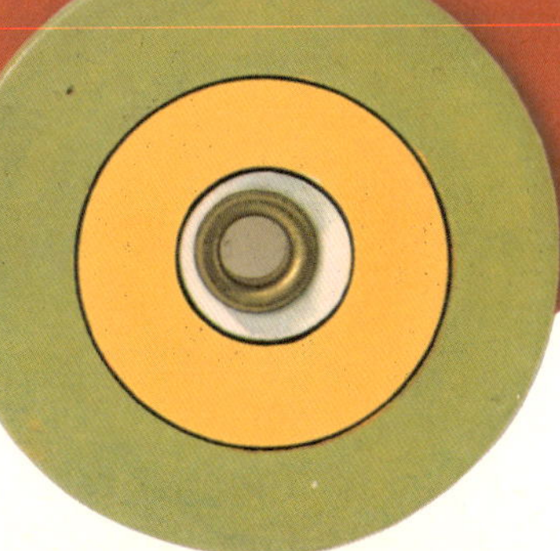

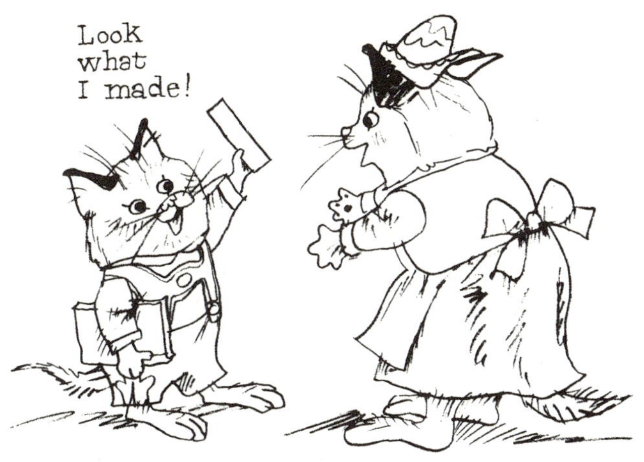

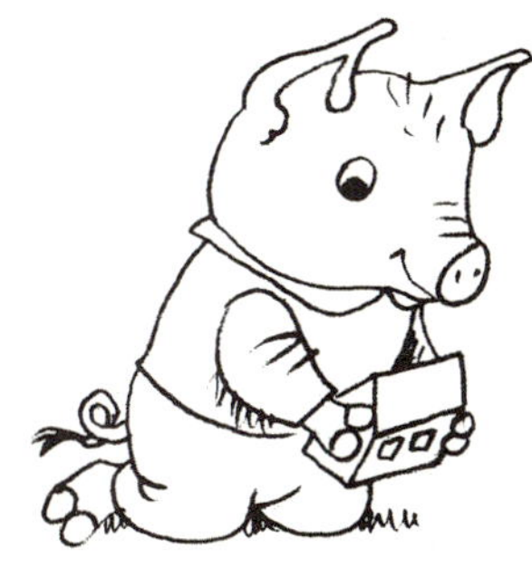

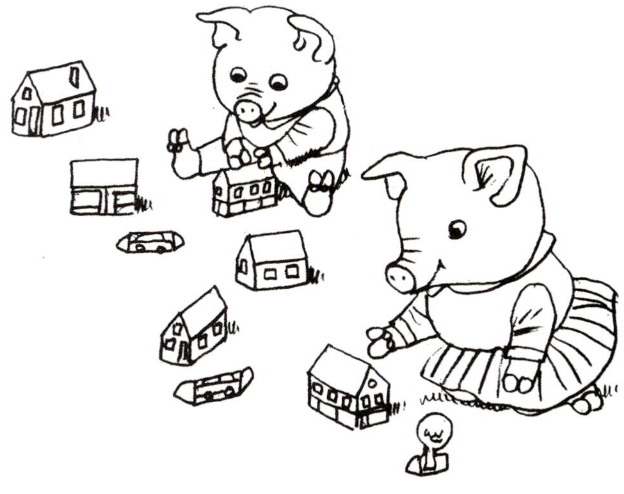

characters and objects that would stand out from the pages or move when tabs were pushed or pulled. In one of the situations, he used Lowly Worm as an arrow that actually moved across two pages. Whatever challenge the publishers threw at him, Dick seemed able to meet it. He even created a *Lowly Worm Car and Truck Book* in the shape of an apple, with wheels that actually turned, so a child could roll the book along on the floor.

When activity books became especially popular, Dick created both the *Best Rainy Day Book Ever* and the *Best Make-It Book Ever* with the assistance of Random House children's book editors. During the book's preparation, these editors could often be seen standing in the office hallways trying out paper airplanes and other objects that Dick designed for young readers to put together.

Board books, fragrance books, books with holes die-cut through the pages, all seemed to become something special when Scarry went to work on the concept. They also sold in large quantities in the stores without competing with his major titles.

Drawings from *Best Rainy Day Book Ever*

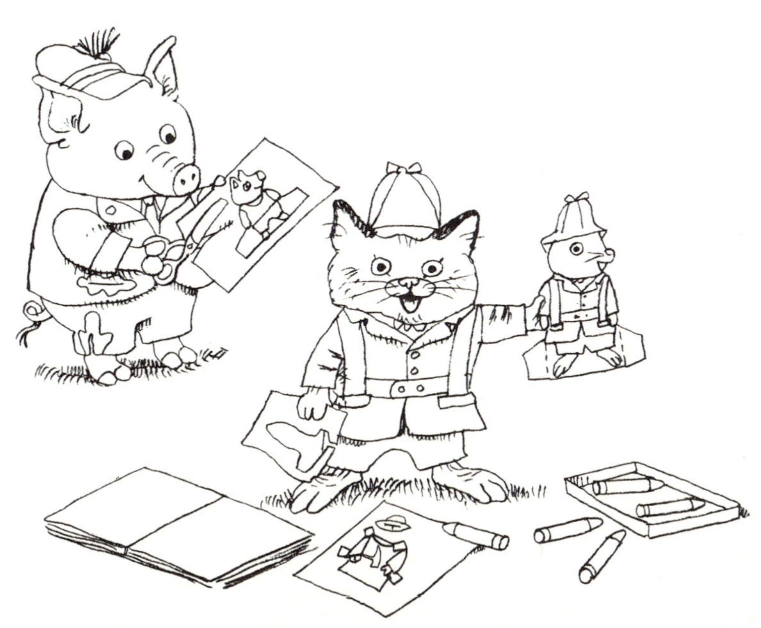

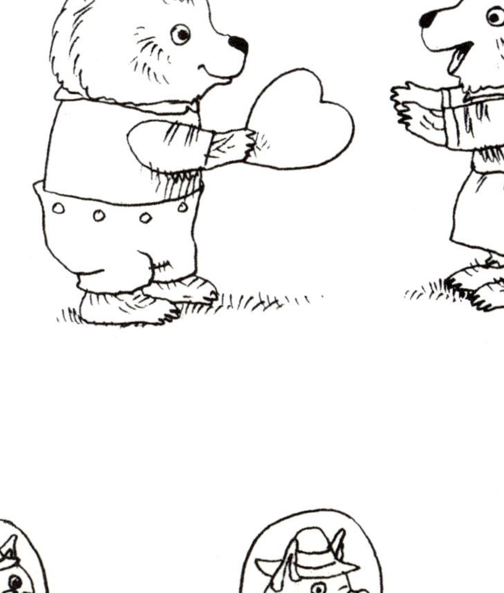

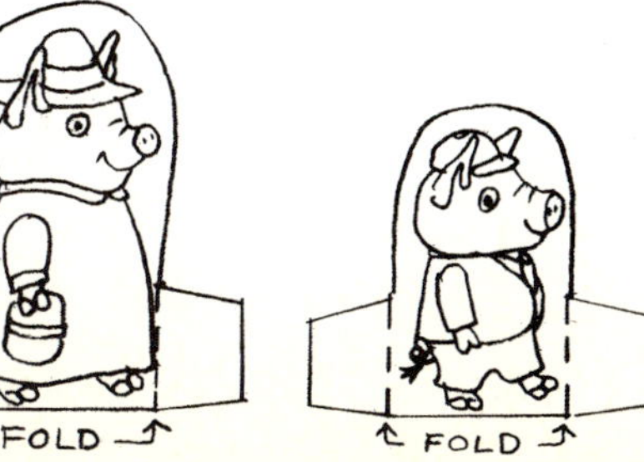

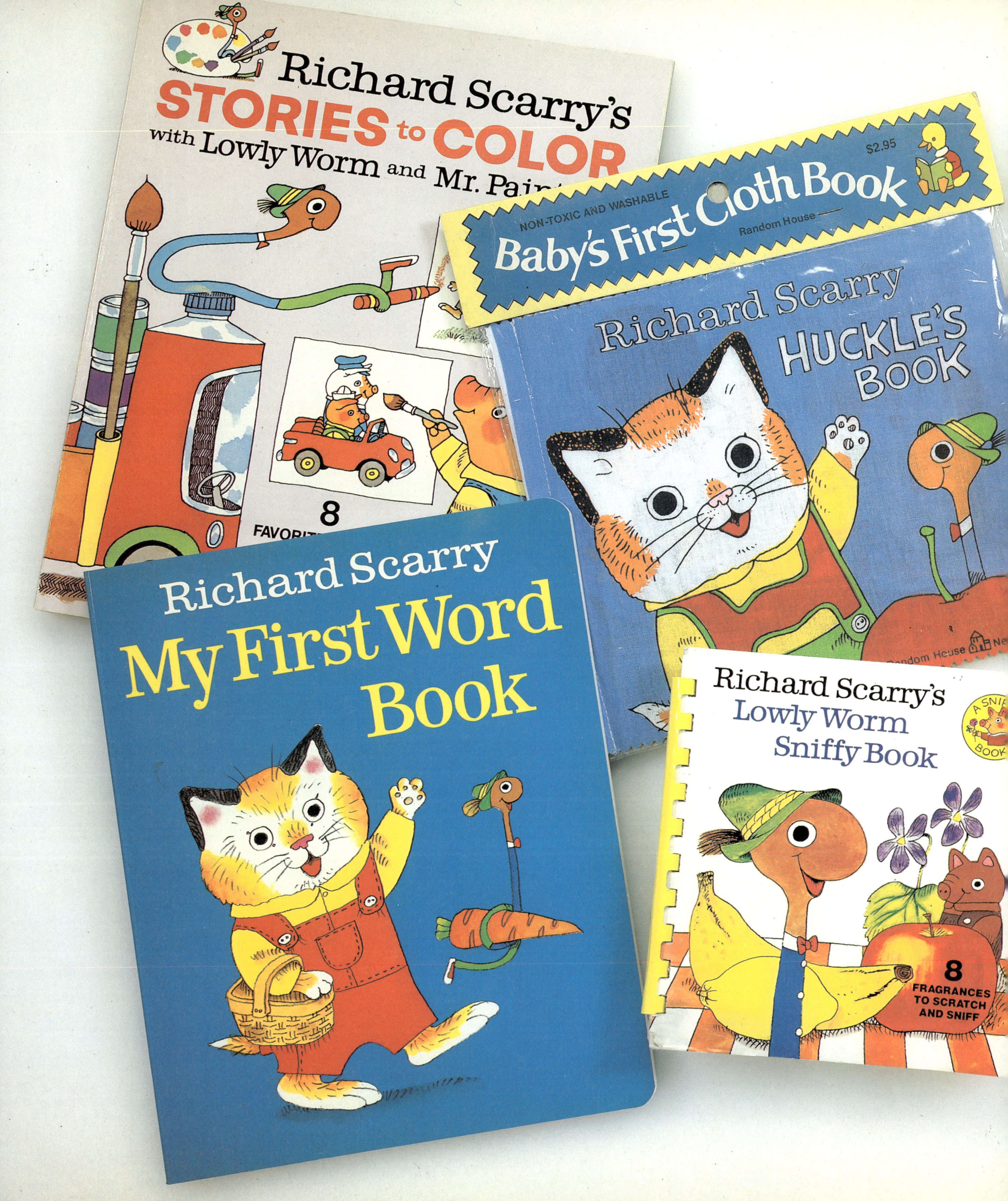
Richard Scarry's
STORIES to COLOR
with Lowly Worm and Mr. Pain
8
FAVORIT
$2.95
NON-TOXIC AND WASHABLE
Baby's First Cloth Book
Random House
Richard Scarry
HUCKLE'S BOOK
Richard Scarry
My First Word Book
Richard Scarry's
Lowly Worm
Sniffy Book
8
FRAGRANCES
TO SCRATCH
AND SNIFF

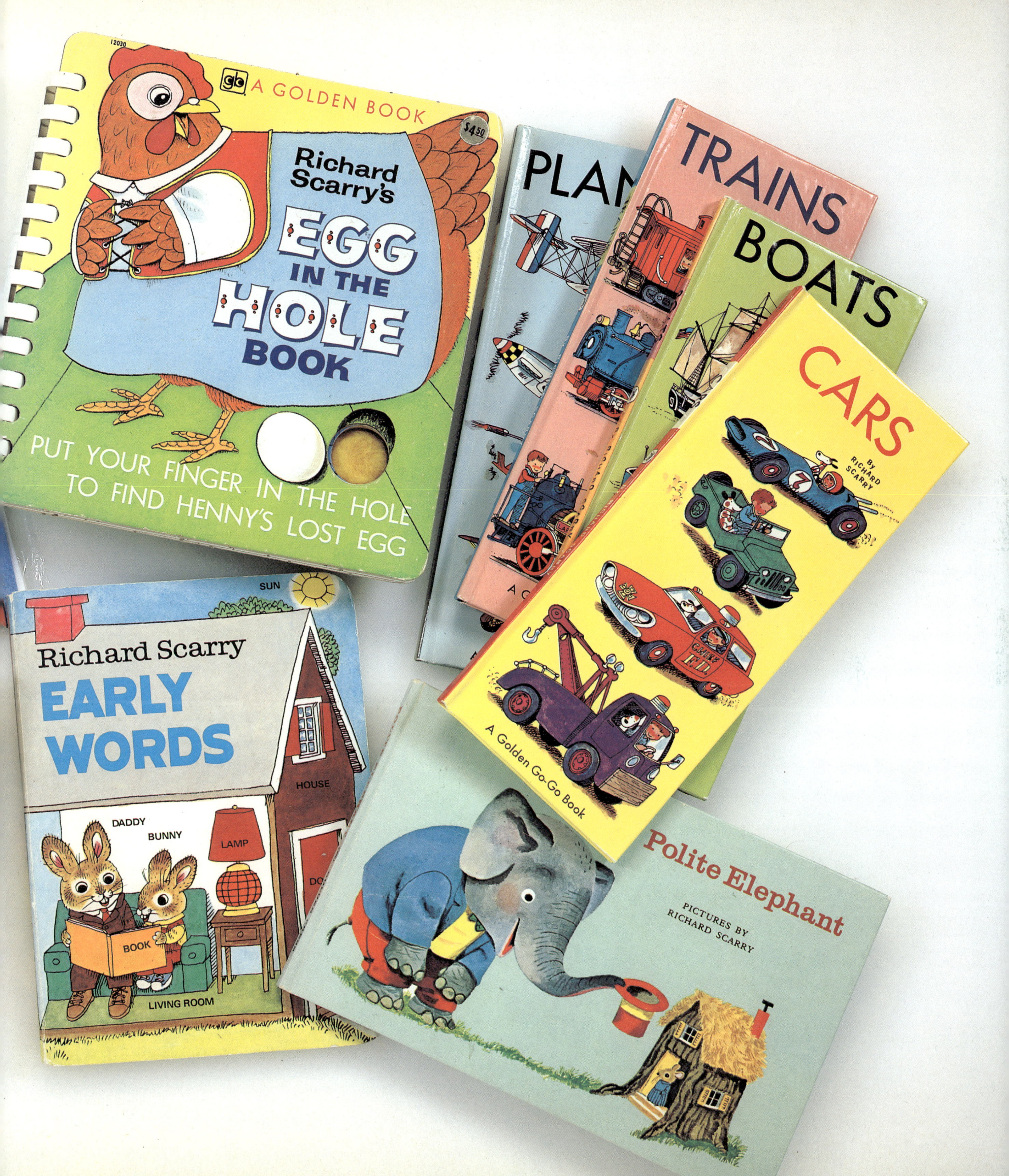

12030
A GOLDEN BOOK
$4.50
Richard Scarry's
EGG IN THE HOLE BOOK
PUT YOUR FINGER IN THE HOLE TO FIND HENNY'S LOST EGG
TRAINS
BOATS
CARS
By RICHARD SCARRY
A Golden Go-Go Book
SUN
Richard Scarry
EARLY WORDS
HOUSE
DADDY
BUNNY
LAMP
BOOK
LIVING ROOM
Polite Elephant
PICTURES BY RICHARD SCARRY

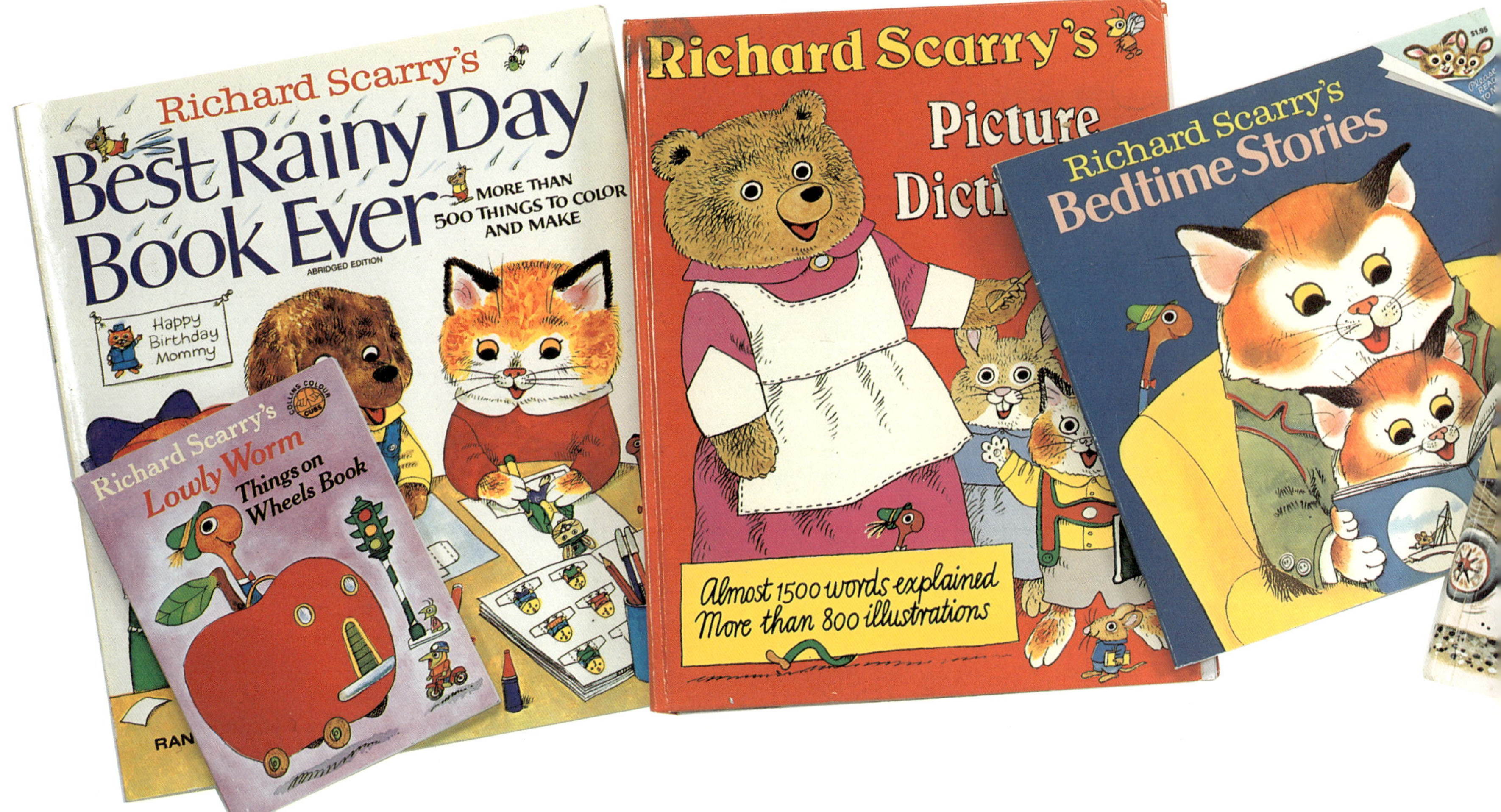

NEW BOOKS FROM OLD BOOKS

After Scarry left Western Printing and signed with Random House, the editors at Golden Press began looking through all the books he had created for them, trying to find a way to create some new titles by combining and reformatting work from older books. Their contracts with Scarry, up until the time he left, gave them sweeping rights to do anything they wished with his material. In the fall of 1968 Golden Press brought out a thick volume called *Richard Scarry's Best Storybook Ever.* This was created by pulling together material from a number of sources such as Little Golden Books, Shape Books, the *Teeny Tiny Tales* that he had created for the frame-tray assortment. Even the text and illustrations from *I Am a Bunny* were included. A great deal of the material had to be resized and reformatted.

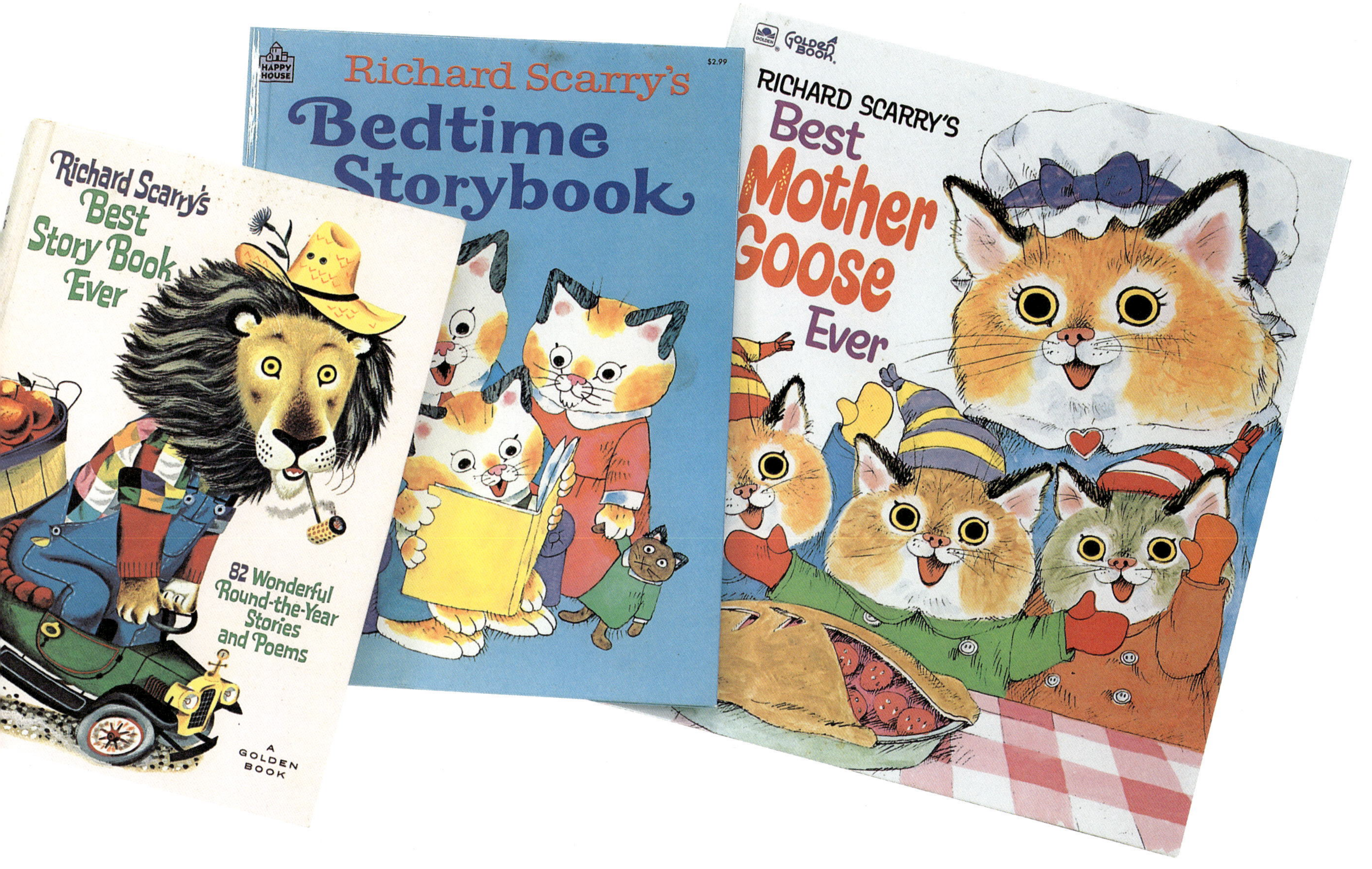

In 1967 Scarry had created a set of four small oblong picture books in a slipcase. The titles of the books were *Planes*, *Cars*, *Trains*, and *Boats*; and the overall name of the package was *My Golden Go-Go Library*. In 1974 Golden Press combined the four small books into one large volume called *Hop Aboard! Here We Go!* Again, the text and illustrations were resized and reformatted. This new, larger book sold very well, but as Western continued to pursue this practice, the book-buying public became somewhat confused, for Random House was issuing new Scarry material at the same time.

Later, after the Random House Picturebacks proved very successful, Golden produced a series of *Look-Look Books* in exactly the same format except that their books contained only twenty-four pages while the Random House books had thirty-two pages. By cutting up and reusing old Scarry material, the Golden Press editors managed to create ten new Scarry titles for their new paperback series.

Foreign publishers also frequently devised new formats for the Scarry books licensed to them by Random House and Western. In England, William Collins took material from *What Do People Do All Day?* and *The Great Big Schoolhouse*, and cut up the art and text to fit a small paperback format. These Collins Cubs, as they were called, sold extremely well in England and Australia; but when Random House tried to do the same thing, using the British films, the small books were not at all successful. Americans simply didn't take to such a format.

Other European publishers made similar changes, contending that a different kind of format would be more successful in their market. In most cases, Scarry was allowed to see the new formats and make any refinements he wished. By this time, he had become so important to their lists that they didn't want to offend him.

While he was still alive, the derived books and products captured some of Richard Scarry's interest, but he gave most of his attention to his new projects. Those books continued to be remarkably and consistently good, and to sell well. There is no doubt that his major, original picture books will continue to delight parents and children for years, for there has never been anyone quite like him in the realm of children's books.

Opposite: Scarry's *Biggest Word Book Ever!* measured a full twenty-four inches in height, taller than many of it's readers. Despite a price just under $30, making it the most expensive children's book of its day and one of the costliest ever, the book sold very well, was translated into several languages, and was taken by The Book-of-the Month Club.

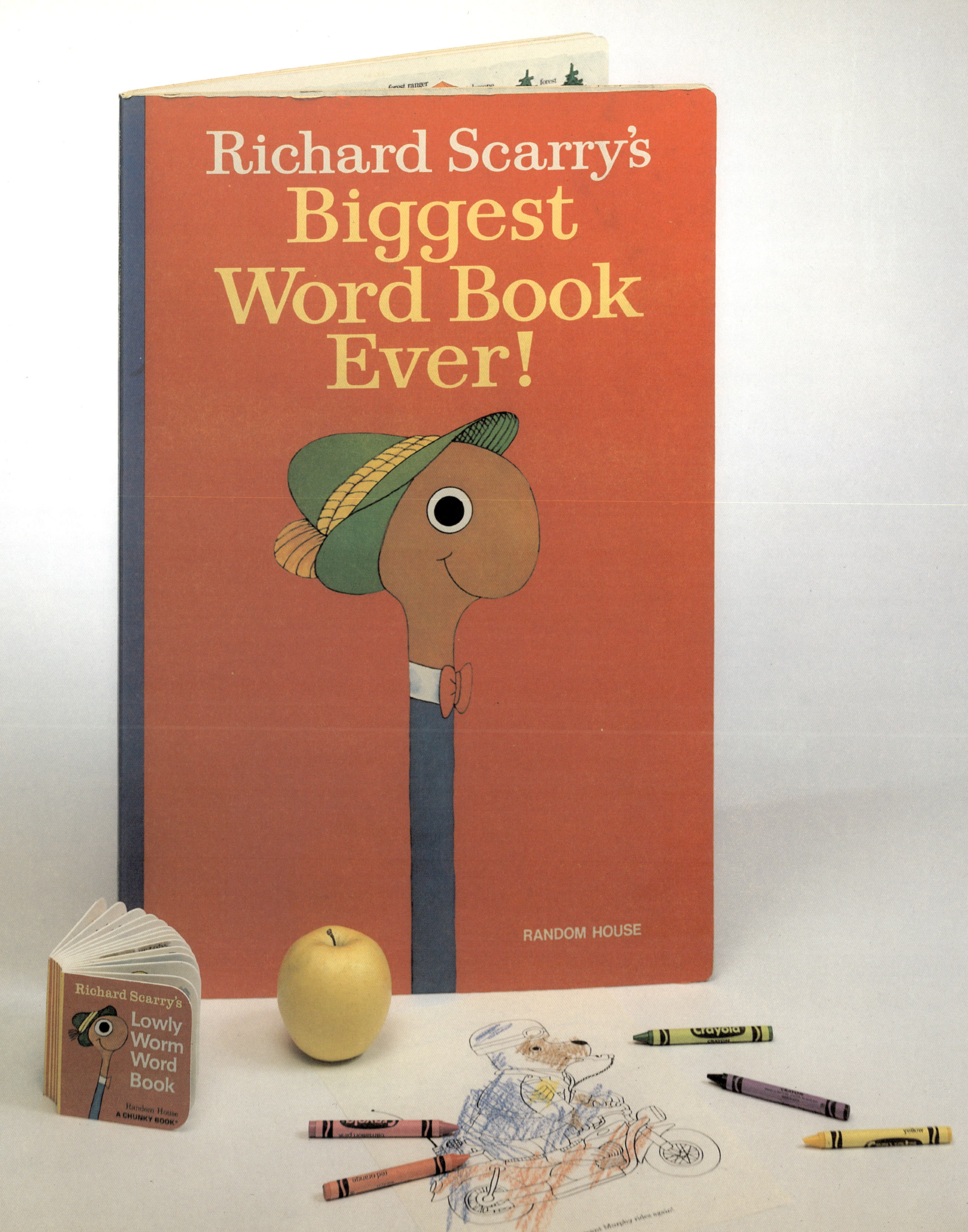

Richard Scarry's
Biggest
Word Book
Ever!
RANDOM HOUSE
Richard Scarry's
Lowly
Worm
Word
Book
Random House
A CHUNKY BOOK
Crayola
yellow

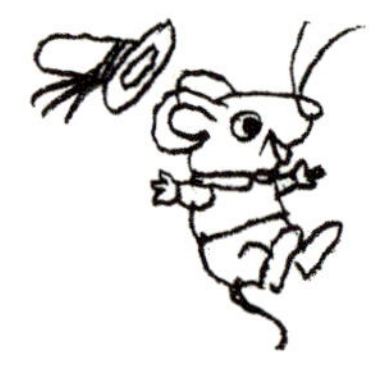

SELECTED WORKS AND PUBLICATION DATES

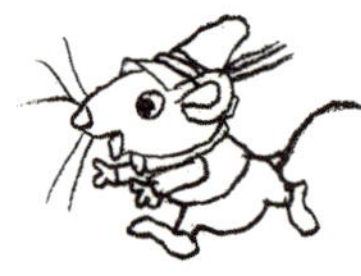

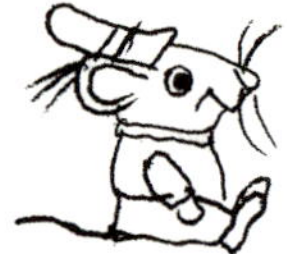

SELECTED LIST OF BOOKS ILLUSTRATED BY RICHARD SCARRY

(LGB indicates a Little Golden Book)

Mouse's House by Kathryn Jackson, Simon & Schuster, 1949
Two Little Miners (LGB) by Margaret Wise Brown and Edith Thacher Hurd, Simon & Schuster, 1949
My Little Golden Dictionary (LGB) by Mary Reed and Edith Oswald, Simon & Schuster, 1949
Let's Go Fishing by Kathryn Jackson, Simon & Schuster, 1949
Duck and His Friends (LGB) by Kathryn and Byron Jackson, Simon & Schuster, 1950
Brave Cowboy Bill (LGB) by Kathryn Jackson, Simon & Schuster, 1949
The Animals' Merry Christmas by Kathryn Jackson, Simon & Schuster, 1950
Little Benny Wanted a Pony (LGB) by Olive O. Barrett, Simon & Schuster, 1950
Albert's Stencil Zoo (LGB) by Jane Werner, Simon & Schuster, 1951
Danny Beaver's Secret (LGB) by Patricia Scarry, Simon & Schuster, 1953
The Gingerbread Man (LGB) by Nancy Nolte, Simon & Schuster, 1953
The Animals of Farmer Jones (LGB) by Leah Gale, Simon & Schuster, 1953
The Party Pig (LGB) by Kathryn and Byron Jackson, Simon & Schuster, 1954
Little Indian (LGB) by Margaret Wise Brown, Simon & Schuster, 1954
Pierre Bear (LGB) by Patricia Scarry, Simon & Schuster, 1954
Smokey the Bear (LGB) by Jane Werner, Simon & Schuster, 1955
The Golden Book of 365 Stories: A Story for Every Day of the Year by Kathryn Jackson, Simon & Schuster, 1955
The Bunny Book (LGB) by Patricia Scarry, Simon & Schuster, 1955
Golden Bedtime Book by Kathryn Jackson, Simon & Schuster, 1955
Rudolph the Red-Nosed Reindeer (LGB) by Barbara S. Hazen, Golden Press, 1958
Cowboys and Indians (LGB) by Willis Lindquist, Golden Press, 1958
Colors (LGB) by Kathleen N. Daly, Golden Press, 1959
Just For Fun (LGB) by Patricia Scarry, Golden Press, 1960
Chicken Little (LGB) by Vivienne Benstead, Golden Press, 1960
The Country Mouse and the City Mouse (LBG) by Patricia Scarry, Golden Press, 1961
Good Night, Little Bear (LGB) by Patricia Scarry, Golden Press, 1961
My Little Golden Book of Manners (LGB) by Peggy Parrish, Golden Press, 1962
Tommy Visits the Doctor (LGB) by J. Seligmann and M. Levine, Golden Press, 1962
Nonsense Alphabet by Edward Lear, Doubleday, 1962

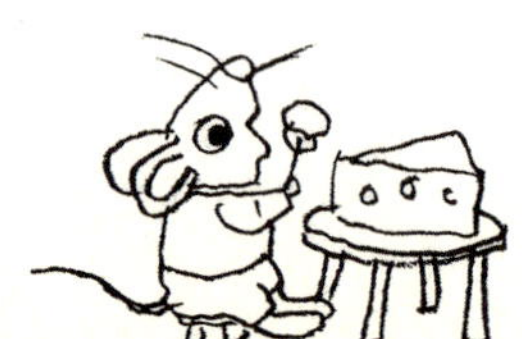

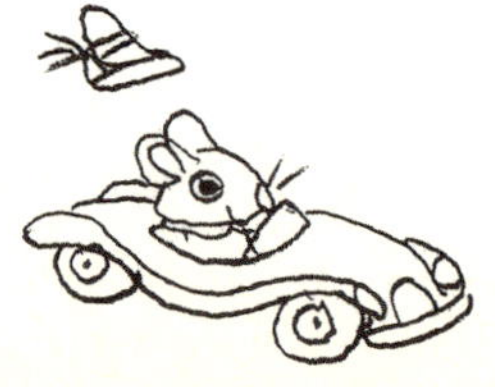

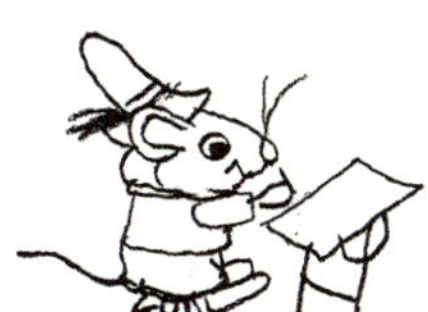
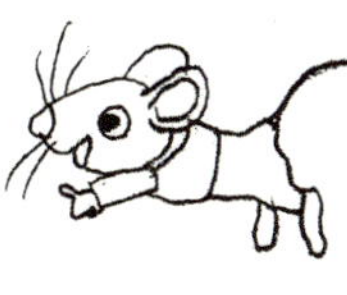
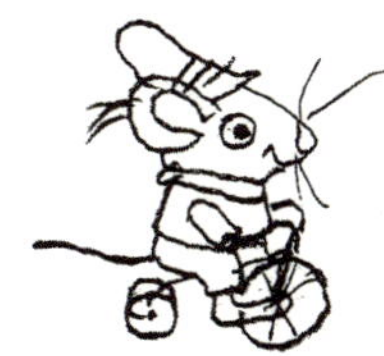
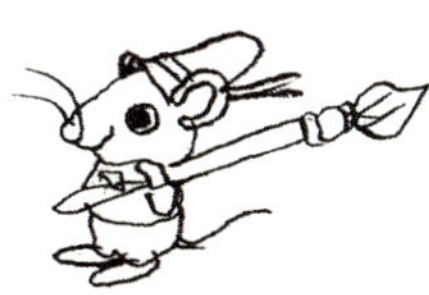

I Am a Bunny by Ole Risom, Golden Press, 1963
Chipmunk's ABC (LGB) by Roberta Miller, Golden Press, 1963
Fables by Jean de la Fontaine, Doubleday, 1963

SELECTED LIST OF BOOKS WRITTEN AND ILLUSTRATED BY RICHARD SCARRY
(LGB indicates a Little Golden Book)
Note: This list does not contain titles derived from already published material.

The Great Big Car and Truck Book, Simon & Schuster, 1951
Rabbit and His Friends (LGB), Simon & Schuster, 1953
Nursery Tales, Simon & Schuster, 1958
Cars and Trucks (LGB), Golden Press, 1959
Naughty Bunny (LGB), Golden Press, 1960
Tinker and Tanker, Doubleday, 1960
Tinker and Tanker Out West, Doubleday, 1961
Tinker and Tanker and Their Space Ship, Doubleday, 1961
Tinker and Tanker and the Pirates, Doubleday, 1961
The Hickory Dickory Clock Book, Doubleday, 1961
Tinker and Tanker Knights of the Round Table, Doubleday, 1963
Tinker and Tanker in Africa, Doubleday, 1963
The Rooster Struts, Golden Press, 1963
Polite Elephant Book, Golden Press, 1963
Richard Scarry's Best Word Book Ever, Golden Press, 1963
Feed the Hippo His ABC's, Golden Press, 1964
Is This the House of Mistress Mouse?, Golden Press, 1964
The Animals' Mother Goose, Golden Press, 1964
The Bunny Book, Golden Press, 1965
Teeny Tiny Tales (16 books in a frame tray), Golden Press, 1965
Richard Scarry's Busy, Busy World, Golden Press, 1965
Richard Scarry's Storybook Dictionary, Golden Press, 1966
Richard Scarry's Egg in the Hole Book, Golden Press, 1967
My Golden Go Go Library (a boxed set of 4 titles including *Trains, Planes, Boats, and Cars*), Golden Press, 1967

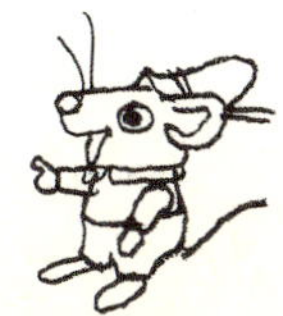
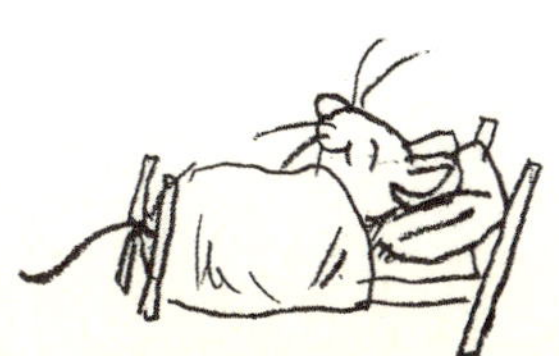

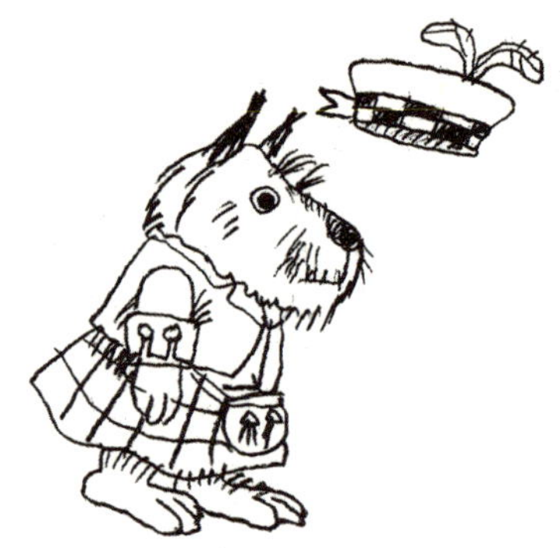

The Early Bird, Random House, 1968
What Do People Do All Day?, Random House, 1968
The Great Pie Robbery, Random House, 1968
The Supermarket Mystery, Random House, 1968
Richard Scarry's Great Big Schoolhouse, Random House, 1969
Richard Scarry's ABC Word Book, Random House, 1971
Richard Scarry's Great Big Air Book, Random House, 1971
Richard Scarry's Funniest Storybook Ever, Random House, 1972
Richard Scarry's Find Your ABC's (paper), Random House, 1973
Richard Scarry's Please and Thank You Book (paper), Random House, 1973
Richard Scarry's Cars and Trucks and Things That Go, Golden Press, 1974
Richard Scarry's Great Steamboat Mystery (paper), Random House, 1975
Richard Scarry's Best Counting Book Ever, Random House, 1975
Richard Scarry's Animal Nursery Tales, Golden Press, 1975
Richard Scarry's Early Words (board), Random House, 1976
Richard Scarry's Color Book (board), Random House, 1976
Richard Scarry's Busiest People Ever, Random House, 1976
Richard Scarry's Best Make-It Book Ever (paper), Random House, 1972
Richard Scarry's Punch-Out Toy Book, Random House, 1978
Richard Scarry's Postman Pig and His Busy Neighbors (paper), Random House, 1978
Richard Scarry's Lowly Worm Sniffy Book, Random House, 1978
Busy Town, Busy People, Random House, 1978
Little ABC, Random House, 1978
Richard Scarry's Mix or Match Storybook, Random House, 1978
Richard Scarry's Best First Book Ever, Random House, 1979
Richard Scarry's Busytown Pop-Up Book, Random House, 1979
Richard Scarry's Peasant Pig and the Terrible Dragon, Random House, 1980
Richard Scarry's Lowly Worm Word Book (chunky board), Random House, 1981
Richard Scarry's Best Christmas Book Ever, Random House, 1981
Richard Scarry's Busy Houses, Random House, 1981
Lowly Worm Cars and Trucks Book, Random House, 1983
The Best Mistake Ever! (paper), Random House, 1984
Richard Scarry's Lowly Worm Bath Book, Random House, 1984
Richard Scarry's Pig Will and Pig Won't: A Book of Manners, Random House, 1984
Richard Scarry's Biggest Word Book Ever!, Random House, 1985
My First Word Book (board), Random House, 1986
Richard Scarry's Lowly Worm's Schoolbag, Random House, 1987
Richard Scarry's Just Right Word Book, Random House, 1990
Richard Scarry's Cars and Trucks from A to Z, Random House, 1990

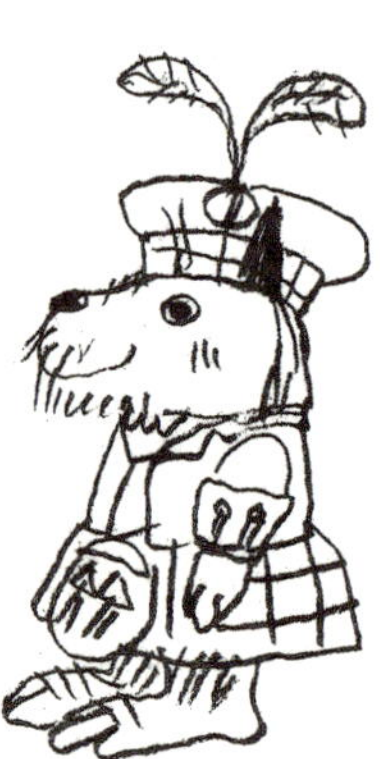

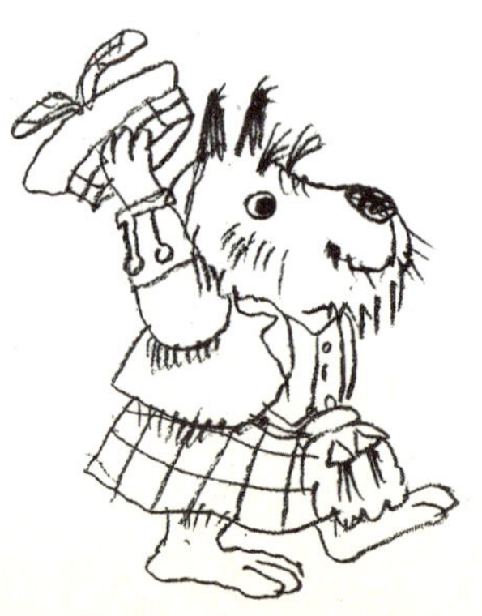

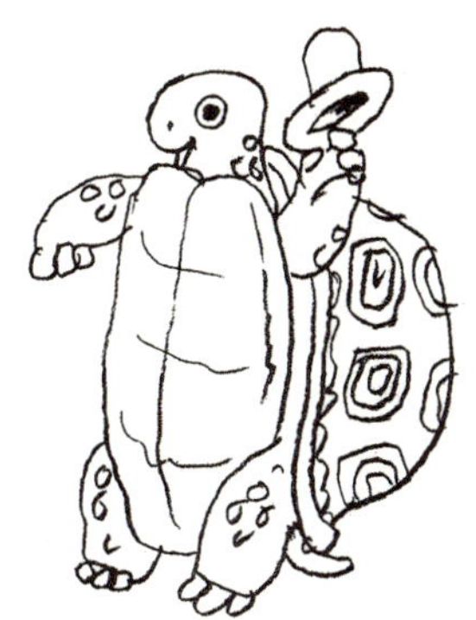

CREDITS AND PERMISSIONS

Publisher's Note: Photographic copies of Richard Scarry original illustrations and printed books and covers were made by Manhattan Color Graphics Inc., a Color Wheel Company, and Lynton Gardiner. Biographical photographs of Richard Scarry, his family, and friends are from family archives. Efforts have been made to trace the photographers and identify their contributions, but the sources are unknown, with a few exceptions. The photograph on page 44 of the Scarry family sailing is by Peter Barlow, the postcard view of Cap Ferrat on page 100 is by Yvon, and the portrait of Richard and Patsy Scarry in Gstaad (page 115) is from the magazine Jours de France, *photographer unknown. The publisher wishes to thank all those whose work appears here.*

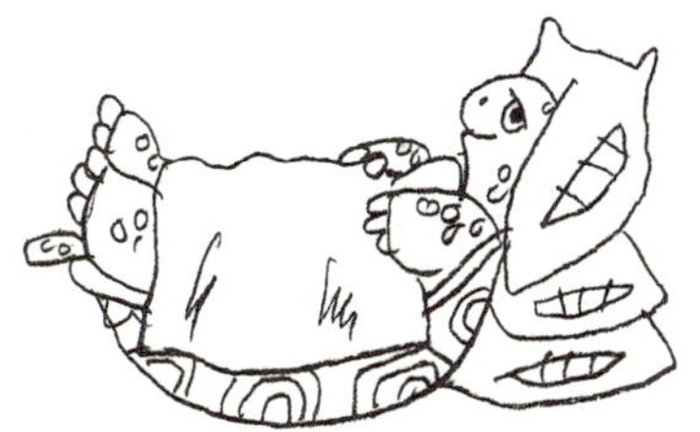

Illustrations by Richard Scarry from the following books are used by permission of Doubleday, a division of Bantam Doubleday Dell Publishing Group, Inc.: *Tinker and Tanker* by Richard Scarry. Copyright © 1960 by Doubleday, a division of Bantam Doubleday Dell Publishing Group, Inc.; *Tinker and Tanker Knights of the Round Table* by Richard Scarry. Copyright © 1963 by Richard Scarry

Illustrations by Richard Scarry from the following books are used by permission of Golden Books Publishing Company, Inc.: *Best Word Book Ever.* © 1963 Golden Books Publishing Company, Inc. © 1980 Richard Scarry; *Storybook Dictionary.* © 1966 Richard Scarry; *Cars and Trucks and Things That Go.* © 1974 Richard Scarry; *Boats Go Go Library.* © 1967 Richard Scarry; *Cars Go Go Library.* © 1967 Richard Scarry; *Planes Go Go Library.* © 1967 Richard Scarry; *Trains Go Go Library.* © 1967 Richard Scarry; *Egg in the Hole Book.* © 1967 by Golden Books Publishing Company, Inc.; *Polite Elephant.* © 1963 by Golden Books Publishing Company, Inc.; *Best Stories Ever, Look and Learn Library.* © 1971 by Richard Scarry

Illustrations by Richard Scarry from the following books are used by permission: *Busy, Busy World.* © 1965 Golden Books Publishing Company, Inc.; *Two Little Miners.* © 1949 Golden Books Publishing Company, Inc.; *The Bunny Book.* © 1955 Golden Books Publishing Company, Inc.; *Just For Fun.* © 1960 Golden Books Publishing Company, Inc.; *Good Night, Little Bear.* © 1961 Golden Books Publishing Company, Inc.; *Country Mouse, City Mouse.* © 1961 Golden Books Publishing Company, Inc.; *Pierre Bear.* © 1954 Golden Books Publishing Company, Inc.; *Naughty Bunny.* © 1959 Golden Books Publishing Company, Inc.; *Nursery Tales.* © 1948 Golden Books Publishing Company, Inc.; *Chipmunk ABC.* © 1963 Golden Books Publishing Company, Inc.

Covers from the following books, illustrated by Richard Scarry, are used by permission of Golden Books Publishing Co., Inc.: *Best Storybook Ever.* © 1968, 1950 by Golden Books Publishing Company, Inc., "The Storybook Dictionary," © 1966, and "The Golden Go-Go Library" © 1967 by Richard Scarry; *Best Mother Goose Ever.* © 1970 Richard Scarry

Covers from the following books, illustrated by Richard Scarry, used by permission: *Little Indian.* © 1954 Golden Books Publishing Company, Inc.; *Rabbit and His Friends.* © 1953 Golden Books

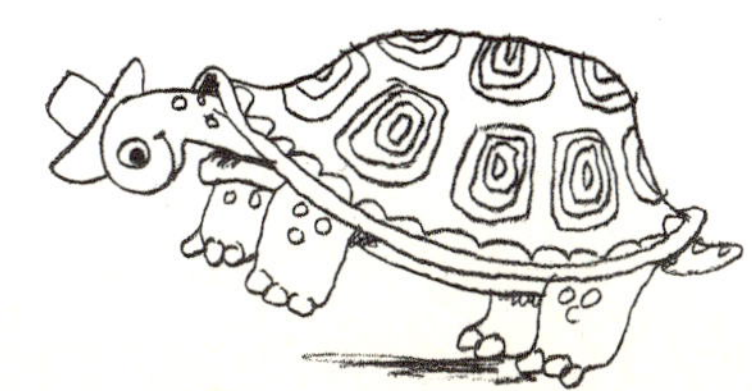

Publishing Company, Inc.; *Smokey the Bear.* © 1955 Golden Books Publishing Company, Inc.; *I Am a Bunny.* © 1963 Golden Books Publishing Company, Inc.

Photos from an article written by Nancy Williams from *The Westerner,* an in-house magazine of Western Publishing Company, Inc., February 1950, used by permission of Golden Books Publishing Company, Inc.

Illustrations by Richard Scarry from the following books are reprinted by permission of Random House, Inc.: *Richard Scarry's Great Big Schoolhouse* by Richard Scarry. Copyright © 1969, 1979 by Richard Scarry; *What Do People Do All Day?* by Richard Scarry. Copyright © 1968 by Richard Scarry. Copyright renewed 1996 by Richard Scarry II; *Richard Scarry's Great Big Air Book* by Richard Scarry. Copyright © 1971, 1982 by Richard Scarry; *Richard Scarry's Best Counting Book Ever* by Richard Scarry. Copyright © 1975 by Richard Scarry; *Richard Scarry's Funniest Storybook Ever* by Richard Scarry. Copyright © 1972 by Richard Scarry; *Richard Scarry's Best First Book Ever* by Richard Scarry. Copyright © 1979 by Richard Scarry; *Richard Scarry's Biggest Word Book Ever* by Richard Scarry. Copyright © 1985 by Richard Scarry; *Richard Scarry's Best Make-It Book Ever* by Richard Scarry. Copyright © 1977 by Richard Scarry; *Richard Scarry's Best Rainy Day Book Ever* by Richard Scarry. Copyright © 1974 by Richard Scarry; *Richard Scarry's Best Color Book* by Richard Scarry. Copyright © 1976 by Richard Scarry; *Richard Scarry's Please and Thank You Book* by Richard Scarry. Copyright © 1973 by Richard Scarry; *Postman Pig and His Neighbors* by Richard Scarry. Copyright © 1978 by Richard Scarry; *Richard Scarry's Lowly Worm Car and Truck Book* by Richard Scarry. Copyright © 1990 by Richard Scarry; *Richard Scarry's Best ABC Video Ever* by Richard Scarry. Copyright © 1969–89 by Richard Scarry. Copyright © 1989 by Random House, Inc.; *Richard Scarry's Lowly Worm Sniffy Book* by Richard Scarry. Copyright © 1978 by Richard Scarry; *Richard Scarry's My First Word Book* by Richard Scarry. Copyright © 1986 by Richard Scarry; *The Early Bird* by Richard Scarry. Copyright © 1968 by Richard Scarry. Copyright renewed 1996 by Richard Scarry II; *Richard Scarry's Busy Houses* by Richard Scarry. Copyright © 1981 by Richard Scarry; *Richard Scarry's Little World Book* by Richard Scarry. Copyright © 1978 by Richard Scarry; *Richard Scarry's Lowly Worm School Bag* by Richard Scarry. Copyright © 1987 by Richard Scarry; *Richard Scarry's Lowly Worm Coloring Book* by Richard Scarry. Copyright © 1983 by Richard Scarry; *Richard Scarry's Busy Town Pop-Up Book* by Richard Scarry. Copyright © 1979 by Richard Scarry; *Richard Scarry's Best Christmas Coloring Book Ever!* by Richard Scarry. Copyright © 1985 by Richard Scarry; *Richard Scarry's Toy Book* by Richard Scarry. Copyright © 1978 by Richard Scarry; *Huckle Cat's Busiest Day Ever* by Richard Scarry. Copyright © 1993 by Richard Scarry; *Richard Scarry's Lowly Worm Story Book* by Richard Scarry. Copyright © 1972, 1977 by Richard Scarry; *Richard Scarry's Find Your ABCs* by Richard Scarry. Copyright © 1973 by Richard Scarry; *Richard Scarry's Bedtime Stories* by Richard Scarry. Copyright © 1978 by Richard Scarry; *Richard Scarry's Great Steamboat Mystery* by Richard Scarry. Copyright © 1975 by Richard Scarry; *Richard Scarry's Supermarket Mystery* by Richard Scarry. Copyright © 1969 by Richard Scarry; *Richard Scarry's Early Words* by Richard Scarry. Copyright © 1976 by Richard Scarry; *Richard Scarry's Stories to Color* by Richard Scarry. Copyright © 1978 by Richard Scarry; *Richard Scarry Huckle's Book* by Richard Scarry. Copyright © 1979 by Richard Scarry; *Richard Scarry's Biggest Word Book Ever* by Richard Scarry. Copyright © 1985 by Richard Scarry

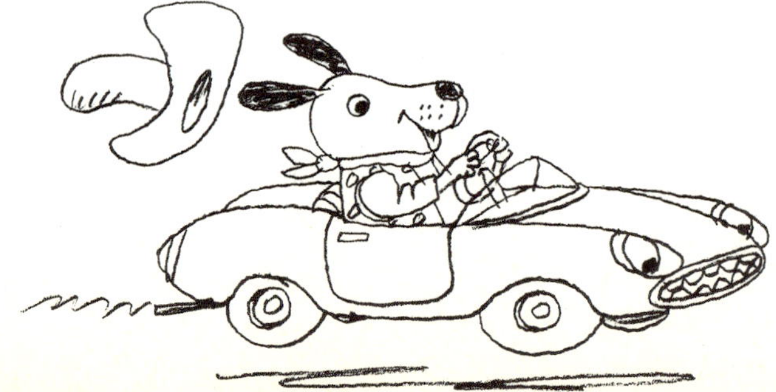

ACKNOWLEDGMENTS

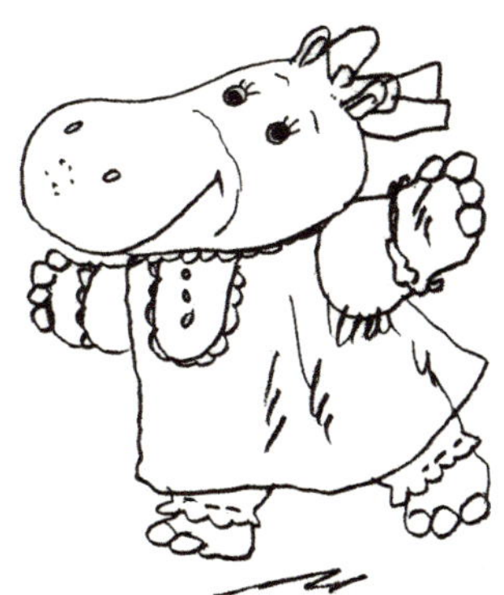

The authors would particularly like to thank:

Dick and Patsy Scarry for their generosity in providing personal photographs and for their patience in sitting through many hours of taped interviews at the beginning of this project;

Huck Scarry for supplying additional family photographs, as well as copies of several of Richard Scarry's early books, and for sharing some family anecdotes;

Erik and Lenore Blegvad, Jane Werner Watson, Mike Smollin, and Peter Spier for writing colorful vignettes drawn from their memories of Dick Scarry;

Ray Butman for allowing us access to his unpublished course paper, "The History of Richard Scarry and His Works."

In addition, the following have all been most helpful:

Carol Christiansen, Grace Clarke, Remo Cosentino, Michel Duplaix, Ellen E. Embardo, Patricia Flynn, Bernette Goldsen Ford, Stanley Garrett, Cathy Goldsmith, Judith Gray, Gerald Harrison, Linda Hayward, Andrea Hein, Terry Helton, Mary Janaky, Kathleen Daly Korybut, Sidney Kramer, Nancy Nolte, Catherine Ratzberg, Robin Warner, and Thomas Wilsted.

Last, but by no means least, the authors are especially indebted to their editor, Robert Morton, and his assistant, Nola Butler, as well as to the art director, Ellen Nygaard Ford. They were patient, understanding, and extremely helpful.

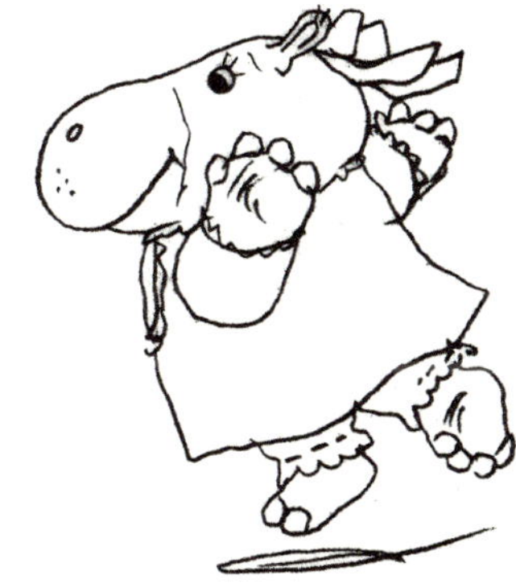

Pages 152–59: Line drawings from the collection of Ole Risom

Page 160: From *Richard Scarry's Best Stories Ever*

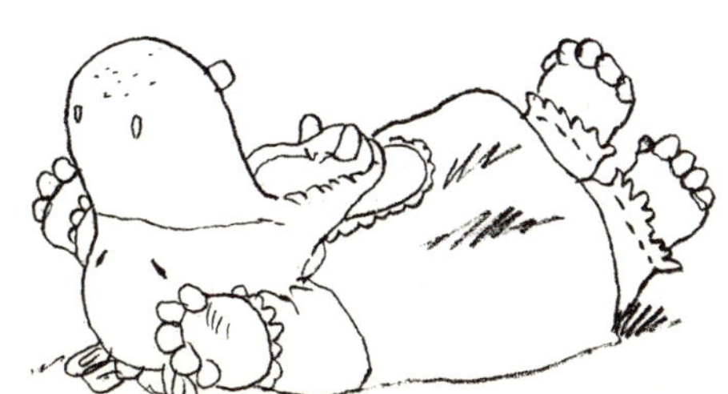

INDEX

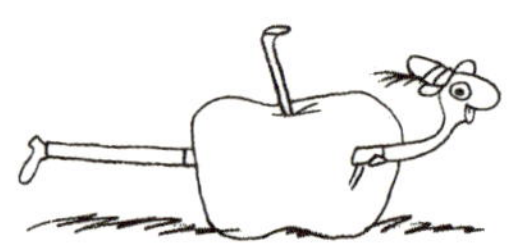
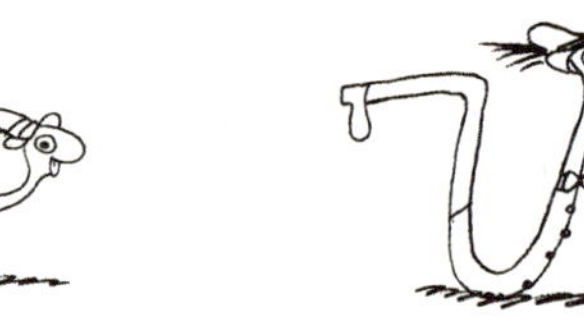
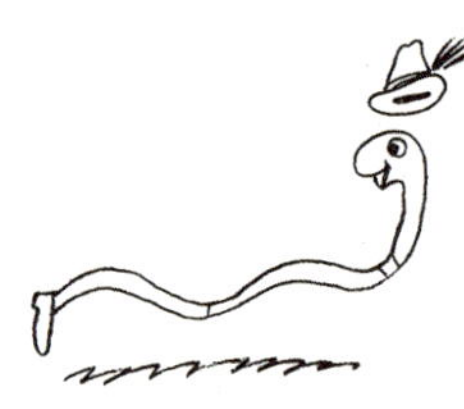
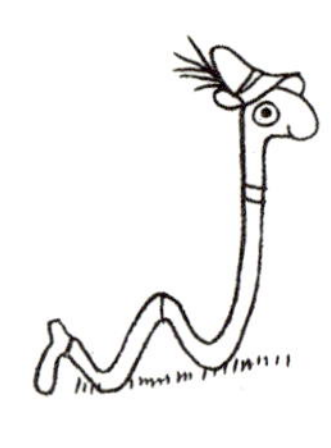
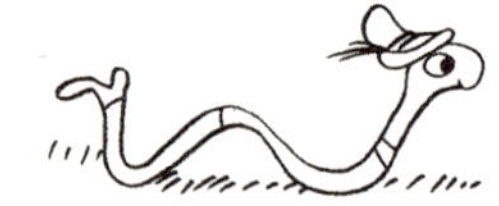

Page numbers in *italics* refer to captions.

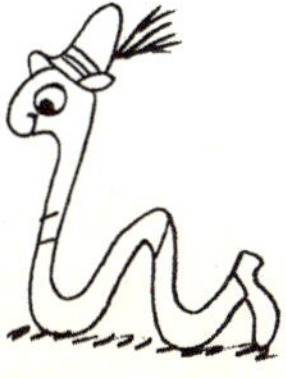

The End

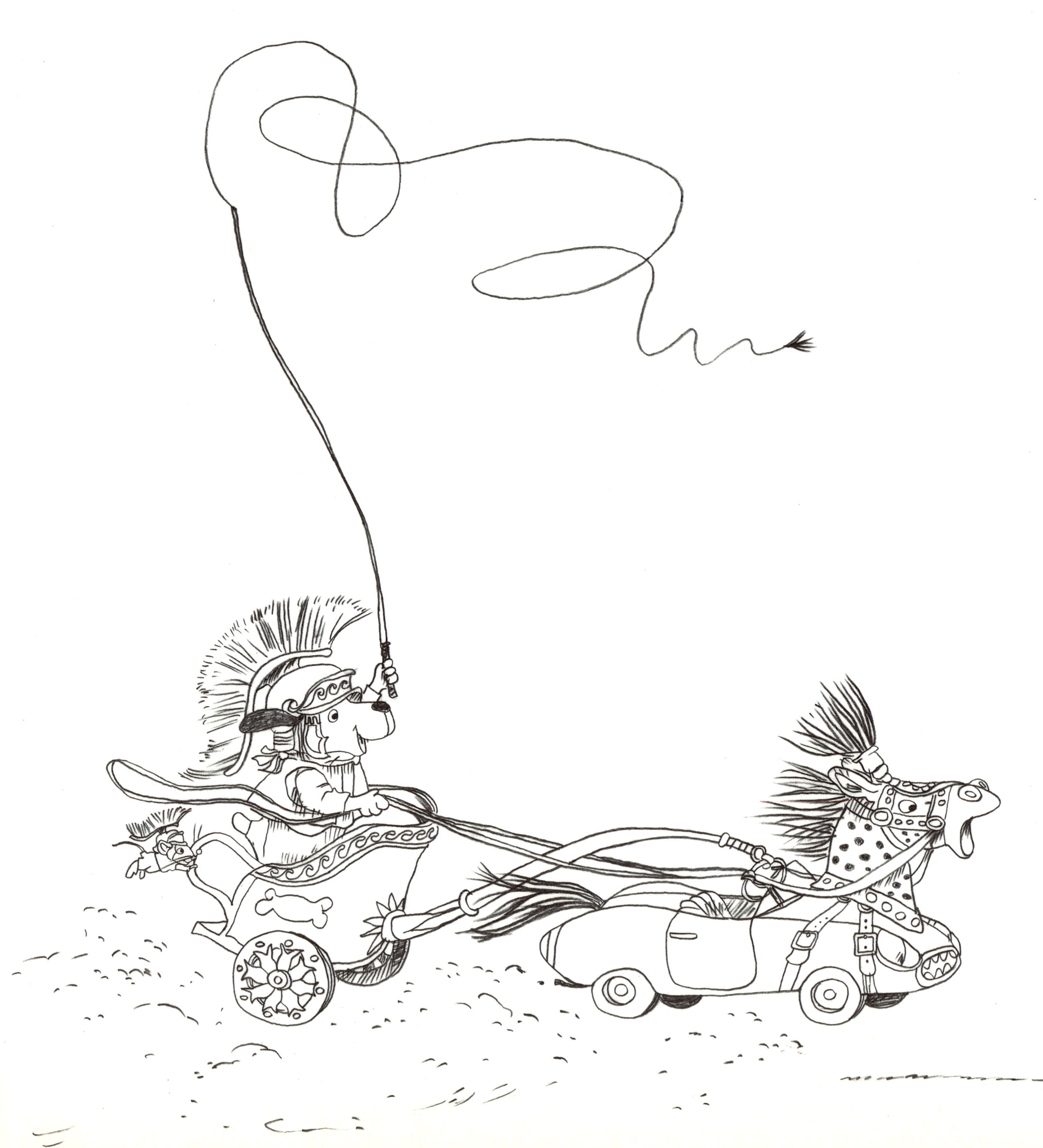